Foundations
Series

Apologetics by the Book

Cliff McManis

GBF Press
Sunnyvale, CA

Dedicated to Dr. George Zemek:
exacting exegete,
passionate teacher,
exemplary scholar,
personal friend,
biblical apologist.

CONTENTS

Introduction

Apologetics by the Book is a revision and expansion of my 2011 book called, *Biblical Apologetics: Advancing and Defending the Gospel of Christ*. I had three main goals in writing this updated version:

First, I wanted to make the book more accessible to the average Christian reader. The first version was geared toward a post-graduate level seminary class. So it included much of the attendant specialized jargon that typifies the field of apologetics and theology on a formal level. Originally, I did intentionally try to stay away from a preponderance of philosophical terminology as well as esoteric nomenclature found in formal metaphysical studies, but some confusing and high-powered terms could not be avoided, like "ontological" and "epistemology." Although, *ontos* is a biblical word, used in Revelation 1 and so is epistemology, used by the biblical author in the Book of James.

In light of this first goal I reworked every chapter, trying to simplify the terminology and concepts. I also eliminated the Hebrew and Greek fonts wherever they occurred and transliterated all the biblical terms so they can be pronounced in English. Overall, apologetics is a meaty, and for many, an unavoidably complicated topic, so the present book still poses a challenge for some readers. Nevertheless, I trust in the end it will prove to be more "reader friendly," useful and edifying.

Second, since I wrote the 2011 version I have been able to interact with many evangelicals who specialize in the study of apologetics and so I have been able to incorporate the fruits of some of that interaction into the present volume. This has added depth, breadth and clarity in my thinking on certain topics throughout. For example, I had deliberate, sometimes lengthy, personal conversations and interactions with the authors of the book, *Five Views on Apologetics*

(Zondervan), the book I profiled in my 2011 volume. I was an antagonist in 2011 of the five views presented in that book, so it was helpful to interact personally with those authors, with the goal of accurately representing their views. I did not interact with Paul Feinberg, as he went to be with the Lord in 2004.

Also since 2011 I have been able to travel around the world, teaching apologetics at various seminaries to pastors living in Kiev, Novosibirsk, Honduras, Ghana, India and St. Petersburg, Russia and in other contexts as well. These pastors all proved to be faithful, courageous shepherds of Christ's Church who are committed to feeding and protecting God's truth and God's people in the local church. They had voracious appetites for *Biblical Apologetics* and they helped me fine-tune my thinking in many areas, confirming my original conviction, that God's Word, the Bible, is sufficient and perspicuous for every culture, language and people group.

A third goal I had was to bring the book up to speed in light of current theological trends swirling around in the evangelical world as well as to incorporate highlights from certain books on apologetics that were written since 2011. A couple recent books of note include John Piper's, *A Peculiar Glory* (2016) and Voddie Baucham's, *Expository Apologetics* (2015). I particularly appreciated these works since they were written by experienced, faithful pastors, who have the priority of "internal apologetics," shepherding the sheep in their local churches that Christ has entrusted to their care (1 Pet :1-5). And with respect to scholarship, neither man is a slouch, but rather highly competent in discussing the pertinent issues.

As with my first book, this volume is also dedicated to Dr. George Zemek, the academic dean of The Expositors Seminary in Jupiter, Florida. After thirty years now, he continues to be a source of wisdom and encouragement for me in my life-long pursuit of teaching and doing biblical apologetics.

I want to thank my good friend, fellow colleague, and fellow Elder, Dr. Derek Brown, managing editor of GBF Press in Sunnyvale, CA for encouraging me to do a "make-over" of *Biblical Apologetics* and for taking the lead in getting the present volume published. I also want to thank my daughter, Breanna Lynn (McManis) Paniagua for the countless hours of tedious labor it took to format and edit the manuscript. Thanks also to Rebecca Milco for your fantastic, detailed work in editing, proofreading and thoughtful suggestions for improvement. Thanks to Levi Gill for help with formatting. Thanks to Jasmine Patton and Alyssa Shields for help with editing the Scripture index. And a huge thanks to fellow Elder at Grace Bible Fellowship, Bob Douglas, for the many hours invested in cover layout and design.

My prayer is that God might use this book to edify the saints and encourage them to be informed, faithful and courageous defenders and practitioners of the faith once-for-all delivered to the saints (Jude 3).

Clifford B. McManis
GBF Press
Cupertino, CA
1 Corinthians 15:58
October, 2017

Foreword

We think of the apostle Paul as a great preacher, missionary, and church planter—and he was all of those things. But Paul described his own calling this way: "I am appointed for the defense of the gospel" (Philippians 1:16).

The defense of the gospel—the discipline known as *apologetics*—has fallen on hard times in our generation. Most Christians think of it as a philosophical exercise rather than (as Paul saw it) a vital application of biblical doctrine. Some think it's a discipline best relegated to the academic arena, handled only by specialists who have attained advanced degrees, as if it should be kept out of the hands of the laity or the life of the local church. Some insist that contextualization, not apologetics, is the most effective way to advance the kingdom of Christ in a hostile culture.

Cliff McManis rightly understands that biblical apologetics is an exegetical, theological, and pastoral duty. Indeed, at the most basic level, it is *every* believer's duty to "sanctify Christ as Lord in your hearts, always being ready to make a defense to everyone who asks you to give an account for the hope that is in you " (1 Peter 3:15). That may be the most succinct biblical description of Christian apologetics.

Pastor McManis furthermore believes (as Paul did, and as I do) that a proper defense of the Christian faith is not to be done with persuasive words of human wisdom (1 Corinthians 2:4) but by proclaiming the truth of the Word of God itself, which is "living and active and sharper than any two-edged sword, and piercing as far as the division of soul and spirit, of both joints and marrow, and able to judge the thoughts and intentions of the heart" (Hebrews 4:12). As Charles Spurgeon famously said, the Bible is like a lion. You don't need to defend a lion. Let it out of its cage. It will defend itself.

This approach has been labeled "presuppositional apologetics," because it attacks worldly wisdom at the level of fundamental presuppositions. It challenges the notion that human reason is in any way more authoritative or more reliable than God's Word. It repudiates the assumption that fallen creatures have any right to question or pass judgment on God's actions, His decrees, or His commandments. It rejects any assertion that common ground exists between belief and unbelief, light and darkness, righteousness and sin, or Christ and Belial (2 Corinthians 6:14-15).

The book you are holding in your hands is perhaps the simplest, most straightforward summary and how-to guide for presuppositional apologetics now in print. It is both informative and practically helpful. I believe you will find it an extremely useful tool whether you are an apologetics professor at the seminary level seeking supplemental reading material or just a simple lay person looking for practical answers.

Pastor McManis writes with crisp clarity in a way that is certain to give you fresh insight into what Scripture teaches about the defense of the Christian faith. I wish this book had been available when I was studying apologetics in seminary.

John MacArthur
Grace Community Church
Sun Valley, CA, 2011

Preface

Over the course of many years of teaching, several ideas about books that need to be written have come to mind. A few of those ideas, by the grace and enablement of God, I have brought to fruition, a few remain on the drawing board, and a few of the ones that had been on that drawing board ended up in another category appropriately labeled "someone beat me to the punch." When that occurred I sometimes felt regret because I didn't get to write on that topic as I had it framed up in my mind. However, although the textbook in your hands dealing with apologetics from a presuppositional standpoint had been at the top of my drawing board list for years, I am thankful in the providence of God that Cliff McManis "beat me to the punch."

There is great joy when former students rise to higher levels of ministry accomplishments that honor Christ and advance His Kingdom. The publishing of this volume authored by Dr. McManis I look upon as Exhibit A in this regard. Having had the privilege of reviewing its pre-publication drafts chapter by chapter was a gratifying experience. Many times I thought to myself, "I would have never thought of developing that important argument or phrasing that important point so clearly and cleverly." Those touches of attention-arresting wordsmithing become an effective means of both exposing the futilities of verificationalist systems and correspondingly of establishing the superiority of a presuppositional methodology. Just a glance at most of the author's chapter titles and their subheadings draws the reader with anticipation into their ensuing points of development.

These and other factors of writing style accomplish much in alleviating the heavy-duty nature of the subject matter yet without neglecting a credible interaction with the substance of a discipline that traditionally has been presented and debated in an esoteric fashion. Cliff has rescued the discipline from the elite circle of the

"intelligentsia" and returned it as a biblical theology of truth communication to the common people (i.e. to *all* believers). This volume
will be of great help in the restoration of the practicality of biblical
apologetics as it was exemplified in the early Church. Hopefully,
today's readers will be able to understand and put into practice the
true nature of Peter's command in 1 Peter 3:15 as it is strategically
situated *in its defining context.*

George J. Zemek
The Expositors Seminary
Jupiter, Florida
September, 2011

by Christian philosophers and scholars. This book is an attempt to examine everything carefully that is being propagated in the current field of Christian apologetics. The verse above says we need to "abstain" (NIV = "avoid") from every form of evil. Wrong teaching about the Bible and the faith is evil. We need to take it very seriously.

On the other hand, this is not to imply that the men I disagree with are evil, because they are not. Most of them are men I admire and whom I have learned from over the years—some on a personal basis. Take William Lane Craig for example—the world famous Christian philosopher. He was my theology teacher at Westmont College in Santa Barbara my sophomore year in 1987. That was a great class and I learned much as a new, green believer. The first time I ever spoke to a crowd of people, was alongside Dr. Craig, when we both addressed about 400 college students at an evening vespers service. We pumped iron in the same weight room daily. He was, and still is, a gracious, winsome believer. It just so happens that I totally disagree with him on his approach to apologetics and I hope he amends his views and brings them more in keeping with the fidelity of Scripture. Maybe this book will help.

Or take another example—Dr. Norman Geisler; known back in my seminary days as "Stormin' Norman," in light of his great passion and acumen as a skilled debater of atheists and heretics. He also has a great dry wit that is entertaining. I consider him to be one of the greatest Christian scholars alive today in light of his prolific writings that cover such a broad range of topics. To this day his books *Inerrancy*, *A General Introduction to the Bible*, *Christian Ethics*, *A Popular Survey of the Old Testament*, and *Answering Islam* are some of the best books ever put in writing on those respective topics. I have met him personally on several occasions and have corresponded with him in writing on apologetics over the years. He is always accommodating and gracious. But he is also a bull-dog and is not afraid of a skirmish. In this book I take issue with Geisler's presuppositions and methodology on apologetics. And even though I disagree with his apologetical methodology, his encyclopedia on Christian apologetics is a fantastic resource.

Then there are the presuppositionalists—Frame, Bahnsen and Van Til. In this book I propose that Frame is not a consistent presuppostionalist. William Lane Craig acutely makes the same diagnosis in *Five Views on Apologetics*.[1] So that just leaves Bahnsen and

Van Til. I am most aligned with these two men in apologetical methodology, but there are times when I take issue with them. Occasionally I lump them in the group with other "traditional apologists" when I believe they are being too philosophical and not strictly scriptural (Van Til admitted this shortcoming about himself later in life).[2] They were, after all, first and foremost philosophers and not biblical exegetes. What is the difference between my view and these two men? I'd say they were philosophical presuppositionalists whereas I am a scriptural presuppositionalist. Frequently our views harmonize, and at other times there is dissonance. Nevertheless, I admire these two men tremendously. I believe they were in the elite category of true brilliance when it came to original thinking and intellectual aptitude and prowess in the field of apologetics. And I believe that today they are bona fide scriptural presuppositionalists!

In addition, a word needs to be said about the popular theologian and philosopher, R. C. Sproul. Known by most as the stalwart defender of Reformed theology and the doctrine of *sola fide*, surprisingly few seem to be familiar with his almost Roman Catholic approach to apologetics. It is quite bizarre. He wrote a classic book on the holiness of God that all Christians should have on their bookshelves, and at the same time he writes books on apologetics that would make Aquinas and Aristotle leap for joy while at the same time cause Luther and Calvin to howl. Sproul's Achilles' heel that explains the odd discrepancy between his Protestant bibliology and his apologetically Romanist anthropology is due to the fact that he is first and foremost a classical philosopher and not a trained exegete nor biblical theologian. He prefers Latin[2] over Hebrew and Greek, and gravitates toward metaphysics and philosophy before theology and biblical exposition. As a result, his writings on apologetics get a thorough scouring in the light of Scripture in this book. The end result is eye-opening.

The reader might ask, "Who does McManis agree with? He takes everyone to task!" Not really. In reality it is just a handful of philosophers that I disagree with. There are countless others that I do agree with, most of them unnamed, and they are usually pastors and biblical theologians who put a premium of scriptural fidelity and authority—Church men typically. Some famous and some not-so-famous. Among the notable ones are Luther, Calvin, Spurgeon, Reymond, and MacArthur, to name a few.

Yet, one deserves special mention—a mentor of mine in the field of biblical apologetics, Dr. George J. Zemek. Since 1975, Dr. "Z" has been a teacher of theology, the biblical languages and apologetics at several seminaries, including *Grace Theological Seminary*, *The Master's Seminary* and *The Expositors Seminary*, in addition to being a shepherd in the local church. His tome on the exegesis and theology of biblical apologetics, written as his doctoral thesis at *Grace Theological Seminary* in 1982, is masterful and unparalleled. Thanks to Dr. "Z" for reviewing the initial drafts of this book as I trudged through each chapter—your insights and recommendations were keen, exacting and greatly appreciated.

Finally, the reader needs to be aware that I use the book, *Five Views on Apologetics*, as a sparring partner throughout my book. There are countless books written on apologetics, but the *Five Views* book is highly popular, has a wide reading audience and is perennially referred to as the modern-day standard summarizing all acceptable evangelical positions on Christian apologetics. I use it as a text in my apologetics class. It's a good, representative distillation of what constitutes, and what is wrong with, traditional apologetics—the approach to apologetics I set out to debunk. It is the ideal tool for instructing by way of comparing and contrasting. My prayer is that God and His Spirit might use the current study to better prepare apologists everywhere—all believers—in their ongoing task of defending and advancing the gospel of Jesus Christ to the uttermost parts of the earth.

For His glory,
Cliff McManis
Cupertino, CA
August, 2011
1 Corinthians 15:58

Notes

1. *Five Views On Apologetics*, edited by Steven B. Cowan, counter-point series, (Grand Rapids, MI: Zondervan, 2000), 233.

2. Van Til admitted his shortcoming when confronted by Berkouwer: "I agree that my little book on The Sovereignty of Grace should have had much more exegesis in it than it has. This is a defect. The lack of detailed scriptural exegesis is a lack in all of my writings." Cornelius Van Til, *Jerusalem and Athens: Critical Discussions on the Philosophy and Apologetics of Cornelius Van Til*, ed. E. R. Geehan (Phillipsburg, NJ: P & R Publishing, 1980), 203.

3. For example, see Sproul's book, *Willing to Believe: The Controversy over Free Will* (Grand Rapids, MI: Baker Books, 1997, 7). He lists a "Latin Glossary" in the Table of Contents, cataloguing over sixty-five Latin words and phrases. The book purports to be a definitive biblical approach to the topic at hand, yet he lists no Hebrew or Greek glossary, and not one of the listed Latin words is actually found in the New Testament. This is typical of his books. Cf. *What is Reformed Theology? Understanding the Basics*, (Grand Rapids, MI: Baker Books, 1997), 225-226. See chapter 8 on "Faith: The Gift of God" for further discussion on the value and limits of Latin in biblical studies and theology.

1

Breaking Through the Maze of Confusion

Facing the Competition

Apologetics, or defending the faith, is an imperative for every Christian. God has called all believers to defend the faith. Peter exhorted all believers in his day to always be "ready to make a defense to everyone who asks you to give an account for the hope that is in you" (1 Pet 3:15). And God has also called all believers to advance the faith. Jesus commanded believers to, "Go therefore and make disciples of all nations" (Matt 28:19). Defend and advance—that is the mission. But many Christians feel inadequate to fulfill this heavenly mission without proper training, direction and guidance. Where does a Christian go to get practical help for doing the work of apologetics? New believers in particular frequently have great zeal and boldness and could benefit from good resources on how best to approach this Christian discipline.

In answering the question, "How should Christians do apologetics?" there is a surprisingly vast array of conflicting answers given by the Christian community. As a result, the average Christian can become quite confused about the whole topic of apologetics. Some might answer the question by saying, "Leave apologetics to the experts." Others might say, "Just go out and share the gospel—it's easy and anyone can do it." Those are the opposite ends of the spectrum, and there are countless combinations between the two.

On a popular level, many evangelicals keep pointing to a book called *Five Views On Apologetics* that came out in 2000 as a starting point to answer the apologetics question. The book presents five supposed different approaches to defending Christianity by five professing Christians. I have been using this book every year in my apologetics class at The Cornerstone Seminary since 2006. The five views represented are as follows: (1) classical apologetics; (2) evidential apologetics; (3) cumulative case apologetics; (4) Reformed epistemology apologetics; and (5) presuppositional apologetics. The implication in the book is that these five views represent every legitimate approach there is to know in the pursuit of defending the Christian faith.

As my MDiv students trudge through the highly philosophical and esoteric book, inevitably, before we are half way through, I begin to hear an undercurrent of rumblings, grumblings and questions about the book. A typical groaning refrain I hear from the students is, "This book is very frustrating!" When I ask, "Why?" the response is usually, "Where's the Bible in all this? It's all man-made musings!"

After reading the book carefully about fifteen times over the course of several years, I whole-heartedly agree with my students. This book has gnawed at me since the first time I read it—and it continues to gnaw at me as I read it annually in preparation for teaching my class. What nags at me about the book is my growing conviction that a fully-orbed, strictly biblical position of apologetics is not consistently defended among the five positions offered. All five views explain apologetics from primarily a philosophical perspective, and not from a biblical or scriptural one. In the following pages of this book I propose that apologetics needs to be explained from a biblical perspective, not a philosophical one. As such I offer a sixth view: "biblical apologetics."

The above five views are the exclusive, popularly accepted approaches to Christian apologetics. Supposedly, they all have distinctive features that set them apart from each other, yet in reality there is much overlap with most of them. Generally speaking, the first four probably have more similarities than differences. In contrast, presuppositional apologetics is the most distinct as a system among the five views, and is often pitted as a strong contrarian rival to the other four views. But as I already suggested, none of the five views sufficiently reflects what I call biblical apologetics. For the sake of argument in this book I will refer to the five above views as the "traditional approach" to apologetics. I will compare and contrast the traditional approach with biblical apologetics throughout.

Biblical Apologetics

I define biblical apologetics as follows: the biblical mandate for every Christian to advance and defend the gospel of Jesus Christ as they live the Christian life, in the power of the Holy Spirit, by exposing and subjecting all contrary beliefs to Christ's revelation as found in Scripture. The goal of this book is to expand upon this definition in a comprehensive manner by showing its biblical lineage and by comparing and contrasting it with generally accepted traditional definitions of apologetics. But before delineating a full-fledged explication of my proposed working definition, it will prove instructive to first give a summary overview of the traditional definitions and their peculiar nuances and points of emphasis.

The Biblical Approach...?

Is there a definitive biblical approach to apologetics? Dr. Kelly James Clark, who wrote the chapter on Reformed epistemology in *Five Views*, disparages the idea of there being a "biblical" view of apologetics, and thinks it's arrogant to claim that you have the "biblical approach." He avers, "I cringe when people claim that their apologetic approach is *the* biblical approach."[1] Further, he asserts, "a coercive case from Scripture cannot be made for one's apologetic approach."[2] Similarly, Boa and Bowman, two pop apologists, say, "no specific system or theory of apologetics is outlined in the New Testament."[3] Despite Clark and Boa and Bowman's agnostic pessimism on the matter, I propose that a coercive case establishing a biblical apologetic is not only possible, but also required. In other words, one could ask, "Does the Bible have a complete theology of apologetics?" Absolutely! Or another way to ask it is, "Does the Bible give sufficient information to the believer in how to defend the faith in a systematically consistent manner?" Once again, the answer is "Absolutely." That is true because of biblical sufficiency—the Bible is sufficient for everything pertaining to life and godliness (2 Pet 1:3). Scripture clearly teaches, by precept and by precedent, a thorough and consistent "biblical apologetic." This book argues that biblical apologetics is the clear, definitive Christian approach to apologetical methodology. In the chapters ahead, we will flesh out the pertinent Scriptures to make that case.

This book will also address apologetical *methodology*. Methodology pertains to how we do something—what the procedure entails. Apologetics has to do with defending the Christian faith (1 Pet 3:15;

Jude 3). So apologetical methodology addresses the manner, methods and even the starting point of how we go about defending the faith. Frequently, how one defines something will dictate the procedure of implementation. How we do something matters greatly (Col 3:17), especially when it comes to guarding and advancing the Christian faith, obeying God and interfacing with a lost world (Col 4:6). Sadly, many so-called apologetical experts disagree and allege that methodology does not matter—they would argue that the ends justify the means. In their book on apologetics, Kreeft and Tacelli reject the importance of methodology outright: "An introduction to apologetics usually deals with methodology. We do not. We believe that nowadays second-order questions of method often distract attention from first-order questions of truth."[4] They aver that addressing apologetical methodology is a peripheral, annoying sidebar of inferior significance when it comes to defending the faith. They don't think "how" one does apologetics matters much. In contrast, the Bible cares much about how we do things with respect to the disciplines of the faith. Paul warned the Corinthian Christians in his day to, "Be imitators of me, just as I also am of Christ" (1 Cor 11:1). Paul modeled "how" to live the Christian life in every respect and he knew it mattered greatly.

Establishing a proper biblical methodology for apologetics is paramount, a "first-order question," and the first necessary step for laying a solid foundation for successfully carrying out the apologetic task. Pragmatics in theology often has perilous ramifications. God commanded Christians to do "all to the glory of God" (1 Cor 10:31); that includes our methods of apologetics.

Apologetics: a Summary of Typical Definitions

What is apologetics? The answer to this question gets prickly and ushers one immediately into an intramural squabble among Christian scholars, apologetics "experts" and even ordinary, everyday believers. This has been the case for the past couple centuries. Bernard Ramm, a respected apologist of the twentieth century, concedes: "No uniform phrase has been adopted to express the idea of Christian apologetics."[5] A hundred years ago, one of the most respected evangelical theologians and apologists, B. B. Warfield, noted the same thing:

It must be admitted that considerable confusion has

reigned with respect to the conception and function of apologetics...Nearly every writer has a definition of his own, and describes the task of the discipline in a fashion more or less peculiar to himself.[6]

Despite the above caveats, countless definitions abound and are continually being suggested by various theologians and philosophers. Following are typical samplings from more recently established and well-known sources:

> It is...the function of apologetics to investigate, explicate and establish the grounds on which a theology—a science, or systematized knowledge of God—is possible.[7]

> On the technical level apologetics is the defense and presentation of the truth of Christian faith on intellectual and moral grounds. As such, it is the work of the theologians and philosophers. But on the everyday level apologetics is simply the matter of facing up to the questions of what we believe and why?[8]

> The Science and art of defending Christianity's truth claims.[9]

> Christian Apologetics is the scientific vindication of the divine authority of the Christian religion.[10]

> Defense of Christianity in the face of the various attacks made upon it by the unbelieving world.[11]

> Christian apologetics has three great tasks: reasoning for the existence of God, establishing the deity of Christ, and defending the inspiration of Scripture.[12]

> Christian apologetics is the comprehensive philosophical, theological, and factual demonstration of the truthfulness of our Christian religion.[13]

> Apologetics is that branch of Christian theology which answers the question, Is Christianity rationally defensible?[14]

Apologetics is the vindication of the Christian philosophy of life...apologetics deals mostly with philosophy.[15]

Apologetics is the reasoned defense of the Christian religion.[16]

Apologetics is the area of study purely devoted to the justification and defense of the Christian faith....Our goal as apologists is not to prove Christianity, but to show that it is a credible religion...to clearly show the challenger that the basic truths of Christianity are possible, if not probable....Apologetics should be considered under the heading of **pre-evangelism**...the student of apologetics ...should be able to convey that Christianity is free from contradiction and that the doctrines therein are reasonable.[17]

Apologetics is that branch of Christian theology that seeks to give a rational defense of Christian truth claims.[18]

Apologetics means a justification, a vindication, a satisfactory explanation. Apologetics is the science which explains and justifies the [Christian] religion as the true religion... Apologetics is a *human* science, for it draws its facts from history and philosophy (i.e., *human* sources) and develops its proofs by unaided human reason... Apologetics does not call upon Divine Revelation (as the *divine* science of theology does) for its fundamental proofs.[19]

That is an abudance of definitions. But the redundancy illustrates an important point—there is little variance as to the main points of emphasis in the traditional definitions of apologetics. The above definitions are monolithic in their primary delineation of what constitutes Christian apologetics. Although articulated in various ways, there are common themes to the above definitions that classify them under the same genus. Interestingly, the authors who wrote the above views include those who are Catholic, Protestant, Calvinistic and Arminian alike. For the most part, they all exhibit, or presuppose, some or all of the following eleven traits, to varying degrees, that inherently put them in conflict with what I will present as biblical apologetics. The eleven traits of traditional apologetics include the following: (1) rationalism; (2) philosophy; (3) natural theology; (4) pre-evangelism; (5) selectivity; (6) formalism; (7) probability; (8) appeasement; (9) novelty; (10) obfuscation and (11) integration. Each of these eleven definitional and functional traits warrants a brief diagnosis. These diagnostic vignettes will be expanded upon in greater detail throughout the remainder of the book.

Examining the Definitions
(1) Rationalism vs. Revelation
First, many of these definitions imply apologetics is simply a "rational" pursuit. They try to reach God by finite, human means. By "rational" they mean apologetics begins with and puts a premium on "human wisdom" or "the laws of logic." Or stated another way, apologetics begins with sheer human reason and not divine revelation. This perspective presupposes that "the human mind is sufficient." Apologetics begins with what man thinks, not what God thinks. Scripture is not to be our starting point—the Bible cannot be assumed to be true from the get-go. Anselm (1033-1109) and Aquinas (1225-1274) stand out as exemplars of this approach in Church history, systematizing and propagating it on a universal level.

And so it remains the dominant view today. For example, Glenn is clear and emphatic on this point: "Apologetics is a *human science*...for it develops its proofs with unaided reason." In other words, he is saying that apologetics is dependent solely upon the finite human brain to explain, validate, justify, define and vindicate all of life's transcendent metaphysical and ontological realities from a theistic point of view, and whatever you do as an apologist, you can't use the Bible to prove or establish any of it as true. Glenn continues dogmatically: "Apologetics does not call upon Divine Revelation... for its fundamental proofs." In other words, he says we cannot begin with the Bible in our Christian apologetics work. His reason? He essentially goes on to say that we first have to assume the Bible is not true, or grant the atheist or skeptic his presupposition up front, and then try to prove that the Bible is true (the Christian presupposition) by using sheer human logic or reason.

In the same vein, Habermas, the evidentialist apologist from Liberty University, agrees and is unapologetic about his "no-Bible!" approach to apologetics, for his "method does not begin with a belief in the inspiration of Scripture, no matter how well this may be established. In fact, this approach does not even require that Scripture have the quality of general trustworthiness…the trustworthiness and inspiration of Scripture… are simply not required in order to establish the central tenets of the Christian position."[20] I say just the opposite: it is impossible to establish any of the central tenets of Christianity apart from Scripture. Yet according to the traditional "Christian" apologists, the unbeliever gets to keep his presuppositions, but the Christian has to jettison his from the start!

Mayers says the Christian must do apologetics using "the rules of logic first delineated and clarified by Aristotle."[21] Sproul, Gerstner and Lindsley make the same argument in their book. They openly "affirm the *primacy of the mind*" in apologetics.[22] This is in contrast with biblical apologetics which affirms "the primacy of Scripture" or "the primacy of God's mind" in defending the faith. What is God's mind? What are God's thoughts? What are God's views on reality? They are clearly revealed in Scripture (1 Cor 2:1-16), and they are ontologically superior to the thoughts and reasoning of man. God declared, "'For My thoughts are not your thoughts, nor are your ways My ways,' declares the LORD. 'For as the heavens are higher than the earth, so are My ways higher than your ways and My thoughts than your thoughts'" (Isa 55:8-9). God defines reality for us. On the contrary, Sproul *et al* argue that apologetics needs to begin with human logic, the theistic arguments and natural theology, not Scripture or special revelation. In contrast, biblical apologetics begins with God's logic, divine arguments and revealed theology; we must subject all human wisdom to God's mind as revealed in Scripture and reject altogether the notion of "natural theology."

One of the foremost respected evangelical apologists of today, William Lane Craig, also argues that apologetics begins with, and depends on, human wisdom apart from the Bible. He says apologetics "is a rational defense" of the Christian faith.[23] By "rational" he means human logic apart from Scripture. He means the laws of logic, natural theology and the theistic arguments like the *kalam* cosmological argument. He is adamant about dependence upon "brain power" in contrast to using Scripture when doing apologetics. It is strictly a human endeavor. He asserts, "the use of argument and evidence assumes a primary and appropriate role, while the work of the Holy Spirit plays no part in the demonstration proper."[24] Note how he alleges that the Spirit of God is banished to the sidelines when it comes to doing Christian apologetic work. Further, he goes on to say, "our beliefs...are based on rational arguments."[25] This statement is alarming, especially when it comes from a high-profile evangelical Christian. In contrast, biblical apologetics says human logic is subservient to God's logic, while God's Word and the Spirit of God assume front and center stage in the work of defending the faith.

Traditional apologists who champion the rationalist approach to apologetics unwittingly ignore the noetic effects of the Fall on man's ability to reason independently while at the same time undermine the doctrine of the sufficiency of Scripture, thus illustrating its inadequacy as a legitimate approach.

(2) Philosophy vs. Theology

Second, many of the traditional definitions and approaches put a premium on "philosophy" when it comes to the apologetic task. This goes hand-in-glove with the rationalist approach previously mentioned. This view postulates that apologetics falls under the discipline of philosophy proper. One such popular evangelical apologist, Douglas Groothuis of Denver Seminary, says, "apologetics...walks arm in arm with philosophy...A Christian-qua-apologist, then must be a good philosopher...This is nonnegotiable and indispensable."[26] Colin Brown clearly stated that "apologetics...is the work of the theologians and the philosophers."[27] Keyser said, "Apologetics is the scientific vindication" of the Christian religion.[28] By scientific, he means philosophy. Glenn says it's "a human science."[29] Even the great Reformed presuppositionalist, Cornelius Van Til, said, "apologetics deals mostly with philosophy."[30] William Craig purports that the work of real apologetics is reserved for the elite, trained, professional philosophers, and apologetics needs to be discussed in the vortex of "current philosophical discussions."[31]

The *Five Views* book on apologetics takes this same posture, for all five authors chosen for the book were selected based on their professional training and work in the area of religious philosophy. Alvin Plantinga, a world-renowned philosopher, and one of the most revered apologists today, also believes that apologetics is "an exercise in Christian philosophy."[32] Ramm was extreme on this point. He said, "no person can really dare to enter the area of Christian apologetics in a competent way without some mastery of the history of philosophy."[33] How discouraging! To think that in order for me to obey the basic Christian imperative of 1 Peter 3:15 I first have to become a master in the history of philosophy? I think not.

Sadly, lots of Christians think this way. Every time I teach apologetics, be it in a Sunday school class, at various seminars and conferences around the world, and even annually at my own seminary, I usually begin by asking the students or the audience, "Who are the greatest apologists of today?" And the answers are predictable. They shout out, "Craig, Plantinga, Geisler, Habermas, Frame, Clark, Moreland, Schaeffer" and the like. Every one of these men is first and foremost a professional philosopher or scientist of metaphysics. Hardly ever do I hear people shout names like, "Pastor John Piper, John MacArthur, Warren Wiersbe, Mark Dever, Alistair Begg, Tony Evans, Albert Martin, Nick Haight…Charles Spurgeon"…men who are pastors; men of the Word. The true apologists are believers who lean on God's Word and biblical theology to defend and advance the faith; they don't lean on the man-made wisdom that is philosophy.

In stark contrast, biblical apologetics is not primarily, or even secondarily or tangentially, for the philosopher. God even gives explicit warnings against the dangers and the allure of philosophy. "See to it that no one takes you captive through philosophy and empty deception, according to the tradition of men, according to the elementary principles of the world, rather than according to Christ" (Col 2:8). Christianity and the Bible are in the realm of theology (the study of the words of God), not philosophy. Apologetics is not a task reserved for professional philosophers, but for every born-again, Bible-believing child of God (1 Pet 3:15).

(3) Natural Theology vs. Natural Revelation

Third, traditional apologetics presupposes the legitimacy of natural theology and confuses natural theology with natural revelation. There is biblical warrant for what is called natural revelation, but not so for natural theology. What is natural theology? One source summarizes it this way: "Natural theology is the practice of philosophically reflecting on the existence and nature of God independent of …divine revelation or scripture."[34] Natural theology is philosophical theology —humanly concocted religious thought issuing from finite and fallen observations and speculations about ultimate realities. Simply, natural theology is doing theology without the Bible…a frightening prospect.

Traditional apologists say the Bible sets a precedent for utilizing philosophy and unaided human reason under the rubric of natural theology. Natural theology includes variations of modernized Greek philosophy, the theistic arguments, the laws of logic, sheer human reason, sense perception, historical evidences, theoretical calculus, modern secular scientific hypotheses and theories, etc. Traditionalists say natural theology, which is not explicitly in the Bible, is based on and flows from natural or general revelation, which is clearly taught in Scripture. A classic litmus passage from which natural theology can supposedly indirectly be drawn is Romans 1:19-20.

Traditional apologists' main creed is that we can't start with the Bible when talking to unbelievers, but rather we must use natural theology first. And what justification do they give for beginning apologetics with natural theology and not the Bible? The Bible! The Bible gives examples of extrapolating natural theology from natural revelation, so they say. This is circular reasoning of the first order.

Craig argues that he can utilize natural theology, (like the *kalam* cosmological argument and human evidences) because Isaiah 35:5-6; Luke 11:20, 24:25-27; John 3:2, 20:31; Acts 2:22, 14:17, 17:2-3; and Romans 1:19-20 provide "a legitimation of natural theology."[35] So he can reason and argue without the Bible because the Bible says he can reason and argue without the Bible.

Sproul, Gerstner and Lindsley say the same thing. They aver that Paul utilized natural theology to argue for the resurrection in 1 Corinthians 15: "Paul's reasoned defense...stands as a clear example of apostolic appeals to reason and to empirical data to support a truth claim."[36] Is 1 Corinthians 15 natural theology—human reasoning apart from divine revelation—as they allege? I think not. The whole book of Corinthians is divine revelation, not natural theology. They go on to say Jesus used "calculus" to condemn certain cities in Matthew 11:20-24. We say, no, Jesus used divine revelation in Matthew 11:20-24. The authors confuse natural theology with special revelation as well as natural revelation. They say point blank, "natural theology refers to knowledge of God acquired through nature."[37] They are dead wrong here. That is a definition of natural revelation, not natural theology.

Biblical apologetics recognizes special (divine) revelation and natural (general) revelation, makes the proper distinction between natural revelation and natural theology, and shows from Scripture why natural theology is totally illegitimate. This will be thoroughly addressed in chapter four.

(4) Pre-evangelism vs. Authoritative Proclamation

Fourth, traditional definitions of apologetics tend to downplay the role of evangelism. Some extricate evangelism from the apologetic task altogether. Traditional apologists have introduced a novel, unbiblical concept of "pre-evangelism" to justify the need of philosophical apologetics before getting to biblical evangelism when interfacing with an unbeliever. The idea of "pre-evangelism" is that unbelievers need to be "primed" before they can hear biblical truth, or else they will simply reject it out of hand. Hardy writes, "Apologetics should be considered under the heading of **pre-evangelism.**"[38] Sproul and company downplay evangelism in favor of natural theology.[39] Craig is hard-line here and asserts that evangelism has little, if anything at all, to do with apologetics.[40] Howe also is hard-line, asserting "a clear distinction between biblical *witness* and biblical *defense* must be made and maintained."[41] Biblical apologetics, on the other hand, teaches that evangelism and apologetics are inextricably linked (1 Pet 3:15). This will be explored in detail in chapter two.

Biblically speaking, there is no such thing as "pre-evangelism" as the traditional apologists define it and use it. Francis Schaeffer was the first to formally use the term in his writings, and since him many routinely follow suit without question. But it is a man-made concept that actually undermines biblical evangelism and apologetics. Sproul, who advocates the non-biblical notion, says *"pre-evangelism...*is involved in the data or the information that a person has to process with his mind before he can either respond to it in faith or reject it in unbelief."[42] The content or the substance of pre-evangelism for Sproul is natural theology—man-made wisdom and philosophy void of Scripture. Of course he has no Bible verse to justify his mandate for human pre-evangelism, because there is no such thing.

God's mandate for every Christian to engage in evangelism with a hostile world does not need a crutch or a man-made jump-start like the fabricated notion of "pre-evangelism." Jesus and the apostles never mentioned, taught, commanded, or practiced anything called "pre-evangelism." Scripture is clear about Jesus' *modus operandi*: "Jesus came...preaching the gospel of God, and saying, 'The time is fulfilled and the kingdom of God is at hand; repent and believe in the gospel'" (Mark 1:14-15). Read the Book of Acts and note how Paul and his ministry partners go into city after city, country after country, proclaiming the gospel cold-turkey to absolute strangers—and virtually every time he did, Scripture says "the Gentiles...believed" (Acts 13:48; cf. 13:12; 14:1, 21; 16:14, 31-34; 17:4, 12, 34; 18:8). There are no prerequisites for evangelism.

Those who say that pre-evangelism is required in order to prepare the hearts of hardened unbelievers so they can get to a point of believing fail to recognize that general revelation and the convicting work of the Holy Spirit do that very thing. God uses general revelation (conscience and creation) to convict sinners about His existence (Rom 1). And the Holy Spirit was sent by Jesus to always be working on the hearts and minds of all unbelievers everywhere, convicting them of sin, righteousness and judgment (John 16). So God does prepare the hearts of all sinners sufficiently through His own means so that all people are without excuse as soon as they hear the complete gospel. God does His own pre-evangelism.

(5) Selectivity vs. Holistic

Fifth, traditional approaches to apologetics are selective and lack balance either in emphasis, scope or both. Biblical apologetics is holistic, or comprehensive. Regarding emphasis, traditional apologetics usually takes a strictly defensive posture with apologetics. But biblical apologetics entails advancing the faith in the face of opposition just as much as defending the faith. Lewis defines apologetics as "the science and art of defending Christianity's truth claims."[43] Halsey says it is the "Defense of Christianity in the face of various attacks."[44] Pinnock opines it is "the defense of the truthfulness of the Christian religion."[45] Carnell claims that apologetics is preoccupied with one question: "Is Christianity rationally defensible?"[46] Sproul et al declare it is "the reasoned defense of the Christian religion."[47] Craig alleges apologetics "seeks to give a rational defense" of Christianity[48] and he dogmatically asserts that evangelism (an offensive task) has nothing to do with apologetics. So he dichotomizes the believer's witness to the world. For all these traditional apologists the work of apologetics is one-dimensional—strictly a defensive endeavor. Interestingly, B. B. Warfield held the opposite extreme. For him, apologetics was strictly positive, and in fact there was no need for the defensive component at all—it exists essentially "as a positive and constructive science."[49]

In contradistinction to all these examples, biblical apologetics is defensive in nature as well as positive, offensive, or proactive in nature—it is holistic; our witness to the world is twofold or multi-dimensional. Guarding the faith entails forward advances, offensive maneuvers and even preemptive actions on behalf of Christ in the midst of a hostile and unbelieving world. Jesus said He would build His Church, not just defend it, parrying and absorbing the blows from the enemy (Matt 16:18). Jesus commanded His disciples to go, advance and infiltrate the hostile world, courageously in the power of the Holy Spirit, to propagate the truth of the gospel (Matt 28:18-20; Acts 1:8). And Scripture also clearly shows the gospel needs to be defended (Phil 1:17). So, biblical apologetics is aggressively and triumphantly proactive as much as it is defensive.

As for scope, traditional apologetics is unilaterally external in approach. Apologetics, they say, is defending the faith against unbelievers outside the church, and the traditional apologists selectively major on atheists. But the Bible clearly mandates that defending the faith needs to be internal as well. The faith needs to be defended and protected within the community of the professing Church. Christians are probably more vulnerable to dangerous heresies circulating and being propagated in churches worldwide than by the false views that are held in the unbelieving world. Paul warned the elders at Ephesus about this very reality and called for internal, as well as external apologetics: "Be on guard for yourselves and for all the flock…I know that after my departure savage wolves will come in among you, not sparing the flock; and from among your own selves men will arise, speaking perverse things, to draw away the disciples after them" (Acts 20:28-30). Internal apologetics—defending the faith *within the Church*—is a key distinctive setting biblical apologetics apart from all other forms of traditional apologetics.

(6) Formalism vs. Personal Lifestyle

Sixth, most traditional definitions refer to apologetics as a "discipline" or a "field of study" as though it is a specialized, and compartmentalized, academic course that only a minority of elite Christians pursue as a major.[50] Earlier, we saw Brown referred to it as "the work of the theologians and philosophers." All the authors of the five views on apologetics (and the authors of most books written on apologetics) are first and foremost philosophers, supposed experts in metaphysical studies. Today, if we need answers we are told to consult the "professional apologists."

When Peter commanded Christians to "set apart Christ" in their hearts as they answer critics of the faith (1 Pet 3:15), he was not referring to an "academic discipline" or a specialized "field of study," but rather to a lifestyle. Defending the faith is a spiritual, spontaneous, daily, personal, informal, responsibility of all Christians.[51] Doing apologetics is not about spewing a rehearsed forty-five minute presentation of the *kalam* cosmological argument to select audiences at intermittent apologetics conferences in exchange for a healthy honorarium and cushy hotel stay. Doing apologetics is about being salt and light in the world, wherever you go, all the time—living an obedient and model Christian life (Matt 5:13-16).

(7) Probability vs. Truth

Seventh, traditional apologetics often has as its goal the establishment of Christianity as a feasible religion in the eyes of the unbelieving world. Or, that the goal of apologetics is to logically argue for the plausibility (not the "certainty") of Christianity's legitimacy. Through apologetics, we are told that we are to try to convince the unbeliever through sheer human reason and logic-chopping arguments that Christianity is humanly possible, intellectually viable, academically conceivable, theoretically sensible, apparently non-inconsistent, or the best of all options.

Listen to a sampling from a flurry of the world's most famous apologists, arguing that the goal of apologetics is not to establish binding, universal truth, but to propose negotiable plausibility: Groothuis says that in apologetics we are to present the Christian worldview to the unbeliever "as a large scale hypothesis" or as "the best hypothesis."[52] Geisler posits that we try to show that the Christian worldview "is most reasonable" compared to other worldviews.[53] Similarly, McCallum says, "we only have to discern that one alternative is more plausible than the others."[54] Tim Keller says, "The theory that there is a God who made the world accounts for the evidence we see better than the theory that there is no God."[55] In other words, we should believe in God, not because the Bible says it's true, but because we have a better theory. Our belief in God is only a theory—it's possible that God might not exist! He says, "there cannot be irrefutable proof for the existence of God."[56] Keller amazingly even concedes with the atheist saying, "the secular view of the world is rationally possible."[57]

J. P. Moreland writes his book on apologetics hoping it "contributes to making the belief that the Christian God exists at least permissible."[58] Craig puts it this way: "using the methodology of classical apologetics, one seeks to show that Christian theism is the most credible worldview."[59] He adds that the aim of apologetics is "to show that God's existence is at least more probable than not... more plausible than their contradictories...extremely plausible... more likely than not."[60] Hardy agrees and says that the goal of apologetics "is to show that it is a credible religion...[and] reasonable."[61]

Plantinga is no different. His apologetic work exists to seek "the rational acceptability of Christian belief" among unbelievers.[62] Sproul says we do apologetics to show "the extreme plausibility" that God may exist.[63] Dulles penned his tome on apologetics, not to establish the certitude of Christianity, but merely to establish "the general credibility of Christianity."[64] Dulles the apologist goes on to say that "we cannot know the exact words used by Jesus" as we read them in the Gospels—nothing is certain.[65]

Most reasonable? At least permissible? Most credible? More probable than not? Extremely plausible? More likely than not? Am I to stake my eternal soul on such a shaky foundation of probabilistic propositions? Did Jesus ever argue for truth with such agnostic paradigms of probabilistic and conditional speculations? Biblical apologetics answers with an emphatic, "No!" Jesus typically made dogmatic assertions regarding ultimate reality in the face of skeptics and doubters by using the phrase, "Truly, truly..." (John 6:47). The Greek word for "truly" is "amen" which means "fixed, certain, reliable, unchanging." This was an emphatic way of saying, "You can absolutely count on it, without a doubt!" Jesus believed in the possibility of knowing spiritual truth with absolute, unshakable certainty. Kelly James Clark is at odds with Jesus when he says, "Gone, I believe, are the prospects for rational certainty."[66]

As an apologist, Greg Bahnsen was unique and refreshing at this point. He wrote,

> God tells us to apply our hearts unto His knowledge if we are to know the certainty of the words of truth (Prov. 22:17-21). It is characteristic of philosophers today that they either deny that there is absolute truth or they deny that one can be certain of knowing the truth; it is either not there, or it is unreachable. However, what God has written to us (i.e., Scripture) can "make you know the

certainty of the words of truth" (vv. 20-21). The truth is accessible![67]

God has already declared that the unbelieving world thinks Christianity is utter foolishness. God said, "For the word of the cross is to those who are perishing foolishness, but to us who are being saved it is the power of God" (1 Cor 1:18; cf. 3:19). No amount of clever intellectual disputations is going to make true Christianity respectable or appealing to the unbelieving world. Further, our job as Christians is not to promote the potential, theoretical plausibility of Christianity as being possibly more likely than not. Our job is to defend and promote its truthfulness. This is how Paul did apologetics, as seen in his testimony before the agnostic governor from Rome when he boldly declared, "I am not out of my mind, most excellent Festus, but I utter words of sober truth" (Acts 26:25). That's why biblical apologetics unapologetically asserts Christianity to be absolutely, categorically, undeniably true. Just like Jesus, we can talk with unbelieving doubters and skeptics, saying, "Truly, truly!"

Sadly I know several Christians who say they are not absolutely certain of anything…including the fact that Jesus died and rose again! There are even professing Christians who promote and laud doubt and skepticism as virtues and as supposed examples of humility. Doubt and skepticism are synonyms for unbelief. Unbelief is the enemy of faith. Extolling doubt, skepticism, unbelief and a lack of child-like faith is categorically unbiblical. Believers are called to "walk by faith not by sight" (2 Cor 5:7). God does not want us to doubt— He wants us to believe (John 14:1); He even commands us not to doubt (Matt 21:21) and has declared that without faith it is impossible to please Him (Heb 11:6). Jesus said you can "know the truth" (John 8:32), not "you can be pretty certain…maybe." God has declared that "whatsoever is not from faith is sin" (Rom 14:23). Doubt and skepticism have their origin in sin. There's no virtue in unbelief. If a person doubts, God says such a person is double-minded and God will not answer the prayers of such a skeptic (James 1:6-8). Satan's full-time job is to create doubt in God's Word (Gen 3:1). The entire epistle of 1 John was written so that Christians would believe unshakably, unreservedly in God's truth as revealed in Scripture. Certitude is the goal; doubt is the enemy. The indwelling Holy Spirit of truth guarantees that reality can be secured in this life. Biblical Christians live and fight for truth—not probability.

(8) Appeasement vs. Accountability

Eighth, traditional apologetics seeks to prove the existence of God. One of the greatest Christian apologists of our generation, Norman Geisler, says that the first goal of apologetics is "reasoning for the existence of God."[68] He also asserts that "God is what is to be proven and we cannot begin by assuming his existence as a fact."[69] Similarly, Moreland conjectures, "Genesis 1 does not merely assume the existence of the God of the Bible."[70] Biblical apologetics says the exact opposite: Genesis 1 presupposes, or assumes, the existence of God. "In the beginning God created the heavens and the earth" (Gen 1:1). The Bible never tries to explain, justify or rationally prove to the unbeliever that God might exist. It is declared *ipso facto* as a given. The only thing the Bible has to say about atheists is the following: "The fool has said in his heart, 'There is no God'" (Ps 14:1). In other words, atheists are fools.

Countless apologetics books written since the time of Thomas Aquinas (AD 1225-1274) major on long-winded, complex, philosophical delineations of the theistic arguments trying to prove or vindicate the possibility or undeniability[71] of God's existence. Reading modern day evangelical apologists one would think that the super-majority of people in the world is atheistic.[72] Just the opposite is true: the super-majority of the people in the world is theistic. With over one billion Muslims, one billion Hindus, nearly one billion people calling themselves Christians and another billion identifying with some kind of theistic religion, there is no shortage of theists in the world. Over ninety percent of Americans say they believe in God. The atheists are the super-minority in the world. As such, biblical apologetics does not assume everyone is an atheist. Just as Scripture makes plain, unbelievers in general believe in God, "holding to a form of godliness, although they have denied its power" (2 Tim 3:5). And similarly Paul says that although unbelievers "knew God, they did not honor Him as God" (Rom 1:21).

The biggest critics of Jesus were religionists—the Pharisees—not atheists. Those who opposed Paul at the Areopagus were not atheists, for they worshipped an "unknown god" (Acts). The great Old Testament apologist, the prophet Elijah, opposed religionists at Mount Carmel, not atheists (1 Kgs 18). When Moses the apologist confronted Pharaoh's priests in 1,400 BC, he was dealing with religionists of the first order, not atheists (Exod 7). The rebellion at

Babel was by religionists, not atheists (Gen 11). As such, biblical apologetics distinguishes itself by addressing people first and foremost, *a priori*, as religious beings, not as those with a religious *tabula rasa*, sterile of any religious beliefs. God put a conscience in every person born into this world which serves as an innate imprint of God's image in them—enabling every person to know intuitively that God exists (Rom 1). All humans are inescapably religious.

(9) Novelty vs. Legacy

Ninth, reading typical traditional apologists one gets the impression that biblical apologetics formally began in the second and third century AD[73] with Justin Martyr (100-165), Irenaeus (120-202), Tertullian (160-225), and Origen (184-254); was bolstered by Augustine in the fifth century; was systematized for the first time with Aquinas (1225-1274); and finally came into its own as a respectable discipline in the modern era thanks to Hugo Grotius (1583-1645),[74] Joseph Butler (1692-1752), William Paley (1743-1805) and their ilk. I propose that such a notion is anachronistic.

First Peter 3:15 is universally recognized as the *locus classicus* of apologetics for the believer—"defend the faith." But all the basic ingredients of 1 Peter 3:15 that are demanded by God are elements that have been true and expected of believers of all ages: sanctify the LORD as holy, fear and trust God, defend the faith. When the Holy Spirit commanded Christians to speak to unbelievers about their faith in the 60's AD when Peter penned his epistle, that was not a novel concept. The idea of defending the faith was not invented for the first time in seed-form in the days of Peter. There was actually a 2,000 year-old-plus legacy of defending divine truth that went before the early church which became a model for them to follow (Rom 15:4).

Peter commanded Christians not to fear critics of the faith, but to speak of the personal "hope" they have come to believe in. That "hope" was the Messiah. This is the same hope that saints before Peter trusted in—John the Baptist had that hope (John 1:29), as did Jeremiah (Jer 31:31-34), Daniel (Dan 2:44; 9:26-27), Ezekiel (Ezek 36:25-31), Micah (Micah 5:2), Isaiah (Isa 7:14; 9:6; 53:2-12), David (Rom 4:6-8), Moses (Gen 3:15; Deut 18:18), Abraham (Gen 12:1-4) and Noah (Heb 11:7).[75] All were men of faith and were criticized for it and defended it tenaciously. As a matter of fact, the command of 1 Peter 3:15 finds its direct historical context in Isaiah 8:11-15 (739-686

BC), where the prophet was commanded not to fear his critics but to "set apart the LORD" in his heart, just as Peter wrote.[76] Nary a word is ever said about the parallel passage of Isaiah 8 when traditional apologists refer to 1 Peter 3:15. Instead, they gravitate immediately to the pagan Greeks—Socrates, Plato and Aristotle—saying these men provide the historical context by which to understand Peter's imperative in 3:15. This enables them to push their philosophically-laden hermeneutic and agenda in the field of Christian apologetics.

Defending the faith in the midst of persecution is no novelty originating from the Patristic period for God's people. God has preserved a legacy for us to model that stretches all throughout redemptive history (Heb 11:1-40).

(10) Obfuscation vs. Perspicuity/Clarity (Theism vs. the Gospel)

Tenth, the traditional approaches of apologetics seek to defend Christianity only in the most universal, broad and inclusive ways, and thus obfuscate the main goal of apologetics. Usually they begin by trying to convince the atheist of theism. Then from there they try to argue for the virtues of monotheism and the possibility of generic Christianity. Groothuis, for example, says, "If the unbeliever is an atheist, we must start from scratch and argue for theism."[77] But the Bible says if the unbeliever is an atheist, then we give him Christ in the form of the glorious gospel, for that is his greatest need and the only power that can save his lost soul (Rom 1:16; cf. 1 Cor 1:17-25; Gal 6:14).

A common refrain in the previous definitions put forth by the traditional apologists was that apologetics sought to vindicate "the Christian religion," leaving the phrase open-ended and imprecise. Plantinga is a prime example of one who seeks to defend generic Christianity when he writes:

> When I speak here of Christian belief, I mean what is common to the great creeds of the main branches of the Christian church, what unites Calvin and Aquinas, Luther and Augustine, Menno Simons and Karl Barth, Mother Teresa and St. Maximus the Confessor, Billy Graham and St. Gregory Palamas—classical Christian belief, as we might call it.[78]

Similarly, Christian philosopher, James E. Taylor of Westmont College, wrote an entire textbook on apologetics to defend only a generic form of Christianity. He notes, "the goal of this book is to defend only 'mere' Christianity" and he goes on to assert that people should believe in Jesus' death and resurrection only if it is "reasonable."[79]

Biblical apologetics could not be any more different. Biblical apologetics has no desire to defend the Neo-orthodoxy of Barth or the Romanism espoused by Mother Teresa. And what good would it be, if through my philosophical arguments and my natural theology that I get an atheist to embrace theism, if that theism is Islam or Mormonism? William Lane Craig actually believes it is a good thing if we can get people to at least become theists through our apologetics. He lauds himself as he tells a story of how he helped a student at the University of Calgary become a theist as a result of debating about the "existence of God"—but the student did not become a Christian.[80] That is nothing to celebrate. The Pharisees whom Jesus condemned as "sons of hell" and "vipers" were theists (Matt 23:15, 33). And Jesus excoriated them for their false religion, saying, "Woe to you, scribes and Pharisees, hypocrites" (Matt 23:15). Satan is a theist (James 2:19; Matt 4:5-6). Demons are theists with some ortho-dox theology about God's existence and nature (Mark 5:7 ff.; James 2:19).

Biblical apologetics is specific, not general. It is like a focused laser, not a flailing searchlight. Biblical apologetics seeks to defend and propagate only scriptural Christianity, with particular emphasis on the gospel and the cross of Christ.[81] As the Apostle Paul declared, "may it never be that I should boast, except in the cross of our Lord Jesus Christ" (Gal 6:14).

(11) Integration vs. Biblical Theology

The final trait, number eleven, that characterizes traditional apol-ogetics is "integration." This last trait really envelops and incor-porates all previous ten traits. Integration is the big umbrella under which all the others fall. Integration is the over-riding paradigm and interpretive lens of all the other ten features. "Integration" as a word or concept by itself is not always bad. It depends upon the context. Integrating sugar in your coffee can be tasty. Integrating cyanide into your brew will kill you. The problem with the traditional apologists is that they try to integrate pagan Greek philosophy with the Bible on many levels. The result is truth compromised—a mongrel human philosophy of sorts.

The early church fathers were notorious for doing this, men like Justin, Origen and even Augustine in his early days. In the Middle Ages, Anselm and Thomas Aquinas were guilty, Aquinas taking integration to an extreme systematic level as he tried to create theology by pouring the Bible through the grid of Aristotelian thought at every turn.

Modern day Christian integrationists abound, with the likes of R. C. Sproul, Bernard Ramm, Clark Pinnock, Norman Geisler, Douglas Groothuis and many more, who allege that Christians need to lean on the wisdom of Aristotle and the Greeks when it comes to establishing a basis or starting point for all rational thought and argumentation. But such is not the case. The Bible is sufficient for the task.

The Bible was not intended to be integrated with any human wisdom. We need to do the work of apologetics, evangelism, witnessing, discipling, counseling, defending the faith, church planting, theology, preaching—all of it that constitutes "ministry"—with the Bible, and the Bible alone. Scripture is sufficient. Chapter 7 will examine further the dangers and inadequacies of integrating pagan thought (so called "wisdom") with the Bible.

Ironically the traditional apologists don't want to "integrate" when it is actually appropriate and biblical. For example, they typically don't want to integrate evangelism with the work of apologetics, when in fact those two enterprises always go hand-in-hand in the Bible, as modeled by the twelve apostles and Paul when they are on the mission field all throughout the Book of Acts.

Part of the genius of the Reformers like Luther and Calvin was their commitment to the purity and the sufficiency of the Bible. They rejected the popular notion of "integration" when it came to apologetics, doing theology or living the Christian life. Listen to Calvin's sober historical analysis on the plague of integration as it leaked subtly into the church from the very onset:

> Among ecclesiastical writers (i.e., Chrysostom, Jerome) ...many of them made too near an approach to the philosophers. Some of the most ancient writers appear to me to have exalted human strengths from a fear that a distinct acknowledgment of its impotence might expose them to the jeers of the philosophers with whom they were disputing...Therefore, to avoid teaching anything

which the majority of mankind might deem absurd, they made it their study, in some measure, to reconcile the doctrine of Scripture with the dogmas of philosophy ...they have bestowed on man more than he possesses for the study of virtue...the Greek fathers, above others ...have exceeded due bounds in extolling the powers of the human will, yet all ancient theologians, with the exception of Augustine, are so confused, vacillating, and contradictory on this subject, that no certainty can be obtained from their writings....Succeeding writers (every one courting applause for his acuteness in the defense of human nature) have uniformly, one after the other, gone more widely astray, until the common dogma came to be, that man was corrupted only in the sensual part of his nature, that reason remained entire, and will was scarcely impaired....Persons professing to be the disciples of Christ have spoken too much like the philosophers on this subject.[82]

In our day it should be noted that there have been a few Christian philosophers who, like Calvin, have categorically rejected the notion of integrating the Bible with Greek philosophy and human wisdom. Formally that would include those who fall in line with Cornelius Van Til and all those who hold to a biblical anthropology and epistemology—popularly known as the pure presuppositionalists.

Where Is the Gospel?

The greatest glaring deficiency in all the above proposed definitions of apologetics is that not one of them specifically mentions the gospel of Christ, or the cross of Christ, as that which especially needs to be defended against a hostile and unbelieving world. To divorce the work of apologetics from the proclamation of the gospel is to miss the whole point of apologetics.

Kelly James Clark, contemporary Christian apologetics "expert," has a radically different view than the apostle Paul did. In *Five Views*, Clark boasts that his approach to apologetics focuses "primarily on belief in God, not belief in Jesus."[83] Clark follows the long tradition established by Anselm (1033-1109), whose method of apologetics proceeded by "leaving Christ out of view (as if nothing had ever been heard of him)."[84] That explains why he never presents the gospel when delineating his apologetical methodology. He is not bothered by this difference at all because he maintains a low view of Scripture. He writes, "I also think a serious reader of Scripture can doubt that God's Word plays a determinative role in the human knowledge of God"[85]

In other words, he believes that our approach to apologetics should not be driven or dictated by Scripture, the gospel or talk about Jesus. But Scripture and Jesus say just the opposite. Jesus came teaching and "preaching the gospel of God" calling all "to repent and believe in the gospel" (Mark 1:14-15). Paul declared, "I am not ashamed of the gospel, for it is the power of God for salvation to everyone who believes" (Rom 1:16). Like Jesus and Paul, biblical apologetics makes the gospel message paramount when talking with unbelievers as we advance and defend the faith. When we do apologetics, we don't defend generic Christianity or general theism; we defend the cross of Christ in all its glory.

Summary

Apologetics is about defending the faith. A debate continues to rage as to what that means and as to how Christians are supposed to engage unbelievers as they seek to defend the faith. Christians need to continue the debate about the nature of apologetics. Iron sharpens iron (Prov 27:17).

Many suggest there are five distinct approaches to Christian apologetics: (1) classical; (2) evidential; (3) cumulative case; (4) Reformed epistemology and (5) presuppositional. It was observed that these five approaches have many overlapping commonalities, with presuppositionalism being the most distinct.

Although the five approaches have different points of emphasis, for the most part they share much in common and as such, are in the same genus. Many suggest that all five approaches stand on equal ground and Christians may employ one, more or all of the different approaches as they do apologetics. A recent book even proposes a new approach, "Integrative Apologetics," with that intent.[86] Biblical apologetics was set forth as the viable alternative to the five traditional approaches. Eleven traits were identified that contrast biblical apologetics with traditional apologetics:

Traditional Apologetics	Biblical Apologetics
1. rationalism	1. revelation
2. philosophy	2. theology
3. natural theology	3. natural revelation
4. pre-evangelism	4. authoritative proclamation
5. selectivity	5. holistic
6. formalism/elitism	6. personal/life-style
7. probability	7. truth/assurance
8. appeasement	8. accountability
9. novelty	9. legacy
10. obfuscation/theism	10. clarity/ gospel
11. integration	11. biblical theology

Sproul, Craig and many others write and speak to support classical apologetics. John Warwick Montgomery, Gary Habermas and others write to promote evidentialist apologetics. Kelly James Clark and Plantinga write to explain warranted apologetics. Geisler writes to defend philosophical apologetics. Paul Feinberg, Tim Keller and Douglas Groothuis defend cumulative case (or "comprehensive") apologetics. Van Til wrote to defend Reformed apologetics. Greg Bahnsen, Francis Schaeffer and John Frame wrote to advance variations of presuppositional apologetics. K. Scott Oliphint and William Edgar argue for covenantal apologetics. Carnell defended rational apologetics. Kenneth Boa and Robert Bowman write to establish integrative apologetics. Clark Pinnock introduced inclusive apologetics. Mark Hanna offers veridical apologetics; Mayers says it's Both/And. Andrew Davison dreams of "imaginative apologetics." Rev. Monsignor Paul J. Glenn and a host of others passionately defend Roman Catholic apologetics. In an attempt to cut through the malaise, I write this book in the defense of biblical, gospel-driven, cross-centered apologetics.

All the above competing definitions and approaches to apologetics that we examined fall short. Some are better than others. A few entail some truth, but are deficient to varying degrees, biblically speaking, while others incorporate down-right compromised premises, methodologies and conclusions throughout. Such deficiencies and compromises will be noted and refuted throughout the book.

Defending and propagating the Christian faith is a command from Scripture and a sobering and serious privilege. With that reminder we now will turn our attention to Scripture for a working definition of biblical, gospel-driven, cross-centered apologetics concurrent with a more thorough examination of the traditional views of apologetics.

Notes

1. Kelly James Clark, in *Five Views On Apologetics*, ed. Steven B. Cowan, (Grand Rapids: Zondervan, 2000), 275.
2. Ibid., 274.
3. Kenneth D. Boa and Robert M. Bowman Jr., *Faith Has Its Reasons: An Integrative Approach to Defending Christianity* (Waynesboro, GA: Paternoster, 2006), 2.
4. Peter Kreeft and Ronald Tacelli, *Pocket Handbook of Christian Apologetics* (Downers Grove, IL: InterVarsity Press, 2003), 10.
5. Bernard Ramm, *A Christian Appeal to Reason* (Waco, TX: Word, Inc., 1977), 14-15.
6. B. B. Warfield, *The Works of Benjamin B. Warfield: Studies in Theology*, 10 vols. (Grand Rapids: Baker Books, 2003), IX: 5.
7. B. B. Warfield, "Apologetics," in *The New Schaff-Herzog Encyclopedia of Religious Thought*, 12 vols., eds. Samuel Macauley Jackson and Charles Colebrook Sherman (New York: Funk & Wagnalls Company, 1908), I:232-38.
8. Colin Brown, *Miracles and the Critical Mind* (Grand Rapids, MI: Eerdmans, 1984), 3.
9. Gordon R. Lewis, *Testing Christianity's Truth Claims: Approaches to Christian Apologetics* (Chicago, IL: Moody Press, 1976), 340.
10. Leander S. Keyser, *A System of Christian Evidence* (The Lutheran Literary Board, 1953), 21.
11. Jim S. Halsey, *For a Time Such as This: An Introduction to the Reformed Apologetic of Cornelius Van Til* (Phillipsburg, NJ: P & R, 1976), 168.
12. Norman Geisler, "Foreword" in *The Resurrection of Jesus: An Apologetic* by Gary Habermas (University Press of America, 1984).
13. Bernard Ramm, *Protestant Christian Evidences* (Chicago, IL: Moody Press, 1967), 13.
14. Edward John Carnell, *An Introduction to Christian Apologetics: A Philosophic Defense of the Trinitarian-Theistic Faith* (Grand Rapids: Eerdmans, 1956), 7.
15. Cornelius Van Til, *Christian Apologetics* (Phillipsburg, NJ: P & R, 1976), 1.
16. R. C. Sproul, John Gerstner and Arthur Lindsley, *Classical Apologetics: A Rational Defense of the Christian Faith and a Critique of Presuppositional Apologetics* (Grand Rapids, MI: Zondervan, 1984), 13.
17. Dean Hardy, *Stand Your Ground: An Introductory Text for Apologetics Students* (Eugene, OR: Wipf & Stock, 2007), 3.
18. William Lane Craig, *Five Views*, 287.
19. Paul J. Glenn, *Apologetics: A Philosophic Defense and Explanation of the Catholic Religion* (Rockford, IL: Tan Books, 1980), xiii-xiv.
20. Gary Habermas, *Five Views*, 187. Zemek insightfully comments, "On account of the prevalence of philosophical approaches, there is an acute need to delineate as thoroughly as possible the implicit system of apologetics which is contained in the Scriptures. The Church of Jesus Christ has been plagued for centuries by Greek philosophy, and this phenomenon is readily demonstrable in the field of apologetics. Bahnsen

adequately surveys the situation when he asserts that 'Socrates transferred the set of authority to man's autonomous reason; Roman Catholic and Arminian apologetics follow suit...'"; George J. Zemek, Jr., "Exegetical and Theological Bases for a Consistently Presuppositional Approach to Apologetics," ThD Thesis, *Grace Theological Seminary*, 1982, 1.

21. Ronald B. Mayers, *Both/And: A Balanced Apologetic* (Chicago: Moody Press, 1984), 9.

22. Sproul *et al*, *Classical Apologetics*, 9. Elsewhere Sproul espouses the autonomy of human reason when he says, "Nobody starts with God except God. You can't start in your mind with God, the knowledge of God, unless you are God. Where we say you start is self-consciousness, and from self-consciousness you move to the existence of God. You don't start with God-consciousness and move to the existence of the self. By necessity human beings, thinking with human minds must start with where they are, with their brain...You cannot start in your thinking with God's thoughts. The only thing you start with is your own self-awareness, and from there you move...if you begin with self-consciousness, and you reason correctly...you will in fact end by necessarily...affirming the existence of God"; Sproul is in gross error here on at least two counts: (1) he says, "Nobody starts with God" when in fact Paul argues in Romans 1 and 2 that everyone starts with God—all people do in fact have an inescapable "God-consciousness"—because the knowledge of God is innate, immediate, and intuitive, for the knowledge of God is imprinted on every human conscience and every human heart by virtue of being made in God's image; (2) Sproul clearly does not understand what Calvin meant by the *sensus divinitatus*, for he alleges here that humans go through a ratiocination process beginning with self, moving to an eventual affirmation or acknowledgement of God's existence, through what amounts to be an *a posteriori* exercise. The *sensus divinitatus* that Calvin taught, accurately from Scripture, is an *a priori* ontological reality, not an empirical epistemological exercise; see R. C. Sproul, lecture: "Theology, Philosophy and Science," <watch?v=a4xyK1t6eyQ>

23. Craig, *Five Views*, 287.

24. Ibid., 38. In contrast to Craig's unhealthy confidence in unaided human wisdom, Stott's counter is the needed biblical balance on the matter: "Like the brilliant intellectuals of ancient Greece our contemporaries have unbounded confidence in human reason. They want to think their way to God by themselves, and to gain credit for discovering God by their own effort. But God resists such swellings of pride on the part of the finite creature. Of course men have been given minds to use...and they are never to stifle or smother them, but they must humble them reverently before the revelation of God, becoming in Paul's word 'fools' and in Christ's word 'babes' (Mt. 6:25). It is only babes to whom God reveals Himself and only fools whom He makes wise"; John Stott, *The Preacher's Portrait* (Grand Rapids: Eerdmans, 1961), 111.

25. Ibid., 54.

26. Douglas Groothuis, *Christian Apologetics: A Comprehensive Case for Biblical Faith* (InterVarsity Press, Downers Grove IL, 2011), 27.
27. Brown, *Miracles*, 3.
28. Keyser, *A System of Christian Evidence*, 21.
29. Glenn, *Apologetics*, xiii-xiv.
30. Cornelius Van Til, *Christian Apologetics*, (Phillipsburg, NJ: P & R Publishing, 2003), 17. Personal friend, disciple and interpreter of Van Til, K. Scott Oliphint admits Van Til was too philosophical. He agrees that Van Til's esoteric style was a hindrance to the average reader: "So much of the material related to this method is mired in deep and complex philosophical concepts and verbiage that it has remained, by and large, inaccessible to any who are not interested or schooled in such things." As a result, Oliphint felt compelled to write an entire book to "translate" and "interpret" Van Til in a language the average Christian can understand; see K. Scott Oliphant, *Covenant Apologetics: Principles & Practice in Defense of Our Faith* (Wheaton, Illinois: Crossway, 2013), 26-28.
31. Craig, *Five Views*, 38.
32. Alvin Plantinga, *Warranted Christian Belief* (New York, NY: Oxford University Press, 2000), xiii.
33. Ramm, *Appeal to Reason*, 25.
34. J. P. Moreland and William Lane Craig, *The Blackwell Companion to Natural Theology* (Malden, MA: Blackwell Publishers, 2009), 1.
35. Craig, *Five Views*, 40-41.
36. Sproul *et al, Classical Apologetics*, 20. Biblical apologetics is closest to presuppositional apologetics of the five options. Biblical apologetics is not averse to "evidence." Many wrongly assume that presuppositionalists don't use evidence or need evidence. That is false. Bahnsen was correct when he said it was erroneous to divide the Christian approaches to apologetics into 2 camps, i.e. the "evidential" vs. the "presuppositional," for the presuppositional approach does in fact welcome evidence and is based on evidence, and so is biblical apologetics. Bahnsen suggested the approaches be categorized as "traditional" vs. "presuppositional," which I also favor; my own rendition for the purposes of this book is "traditional" vs. biblical"; see Greg L. Bahnsen, *An Answer to Frame's Critique of Van Til: Profound Differences Between the Traditional and Presuppositional Approach* (Glenside, PA: Westminster Seminary Bookstore, nd), 1-52.
37. Ibid., 25.
38. Hardy, *Stand Your Ground*, 1. "Pre-evangelism" was fabricated as a way to seek to soften the blow when talking to unbelievers about Christ—a man-made technique to make Jesus, the Bible and Christianity palatable for the sinner, a way to "ease into" the inherently offensive gospel, a civil approach to bend over backwards seeking not to offend the skeptic and to satisfy all their inquiries on all matters. Stott blows this pseudo-spiritual approach to evangelism out of the water as he exegetes the practical implications of 1 Corinthians 1:17-23: "The Apostle proceeds to enforce these general truths with a more particular reference to [unbelieving] Jews and Greeks. *Jews demand signs*, he writes, *and Greeks seek wisdom, but we preach*

Christ crucified (vv. 22, 23). Notice the verbs in this sentence. *The Jews* were making imperious demands, insisting on certain signs before they were prepared to accept the claims of Jesus. *The Greeks* were forever restlessly seeking and searching for wisdom. *But we preach...*that is, our task as Christian preachers is not subserviently to answer all the questions which men put to us; nor to attempt to meet all the demands which are made on us; nor hesitantly to make tentative suggestions to the philosophically minded; but rather to proclaim a message which is dogmatic because it is divine. The preacher's responsibility is proclamation, not discussion. There is too much discussion of the Christian religion today, particularly with unbelievers, as if we were more concerned with men's opinions of Christ than with the honour and glory of Jesus Christ Himself. Are we to cast our Priceless Pearl before swine to let them sniff at Him and trample upon Him at their pleasure? No. We are called to proclaim Christ, not to discuss Him...we are 'heralds,' charged to publish abroad a message which did not originate with us (that we should presume to tamper with it) but with Him who gave it [to] us to publish"; Stott, *Preacher's Portrait*, 110-111.

39. Sproul *et al*, *Classical Apologetics*, 22.

40. Craig, *Five Views*, 287. Contrary to Craig's view, Busenitz gets it right when he says, "Apologetics is not a form of philosophy reserved for professionals or academics. Rightly understood, apologetics is a tool for evangelists to help people see with clarity the truth about the gospel. Apologetics is not primarily concerned with winning arguments, but with winning souls"; Nathan Busenitz, "The Word of Truth in a World of Error: The Fundamentals of Practical Apologetics," in *Evangelism: How to Share the Gospel Faithfully* by John MacArthur (Nashville, TN: Thomas Nelson, 2011), 43.

41. Frederic R. Howe, "Kerygma and Apologia," *Jerusalem and Athens: Critical Discussions on the Philosophy and Apologetics of Cornelius Van Til*, ed. E. R. Geehan (Phillipsburg, NJ: P & R Publishing, 1980), 446-447.

42. R. C. Sproul, *Defending Your Faith: An Introduction to Apologetics*, (Wheaton, IL: Crossway Books, 2003), 23. Geisler also advocates pre-evangelism; see Norman L. Geisler, *Baker Encyclopedia of Christian Apologetics* (Grand Rapids: Baker Academic, 1999), 37. Groothuis, too, advocates the man-made notion of "pre-evangelism": "Apologetics can be used to remove or diminish intellectual obstacles that hinder people from embracing Christ as Lord; thus it serves as pre-evangelism. In some cases—especially in academic settings where unbelief has become second nature for so many—'all this philosophy' *is* required for evangelism to become even a possibility" (*Christian Apologetics*, 28). Notice he says here that evangelism is not even a possibility in some cases without first resorting to philosophy! Also he claims people don't embrace Christ as Lord because of "intellectual obstacles," whereas Jesus said people don't embrace Him because they love their sin, or "the darkness": "This is the verdict: Light has come into the world, but men loved darkness instead of light because their deeds were evil" (John 3:19, NIV).

43. Lewis, *Testing Christianity's Truth Claims*, 340.

44. Halsey, *For a Time Such as This*, 168.

45. Clark H. Pinnock, *Set Forth Your Case: An Examination of Christianity's Credentials* (Chicago: Moody Press, 1975), 3.

46. Carnell, *Christian Apologetics*, 7.

47. Sproul *et al*, *Classical Apologetics*, 13.

48. Craig, *Five Views*, 287.

49. Warfield, *The Works*, IX:4.

50. Robert L. Reymond, *The Justification of Knowledge* (Phillipsburg, NJ: P & R Publishing, 1979), 1-4.

51. Hart correctly observes, "[*apologia*] is used metaphorically…no reference is intended to formal proceedings in a court of law," J. H. A. Hart, *The Expositor's Greek Testament*, 5 vols. ed. Robertson Nicoll, (Grand Rapids: Eerdmans, 1990), V:67. Calvin had it right 500 years ago on 1 Peter 3:15: "The meaning then is, that we ought to be prompt in avowing our faith, so as to set it forth whenever necessary, lest the unbelieving through our silence should condemn the religion we follow….Peter had in view no other thing, than that Christians should make it evident to unbelievers that they truly worshipped God, and had a holy and good religion," John Calvin, *Commentaries on the Catholic Epistles*, trans. By John Owen (Grand Rapids: Baker Book House, 1999), XXII: 108. By contrast, Groothuis wrongly limits the use of *apologia* in the New Testament to "a formal courtroom defense," (*Christian Apologetics*, 24) a definition that does not flow from the composite exegetical pool of New Testament usage, but rather from a strained, eisegetical assumption.

52. Groothuis, *Christian Apologetics*, 49.

53. Norman Geisler and Peter Bocchino, *Unshakable Foundations* (Minneapolis, MN: Bethany House, 2001), 29. Ramm says the same thing: Christianity is "the best of perspectives" among many perspectives and the "largest possible framework," not the right and only truth—just the best perspective; Ramm, *Appeal to Reason*, 18.

54. Dennis McCallum, *Christianity, The Faith that Makes Sense: Solid Evidence for Belief in Christ* (Wheaton, IL: Tyndale House Publishers, 1997), 12.

55. Tim Keller, *The Reason for God* (2008, Dutton New York, NY: Dutton, 2008), 141.

56. Ibid., 127.

57. Ibid., 141.

58. J. P. Moreland, *Scaling the Secular City* (Grand Rapids, MI: Baker Book House, 1987), 13.

59. Craig, *Five Views*, 53. Craig's statement here, that Christianity is "the most credible view" is synonymous with what is often called the Cumulative Case approach to apologetics. This approach argues that Christianity is "the best theory among all theories" in explaining the world in all its component parts. Paul Feinberg (1938-2004) defended the Cumulative Case approach in *Five Views*. Others with similar views include the Anglican, pro-Darwinian theologian, Alistair McGrath (b. 1953), C. S. Lewis (1898-1963), Dorothy Sayers (1893-1957) and G. K. Chesterton

(1874-1936). From this perspective C. S Lewis could say, "I am an empirical theist. I arrived at God by induction."

60. Ibid., 48-51.
61. Hardy, *Stand Your Ground*,1-3.
62. Plantinga, *Christian Belief*, vii.
63. Sproul, *Defending Your Faith*, 50. Sproul's starting point in apologetics is the dubious mantra, "The Bible is generally reliable." He said this at the Shepherd's Conference via video at Grace Church in Sun Valley, CA, 2015 of March. This is a far cry from the resolute declaration of the prophets, Jesus and the apostles who would proclaim with certitude, "Thus saith the Lord!" They believed that God's Word was completely and assuredly reliable.
64. Avery Cardinal Dulles, *A History of Apologetics* (San Francisco: Ignatius Press, 2005), xxi. For over fifty years world renown Oxford Christian apologist, Richard Swinburne, has argued not for the certainty of God's existence, but like others, the mere probability of God's existence. He profers that he "is not concerned primarily with whether this belief is true or with whether we can know it to be true, but with the prior questions of what it means and whether it is coherent; what claim a man who asserts that there is a God is making and whether it is a claim which is coherent"; Richard Swinburne, *The Coherence of Theism* (New York: Oxford University Press, 2010), 1. Contrast that sterile ambivalence with the bold, rhythmic confidence of Steven Curtis Chapman and Toby Mac who say, "It's got to be true!"
65. Ibid., 3. To the choir of reticent voices already listed we can add Bush who yodles the same shaky tune: "We need first to defend the possibility of truth"; *Defending the Faith—Engaging the Culture: Essays Honoring L. Russ Bush*, editors Bruce A. Little and Mark Liederbach (Nashville: B & H Publishing Group, 2011), 77.
66. Clark, *Five Views*, 277.
67. Greg L. Bahnsen, *Always Ready: Directions for Defending the Faith,* ed. Robert R. Booth (Texarkana: Covenant Media Foundation, 1996), 19.
68. Normal L. Geisler, *"Foreword"* in *The Resurrection of Jesus.*
69. Norman Geisler, *Christian Apologetics* (Grand Rapids: Baker Books, 1976), 61.
70. Moreland, *Scaling the Secular City*, 11.
71. Note, Aquinas himself argued for "certainty" and not mere "plausibility."
72. See *Five Views*, 275.
73. We even call them "the apologists"—why don't we call Titus, Timothy, Phillip and Apollos the apologists?
74. Craig, *Five Views*, 28. L. Russ Bush gives a similar pedigree as representative of the development of the formal discipline of apologetics through the ages, twelve men, he says, who "characteristically represent the developments in apologetics studies prior to the nineteenth century"; in chronological order they are Justin Martyr, Athenagoras, Iranaeus, Tertullian, Origen, Athanasius, Augustine, Anselm, Aquinas, Calvin, Joseph Butler and William Paley; *Classical Readings in Christian Apologetics—*

AD 100-1800 (Grand Rapids: Zondervan, 1983), xiv-xvii. One should not be misled to believe that these twelve writers represent an unbroken chain and monolithic approach to defending the faith. For example, Calvin can hardly be called a classical or philosophical apologist. He was first and foremost a biblical exegete and theologian, setting him distinctly apart from most of those in this list of twelve. Edgar and Oliphint propose forty-one names throughout church history up to the present in their two-volume work, *Christian Apologetics: A Primary Source Reader*, see footnote 75.

75. Oliphint and Edgar hint at the Old Testament legacy, but then fail to develop the idea; William Edgar and K. Scott Oliphint, *Christian Apologetics Past and Present: A Primary Source Reader* (Wheaton: Crossway, 2009), 11-12.

76. The conscientious reader will note that in the English text 1 Peter 3:14-16 is one sentence, so verse fifteen can't be read apart from verse fourteen or sixteen, and then massaged eisegetically to conform to one's own liking. Verse fourteen quotes Isaiah 8:12 thus laying the contextual foundation for the imperative in verse fifteen. The point is that God was commanding Isaiah and believing Jews to sanctify the LORD in their lives as they faced opposition. Wiersbe well notes, "The setting of the Isaiah quotation is significant. Ahaz, King of Judah, faced a crisis because of an impending invasion by the Assyrian army. The kings of Israel and Syria wanted Ahaz to join them in the alliance, but Ahaz refused; so Israel and Syria threatened to invade Judah! Behind the scenes, Ahaz confederated himself with Assyria! The Prophet Isaiah warned him against ungodly alliances and urged him to trust God for deliverance. 'Sanctify the Lord of hosts [armies] Himself; and let Him be your fear, and let Him be your dread' (Isa. 8:13)"; Warren W. Wiersbe, *The Bible Expository Commentary: An Exposition of the New Testament*, 2 vols. (Colorado Springs, CO: Chariot Victor Publications, 1989), II: 413.

77. Groothuis, *Christian Apologetics*, 43.

78. Plantinga, *Warranted Christian Belief*, vii.

79. James E. Taylor, *Introducing Apologetics: Cultivating Christian Commitment*, (Grand Rapids: Baker Academic, 2006), 229.

80. Craig, *Five Views*, 288.

81. Lenski, the Bible teacher got it right, because he was driven by Scripture not philosophy. Commenting on the basic thrust of Peter's imperative he says, "Let whoever will constitute himself a judge, the Christian is never to evade or to put him off, he is to be ready to present his case, his defense, to render account as to what his hope embraces, and as to why he holds it in his heart. We may say that he is to be ready always to testify, to correct ignorance about Christ, to spread the gospel light, to win others for Christ, to justify his own hope, and as Peter adds here (v. 16), to silence evil speakers with his good conduct which certainly speaks for itself and puts slander to shame,"; R. C. H. Lenski, *The Interpretation of I and II Epistles of Peter, the Three Epistles of John, and the Epistle of Jude* (Minneapolis, MN: Augsburg Fortress, 2008), 150.

82. John Calvin, *Institutes of the Christian Religion*, 159-160.

83. Clark, *Five Views*, 367. Ironically, in *Five Views*, Clark is supposed to represent Calvin's view; but unfortunately he is the most rank of Arminians. He openly pushes an apologetic that excludes Jesus, but rather puts forth a system to establish generic theism. Calvin blasted such a Christless notion: "after the fall of our first parent, no knowledge of God without a Mediator was effectual to salvation...The more shameful, therefore, is the presumption of those who throw heaven open to the unbelieving and profane, in the absence of that grace which Scripture uniformly describes as the only door by which we enter into life....no worship was ever pleasing to God in which respect was not had to Christ." In other words, it is "shameful" to defend Christianity without Jesus being front and center; *Institutes*, 213.

84. Dulles, *A History*, 101.

85. Clark, *Five Views*, 371.

86. Boa and Bowman, *Faith Has Its Reasons*.

2

Apologia: What Peter Really Meant

The Significance of 1 Peter 3:15

Today's Christian philosophers and theologians all agree that 1 Peter 3:15 is a mandate for the Church to practice apologetics. Most agree that 1 Peter 3:15 is foundational in defining what apologetics is. The problem is that there is great disparity between Christian apologists and biblical expositors regarding what Peter actually meant when he penned this verse. In context, Peter wrote the following:

> [13]And who is there to harm you if you prove zealous for what is good? [14]But even if you should suffer for the sake of righteousness, *you are* blessed. 'And do not fear their intimidation, and do not be troubled,' [15]but sanctify Christ as Lord in your hearts, always *being* ready to make **a defense (*apologia*)** to everyone who asks you to give an account for the hope that is in you, yet with gentleness and reverence; [16]and keep a good conscience so that in the thing in which you are slandered, those who revile your good behavior in Christ may be put to shame (3:13-16).

I concede with many traditional apologists who teach that this verse is foundational for apologetics. Unfortunately this verse is often taken out of context and misapplied by popular Christian apologists and philosophers. The goal of this chapter is to give an exegesis and exposition of 1 Peter 3:15 in its proper biblical context so that it can legitimately inform a truly biblical apologetic. The average apologetics book makes a passing, obligatory reference to 1 Peter 3:15, usually quoting just a portion of the verse with no explanation of its context and then the Christian metaphysician is off to the races in expounding his philosophically-driven treatise of natural theology, supposedly warranted by the meaning of 1 Peter 3:15. A typical example of such exegetical short-circuitry is the popular survey of apologetics referred to earlier, *Five Views On Apologetics*. The authors of that book refer to the verse reference a few times, but the passage is never explained by them in its scriptural context. Worse, they leave it undefined and infuse it with nuances of meaning that are not in the biblical text as Peter intended.[1]

The Proper Meaning of 1 Peter 3:15
Defining 'apologia'
Before examining 1 Peter 3:15 to show what Peter meant by "to make a defense" in context, it's first necessary to expose the counterfeit meaning typically proffered by traditional apologists. A classic example is from William Lane Craig.[2] Craig, and a legion of philosophical apologists, argue that the most important word in 1 Peter 3:15 is *apologia*, translated in English as "defense." Isolating and over-emphasizing *apologia*'s import, they then extrapolate from there, while ignoring the bulk of other equally potent inspired words in the verse, saying *apologia* really emphasizes "giving a lengthy legal defense," or *apologia* means "expounding with unaided human reason seeking to nullify the critic and skeptic with logic-chopping arguments," or the word means "to wax eloquent with Aristotelian logic and philosophical jargon apart from Scripture," or "to muster a flurry of observations from natural theology."[3]

Two huge problems result with such an approach: (1) it's illegitimate to isolate a word in a Bible verse, pulling it out of context and assigning it a nuance foreign to the immediate context; and (2) it's illegitimate to ignore most of the other words in the passage that actually give the passage its true meaning. The end result of this selective eisegetical word-crafting with respect to the misuse of *apologia* in 1 Peter 3:15 is a completely wrong foundation of interpretation and meaning of what Peter was saying. Craig and company try to establish that *apologia* should be understood the way it was commonly used by the Greek pagan world in the fifth century BC, by the likes of the profane Greek philosophers Socrates (c. 469 BC), Plato (c. 428 BC) and Aristotle (384-322 BC). They highlight that the Greeks were intellectuals and for them giving an *apologia* was first and foremost reasoning as a sheer intellectual pursuit, wielding the laws of logic and raw brainpower. In turn, they say, we need to be like Socrates and Plato when we give our "defense" by using unaided human logic and raw intellectual prowess in defending Christianity. In other words, they say you can't begin the work of apologetics by using the Bible. For example, listen to Cowan: "the very word *apologetics* is derived from the Greek *apologia*, which means 'defense.' It was a term used in the courts of law in the ancient world. Socrates, for example, gave his famous 'apology,' or defense before the court of Athens."[4] Pratt echoes the same refrain: "The *Apology of Socrates* is an account of the defense which he offered before the court of Athens."[5]

In similar fashion Bernard Ramm explains with more detail his strained version of the history for the word *apologia*:

> The historical origin of apologetics is to be found in the legal procedures in ancient Athens. The plaintiff brought his accusation (*kategoria*) before the court. The accused had the right of making a reply (*apologia*) to the accusation …The classic example of the apology is of course the famous *Apology* of Socrates before the Athenian court of law preserved for us in the *Dialogues* of Plato.[6]

Ramm goes on to say that just as the Greeks understood the use of *apologia* in a secular, legal, philosophical and rationalistic context, so must the Christian. Based on this one word and their nuanced massaging of its meaning, traditional apologists insist that apologetics is primarily a philosophical enterprise based on natural human reason and the laws of logic apart from the use of special revelation. The Greeks reasoned from logic, not Scripture—so then must we.

Exegetical Fallacies

The standard traditional apologists' definition and application of *apologia* as used by Peter is flawed. This should not be totally surprising in light of the fact that traditional apologists are first and foremost philosophers and not skilled biblical exegetes. When handling *apologia* this is readily apparent as they commit a basic exegetical howler when dealing with this word. They assume that the way a word was once used in a certain context in a different time period by a different author in a different culture means the exact same thing in another context, by a different author in a different time period and culture. But this is not the case. Manipulating one word and infusing it with a strained meaning can wreak much havoc. Building an entire discipline, theological system or methodological approach upon a contrived, isolated meaning of one word from the Bible is dangerous. Sadly it is very common among everyday Christians as well as professional theologians, apologists and philosophers. Carson gives this sobering reminder regarding common word-study fallacies in exegesis:

> **Semantic obsolescence**—In some ways, this fallacy is the mirror image of semantic anachronism. Here the interpreter assigns to a word in his text a meaning that the word in question used to have in earlier times, but that is no longer found within the live, semantic range...Some words, of course, simply lose their usefulness and drop out of the language...far trickier are those that remain in the language but change their meaning. So also in biblical languages...a Greek word that means one thing in classical Greek and another in the New Testament, can easily lead the unwary into the pitfall of this third fallacy...In short, words change their meaning over time.[7]

So it is with *apologia* as used by Peter in 3:15. The way Plato used this word in 400 BC as a pagan, in a pagan culture, with a pagan worldview is not identical to how the born-again, Spirit-led Hebrew Apostle of Palestine used this word in AD 64.

The careful English reader should note that 1 Peter 3:14-15 is actually referring to Isaiah 8:12-13 (739-686 BC). The Hebrew Old Testament is the historical context for *apologia*, not Plato's Greek pagan use of it. Isaiah the prophet was commanded not to fear his critics but to "set apart the LORD" in his heart, just as Peter wrote. Nary a word is ever said about the parallel passage of Isaiah 8 when traditional apologists refer to 1 Peter 3:15.[8] Instead they gravitate immediately to the pagan Greeks—Socrates, Plato and Aristotle— saying these men provide the historical context by which to understand Peter's imperative in 3:15. This enables them to push their philosophically-laden hermeneutic and metaphysical agenda in the field of Christian apologetics.

In his classic work on linguistic and exegetical studies of the biblical languages, Leon Morris reiterates this basic hermeneutical principle, warning against the perils of flippant, shallow word studies that pop apologists frequently employ:

> And in any case the meaning of a word is to be determined in the last resort by the way people used it. We cannot say that, since a verb is formed in such and such a fashion, therefore the Greeks must have understood it to mean so and so....in many profane contexts the thought is...in striking contrast with the use in the Bible.[9]

In light of the above it is imperative then that "*apologia* not be extracted from a strictly secular background and then taken as a frozen technical term used to define all stages of the Christian discipline."[10] Hart gives the true meaning of *apologia* from an exegetical perspective explaining how Peter used the word in context:

> Properly *speech in defense, apologia*, is used metaphorically here as by St. Paul in I Cor. ix. 3, *ho houtos eimi emos apologia ho anakrino ego*; where also, though another technical word is introduced, no reference is intended to formal proceedings in a court of law.[11]

It is a well established fact that one of the most popular New Testament Greek words, *agape* ("love"), has no exact equivalent in secular or classical pre-biblical Greek in terms of its apostolic meaning. Words can change over time. A. T. Robertson has done a great service to the Church by reminding us of the proper approach when doing word-studies from the Bible.[12] He showed that every word needs to be examined in light of three considerations: (1) each word's root and etymology needs to be examined; (2) the word's historical development needs to be weighed; (3) finally, the immediate context of any given word needs to be considered and its immediate contextual meaning can even override and defy the first two points of consideration.

So then, traditional apologists are really guilty of two key exegetical blunders. First, they misrepresent the actual meaning of the way Peter used the word *apologia*, and second, they try to milk too much out of one word by attempting to construct an entire field of discipline out of one isolated term. Biblical scholar and exegete Bill Barrick comments on the dangers of this second common fallacy. He says word studies are of minimal value when used alone because "terms are more constrained by context and usage within bound phrases than by etymological considerations." In other words, etymological studies done in isolation are too myopic and have relevant meaning only in relation to other words and phrases. He further adds, "Lexical analyses too often pay too little attention to entire phrases and the overall context—both being the better determiners of an individual word's meaning in a particular passage."[13] A legitimate examination of what Peter meant by *apologia* can only be determined by a holistic approach that includes the word usage of *apologia* throughout the whole New Testament in addition to examining 1 Peter 3:15 in light of the whole context of Peter's epistle. With that in mind, we now turn to see what Peter really meant.

A Scriptural Defense

Peter exhorts his readers to "give an *apologia*" for their hope. *Apologia* is made up of two Greek words, the preposition *apo* plus *logia*. *Apo* is "from" and *logia* is related to *logos*, meaning "word, a speech, verbal communication." The compound word means a "verbal defense or explanation." *Apologia* can refer to a formal setting for giving a defense as in a court of law or it can also be informal, explaining oneself in spontaneous discourse and dialogue.[14] The immediate context determines the meaning of how it is being used. Some popular English Bibles translate *apologia* here as "give/make a defense" (NASB; ESV; NKJV). But the NIV, the KJV and The NET Bible all translate it as "give an answer," which is also legitimate. This second, informal translation is more in keeping with how *apologia* is used throughout the New Testament.

Aside from deciding on the best translation there is also debate over its *interpretation* and *application*. The dispute arises over the content and method of that defense. As for the method, traditional apologists say we need to defend ourselves after the manner of Socrates and Plato. Biblical apologetics says we need to defend ourselves after the manner of the Old Testament prophets, Jesus and the apostles. As for the content of our defense, traditional apologetics says we resort to sheer human wisdom, the laws of logic and natural reason apart from Scripture. Biblical apologetics says we reason from Scripture with Scripture in making our defense.

Paul used the word *apologia* in the same manner as Peter. In Philippians he writes, "For it is only right for me to feel this way about you all, because I have you in my heart, since both in my imprisonment and in the **defense** [*apologia*] and confirmation of the gospel, you all are partakers of grace with me....knowing that I am appointed for the **defense** [*apologian*] of the gospel" (1:7, 16). It is clear what Paul was defending—the gospel. He was not defending theism, or the probability of God's existence. He was defending specific truths about the life, death and resurrection of Jesus Christ, the content of which is special revelation. And it was based on revealed truth from God, not natural human reason or the laws of logic.

Defending with Scripture

Thousands of times the Old Testament prophets, from Moses to Malachi, customarily used the refrain, "This is what the LORD says" as they preached, taught and defended the faith (Exod 7:17; Mal 4:3). They were wielding words they received directly from God—that is special revelation. Jesus' favorite phrase when teaching, preaching and especially when He was defending the faith against critical religious enemies (Mark 7:6) and even Satan himself (Matt 4:4), was, "It is written...." Jesus' highest authority for defending truth was written Scripture (John 6:45; 10:35-38). Also, the apostles were sent to teach, preach, reprove, rebuke and exhort with God's Word: "they were all filled with the Holy Spirit, and began to speak the word of God with boldness" (Acts 4:31). The apostles were dependent upon divine revelation, not finite human reason or man-made natural theology, as they advanced and defended the faith.

The key difference between traditional apologetics and biblical apologetics is not whether one employs reason while the other does not. Traditional apologists often accuse their critics of this very thing. When folks like me warn Christians of depending upon raw human wisdom in apologetics, traditional apologists interpret that to mean that we reject reasoning, logic and thinking altogether. Dean Hardy is typical when he suggests that if you don't accept his premise and methodology in doing apologetics in the classical manner, utilizing man-made theistic arguments and the laws of logic, then one is infected with "anti-intellectualism."[15] Sproul *et al* make the same accusation, labeling non-traditional apologists "fideists" and "anti-apologists."[16]

The biblical position being proposed is not anti-intellectual or opposed to reasoning as some will suggest. Just the opposite is true.

The greatest intellect in the universe is God. He is the quintessential thinker and has an infinite mind (Rom 11:33). He knows all truth and even defines reality (Ps 139). He has revealed His mind through revelation and He has preserved it for us today in Scripture. Scripture is sufficient for every task of Christian ministry, including apologetics: "All Scripture is inspired by God and profitable for teaching, for reproof, for correction, for training in righteousness; so that the man of God may be adequate, equipped for every good work" (2 Tim 3:16-17). The mysteries of God and the very mind of Christ are found in Scripture (1 Cor 2:1-16). When we engage in apologetics we engage in the highest form of thinking and intellectual activity possible as we reason with unbelievers using Scripture. We reason with the Scriptures and we reason from the Scriptures. As we defend the faith, we use God's thoughts and His reason as found in the Bible.

Sproul *et al* suggest that Paul at times defended the faith, reasoning with unbelievers using sheer "appeals to reason and to empirical data" apart from special revelation.[17] That simply is not true. In Acts 17 Paul went to Thessalonica for the first time and engaged with unbelievers. He engaged in apologetics. "And according to Paul's custom, he went to them, and for three Sabbaths reasoned with them from the Scriptures" (v. 2). Notice Paul used reason—he employed his mind full-throttle. But the content and the methodology of his reasoning were dictated by "the Scriptures." This passage says this "was his custom." He did not deviate from using God's direct revelation depending upon his audience or the circumstances. He always reasoned from the Scriptures or utilized direct revelation as an apostle. He never resorted to sheer human wisdom, the Aristotelian laws of logic, man-made theistic arguments or raw empirical data to defend or proclaim the faith.

Give a Biblical Defense!

When Peter says we need "to make a defense" to everyone who asks us about our hope, we follow the example of the prophets, the apostles and Jesus Himself. We reason with unbelievers, depending upon the revealed mind of God as found in the Scriptures. Peter's custom was to defend the faith by reasoning from the Scriptures. There was no one more hostile to Christianity than the unbelieving Jews who murdered Jesus. And Peter addressed and reasoned with those very people by using Scripture (Acts 2:22-24). We must do the same.

Give Real Answers

When Peter exhorts Christians to "give an answer" to unbelievers, traditional apologists assume Peter meant that we can't use Scripture—we must give answers not using the Bible! They say the "answer" must be non-biblical, based on neutral logic, flowing strictly from unaided human reason, in a formal, forensic and philosophical capacity. That is a colossal, misguided assumption. When he commanded believers to "give an answer" Peter may actually have been thinking that we should give true, real-life, biblical answers or reasons for our hope in Christ.

Here are some great "answers" that we can share with unbelievers when they ask about our faith: (1) "I believe in Jesus because He promised to rescue me from the devil and eternal hell." (2) "I believe in Jesus because He promised to give me eternal resurrection life in the future." (3) "I believe in Jesus because He promised to forgive all my sin and relieve my guilt." (4) "I believe in Jesus because He promised to give me eternal life right now, in this life." These are all good, legitimate, true, powerful answers that flow from Scripture. These are not hypothetical either—these are reasons people have given to me over the years telling me why they became Christians. I have never had anyone tell me, "I became a believer because of the consistency in the byproducts of natural theology's *kalam* cosmological argument as it rationally tipped the scale in favor of the theoretical 'actual undeniability' of the existence of God and the 'unaffirmability of the converse alternatives'." Further, the answers above are not anti-intellectual or fideistic in nature either, as traditional apologists will allege. They are grounded in eternal truth, in the historical realities of Christ's life, death and resurrection, and in the unchanging God of the universe.

Efficacious Living

Another basic point about how Peter used the word *apologia* is paramount and that has to do with its function in the sentence and how it relates to other words in the verse. Traditional apologists would have us believe that the main verb in 1 Peter 3:15 is "to give a defense." But it is not. As a matter of fact the word "defense" (NASB) or "answer" (KJV) is not even a verb. The word is *apologian* which is a noun, functioning as the object of a prepositional phrase. And the whole prepositional phrase is subordinate to and modifies the main verb which is "sanctify" (NASB) ["set apart" (NIV); "honor" (ESV)]. "Sanctify" (*hagiasate*) is a second person plural aorist active imperative from *hagiazo*, meaning "to treat as holy, to hallow, to set apart." In this context it means to "treat as holy, reverence of persons" (cf. Isa 8:13).[18] So the command "to sanctify" is the main verb in the sentence, and as such, "to sanctify" the Lord Christ in the heart is the primary action in the work of apologetics. The main action in apologetics, according to this verse, is not "reasoning" or "arguing" or "debating" or "waxing eloquent." But chronologically and methodologically, the emphasis is on personally setting apart Christ as Lord with a focused, hallowed reverence. There are two basic practical implications that flow from this reality.

First, apologetics begins with revering the Lord Christ personally in our hearts. Significantly the word "Lord" is the first word in the sentence which makes it emphatic and so Jesus is to be preeminent in our apologetics work; He is the focal point; He is the epicenter and circumference of all conversation when engaging with unbelievers. Jesus Christ in His matchless glory is to be the overriding and underlying theme in all our discussions with skeptics. We are to "glory in Christ Jesus" (Phil 3:3). Any apologetics discussion that neglects Christ as front and center is a cipher, amounting to wood, hay and stubble. Kelly James Clark boasts that his whole apologetics approach focuses "primarily on belief in God, not belief in Jesus."[19] That is inexcusable and profits nothing. Rather, Peter exhorts that we are to be Christocentric in apologetics. If we start out with the risen Christ as preeminent in our hearts, then He will also be preeminent in our thoughts and words as we dialogue with others. It is all about Christ. As Paul said, "For to me, to live is Christ" (Phil 1:21).

Second, revering the Lord Christ as holy entails fearing Him, which in turn prompts the believer to live a life of holiness and purity in honor of Christ as the Master. A holy, obedient, moral godly life will then be used by God as an adjunct, efficacious witness to the unbeliever in the apologetic process. When Christians live godly lives they shine as lights in a dark world. God uses the light of holiness to help convict unbelievers of their darkened minds and their hardened hearts. God promised that when Christians live godly they will then prove "to be blameless and innocent, children of God above reproach in the midst of a crooked and perverse generation, among whom you appear as lights in the world" (Phil 2:15). Jesus said the same thing when He declared to believers, "You are the light of the world" (Matt 5:14). He meant that believers have been sanctified by a holy God and as a result they reflect, even radiate, God's holiness as they live in this sinful world. Unbelievers living in darkness will take note of holy believers, and their sanctified lives will be an apologetic used by God to draw sinners to Himself. Jesus made this very point when He said, "Let your light [i.e., 'holy life'] shine before men ['unbelievers'] in such a way that they may see your good works, and glorify your Father who is in heaven" (Matt 5:16). This is an amazing promise. God promises to use the holy life of a believer as an apologetic. Who is it that glorifies the Father who is in heaven? Only believers can do that. So Jesus makes it clear here that some unbelievers are going to be drawn to Christianity when they see the unique, inexplicable, transformed, holy lives of saints walking in obedience to God in the midst of a corrupt society.

Traditional apologists hardly ever make a priority of the efficacious power that godly living has in the apologetics process. Their emphasis is always on talk—rational argumentation, logic-chopping discourses, verbalized philosophical syllogisms, indubitable spoken insights, incontrovertible circumlocutions and veridical disputations. But everyone knows, talk can be cheap. A welcomed exception on this point comes from presuppositionalist John Frame. He writes,

> Our communication with unbelievers consists not only of what we say, but also of how we live before them. If our life contradicts our doctrine, then our apologetics is hypocritical and loses credibility. But if our life and doctrine are consistent, then those who try to make us look bad will themselves lose credibility. They will, in the end at least, be ashamed....don't be an apologist unless your first loyalty is to God—not to intellectual respectability, not to truth in the abstract, not to the unbeliever as such, not to some philosophic tradition.[20]

Ravi Zacharias also gets it on this point when he says,

> the apologist's task begins with a godly walk. One ought to

take time to reflect seriously upon the question, *Has God truly wrought a miracle in my life? Is my own heart proof of the supernatural intervention of God?*'...before the answer is given, the one giving the answer is called to a certain prerequisite. *The lordship of Christ over the life of the apologist is foundational to all answers given*....The way the Christian's life is lived will determine the impact upon believers and skeptics alike....This call to a life reflecting the person of Christ is the ultimate call of everyone who wishes to do apologetics because of the snare of argument and its overriding appeal that suppresses the devotional side of truth.[21]

John Piper also understands that changed, godly lives are used by God in the apologetics task; he writes,

The Scriptures manifest themselves to be the word of God by their display of this peculiar glory of God in the transformation of selfish people into God-centered, Christ-exalting servants who live for the temporal and eternal good of others. More specifically, the Scriptures show themselves to be God's word both *by the new life they exhibit and by the new life they create.*[22]

Jesus put a premium on godly living with respect to apologetics. He told His apostles, "By this all men will know that you are My disciples, if you have love for one another" (John 13:35). What is a primary goal of apologetics? It is to get unbelievers to know what Christianity truly is. Here Jesus gives one of the priorities the Church needs to keep paramount in the apologetics process. Believers need to live godly lives, characterized by holy love for each other, and as a result unbelievers will know who Christ truly is and what Christians are really about.

Similarly in John 17 Jesus said when believers live godly lives that are characterized by unity, then their very lives will be efficacious apologetically toward unbelievers. As He prayed to the Father, Jesus asked that true believers "may all be one; even as Thou, Father, art in Me, and I in Thee, that they also may be in Us; that the world may believe that Thou didst send Me" (17:21). Notice that Jesus said some unbelievers will "believe" as a result of being influenced by the way believers live their lives. Apologetics is not solely about what we say; it is also about how we live. Our very personal lives have apologetical implications. Of course, no one will be saved or come to believe apart from the verbal proclamation of the gospel message (Rom 10:14-15), but God clearly promises to use godly living in conjunction with the proclaimed good news to bring unbelievers to repentance.

Even if unbelievers see our godly lives and refuse to repent and believe in Christ, God will still use our holy living in an efficacious manner. Peter explains this reality in the immediate context of our very apologetics passage that is under consideration: "keep a good conscience so that in the thing in which you are slandered, those who revile your good behavior in Christ will be put to shame" (1 Pet 3:16). Here is an amazing implication for apologetics. When Christians live holy, courageous, uncompromising lives among unbelievers, they will always force the issue with unbelievers. Unbelievers will be forced into a corner to choose one or the other— godliness or worldliness. They will either be attracted to the godly lives of Christians and be on their way to transformation, or they will be repulsed and hardened by godliness and shun it to their own demise. Their repulsion may even turn into persecution—verbal, social, physical, or a combination of all three.

> Believers should not be surprised if they suffer in spite of the fact they are living godly lives. They should be prepared to give the right kind of answer in the face of rejection or persecution. They should not retaliate in self-defense or seek revenge. The best "answer" they can make is to live in such a way no one will believe the accusations.[23]

With either response from unbelievers, positive or negative, more of the light of God's truth will have been exposed into their lives, and as a result they will become all the more accountable to their Creator. Godly living, then, is inextricably bound up with the apologetics task as given in 1 Peter 3:15.

Peter's Audience
Garden Variety Sinners
Next to be considered in 1 Peter 3:15 is Peter's audience. To whom

was he writing? The cursory manner in which traditional apologists allude to this verse, one would think that Peter was writing to an elite group of professional PhD's who composed *The First Hellenistic Evangelical Philosophical Society.* Such was not the case. Peter wrote to "those who reside as aliens scattered throughout Pontus, Galatia, Cappadocia, Asia, and Bithynia, who are chosen" (1:1). Based on this verse and the content of his entire letter it is clear Peter was writing to all Christians at local churches within the Roman Empire that today constitute Turkey. They were regular, everyday, average believers who composed the normal local church body. And Peter commanded these lay people to always be ready to "give a defense" for their faith. Who is supposed to employ apologetics? All Christians are, not just the elite professionals. The command to defend the faith was one of about thirty commands Peter gave to all believers in these churches. And every believer was expected to obey all of them.

These Christians, many of whom were Gentiles, converted to Christ from paganism. Peter reminds them of their godless history: "For the time already past is sufficient for you to have carried out the desire of the Gentiles, having pursued a course of sensuality, lusts, drunkenness, carousing, drinking parties and abominable idolatries" (4:3). This group sounds much like modern secular America. Before these Gentiles got saved they were an eclectic mix of idol worshippers, Gnostics, agnostics, skeptics, hedonists, secularists and probably even some atheists. No doubt some were outwardly hostile to Christianity, as Peter makes it clear that was the milieu of the culture when he wrote (3:13-14).

These are the kind of people that traditional apologists tell us we are confronted with today. And they tell us we need to confront these unbelievers first, not with the Bible and special revelation, but with human reason, the laws of logic, the man-made theistic arguments and raw empirical data. Traditional apologists say these unbelievers can't handle Bible truths up front because the Bible is a stumbling block to them. One traditional apologist puts it this way:

> [Paul] understood that some non-Christians would have intellectual barriers between them and the Lord. He sought to knock down those walls so that the pathway to Christ would be clear.[24]

He goes on to say that before a Christian can use the Bible or share gospel truth with some unbelievers, one first needs to employ traditional apologetics to woo the skeptic. The Bible first has to be proved to be plausible and it has to earn credibility in the minds of unbelievers before it can be cracked. Skeptics first need to be warmed up to the idea of monotheism before progressing into weightier truths. The pump needs to be primed with the law of non-contradiction before the doctrine of the resurrection is sprung on them. Clark claims that by using rational arguments in apologetics before we get to gospel truths, we will "be assisting people in the removal of barriers to belief. We can help some of the scales fall off."[25] Plantinga goes so far as to say that rational arguments and man-made theistic arguments, including natural theology, can even "be useful in helping someone move from unbelief to belief."[26] Sire says when a "barrier to belief is intellectual doubt" then "clever rhetoric with sound reasoning" may move the unbeliever from doubt to faith.[27] Clever rhetoric? Similarly, Taylor says, "objective reasons, arguments, and evidences…help faith grow…and prevent faith from dying."[28]

Saving Faith

In stark contrast, the Bible is clear—faith, the ability to believe spiritual truth, comes from one place only. Faith is a gift from God (Eph 2:8) and comes only from hearing teaching and preaching about Christ: "faith comes from hearing, and hearing by the word of Christ" (Rom 10:17). Faith is the by-product of special revelation alone, not natural theology, archaeological evidences, raw human reason or clever rhetoric.

So how were these pagan, Gnostic, Hellenized, skeptical Gentiles that Peter wrote to won to Christ? Did they enter the starting gate of faith by first hearing the *kalam* cosmological argument that had not been invented yet? Or was pre-faith faith created as first-century apologists used the laws of logic invented by pagan Greek, pantheistic philosophers like Socrates, Plato and Aristotle? I think not. Peter is clear. In the first chapter he reminds them about the means of their glorious conversion:

> Since you have in obedience to the truth purified your souls for a sincere love of the brethren, fervently love one another from the heart, for you have been born again not of seed which is perishable but imperishable, *that is,* through the living and enduring word of God. For, "*All*

49

flesh is like grass, and all its glory like the flower of grass. The grass withers, and the flower falls off, but the Word of the LORD endures forever." And this is the word which was preached to you (1:22-25).

They were saved as they heard the Word of God preached to them. They obeyed the truth of special revelation. The gospel purified their souls, not sheer human logic and rationalistic argumentation.

No Compromise

Peter also reminded the believers to "sanctify Christ as Lord in your hearts" as they defended their faith. This assumes that those who practice apologetics are godly, reverent believers. And they are believers who "sanctify Christ" in their hearts. That means they make Christ the priority in their whole life—their thoughts, actions and words. They submit to His Lordship. They depend on His strength, Spirit and truth as they give their defense.

This is contrary to what some traditional apologists suggest we do in apologetics. Craig suggests we use the *kalam* cosmological argument to create faith in the skeptical unbeliever. He goes even further by claiming, "I and many others have seen people come to believe in God (and even Christ) on the basis of the *kalam* cosmological argument."[29] This is ludicrous. No one has ever come to Christ on the basis of the *kalam* cosmological argument, "for there is salvation no one else; for there is no other name under heaven that has been given among men by which we must be saved" (Acts 4:12). People come to Christ only through the gospel (Rom 1:16). The *kalam* cosmological argument actually derives predominantly from Muslim theologians and even has origins in the teachings of the pagan Greek philosophers, Plato and Aristotle. It contains no gospel and is totally void of biblical truth or references to Christ and His atoning work. When we employ apologetics we need to set our hearts, thoughts and methodology apart under the Lordship of Christ and not be dependent on the wisdom of the world as found in pagan philosophy or false religion.

Defend the Hope

When Peter commanded these believers to give a defense, what were they supposed to defend? Traditional apologists are almost unanimous here. They typically put the emphasis on the method, "give a defense," to justify their use of philosophical argumentation instead of using the Scriptures to make a defense. And when they do speak of the content to be defended, it is not "the hope" as Peter urges here. The content they say we are to defend is generic theism and the possibility of religion—the first order of business is "reasoning for the existence of God."[30] Craig says we are to defend the plausibility of God's existence as being more likely than not.[31] That is not at all what Peter was saying in 1 Peter 3:15. Rather, he was commanding all Christians to give a defense for "the hope" that was in them. And what was their "hope"? It was not the plausibility of God's existence as being more likely than not. Their hope was in Christ, so our love for Christ is what we defend.

Peter already told his readers in the first chapter that they were "born again to a living hope through the resurrection of Jesus Christ from the dead" (1:3) and to fix their "hope completely on the grace to be brought to you at the revelation of Jesus Christ" (1:13). Paul similarly wrote of "Christ Jesus, who is our hope" (1 Tim 1:1) and "Christ in you, the hope of glory" (Col 1:27). The hope that is in us that we defend is the hope of the gospel, the reality that Christ Jesus has saved us through His death and resurrection and as a result we will also be saved in the future from hell and will instead inherit eternal glory. It is our faith in Christ on a very personal level that we are to defend. It is our testimony.

John Calvin, the conscientious, careful and unrivaled biblical exegete got it right on this verse when he wrote the following in the 1500's:

> It is the general doctrine that is meant, which belongs to the ignorant and the simple. Then Peter had in view no other thing, than that Christians should make it evident to unbelievers that they truly worshipped God, and had a holy and good religion...*Hope* here is by metonymy to be taken for faith. Peter...does not require them to know how to discuss distinctly and refinedly every article of the faith, but only to show that their faith in Christ was consistent with genuine piety.[32]

In true, biblical apologetics, we first and foremost defend our personal faith and belief in the gospel of Jesus Christ.

In the same era as Calvin, the fiery German Reformer, Martin

Luther, also understood what "the hope" was that God called us to defend. He was frustrated by traditional apologists in his day (he calls them "sophists") who followed the model of Aquinas who tried to mix the Bible with the teachings of the pagan Aristotle, and as a result Luther believed the simple meaning of 1 Peter 3:15 was being obfuscated by the theological elitists. Listen to him fume a bit in his commentary on 1 Peter 3:15, explaining what "the hope" is that we are to defend as believers:

> We must here acknowledge that Peter addressed these words to all Christians—clergy and laity, male and female, young and old—of whatever state or condition they may be. Hence it follows that every Christian should know the ground and reason of his faith, and he should be able to maintain and defend it...the devil has hit on a fine trick to tear the Bible out of the hands of the laity; and he has thought thus: "If I can keep the laity from reading the Scriptures, I will then turn the priests from the Bible to Aristotle," and so let them gossip as they will....
>
> But look now at what Peter tells us all, that we should give answer and show reason for our faith...Therefore we must know what we believed, namely, what God's Word is, not what the pope and the holy fathers believe or say. For you must not put your faith at all in persons, but in the Word of God.
>
> So when anyone assaults you, and like a heretic asks why you believe you shall be saved through faith, here is your answer: "Because I have God's Word and the clear declarations of Scripture for it." As Paul says in Romans 1:17, "The just shall live by faith"....
>
> But the sophists also have perverted the text, as though one were to convince the heretics with reason, and out of the natural light of Aristotle. Therefore they say, "It is here rendered in Latin, *Rationem reddere*," as if Peter meant it should be done with human reason. Because, they say the Scriptures are far too weak that we should silence heretics with them. The method by which, according to them, it must be shown that the faith is a right one, must agree with reason and come forth from the brain. But our faith is above all reason, and it alone is the power of God.

Therefore, if the people will not believe, then be silent; for you are not responsible for compelling them to hold the Scriptures as the Word or Book of God. It is enough that you give your reason from the Scriptures.[33]

Luther knew Peter was calling us to defend our hope, which is the truth of the gospel of Christ found only in the Scriptures.

Gospel Apologetics

One of the most fundamental and obvious truths about 1 Peter 3:15 is its inescapably evangelistic overtones. Peter's use of *apologia* is inherently related to the good news of Christ. His imperative here is a basic call to proclaim the gospel. In effect, Peter was saying: "when people ask you about your hope in Christ, explain yourself." This means witness; give your testimony—proclaim the details of the gospel; tell people of the glories of Christ and His beauty as described in Scripture and as realized in your own repentance and belief. The content of the gospel has supernatural, inherent, eternally life-changing power. God emphatically declared: "the gospel...is the power [*dunamis*] of God for salvation" (Rom 1:16). Paul also proclaimed, "the word of the cross is to those who are perishing foolishness, but to us who are being saved it is the power of God" (1 Cor 1:18). Do you want innate, supernatural, life-changing power? Power that impacts human hearts like nothing else? Then preach the gospel. The gospel is its own apologetic!

The Gospel's Electrifying Power

When the gospel is proclaimed to any unbeliever, unseen, super-natural realities and transactions take place. The truth of God's Word penetrates the ears (Rom 10:14), enters the mind (1 Cor 15:2), while violently invading the conscience of the sinner (Heb 4:12); the Holy Spirit intrudes and carries the truth even further, deep into the human heart; acting as the prosecuting attorney He uses spiritual truth to pierce the very soul and spirit of the unbeliever, like un-bridled electricity, stirring up guilt over sin—known and hidden (John 16:8-11). Regardless of the unbeliever's response, God's Word and His Spirit have done their work—and amazingly, God's Word continues to work on the heart of that sinner, for days, years and even decades. A supernatural seed has been planted, watered or cultivated (1 Cor 3:6-9). God's living Word, ensconced in the gospel, is invariably dynamic and efficacious. God Himself testifies to this, declaring,

> So shall My word be which goes forth from My mouth;
>   It shall not return to Me empty,
> Without accomplishing what I desire,
>   And without succeeding *in the matter* for which I sent it.
>   (Isa 55:11).

Proclaiming the gospel of Jesus Christ is the most potent, lasting, penetrating, life-changing, liberating thing a Christian can articulate to any unbeliever, under any circumstances. God's powerful, living Word in the Scriptures never returns void.

Paul's Gospel Defense

Consistently in the New Testament, *apologia* more often refers to a Christian presenting the gospel, or a personal testimony, as opposed to the presentation of a secular legal brief. This was true of the apostle Paul (see chart at the end of the chapter). Sometimes Paul used the word *apologia* in an informal sense and sometimes in a formal sense, but every time he gave his *apologia*, or defense—every time he practiced apologetics—the presentation of the gospel was at the heart of his presentation. In Acts 22 Paul gave his "defense" to the Jews of Israel (22:1). He was not in court before pagan atheists. Paul was not formally on trial. The apostle was speaking spontaneously, just after being subjected to a beating, in the midst of a public tumult instigated by hostile, unbelieving Jews from Asia who incited the local Jews of Jerusalem against Paul. He was in the temple with monotheistic Jews, many of whom despised Jesus. The content of Paul's "defense" or apologetic argument incorporated his salvation experience (22:1-16), divine revelation (22:7, 17) and climaxed as he spoke of his belief in the risen Lord Jesus Christ (22:8). That's biblical apologetics. In the face of critics, Paul did not give the cosmological argument, or resort to the laws of logic, or try to establish the probability of God's existence. He preached the life-changing gospel of Jesus Christ from his own personal experience. Any Christian can do that.

The next day Paul gave a second defense, this time to the Sanhedrin, with Ananias presiding. In this apologetic presentation he culminated with the statement: "I am on trial for the hope and resurrection of the dead!" (Acts 23:6). That is simple, classic, undiluted, gospel truth. His formal defense before violent critics was a simple delineation of the gospel from his personal experience...nothing more.

Five days later, Paul was escorted under Roman guard to Caesarea for a third defense before the governor Felix, Ananias and the elders. Paul began, "I cheerfully make my defense [*apologia*]" (Acts 24:10). What was Paul's defense? What was his apologetic argument before Felix, the pagan Roman governor? Was it the ontological, teleological, moral or transcendental argument? Did he try to find common ground in empirical data and sense perception? Did he utilize man-made natural theology devoid of divine revelation? No. The first thing he said was that he worshipped God (24:11). Next he said he believed in the Scriptures (24:14). Then he said his "hope" was in the "resurrection" (24:15). He went on to make his main point, when Felix heard Paul "speak about faith in Christ Jesus" (24:24). Paul's entire apologetic presentation evolved around the gospel of Jesus Christ from personal experience. Every Christian can do the same.

Paul remained imprisoned for two years after his defense before Felix. The next event in the book of Acts has Paul once again giving his "defense" [*apologia*] (25:8), this time before Festus, another pagan Roman governor. The first thing Paul said to Festus was that he had been faithful to the Old Testament Scriptures, "the law of the Jews" (25:8). He then relayed to Festus his faith in the resurrected Jesus Christ (25:19). Paul's apologetic argument, once again, amounted to a gospel presentation.

Next, Festus invited King Agrippa to hear Paul's story, and so once again, for the sixth time, before Agrippa, "Paul stretched out his hand and proceeded to make his defense [*apologia*]" (Acts 26:1; cf. 26:2). The fact that Paul stretched out his hand meant he was in preaching mode! The first line of Paul's apologetic argument was over "the hope of the promise made by God" to the Jews in Scripture (26:6). What was that hope? It was hope in the resurrection (26:8). Next, once again, Paul gives his salvation story (26:9-18), refers to Scripture (26:22) and ramps it up with a convicting gospel presentation: "I stand to this day testifying...that the Christ was to suffer, and that by reason of His resurrection from the dead He would be the first to proclaim light both to the Jewish people and to

Gentiles" (26:22-23). Paul then concludes his apologetic argument by pleading with Agrippa, calling him to repentance and belief in the gospel (26:27-29).

So over the course of two years Paul gave his *apologia* six plus times. And each time his defense amounted to a witness for Christ (Acts 23:11), a personal appeal to the power of the gospel. For the apostle Paul, apologetics was about proclaiming and explaining the content, the meaning and the implications of the good news of Jesus Christ as revealed through special revelation.

Our Hope is Christ!
It is clear, then, when Peter commands Christians to give their *apologia* to those who ask about the hope we have, we are to give the gospel of Jesus Christ. Biblical apologetics is inextricably linked to evangelism. Sadly, traditional apologists frequently deny this basic biblical reality. Craig adamantly constructs a false dichotomy between apologetics and evangelism, saying the two are distinct and un-related.[34] And Taylor represents many like him when he falsely asserts, "The evangelist preaches the gospel, and the apologist defends it."[35]

Who are the Apologists?
Everyday Christians
Traditional apologists extricate 1 Peter 3:15 out of its immediate context, isolate it and infuse it with preconceived notions to create a precedent allowing them to forge full steam ahead into an all-out Aristotelian metaphysical philosophy while calling it Christian apologetics. An example is William Lane Craig, who says, "Apologetics is primarily a theoretical discipline."[36] But upon closer examination of the context of 1 Peter 3:15, a far different reality emerges. The reality goes back to two related questions: (1) to whom was Peter writing? and (2) why was he telling them to defend their faith? The first question was answered earlier when it was shown from Peter's epistle that he was addressing *normal* Christians, not the extraordinarily erudite, and that he was addressing *all* Christians in the local churches, not just a few elitist intellectuals who specialized in theoretical calculus. That leaves the second question: why were they being encouraged to defend their hope? The answer is simple: they were being persecuted for being Christians. That is the theme of 1 Peter.

56

In the very first verse of the epistle Peter reminds his readers that they are "aliens." He wanted them to remember up-front that followers of Christ are out of place in this fallen, hostile world. This present world is not their home. As they live the obedient Christian life, they will be going against the grain of society and will incur resistance from all the competing religions, worldviews and ideologies. In the next chapter he reminds them that their Savior was "rejected" by humanity (2:4) because they found Jesus to be "a stone of stumbling and a rock of offense" (2:8). Unbelievers hated Jesus because they were "disobedient," loving instead their own sin. And so Christians would "suffer unjustly" just as Jesus did (2:19). That is exactly what was happening. The believers Peter wrote to were being "reviled" by unbelievers, "suffering unjustly" simply for being Christians, for holding onto the hope of redemption in the resurrected Christ (2:18-25).

In chapter three Peter continues to develop this theme, instructing believers how to live in every area of life in the midst of persecution, rejection and hostility from the unbelieving world. As believers walk through life day to day they will be subject to "harm" and "intimidation" from unbelievers (3:13-14). Christians will be "slandered" and "reviled" by unbelievers for their good behavior (3:16-17), and will "suffer" just as Christ suffered (3:17-18). Being mocked by unbelievers is normative for those who faithfully follow Christ. This is the context of 1 Peter 3:15, the universally acknowledged passage for defining Christian apologetics.

Apologetics is a Lifestyle

There are two practical implications for biblical apologetics that issue from the foregoing reality. First, apologetics is to be employed and practiced as a lifestyle, in an ongoing manner as all believers constantly interface with a fallen world, rubbing shoulders continually with those who despise Christ. Apologetics is a way of life for the Christian. It is similar to being an ambassador for Christ. It's synonymous with the clarion call given to all Christians to live as soldiers for Christ as they are engaged in an ongoing war with unbelief, sin and enmity towards the truth of Christ everywhere they go. As Paul exhorted Timothy, "Suffer hardship with me, as a good soldier of Christ Jesus" (2 Tim 2:3).

In contrast, traditional apologetics can give the impression that apologetics is reserved for special occasions, planned in advance, whereby two predetermined heavyweight intellectuals are scheduled to battle it out like gladiators in the coliseum of a formal, televised debate in front of a live, under-educated audience. For example, James Sire says a main venue in which apologetics occurs is in "formal lectures to primarily nonbelieving audiences."[37] Others imply apologetics takes place at the bi-annual conference of religious philosophers where all patrons must have pre-requisite credentials in metaphysical studies as they exchange highfalutin ideas and "deliver" their theses by way of elitist academic research papers. But that is clearly not what Peter or the Spirit of God had in mind.

An Action, Not an Office

The second implication is that apologetics is something we do, not so much what a person is. When Peter commanded Christians to always be "ready to make a **defense**," he was giving them a practice to follow, not a position to be filled. Paul uses the word *apologia* in a similar manner. In Philippians he reminded his readers that he was "appointed for the **defense** of the gospel" (1:16). Defending the gospel was an action he performed, not an office he filled. He says the same thing in Philippians 1:7. Jesus used the word *apologia* in a similar fashion when He warned His disciples how to react in the face of persecution; He told them to "not worry about how or what you are to speak in your **defense**, or what you are to say; for the Holy Spirit will teach you in that very hour what you ought to say" (Luke 12:11-12). To Jesus, apologetics was an action, not an office.

Traditional apologetics would have us believe that 1 Peter 3:15 gives the precedent for the position, title or office of "apologist." There are countless modern day evangelical scholars who assume the title formally as "apologist." It's on their books and websites, featured among their other credentials and titles. For example, Taylor says, "The evangelist preaches the gospel, and the apologist defends it."[38] James Sire, an advocate of traditional apologetics, says that there are five specific qualifications that make one suited for the position and calling of apologist. He says the first of the qualifications to be an apologist is, "(1) a fascination with and delight in the intellectual life."[39] But in reality there is no such thing in the Bible as the distinct office, calling, or position of "apologist." The only distinct offices delineated in the New Testament that are given by God for the care, administration and oversight of His Church are as follows: apostles, prophets, pastors [i.e. elders], teachers, evangelists (Eph 4:11) and deacons (1 Tim 3:8-13). The notion of a select group of men being "apologists" while all other Christians are not is a misnomer and false construction. That would be like saying some Christians are "saints" or "priests" while others are not. Peter is clear. Every Christian is commanded to do apologetics as a way of life—a lifestyle of giving an account of the hope they have in Christ when challenged by unbelievers.

The Attitude of Apologetics

There is one more invaluable truth about apologetics set forth by Peter in 3:15. It has to do with the Christian's attitude when defending the faith. When one is under duress it is easy to be defensive or caustic to antagonists. So Peter reminds Christians to defend their faith with godly attitudes, namely "gentleness and reverence." "Gentleness" refers to our attitude toward unbelievers, while "reverence" speaks of our attitude before God. "Humility" best summarizes the implications of both terms. Specifically, gentleness means meekness, mildness, friendliness, and moral strength under control. We are not to be domineering, overbearing, belittling or condescending when witnessing to the unbelievers, but rather we are to speak "the truth in love" (Eph 4:15). Greg Bahnsen rightly referred to this approach as "humble boldness."

The goal is not to win the argument by eviscerating the opponent with a verbal tongue-lashing. This is in stark contrast to the goal of the Greeks in Peter's day. From the time of Socrates down to the apostles, the Greeks prided themselves on public disputation and wrangling with antagonists, with the goal of being able to "one-up" the other by out-arguing and humiliating the enemy. Their social interactions were "dog-eat-dog," championing the motto of "the survival of the fittest." The winner was the "king of the hill." They were rhetorical gladiators and proud of it.

> The Greeks liked to debate issues of all kinds...On the contrary, Peter said [believers] should give their witness not in a high-handed, cocksure manner but with "meekness" (*prautetos*, humility, mildness) and "fear" (*phobou*, terror, fear), not of man but of God; that is with reverence and dependence on divine guidance.[40]

In contrast, Peter commands Christians to be motivated by utter humility. But the Greeks regarded "humility" as an undesirable and negative attribute when relating with others. For them it implied inherent weakness and servility. After all, humility means, "lowly" and "insignificant," and if your goal was to win the debate, then the last thing the Greek philosophers wanted to be was insignificant. The Greeks had a radically different perception of humility than what the Bible taught about this highest, Christ-like virtue:

> The different estimation of the word group *tapeinos* [*humble*] in Greek literature and the Bible is governed by the different understanding of man. The Greek concept of free man leads to contempt for lack of freedom and subjection. This qualifies *tapeinos* and derivates negatively.... *tapeinos* has the derogatory negative sense found in the Greeks.[41]

This difference is graphically illustrated when Paul, the humble man of God, was debating with the pagan Greeks at Athens, telling them about Jesus and His death and resurrection. The Greek philosophers responded to Paul by calling him an "idle babbler" and a "proclaimer of strange deities" (Acts 17:18). In other words they were calling him an "uneducated idiot" and a "delusional fool." They were arrogant, condescending and personally insulting. In the ensuing dialogue, Paul is the very antithesis in demeanor toward them, even though Paul knew they were wrong and truly ignorant. He spoke the truth in love to them, treated them with dignity, and desired their spiritual salvation, as he pleaded with them to turn to Christ and be saved. Their response was mixed. Some of them were intrigued and curious by what he said, yet others "began to sneer" at him (17:32). The latter just could not shake their innate attitudes of intellectual pomposity and superiority that pulsed through their veins, being by-products of the pagan Greek culture that despised humility and gentleness.

For Christians engaged in apologetics the goal is to accurately represent Christ and His gospel in a godly manner. "Reverence" refers to our continual attitude of awe toward God in light of the reality that we were once His enemies (Rom 5:8), children of wrath (Eph 2:3), sons of the devil (1 John 3:8) and no better than any unbeliever we may be confronted with. We did not get saved by God because we were worthy or because we earned it. We were undeserving and yet God graciously saved us anyway.

"Reverence" also flows from the understanding that we owe our very lives to the Savior, Jesus Christ who was incarnate "gentleness" who always modeled perfect humility and deference toward others. Jesus described Himself as such, saying, "I am gentle and humble in heart" (Matt 11:29). In awe of Christ as the God-Man, the Christian is always to live before God in fear and trembling—which Peter calls reverence.

That sense of awe should permeate the tone of our witness to unbelievers. Paul says it best when he commanded believers to,

> malign no one, to be peaceable, gentle, showing every consideration for all men. For we also once were foolish ourselves, disobedient, deceived, enslaved to various lusts and pleasures, spending our life in malice and envy, hateful, hating one another. But when the kindness of God our Savior and His love for mankind appeared, He saved us, not on the basis of deeds which we have done in righteousness, but according to His mercy, by the washing of regeneration and renewing by the Holy Spirit (Titus 3:3-5).

Summary

It has been shown that 1 Peter 3:15 is a key paradigmatic passage in defining and giving precedents for the discipline of Christian apologetics, and nine resultant truths surface as paramount: (1) In the context of 1 Peter 3:15, Peter used the word *apologia*, "defense," in an informal, spiritual, religious and theological manner after the model of Jesus (Luke 12:11-12), not in a formal, secular, legal and philosophical manner typified by the Greek pagans, Socrates and Plato. (2) Peter also taught that the holy life of a Christian is used by God as an apologetic. Apologetics is not only about speaking, but it also entails living. This is highlighted by Peter's use of *hagiazo*, the command for believers "to sanctify" Christ as Lord in a personal way. (3) Peter also made it clear that Christians are to defend their faith with the content of divine revelation, utilizing God's thoughts as preserved in Scripture. We are not to defend our faith with human reason and logic apart from special revelation, as traditional apologetics argues. (4) Apologetics is to be practiced by all Christians and the same approach is to be used when dealing with all unbelievers. Unbelievers need faith, and only the gospel as found in Scripture can impart saving faith. Natural theology, sheer human reason and the laws of logic cannot conjure up faith in unbelievers as traditional apologetics would have us believe. (5) Christians are to defend their "hope," that is their faith in Jesus Christ and the basic realities of the gospel. Peter was not asking believers to defend the plausibility of God's existence as traditional apologetics assumes. (6) Apologetics is evangelistic. That is how Peter and Paul used the word *apologia*. Every Christian should always be ready to present the gospel to anyone at any time. (7) Apologetics is a way of life for all Christians as they interface with unbelievers daily. Apologetics is not a formal discipline reserved for special, pre-planned orchestrated intellectual cage-match debates between two select academic opponents as traditional apologetics at times tends to portray. (8) Apologetics is a practice to be employed, not a position to be filled. In the New Testament there is no special office for the select few who are uniquely called to serve as "apologists." All Christians are called to practice apologetics as a way of life. (9) Finally, Christians are to engage in apologetics with an attitude of gentleness and humility toward unbelievers, while maintaining an attitude of awe and reverence before God.

The key to understanding what Peter really meant in 3:15 is always to remember his overriding themes of persecution that the saints were undergoing at the time, and their resultant expectation and opportunity to respond to this religious persecution with godly humility. Persecution and humility—this is the true context of Peter's words. As such, Peter's words fall outside the pale of any controlling technical or philosophical background. He is not utilizing technical terms demanding sophisticated, defensive responses, but pastoral urgings that a persecuted people simply explain the basis of their seemingly inexplicable hope in Christ.

Notes

1.   John Frame, *Five Views on Apologetics*, ed. Steven B. Cowan (Grand Rapids: Zondervan, 2000), 214-215.

2.   William Lane Craig, *Apologetics: An Introduction* (Chicago: Moody Press, 1984), 23.

3.   Bickel and Jantz really go astray, saying apologetics comes from the Latin word in 1 Peter 3:15, *apologia*. Hardy makes the same elementary blunder. *Apologia* does not come from the Latin—it comes from the Greek New Testament! See, Bruce Bickel and Stan Jantz, *Evidence for Faith 101: Understanding Apologetics in Plain Language* (Eugene, Oregon: Harvest House Publishers, 2008), 15 and Dean Hardy, *Stand Your Ground: An Introductory Text for Apologetics Students* (Eugene, OR: Wipf & Stock, 2007), 1.

4.   Steven B. Cowan, *Five Views*, 8. John Milbank is equally misguided and his extended essay is a classic example of eisegetical overreach, as he fabricates an entire esoteric and overly-sophisticated category of apologetical thought based on a stilted and forced etymological analysis of one prefix in the Greek word, *apologia*. He milks, and bleeds *apo-* for pages in an attempt to lay the foundation for the highly questionable and subjective motif of "imaginative" apologetics. Milbank contends, "*apologia* in ancient Greece referred primarily to the defence speech spoken at a trial….the *apologia* of Socrates…was a defence before the city… 'apology' turns out to be *theologico-politcal* in some fundamental and constitutive sense. And yet this sense is thoroughly ambivalent…For this reason today apologetics, which is to say Christian theology as such, faces the integral task of at once defending the faith and also of defending a true politics of civic virtue (rooted in Platonic and Aristotelian assumptions), besides a renewed metaphysics of cosmic hierarchy and participatory order"; Milbank could not be more wrong when it comes to how *apologia* is used by the New Testament authors. See John Milbank's Foreword, "An Apologia for Apologetics," in *Imaginative Apologetics: Theology, Philosophy and the Catholic Tradition*, ed. Andrew Davison (Grand Rapids: Baker Academic, 2011), xiii-xxii.

5.   Richard Pratt, *Every Thought Captive* (Phillipsburg, NJ: P & R, 1979), 2.

6.   Bernard Ramm, *Varieties of Christian Apologetics* (Grand Rapids, MI: Baker Book House, 1976), 11. In contrast to Ramm and the traditional apologists, the truth is quite to the contrary when reading *apologia* in its biblical contexts; Selwyn explains, "*apologia* and its cognates are used both of public self-defense (as in Lk. xii. and xxi., Acts xix. 33, xxii. 1, xxvi. 1, 2, 24) and of more private and less formal utterances (as in 2 Cor. vii. 11). Its application to written treatises such as Plato's *Apology* does not seem to occur in Christian literature before the second century, where we have the Apologies of Justin, Aristides, and the anonymous author of the *Epistle to Diognetus*. The first sense is not excluded here, but the second must be chiefly in mind, for *aitounti* is a quite informal term, and indicates conversation rather than police enquiry"; Edward Gordon Selwyn, *The*

First Epistle of St. Peter: The Greek Text with Introduction, Notes and Essays (London: The Macmillan Press, LTD, 1946, 1971), 193.

7. D. A. Carson, *Exegetical Fallacies* (Grand Rapids, MI: Baker Books, 1996), 35-36.

8. In his recent 2015 book on apologetics, Voddie Baucham actually dedicates a whole chapter to the meaning of 1 Peter 3:15 in its proper context in a similar fashion I did when I first wrote this chapter in 2011. And Baucham properly attests to the import of Isaiah's influence on Peter's imperative: "In words reminiscent of Isaiah, Peter urges: 'But in your hearts honor Christ the Lord as holy' (1 Pet. 3:15). Peter is here adapting the prophet's words in Isaiah 8:13: 'But the LORD of hosts, him you shall honor as holy. Let him be your fear, and let him be your dread.' The context in Isaiah is informative, as Simon Kistemaker observes: 'In his day, Isaiah told the people not to fear the invading Assyrian armies but to revere God. In his epistle, Peter has the same encouraging message'"; *Expository Apologetics: Answering Objections with the Power of the Word* (Wheaton: Crossway, 2015), 43.

9. Leon Morris, *The Apostolic Preaching of the Cross* (Grand Rapids, MI: Eerdmans Publishing, 2001), 252.

10. George Zemek, "Christian Apologetical Methodology," unpublished class syllabus (Sun Valley, CA: The Master's Seminary, 1992), 2.

11. J. H. A. Hart, *The Expositor's Greek Testament*, ed. W. Robertson Nicoll, 5 vols. (Grand Rapids, MI: Eerdmans Publishing, 1990), V:67; in addition to Hart, Schreiner does a superb job with the exegesis of the passage, thus unfolding clearly Peter's intended use of *apologia* here based on the context, which in the balance is in an informal usage, for the imperative is for "all" (*panti*) believers, not just those restricted to formal courtroom settings; Thomas R. Schreiner, *1, 2 Peter, Jude: An Exegetical and Theological Exposition of Holy Scripture* in *The New American Commentary, Vol. 37* (Nashville: Broadman and Holman Publishers, 2003), 174.

12. A. T. Robertson, *A Grammar of Greek New Testament in the Light of Historical Research* (Nashville, TN: Broadman Press, 1934), 173.

13. William D. Barrick, "Noah's Flood and Its Geological Implications," *Coming to Grips with Genesis: Biblical Authority and the Age of the Earth*, eds. Terry Mortenson and Thane H. Ury (Green Forest, AR: Master Books, 2009), 280-81.

14. Charles Bigg, *A Critical and Exegetical Commentary on the Epistles of St. Peter and St. Jude* (Charleston, SC: BilioLife, n.d.), 158.

15. Hardy, *Stand Your Ground*, 7.

16. R. C. Sproul, John Gerstner and Arthur Lindsley, *Classical Apologetics: A Rational Defense of the Christian Faith and a Critique of Presuppositional Apologetics* (Grand Rapids, MI: Zondervan Publishing House, 1984), 17.

17. Ibid., 20.

18. William F. Arndt and F. Wilbur Gingrich, *A Greek-English Lexicon of the New Testament* (Chicago and London: The University of Chicago Press, 1979), 9.

19. Clark, *Five Views*, 367; Clark's non-Jesus apologetic should be contrasted with Piper's powerful, fully Christocentric apologetic that sets the glory of Christ's beauty front and center: "the way the Scriptures convince us is by the revelation of a *peculiar* glory. In other words, the power of Scripture to warrant well-grounded trust is not by generic glory. Not, as it were, by mere dazzling. Not by simply boggling the mind with supernatural otherness. Rather, what we see as inescapably divine is a peculiar glory. And at the center of this peculiar glory is the utterly unique glory of Jesus Christ"; John Piper, *A Peculiar Glory: How the Christian Scriptures Reveal Their Complete Truthfulness* (Wheaton: Crossway, 2016), 284.

20. John M. Frame, *Apologetics to the Glory of God: An Introduction* (Phillipsburg, NJ: P & R Publishing, 1994), 27-28; cf. John Frame, *Apologetics: A Justification of Christian Belief* (Phillipsburg, NJ: P & R Publish-ing, 2015), 27. John Frame (b. 1939) is considered by many to be the greatest proponent of presuppositional apologetics today. Although he studied under Cornelius Van Til (1895-1987), he deviates from Van Til's apologetic in significant ways. The term "presuppositionalism" seems to have been coined in the late 1930's or early 1940's by J. Oliver Buswell (1895-1977) who had at the time been reviewing some of Van Til's early apologetics work and had been corresponding with him personally. Buswell seems to have crafted the term from Allan MacRae's (1902-1997) reference to "presuppositionism." Van Til preferred the term "transcendental." Van Til was greatly influenced by the Dutch Reformed theologian and states-man, Abraham Kuyper (1837-1920). Van Til's greatest protégé was Greg Bahnsen (1948-1995).

21. Ravi Zacharias, *Beyond Opinion: Living the Faith We Defend* (Nashville, Tennessee: Thomas Nelson, 2007), 305-06.

22. Piper, *A Peculiar Glory*, 254.

23. Ralph Harris, Stanley Horton, Gayle Garrity, *The Complete Biblical Library: Hebrews—Jude*, 10 vols. (Springfield, Missouri: World Library Press, 1989), IX:293.

24. Hardy, *Stand Your Ground*, 6.

25. Clark, *Five Views*, 280.

26. Quoted by Craig in *Five Views*, 45.

27. James W. Sire, *A Little Primer on Humble Apologetics* (Downers Grove, IL: InterVarsity Press, 2006), 32-33.

28. James E. Taylor, *Introducing Apologetics: Cultivating Christian Commitment* (Grand Rapids, MI: Baker Academic, 2006), 17.

29. Craig, *Five Views*, 176.

30. Norman Geisler, "Foreword" in *The Resurrection of Jesus: An Apologetic*, by Gary Habermas (University Press of America, 1984).

31. Craig, *Five Views*, 51.

32. John Calvin, *Calvin's Commentaries: Commentaries On the Catholic Epistles*, trans. by John Owen (Grand Rapids, MI: Baker Book House, 1999), XXII: 108-09. In his commentary on Peter, Hiebert is clearer than most about what "the hope" is as defined by the context of the whole epistle; for him it is obviously a gospel-saturated, Christ-centered hope: "It is the

living hope (1:3) to which we have been begotten by God, a hope centered in the God who has revealed Himself in Christ, imparting present salvation and the hope of future glory (1:20-21). The experience of present salvation brings with it an assured hope concerning the future (Rom. 8:23-24): the blessed return of our Savior and Lord"; D. Edmond Hiebert, *1 Peter* (Chicago: The Moody Bible Institute, 1992), 228; Kelly distills as follows: "We note that, as at i. 3, 21, **hope** is for the writer a conception of primary importance, expressing as it does a cardinal aspect of the gospel"; J. N. D. Kelly, *The Epistles of Peter and of Jude*, in *Black's New Testament Commentary* (London: Hendrikson Publishers, 1969), 143; Hillyer renders, "They are expected to say what Christ means to them"; Norman Hillyer, *1 and 2 Peter, Jude: New International Commentary*, vol. 16 (Peabody, Mass.: Hendrickson Publishers, 1994), 109.

33. Martin Luther, *Commentary on Peter & Jude* (Grand Rapids: Kregel Publications, 1990), 158-161.
34. Craig, *Five Views*, 287.
35. Taylor, *Introducing Apologetics*, 13.
36. Craig, *An Introduction*, xi.
37. Sire, *Humble Apologetics*, 55.
38. Taylor, *Introducing Apologetics*, 13.
39. Sire, *Humble Apologetics*, 94.
40. Harris, *The Complete Biblical Library*, 293.
41. Gerhard Kittel and Gerhard Friedrich, eds., *Theological Dictionary of the New Testament*, (Grand Rapids, MI: Eerdmans Publishing, 1975), VIII: 11, 19.

Passage & Audience	Location & Setting	Occasion & Speaker	Content of Paul's *Apologia*
Acts 22:1-21 A mixed public crowd: (1) unbelieving Jews from Asia; (2) Luke; (3) Lysias (4) 2 centurions; (5) hundreds of Roman soldiers; (6) Jewish Christians; (7) hundreds of pilgrim Jews celebrating Pentecost	Jerusalem, outer temple court; on the stairs outside the Roman barracks just next to Fort Antonia Setting: informal, spontaneous address by Paul, not a trial	April AD 56 or 57, Pentecost Speaker: Paul	"Brethren and fathers, hear my defense (*apologias*) ..." Paul gave his personal testimony telling of his conversion; Jesus appeared to him in a vision, confronted him, saved him, and commissioned him
Acts 23:1-10 (1) 71 members of the Sanhedrin composed of the high priest Ananias (AD 47-58), Sadducees, Pharisees, elders, scribes; (2) the Roman commander Claudius Lysias	Jerusalem, near the Court of the Gentiles Setting: formal, a hearing before the Sanhedrin	One day after Paul's first defense before the Jewish mob in the temple Speakers: Paul, Ananias, scribes	Paul gives a brief testimony then shouts, "I am a Pharisee!" and "I am on trial for the hope and resurrection of the dead!"
Acts 24:10-23 (1) Felix, Roman governor of Judea (AD 52-59); (2) Ananias; (3) some elders; (4) Tertullus the Jewish lawyer	Caesarea Maritima, Herod's palace Setting: a formal hearing (24:4)	A week after the hearing before the Sanhedrin (24:1) Speakers: Paul, Tertullus, the Jews	"I cheerfully make my defense (*apologoumai*)" "for the resurrection of the dead I am on trial"
Acts 24:24-27 Felix & his Jewish wife Drusilla	Caesarea, Herod's palace Setting: informal, many private conversations with Felix	"some days later" Speakers: Paul and Felix	"Paul...[spoke] about faith in Christ Jesus" and about "righteousness, self-control and the judgment to come"
Acts 25:1-12 (1) Porcius Festus, Roman procurator of Judea appointed by Nero (AD 59-62); (2) chief priests; (3) leading Jews from Judea	Caesarea, "before Caesars' tribunal" (25:10) Setting: formal trial	AD 59, the first year of Festus' governorship Speakers: Paul, the Jews,	"Paul said in his own defense (*apologoumenou*), 'I have committed no wrong...I have done no wrong...I appeal to Caesar!'"
Acts 25:23-26:1-32 (1) King Herod Agrippa II & (2) Bernice; (3) chiliarchs; (4) prominent men of the city; (5) Festus	Caesarea, "the auditorium" (25:23) Setting: formal "investigation" (25:26), "amid great pomp"	AD 59, Agrippa's courtesy visit from Caesarea Philippi to Festus in Caesarea Maritima	Paul made "his defense" (*apelogeito*) (26:1); Paul gives his personal testimony; "I am now standing on trial for the hope of the promise made by God"; "I saw a light from heaven...the Lord"; "Christ was to suffer"

3

Defending the Church from the "church": The Priority of Internal Apologetics

Protecting the True Church

Not everyone who attends church should be at church. Not everyone who goes to church is a Christian. Not everyone who says, "I'm a Christian" is truly born again. Not everyone who looks like a sheep is a sheep; some people are wolves and snakes dressed in sheepskin. Jesus said it this way,

> [15] Beware of the false prophets, who come to you in sheep's clothing, but inwardly are ravenous wolves. [16] You will know them by their fruits. Grapes are not gathered from thorn *bushes* nor figs from thistles, are they? [17] So every good tree bears good fruit, but the bad tree bears bad fruit. [18] A good tree cannot produce bad fruit, nor can a bad tree produce good fruit. [19] Every tree that does not bear good fruit is cut down and thrown into the fire. [20] So then, you will know them by their fruits.

> [21] Not everyone who says to Me, "Lord, Lord," will enter the kingdom of heaven, but he who does the will of My Father who is in heaven *will enter.* [22] Many will say to Me on that day, "Lord, Lord, did we not prophesy in Your name, and in Your name cast out demons, and in Your name perform many miracles?" [23] And then I will declare

to them, "I never knew you; 'Depart from Me, you who practice lawlessness'" (Matt 7:15-23).

In light of this sobering prospect, we need to protect the Church of Christ from imposters and deceivers who are in the church but don't belong there. We need internal apologetics.

M. I. A.

I don't know of a book on Christian apologetics that ever mentions "internal apologetics."[1] It is a subject that is clearly missing in action. That is highly unfortunate, because I contend that the New Testament speaks to internal apologetics more than any other kind of apologetics.

All would agree that basic to the task of apologetics is defending the faith—defending and guarding biblical truth. But every other book I have seen focuses on defending the faith against the unchurched—against atheists, agnostics, skeptics, cultists, evolutionists, humanists, the irreligious anti-Christian, anti-Bible people of the world. Taylor is representative of the traditional apologists' view here: "Christian apologetics" is for "critics, seekers, and doubters."[2] That is not the focus of apologetics work in the New Testament. Rather, internal apologetics is dominant. Internal apologetics is the deliberate call of the church, and church leaders in particular, to safeguard biblical doctrine within the confines of the professing church. External apologetics is defending and advancing biblical truth in the world to unbelievers. To make the case for the primacy of internal apologetics, we will survey the conspicuous apologetics texts in the New Testament and accentuate their implications for the apologetic task. But first, a true, modern day case study is telling.

Friendly Fire

John MacArthur, pastor at Grace Community Church since 1969, is one of the foremost Christian apologists (if you'll allow me to use that title) of today. Few pastors alive today can say they have been a teaching shepherd at the same church for nearly fifty years. And even fewer can say they have been as consistent, faithful and influential as Pastor John for such a long period of time. In recent years Dr. MacArthur has repeated a story that has direct relevance and profound implications regarding internal apologetics.

John entered seminary right out of college. He was passionate, enthusiastic and had high expectations for his training in divinity. His mentor quickly became the inimitable Jewish Christian scholar, Dr. Charles Lee Feinberg. John recounts how he buckled down and gave seminary his all in anticipation of graduation, upon which he would go to a church. The church would serve as his barracks from which he would be ready to take on the onslaught of hostility, heresy, heat and head-on attacks directed toward the precious doctrines of the Bible from the atheistic, anti-Christian, unbelieving world.

To John's astonishment, the enemy he expected never showed up for battle. But there was a battle—actually many battles, and they have been non-stop for five decades. Surprisingly, the heretical frontal attacks waged on basic biblical truths were coming from within the church, not outside the church, being initiated by professing Christians, and many times by pastors and highly esteemed theologians. It wasn't until years had passed when he finally realized that most of his time and energy would be spent warding off friendly fire instead of sorties coming from the unchurched. After being the pastor at Grace Church for twenty-five years, he observed,

> Your church's greatest enemy isn't the government, the culture, Hollywood producers, or the liberal media. Scripture states and history confirms that churches are strengthened under persecution and adversity. If our churches are to be destroyed, or rendered ineffective and stagnant, that will happen at the hands of her own people...One of my greatest fears for the church I pastor is that we would unwittingly abandon the vital principles that keep us healthy, growing, and strong. The day we cease clinging to those principles is the day we grow cold and dishonor God before a watching world...
>
> When I came out of Seminary I really did not expect to fight the battles I have fought. I never thought I would spend most of my life on the broader evangelical front defending the gospel and sound doctrine.[3]

Initially John was surprised by the fact that, as a pastor, doing the work of apologetics would primarily entail saving the church from dangerous teachings coming from within the church. But now he realizes that this is not strange at all. This is actually the picture clearly portrayed in the New Testament and the early church. Jesus and the apostles forewarned future generations, by practice and by precept, that basic to the church shepherds' task would be the work of apologetics within their own ranks, defending the faith among the professing faithful.[4]

A Biblical Paradigm for Internal Apologetics: Acts 20

First Peter 3:15 is a verse about apologetics. But it's not the only verse about apologetics. And I would argue it is not even the primary text about biblical apologetics—it's just one of dozens of verses on the topic. If we had to pick a paradigmatic text on defending the faith, that addresses internal as well as external, proactive and defensive—truly comprehensive biblical apologetics, then I would recommend Acts chapter twenty. The pertinent portion of it reads as follows:

> From Miletus he [*Paul*] sent to Ephesus and called to him the elders of the church. And when they had come to him, he said to them…"I did not shrink from…solemnly testifying to both Jews and Greeks of repentance toward God and faith in our Lord Jesus Christ…I do not consider my life of any account as dear to myself, so that I may finish my course and the ministry which I received from the Lord Jesus, to testify solemnly of the gospel of the grace of God….I went about preaching the kingdom….Be on guard for yourselves and for all the flock, among which the Holy Spirit has made you overseers, to shepherd the church of God which He purchased with His own blood. I know that after my departure savage wolves will come in among you, not sparing the flock; and from among your own selves men will arise, speaking perverse things, to draw away the disciples after them. Therefore be on the alert, remembering that night and day for a period of three years I did not cease to admonish each one with tears" (20:17-18, 20-21, 24-25, 28-31).

If there ever was an exemplar of Christian apologetics, it was the apostle Paul. This passage is the quintessential apologetics practicum, as it is charged with timeless, prioritized principles for defending the faith issued by Paul to fellow leaders in the church of Ephesus.

The Nomenclature of Apologetics

First of all, Acts 20 is clearly apologetical in nature. Its tenor is inherently defensive and protective. Paul commands the elders to "be on guard" (20:28), to "be on the alert" (20:31) and to "admonish" or "warn" (20:31). These phrases constitute the parlance of apologetics. The elders, or pastors, of the church are called to carry out apologetics as a life's calling. They are God's "overseers" (20:28). They are to protect, defend, watch out for and guard on God's behalf.

The Beneficiaries of Apologetics

The second point to consider is what the elders guard. They are to guard the sheep—the people of God. They are to be on guard "for all the flock" (20:28). According to Paul that is priority number one. The work of apologetics is first and foremost "internal," safeguarding the church, the people of God, the precious Bride of Christ "which He purchased with His own blood" (20:28). This is true all throughout the New Testament.

Apologetics and Gospel Truth

Third, this passage makes it clear that the work of apologetics is inseparable from the proclamation of divine revelation and the contents of the gospel in particular. The munitions in Paul's apologetical arsenal included preaching "repentance toward God and faith in our Lord Jesus Christ" (20:21), declaring "the gospel of the grace of God" (20:24), and "preaching the kingdom" (20:25).

This is all special revelation focused on the person and the work of Jesus Christ as found in the gospel. There's no deferring to natural theology here. Trying to prove the plausibility of God's existence has no place here. Theoretical, non-specific, inane philosophical musings are non-existent. Paul knew that "the power of God for salvation" (Rom 1:16) was found only in heavenly gospel truths. Apologetics is inextricably gospel-oriented and gospel-driven.

Apologetics Starts with the Religious People

Fourth, in Acts 20 religious people are the target-group for internal apologetics, not unchurched atheists and agnostics. Paul calls the elders to protect the sheep from "savage wolves" (20:29). Savage wolves are spiritual and religious false teachers. They are typified by "speaking perverse things," seeking to make "disciples after them" (20:30). These rogue spiritual carnivores were religious theists, not atheistic humanists and skeptics. Traditional Christian philosophers say in unison that the antagonists in the apologetics task are the irreligious, the atheists, the agnostics and the skeptics. Not so for Paul and the rest of the apostles. The greatest threat of false teaching, distortions of truth, insipid worldviews that need to be countered, come from religious teachers, and often they masquerade as "Christians" and "Bible teachers" and even profess to believe in Jesus. That's why Jesus gave the apologetical clarion call when He warned, "Beware of the false prophets, who come to you in sheep's clothing, but inwardly are ravenous wolves" (Matt 7:15). Here we see that even Jesus, like Paul, made a priority of internal apologetics.

Apologetics Starts Inside the Church

And fifth, Acts 20 shows internal apologetics takes place within the church, not in the world! Paul warns, "after my departure savage wolves will *come in among you,* not sparing the flock" (20:29). Like a virus in the bloodstream, so the most dangerous enemies of Christ will be in the church. Like cancer camouflaging as true bodily organs, so the most imminent spiritual threat to believers is in the Body of Christ. Hymenaeus and Philetus were two such churchmen, who were wolves in sheep's clothing and their false teaching "spread like gangrene…men who have gone astray from the truth saying that the resurrection has already taken place, and they upset the faith" (2 Tim 2:17-18). Like weeds choking and strangling the wheat, so truth is undermined most subtly among the saints. Apologetics must begin in the church. The pressing, impending threat is not first outside the church from the Mormons, Muslims or Moonies but from the specious church professors, priests and prophets amidst the people of God.

Church historian, John Hannah, poignantly highlights the forgotten reality that the earliest "apologists" practiced internal apologetics as a priority and in a normative fashion: "THE APOLOGISTS AND AUTHTORITY (150-300 [AD]) The Apologists were those men and writings that directed and defended the church during the period when it began to come under attack from persecutors on the outside and heretics on the inside."[5] Modern day Christian apologetics has all but forgotten to guard against "heretics on the inside." Hannah goes on to identify the aberrant groups inside the church that the apologists took on: the Marcionites and the Montanists.[6] That would be akin to the true church today taking on and exposing the Emerging church and wayward charismatic theology.

In the 1860's James Strong poignantly recognized the need for internal apologetics when he wrote the following:

> The chief task of the apologist for Christianity in the present age (apart from the metaphysical conflict with Pantheism and Positivism...) is to vindicate the authenticity and the early date of the books of the N. T. against the assaults not merely of avowed skeptics, but also of theologians within the Christian Church....[7]

Regarding internal apologetics Paul goes even further, warning the elders that not only will false religious teachers seep into the church from the outside, but also many will actually be indigenous to the church. He writes, "and from among your own selves men will arise" (Acts 20:30) propagating poisoned, quasi-Christian truth, numbing the intellectual and spiritual sensibilities of people in the church. The elders must be on guard and protect against such assaults on the faith that emanate from the compromised clergy. This is internal apologetics. This is a first-order responsibility of true church leadership.

More Evidence Demanding a Verdict
Jude and Internal Apologetics
Paul wrote virtually all of his thirteen epistles to counter false teaching that was going on...*inside the church!* This is also true of the epistles written by James, Peter, John and Jude. This takes us to one of the other most potent apologetic texts in the New Testament, Jude 3-4:

> Beloved, while I was making every effort to write you about our common salvation, I felt the necessity to write to you appealing that you contend earnestly for the faith which was once for all handed down to the saints. For certain persons have crept in unnoticed, those who were long beforehand marked out for this condemnation, ungodly persons who turn the grace of our God into licentiousness and deny our only Master and Lord, Jesus Christ.

Five principles flow from this divine pericope that are instructive relative to apologetics. They are as follows: (1) Jude 3-4 is apologetical in tenor; (2) apologetics is a command for all Christians; (3) apologetics begins in the church, and is therefore internal; (4) the combatants we wrestle with in apologetics are religious people who claim to be Christian; and (5) the faith is what we defend in apologetics.

Like Acts 20, Jude 3-4 is a five-star passage on apologetics. Sadly, the average Christian apologetics book does not even make reference to Jude 3-4. When such a clear and pertinent passage is neglected, then the whole counsel of God is not being brought to bear on the job of apologetics, and as a result that brand of apologetics lacks balance and thoroughness. There are exceptions—some authors do note the importance of Jude 3-4 in an apologetics context, and such authors are typically pastors, not philosophers. Greg Bahnsen was an example.[8] Although he did have a PhD in philosophy, he was also a pastor of a church. Yet his reference to Jude 3 is negligible due to its brevity. Dr. Walter Martin, the original "Bible Answer Man," served in several pastoral roles over his ministry career, and his life's verse was Jude 3. He was rare in that he understood the import of applying the truth of Jude 3 in an apologetic way to the church. His classic, *The Kingdom of the Cults*, belongs in every Christian's personal library. Following is a survey gleaning practical principles of internal apologetics based on Jude.

Jude and the Language of Apologetics

First, Jude utilizes the nomenclature of apologetics. Jude commands Christians to "contend earnestly for the faith" (v. 3). "Contend earnestly" is from the compound Greek word, *epagonizesthai*. It's actually a combination of a preposition, *epi-*, plus the verb, *agonizomai*, from which we get our English word, *agonize*. The addition of the preposition makes the word emphatic or intensive. Hiebert eloquently gives the significance of the word in context:

> *agonizomai*…was much used in connection with athletic contests to describe a strenuous struggle to overcome an opponent, as in a wrestling match. A more general use was in reference to any conflict, contest, debate or lawsuit. It involves the thought of the expenditure of all of one's energy to prevail. Here, as often, the verb is metaphorical, describing the spiritual conflict in which believers engage

...the thought of a defensive conflict comes out clearly in the following dative, 'for the faith.' Mombert pictures the force of the compound verb as 'to fight, standing upon a thing which is assaulted and which the adversary desires to take away, and it is to fight so as to defend it, and to retain it.'[9]

Hortatory phrases calling Christians "to fight" and "to defend" the faith are clearly the work of apologetics. As such, Jude 3-4 needs to be a regular, priority passage in the biblical apologetical lexicon.

Apologetics—the Work of Every Christian

Second, Jude makes it plain that all believers are called to the work of apologetics. His command is written to the "Beloved" (v. 3) who are the same as those in verse one that he addresses as "those who are the called." This is a parallel truth we already saw in 1 Peter 3:15. This is in contrast to most traditional apologists who claim apologetics is primarily for the professional Christian philosophers.

Apologetics Starts Within the Church

Third, Jude says that apologetics is fundamentally internal. Apologetics is doing the work of defending the faith in the face of "certain persons [that] have crept in unnoticed" (v. 4). These are not atheists and irreligious skeptics outside the church. These snakes have crept into the church disguised as devout religious people—professing Christians. They infiltrated all levels of the local church. Jude notes they were "hidden reefs in your love feasts when they feast with you without fear" (v. 12).

Apologetics and Religionists

Fourth, Jude says apologetics is to be employed against those who are religious, people who claim to be Christians. But they are deceptive, dangerous pseudo-Christians. Their hearts were as black and their minds were as corrupt as any atheist or secular skeptic. Jude said they were "ungodly persons" (v. 4), "unreasoning animals" (v. 10), headed for eternal hell (v. 13), "mockers" (v. 18), "worldly-minded, devoid of the Spirit" (v. 19). And they were the greatest threat to the faith in Jude's day. In keeping with what Paul commanded in Acts 20, Jude says apologetics needs to be employed within the confines of the church against influential, errant church-attenders.

Apologetics and the Gospel

Fifth, Jude says we use apologetics to defend "the faith." There is not one example in the New Testament of Jesus or the apostles ever using apologetics for the purpose of trying to prove the possibility of God's existence, or to justify the logical rationality of the Christian worldview. They always defended the faith, the gospel of Jesus Christ. The Greek text literally refers to "the saints' faith." Faith has a definite article—it is specific content: "The content of the apostolic gospel."[10] And the specific content that is to be defended is the special revelation of the gospel of Jesus Christ that was specifically "delivered" in a final form by the apostles as they preached the gospel and then wrote it down to be preserved in perpetuity for the saints of all the ages.

Jesus and Internal Apologetics

Among the Religious Jews

Jesus made a priority of internal apologetics. Jesus was a Jewish rabbi and teacher in the synagogues (Luke 4:14-15). Most of His defensive apologetic work was done within His own ranks, in-house, combating and confuting the false teaching of religionists inside the Old Testament Jewish faith (Matt 12:38). He did not spend His time arguing philosophically with the pagan, polytheistic Romans who reigned over His environs (John 19:10). Nor did He spend time reasoning with Aristotelian logic among the numerous idolatrous Gentiles who resided all over Palestine at the time (Matt 15:21-26).

His ongoing debates were theological and Scriptural, and they were spearheaded at the Jewish leadership, the Sanhedrin, in Jerusalem where the Temple served as the headquarters of their religion (John 8:2, 20-59). The Pharisees, the Sadducees and the scribes were so-called master teachers of the Old Testament, yet it was with these in-house religious teachers that Jesus continually locked horns apologetically. All throughout the Gospel of John, Jesus was defending the faith against the "Jews," a term John uses over seventy times to refer to the Pharisees and scribes of the Mosaic Law. His entire three-year public ministry of teaching, preaching, proclaiming and defending the faith was virtually all internal, reserved for the religious, monotheistic, Jewish Old Testament community.

Among His Own Church

Jesus also practiced internal apologetics with His own church. When addressing the seven churches of Asia Minor, Jesus emphasized the importance of making internal apologetics a priority. The local church and its leaders need to contend earnestly for the faith, protecting its doctrine within the church. Defensive, protective and preventative apologetics needs to begin among the saints, inside the church walls.

Jesus commended the church at Ephesus for practicing internal apologetics, for they aggressively scrutinized every teacher in the church, and if any were false, heretical or subversive they were then summarily exposed and called to account. Jesus lauds them, saying, "you put to the test those who call themselves apostles, and they are not, and you found them to be false" (Rev 2:2). Not only did the saints at Ephesus identify and expose false teaching, they hated false teaching! And so does Jesus! Jesus goes on with His commendation of their admirable internal apologetics saying, "you hate the deeds of the Nicolaitans, which I also hate" (Rev 2:6).

Jesus rebuked the church at Pergamum for tolerating false teaching in the church. He sternly warned them because they had "some who hold the teaching of Balaam" (Rev 2:14) and the saints in this church did not have the courage to confront and expose it. They also tolerated some who held "the teaching of the Nicolaitans" (2:15). Furious over the compromised heresy, Jesus called them to repent or face His judgment from the sword of His mouth (2:16).

The most scathing rebuke Jesus ever gave anyone was reserved for the church at Thyatira. These professing believers failed to practice internal apologetics inside their own church against a false teacher, a self-proclaimed prophetess Jesus called "Jezebel." Her teaching was so abhorrent that Jesus personally threatened to kill her and those who called themselves Christians who followed her false religious teaching (2:22-23).

In Matthew 13 Jesus warned His disciples through a parable that counterfeits would infiltrate the community of the faithful. And He made it clear that the false teachers and pseudo-disciples would worm their way in among God's people until the end of the age:

> Jesus presented another parable to them, saying, "The kingdom of heaven may be compared to a man who sowed good seed in his field. But while his men were sleeping, his enemy came and sowed tares among the wheat, and went away. But when the wheat sprouted and

bore grain, then the tares became evident also.

The slaves of the landowner came and said to him, 'Sir, did you not sow good seed in your field? How then does it have tares?' And he said to them, 'An enemy has done this!' The slaves said to him, 'Do you want us, then, to go and gather them up?' But he said, 'No; for while you are gathering up the tares, you may uproot the wheat with them. Allow both to grow together until the harvest; and in the time of the harvest I will say to the reapers, 'First gather up the tares and bind them in bundles to burn them up; but gather the wheat into my barn'" (13:24-30).

Jesus goes on to explain the meaning of this parable to His disciples by giving seven interpretive clues. He told them (1) the Sower of the good seed is the Son of Man (Jesus); (2) the field is the world; (3) the good seed are true believers; (4) the tares are false believers or children of the devil; (5) the enemy who sowed the bad seeds is the devil; (6) the harvest is the end of the age; (7) and the reapers are the angels of God.

A "tare" is a troublesome and poisonous "weed," also called a "darnel," that looks just like wheat, especially in the earlier stages of growth. This weed could be distinguished from the wheat after maturity, at the time of "the harvest."[11]

Jesus' point was to warn and prepare His followers about the harsh reality that during this era, the time of the Church age, pseudo-believers will always be around, trying to intermix, affiliate with and attach themselves with true believers. And they will look so genuine on the outside that they will have the appearance of true believers, when in fact they are defiled, unregenerate and evil on the inside—complete imposters. And their attack on the Church will not be on a human or natural level.

The strategy to poison and destroy the Church from within is a diabolical satanic ploy, being orchestrated on high with other-worldly intelligence and power. As such, counterfeit Christianity is a formidable foe and is not to be taken lightly, and the only efficacious weapons to wage against it are heavenly and supernatural.

We should not be surprised when false teachers and false doctrine creep into the Church; Jesus said we should expect it. So false disciple-makers, false disciples and false doctrine would always bedevil the true Church until the Second Coming. Hence, the need for ongoing, aggressive apologetics within the church.

From the above examples it is evident that Jesus expected believers to vigilantly defend the faith beginning on the inside. If the Church is weak from false, watered-down doctrine on the inside, it will be inept at defending the assaults that come from without. So for Jesus internal apologetics was to be foundational for the Church.

The Pastoral Epistles On Internal Apologetics

Internal Apologetics in 1 Timothy

In addition to specific passages like 1 Peter 3:15, Acts 20, and Jude 3-4 that are apologetical in nature, there are also entire books in the New Testament that are apologetical. These include the Pastoral Epistles, first and second Timothy and Titus. For example, 1 Timothy concludes with this charge from Paul to his protégé Timothy: "O Timothy, guard what has been entrusted to you" (6:20). This summary statement encapsulates the theme of the whole book, the call for Timothy to defend the faith—to protect the deposit of divine truth that was imparted to him, to do the work of a true biblical apologist. The stakes are high. Timothy was enlisted by God to engage in spiritual warfare, hence the call to arms that begins the epistle: "fight the good fight" (1:18). Similarly, Timothy is reminded that he is a soldier for God: "you man of God...Fight the good fight of faith" (6:11-12). "Guard," "fight," "fight," "fight"—this is the jargon of apologetics.

Apologetics and Religionists

Who does Timothy confront as he fights for the faith and guards the deposit of spiritual truth? He is confronting people and false teaching that are inside the church, miscreant religious teachers and professing believers gone awry (6:21). Timothy was to employ apologetics against so-called believers like Hymenaeus and Alexander (1:20), and false "teachers of the Law" (1:7), as well as religious men who spread "doctrines of demons" (4:1), and those in the church who "advocate a different doctrine" (6:3). Timothy was to put a premium on internal apologetics.

Specialized Internal Apologetics

It was pointed out earlier that Peter encouraged all Christians to be involved in apologetics. But Paul made it clear that there is a specialized kind of apologetics as well—and it is not reserved for the professional philosopher. It is reserved for the pastors, elders and overseers of the church (Acts 20), those that Paul calls the "man of God" (1 Tim 6:11). This truth is accentuated in 1 Timothy and brings to the fore fundamental questions that distinguish traditional apologetics from biblical apologetics. Who is called specifically by God to do the work of specialized apologetics? By what authority does anyone have the right to officially represent God and His Church as an ambassador and under-shepherd, with the specific task of defending the deposit of His truth, once for all delivered to the saints, in the face of opposition? It is not the self-appointed, professionally trained philosopher plying the laws of logic with finite human reason. Scripture says only the man of God, the local church elder, has this delegated divine authority and is called to this specialized task.

Presuppostionalist Greg Bahnsen set himself apart here from traditional apologists when he said, "Paul wrote to Titus that overseers (pastors and elders) in the church are required to be especially adept at refuting those who oppose the truth of God (Titus 1:9)."[12] Bahnsen recognized the specialized call of the pastor with respect to apologetics so plainly taught in Scripture because he himself was a pastor. This also made him unique in that the majority of today's so-called apologetics experts are not pastors in God's local church, but rather are first and foremost "philosophers" and professional academic "professors" and university "scholars." It seems many of them have forgotten the priority of the local church, the only institution Jesus promised to plant, protect and perpetuate all throughout history (Matt 16:18).

The dominant role that the shepherd and elder should play in the intellectual and practical life of the church has been effectually emasculated in the twentieth century. Historically, if someone needed counsel for the soul, a man of God—a pastor—was entrusted with the task—today such persons are referred to the psychiatrist. If a Christian marriage faced challenges, the man of the Book used to have the answers—today church people turn first to the local MFT or clinical psychologist. For centuries, if fellow believers had a conflict, the elders of the church would assist the saints in seeking resolution, utilizing the sufficiency of the Word and prayer—today, a secular lawyer is consulted without a second thought. So it is with apologetics today—when Christians are challenged with scientific and intellectual dilemmas in regard to the faith, the pastor is nowhere on the radar—what we need, we are frequently told, is a traditional apologist, with a PhD in philosophy, astronomy or metaphysics.

Not so for Paul and the book of Timothy. Specialized apologetics was entrusted to the elders and pastors of the church by virtue of the divinely delegated authority granted by Christ Himself. Paul highlights four grounds of delegated authority that church elders and overseers have, making them perfectly suited for the task of internal apologetics that Christian philosophers do not possess.

By What Authority?
Scripture, Pastors and Internal Apologetics

The first source of divine authority given to the church elder for the task of defending the faith is Scripture, the living Word of God. The traditional apologist prides himself on his mastery of man-generated metaphysics. In 1 Timothy Paul repeatedly reminds the church leader that he has been entrusted with the divine deposit of the Word of the living God (6:20). The pastor is to be highly trained as a biblical teacher (3:2) and is not to deviate from the high and holy calling of being enslaved to the ongoing work of Scripturally-driven ministry: "give attention to the public reading of Scripture, to exhortation and teaching" (4:13). Paul goes on in 2 Timothy to tell the pastor to "preach the word" (4:2) for, "All Scripture is inspired by God and profitable for teaching, for reproof, for correction, for training in righteousness; so that the man of God may be adequate, equipped for every good work" (3:16-17).

It is important to remember that there is no higher authority than Scripture, for it reveals the very mind of God. What Scripture says, God says. The Bible does not have derivative authority, but rather it has inherent authority. As a matter of fact, Scripture has binding authority over all other authority structures including the home, government, the Church and elders. The latter have God-ordained authority as well, but they possess delegated authority and not inherent authority.

The Divine Office of Elder and Internal Apologetics

The second source of authority that pastors have is the divine office of elder. The only institution Christ promised to build, bless and perpetuate was the Church (Matt 16:18). Jesus started the Church, is Lord of the Church and purchased its people with His own blood

(Acts 20:28). He instituted its two ordinances and created its two perpetual offices, elder ["overseer" and "bishop" are synonyms] (Titus 1:5) and deacon (1 Tim 3:8) (the Church was built on the foundation of the apostles and prophets). The office of elder is a sacred position endowed with inviolable and supernatural responsibilities, including the special task of defending the faith (1:18-19). God created the sacred ecclesiastical office of elder, delineating specific qualifications (1 Tim 3:1-7), for the specific purpose of overseeing the church, administrating the people of God and defending the faith. Traditional apologists, who are typically secularly trained philosophers, have no divinely prescribed qualifications. Do you want to be designated as an official "philosopher-apologist" today? Then simply have one of your fellow patriots in the apologists' guild declare you one.

As an overseer in the church, Timothy was entrusted with ruling authority from heaven: "Paul, an apostle of Christ Jesus according to the commandment of God...This command I entrust to you, Timothy, my son...fight the good fight" (1 Tim 1:1, 18). Further, Paul says that any man who serves in "the office of overseer" is commissioned with the incomparable task of taking "care of the church of God" (3:1, 5). The church elders are to "rule" in Christ's stead (5:17). Elders are to "fight the good fight" as a holy "charge...in the presence of God" (6:12-13). No such divine calling is granted to the self-appointed Christian philosopher outside the duly recognized offices instituted by Christ Himself.

The Authority of the Church and Internal Apologetics

The third source of authority delegated by God to the pastor, in addition to Scripture and his office, is the Church itself. An elder is an officer of the Church of Christ. And the elder must maintain holy protocol "in the household of God, which is the church of the living God, the pillar and support of the truth" (1 Tim 3:15). Jesus granted the keys of spiritual authority to the Church as a stewardship responsibility: "I will give you the keys of the kingdom of heaven; and whatever you bind on earth shall have been bound in heaven, and whatever you loose on earth shall have been loosed in heaven" (Matt 16:19).

The pastor can defend the faith, internally and externally, with supernatural resources by virtue of his inextricable link to the living Church of God, which is the pillar of truth itself. No philosopher who maintains merely some loose association with a para-church organization, regardless of how educated he may be, can compare to the sanctioned man of God who, in representing and defending the faith, has direct footing in the pillar of God's eternal truth, the Church.

Spiritual Gifts and Internal Apologetics

A fourth source of divine authority the church leader possesses resides in his supernatural, spiritually energized gift as a church leader. Paul told Timothy not to "neglect the spiritual gift within you" (1 Tim 4:14). The role of pastor is a spiritual gift given by God to the church. The role of philosopher is not. Christ explicitly gave gifted men to the Church: "He gave some as apostles, and some as prophets, and some as evangelists, and some as pastors and teachers, for the equipping of the saints for the work of service, to the building up of the body of Christ" (Eph 4:11-12).

No such gifted man as philosopher or apologist is mentioned in Scripture. Pastors and all Christians do the work of apologetics. And the role of philosopher neither entails nor requires any spiritual endowment or recognition whatsoever. In contrast, Paul sarcastically asks rhetorically, "Where is the philosopher of this age? Has not God made foolish the wisdom of the world?" (1 Cor 1:20; NIV). At best the philosopher's wisdom pales in comparison to the wisdom of the man of God who has divine revelation, the Church of Christ and a holy office at his disposal.

So by virtue of the inherent authority in the Word of God and the delegated divine authority in his office, his inextricable association with the Church of Christ and his supernatural gift as pastor, the elder and shepherd has been called and prepared like no other to do the business of defending and guarding the faith through the work of apologetics, internal and external.

Implications

Several implications follow from the above examination of key apologetical texts in the New Testament. It also needs to be noted that not all the pertinent biblical texts related to internal apologetics were even addressed. Contrary to Christian "apologist" Avery Dulles, who contends that "none of the New Testament writings is directly and professedly apologetical,"[13] the truth is that several entire books are explicitly and deliberately apologetical, including 2 Timothy,

Titus, 2 Peter, Jude and 1 John. It is beyond the scope of this book to expound on them all. As such, Acts 20, Jude 3-4 and 1 Timothy will serve as sufficient representations for the following implications.

Reestablishing Biblical Definitions

The first implication is that the standard definition and understanding of "defense" as portrayed by the traditional apologists needs to be scrutinized in light of the biblical data. Traditionalists say that when Peter told believers to give a "defense" (1 Pet 3:15), he was commanding Christians to give a "justification" or "warrant" in the eyes of unbelievers as to why Christianity is valid and worthy of their potential approval.

The traditionalists also typically expunge the word "defense" of any evangelistic overtones or intrinsic ties to special revelation. But that is contrary to what we have seen from the relevant biblical texts above. When the apostles talked about defending the faith, they did not mean "justify" your beliefs in the hopes of appeasing the intellectual unbeliever; they meant "protect" the Church, the sheep and the truth from hostile unbelievers, be they inside the Church or outside the Church, in the power of the Spirit with divine revelation.

Rise Up, O Church of God

A second implication flowing from these imperatives is that the Church needs to wake up. Most of the imminent and ongoing attacks against believers in the New Testament were going on inside the church, being spearheaded by professing religionists and rogue Christians. Churches need to come to grips with the enemy within. The church has let its guard down. Just because people profess to be Christians does not mean they are. Countless churches have bent over backwards to accommodate just about every conceivable heresy in the name of being nice, tolerant, loving, diverse, or innovative. In the meantime the floodgates have been opened so that the church in many quarters today has tolerated a tsunami of compromise and worldly thinking to the point that a true biblical portrait of what the church is to be is a mere shadow of what it should be.

This is nothing new. When the church of Sardis was barely a generation old, Jesus reprimanded the Christians there for being compromisers and accommodators, saying, "Wake up, and strengthen the things that remain, which were about to die" (Rev 3:2). Churches need to reinstitute the basic yet forgotten principle of spiritual discernment: "examine everything carefully; hold fast to that which is good; abstain from every form of evil" (1 Thess 5:21-22). Unbiblical teaching and compromised methodologies are evil and are to be rejected.

Get Some Courage

Third, in addition to being more spiritually discerning, churches need to muster up the courage to point out, expose and remove the enemy within. That means identifying specific damning heresies by name, naming the source and origin of the false teachings that have seeped into the church, identifying the false teachers—alerting the Body of Christ—starting with the local church, and then the universal church, with an all-points bulletin or red alert, shouting it from the rooftops, warning all of God's true sheep of the imminent danger of such dastardly and chimerical leaven of the religious teachers.

Jesus did. He was specific—He was no coward. He howled to the so-called expert Bible scholars of the day, publicly, in front of their disciples, on their home turf: "But woe to you, scribes and Pharisees, hypocrites...blind guides...You fools...whitewashed tombs...You serpents, you brood of vipers, how will you escape the sentence of hell?" (Matt 23:13-33). He repeated the leading pejorative refrain seven times to them, and not because they were hard of hearing. Not a way to win friends, but it did influence lots of people. Most will say, "Well, that's not very loving or Christian to talk to people like that." I can hear it now. But actually Jesus was being very loving for yelling at them like this—Jesus loved the people the Pharisees were leading astray, so Jesus was lovingly protecting the true sheep from the damage of the deceptive Bible teachers, the Pharisees. That was a good thing.

Paul was also specific and named names. He called out the church leaders, "Hymenaeus and Alexander" of the First Emerging Community Church of Ephesus, whom he "handed over to Satan, so that they will be taught not to blaspheme" (1 Tim 1:20). He exposed the infamous church leaders, "Phygelus and Hermogenes," compromisers to the ministry who turned away from the apostolic authority of Paul (2 Tim 1:15). He told the church, in writing, about "Hymenaeus and Philetus," errant Bible teachers whose teachings were spreading like cancer in the church (2 Tim 2:17). Paul publicly decried, for all time, "Alexander the coppersmith [who] did me much harm; the Lord will repay him according to his deeds" (2 Tim 4:14).

These men passed themselves off as pastors, ministers and servants of the Lord, but Paul warned categorically that "evil men and imposters will proceed from bad to worse," inside the church, "deceiving and being deceived" (2 Tim 3:13). The modern day Philetuses and Hermogeneses are among us—what are we doing to expose and stop them? Why are these above verses never in *The Little Bible Promise* books they sell in the local Christian bookstores? Paul says these false teachers, who look so much like true Christians, are actually "rebellious men, empty talkers...who must be silenced because they are upsetting whole families, teaching things they should not teach" (Titus 1:10-11). Silenced? Not in today's Christianity. Rather than silence, we promote, showcase and buy and proliferate their books.

John the apostle was also a courageous shepherd, practicing internal apologetics, and warning the believers about evil false teachers by name when necessary. He tells of the not-so-always-right reverend, "Diotrephes, who loves to be first among them...I will call attention to his deeds which he does, unjustly accusing us with wicked words" (3 John 9-10). This Diotrephes fiend was an authoritative leader in the local church who brokered unrivaled power, as he was able to dictate who could be thrown out of the church (v. 10).

Pastor Peter was no slouch either. Just like Jesus, Paul and John, when the situation called for it, Peter confronted Christianized compromisers to the face with a clarion call to repentance. Remember Ananias who fell over dead at the Sunday evening vespers service (Acts 5). And the charismatic exorcist and professed Holy Spirit healer, Simon, whom Peter rebuked publicly with this retort: "May your silver perish with you, because you thought you could obtain the gift of God with money!" (Acts 8:20). Imagine that! Professing believers manipulating religion, God and Christianity to make a buck.

Pastors, Christians and churches of today need to follow the lead of Jesus, Love-Incarnate, and His apostles, by exercising holy courage and by practicing internal apologetics in the church by "clean[ing] out the old leaven" and "remove the wicked man from among yourselves" (1 Cor 5:7, 13). Admittedly, this is a tremendous challenge due to the push back a discerning pastor will get if he speaks up publicly trying to expose error in the church. Pastors abroad will accuse him of being "unloving" and "divisive" for saying "negative things" about another "brother." Nevertheless, we are bound by

Scripture to please God and not man (Gal 1:10), and to faithfully discharge the pastoral duty of exposing false teaching in the Church through internal apologetics. And further, we are to "mark out" specifically trouble-makers in the Church (Rom 16:17-18). In the words of Calvin, "We must unmask them."[14]

Rise Up, O Man of God

A fourth implication is that the role of pastor or elder needs to be reinstated to its proper place. The position of elder, once again, needs to be recognized as a holy, sacred, divinely instituted office. And the church can no longer allow man-made vocations, contrived parachurch guilds, patrician strongholds, or other competing quasi-religious crafts to intrude on and usurp the fundamental duties of the man of God and under-shepherd of Christ's Church (1 Pet 5:1-5). God has made elders to be the overseers and specialized defenders of His people and His truth in His Church (Acts 20:28).

This means that churches will once again need to make the delineated, God-given qualifications non-negotiable when it comes to ordaining elders in the local church (1 Tim 3:1-7). No more putting men in positions of ecclesiastical leadership based solely on their charismatic and winsome personalities, business acumen, propensity for wealth or because they have advanced degrees in literature, clinical psychology or astrophysics. Churches need courageous, truth-hungry, theologically trained, experienced, Spirit-filled, men of God who have an uncanny and unparalleled mastery and command of the Word of God.

Satan in the Church

A fifth implication is that the Church needs to be reminded of the tactics of Satan. Satan does not disguise himself as an atheist; he disguises himself as a religionist. And he is most effective in undermining the church and confusing believers by using nuanced biblical truth through so-called men of the cloth. "For such men are false apostles, deceitful workers, disguising themselves as apostles of Christ. No wonder, for even Satan disguises himself as an angel of light. Therefore it is not surprising if his servants also disguise themselves as servants of righteousness, whose end will be according to their deeds" (2 Cor 11:13-15). Satan tried to tempt Christ by using the Bible, not criticizing the Bible (Matt 4:1-10). Satan and his minions have not changed their tactics. Hence, it is important for all

Christians and church leaders to give a renewed commitment and prioritization to internal apologetics. We need to guard the truth, defend the faith, protect the sheep, and we need to begin by looking inside the Church.

Over the Top and Out of Control

Today it seems that there is more heresy, false teaching, doctrinal deception and compromise going on within the professing Church than there has been in a long time. Theological distortion and biblical infidelity seem to have leaked into all quarters of the visible Church. It's startling and almost overwhelming. And it is rising at an exponential rate. I'm not sure what to attribute it to, but the reality is starkly undeniable and has become palpably manifest since the time I was in seminary compared to today. It could be that it is simply because we are in the last days, and Paul warned us clearly in his writings that false teachers would go from bad to worse with time until Christ returns.

Compounding that could be the rise of the internet and technological advancements that enable heretics and self-proclaimed false teachers to spread their damnable heresies across the globe in seconds from the lair of their laptops, as they craft their appealing, sleek and colorful websites and blogs of non-stop religious sophistry. Gone are the days where the rigors of a traditional education in a solid seminary and an internship of service in a trustworthy local church served as sources of vetting, training, fine-tuning and verifying a man's aptitude, worthiness and giftedness with respect to teaching the Bible. Today, anyone with a computer can declare himself to be an expert in the Bible or a prophet and at the same time act as the theological Gestapo by attacking God's true and faithful minsters of His Word through character assassinations and smear campaigns for the whole world to see—a nefarious trend that will only worsen with time.

There are so many heresies that have arisen within the evangelical church in the past thirty years it is hard to keep track. But here are some of the main ones I have witnessed. In the 1980's non-Lordship Salvationism came to fruition, espousing the idea that Christians should not call unbelievers to repentance during evangelism because we were told that "repentance" was a human work that compromised grace alone. It was suggested that we are to tell the lost simply, "Believe in Jesus," or as one ardent non-Lordship advocate told me in an effort to straighten me out: "Pastor Cliff, we don't tell unbelievers to repent; we need to tell them that they are already saved; they just don't know it yet."

The 1990's saw the rise of Open Theism by Arminian evangelicals who claimed to believe in inerrancy. They proposed the notion that God does not know the future, rather God is just a good guesser and usually guesses right about how people might react when they hear the gospel. So in effect they dogmatically asserted that God was not omniscient, but He was in the process of growing and learning—God can get better and improve. Which means God is not immutable as the Bible clearly teaches. And their God was not perfect either, another heresy that was utterly blasphemous.

In the late 1990's and early 2000's "the New Perspective on Paul" came to the fore. A spattering of liberal-leaning evangelical Christian scholars informed the rest of us that the Church has misunderstood what Paul taught on justification for the past 500 years, and Martin Luther is the one who led us all astray. We were told that Paul did not teach personal salvation via justification by grace through faith apart from works. Nor did Paul teach the imputation of Christ's righteousness to the believing sinner. Salvation does not refer to personal redemption and forgiveness of sins, but rather it refers to corporate and even national solidarity leading to an eschatological salvation after all our good works are completed and evaluated as a body of work. And furthermore, the Pharisees are good guys not bad guys—forget Matthew 23...try not to focus on that chapter. So says N. T. Wright, E. P. Sanders, James Dunn and other like professed Christian scholars.

The first decade of 2000 saw the rise of the "inerrancy" debate...again. One hundred years ago, in the days of inerrantists like Machen and Warfield, Bible scholars who opposed inerrancy identified as "liberal scholars" and were clearly distinguished from evangelicals. The liberals considered the word "evangelical" to be a term of derision. Fifty years ago, in the early days of inerrantists like J. I. Packer, Harold Lindsell and Carl Henry, anti-inerrantists were clearly identified as neo-orthodox, and they also were not considered evangelical.

In 2017 things have radically changed. The evangelicals (evangelical churches, colleges, seminaries, societies, etc.) have been overrun by Bible scholars who say the Bible is full of errors, anachronisms and myths, yet these same teachers call themselves evangelicals and many of them even claim to believe in inerrancy. How is this possible? The enemy has simply re-framed the debate; they focus the debate today on the meaning of "inerrancy" and in many cases they have successfully defined the term out of existence. So today countless evangelical scholars suggest "inerrancy" does not mean "absolutely without error," but rather it refers to God's amazing ability "to speak truth through error" or "in spite of error."

So an evangelical can say Paul misspoke in Romans 5 when he wrote about Adam being a real man when in fact, we are told, that Adam was not a real man...yet the Bible's integrity is preserved because God "accommodated" Paul's ignorance and was still able to use Paul as an apostle to write some "inspired truths" in the Bible. Again they say Jesus referred to a man named Noah in the Gospels when in fact Noah never existed, but the Bible is true because "God accommodated to the average Jew's understanding of the day"—i.e., the Jews 2,000 years ago all naively and ignorantly believed Noah was actually a real person. God "accommodated" to the ignorance of the people in that day. Sound like a bunch of hogwash, gobbledygook and balderdash? Well, it is.

True people of God, who love Christ and His flawless Word, cannot tolerate such egregious compromise that is rampant in the Church. God needs to raise up, in every generation, prayerful, courageous, Spirit-led, Christ-centered, gospel-driven biblical apologists who will work on the front lines in the spiritual battle carrying out internal apologetics for the protection and purity of the Church, the precious Body and Bride of Christ.

Summary

Contemporary books on apologetics almost never talk about "internal apologetics," and only address external apologetics. Internal apologetics is defending the faith inside the church. Internal apologetics is commanded in many New Testament passages including Acts 20, Jude, 1 Timothy and 2 Timothy. Jesus and the apostles practiced internal apologetics. Internal apologetics was also a priority for the apostolic and early Church fathers. Internal apologetics needs to be spear-headed by qualified, trained, Spirit-filled, godly pastors and elders in the local churches, who in turn can train their people and model for them a biblical lifestyle of apologetics. Logically, internal apologetics is a prerequisite for effective external apologetics, being that Christians first need to be equipped properly with biblical doctrine and a biblical methodology before they can successfully engage the unbelieving world in defending and advancing the gospel of Jesus Christ.

Notes

1. Stackhouse mentions the phrase once in his book, but does not mean the same thing by it that I do in this chapter; John G. Stackhouse, Jr., *Humble Apologetics: Defending the Faith Today* (New York, NY: Oxford University Press, 2002), 118. Despite his Arminian and rationalistic approach to external apologetics, Norm Geisler is to be commended for his life-long commitment to internal apologetics, as he has exposed errant teaching in the Church and unmasked wayward professing Christians like few have done in our generation. Especially helpful has been his work with inerrancy for half a century in relation to liberalism, postmodernism, Open Theism, higher criticism and countless other "isms" that certain scoundrels have tried to smuggle into the Church.

2. James E. Taylor, *Introducing Apologetics: Cultivating Christian Commitment* (Grand Rapids, MI: Baker Academic, 2006), 76.

3. Iain H. Murray, *John MacArthur: Servant of the Word and Flock* (Carlisle, PA: The Banner of Truth Trust, 2011), 153, 209.

4. For a thorough portrait describing the nature of MacArthur's ministry that has been defined by a healthy dose of practicing internal biblical apologetics as a shepherd, elder and Bible teacher, see Ian Murray's biography of MacArthur, especially pages 111-127.

5. John Hannah, *Our Legacy: The History of Christian Doctrine* (Colorado Springs, CO: Navpress, 2001), 40.

6. Ibid., 41.

7. John McClintock and James Strong, "Evidences of Christianity" in *Cyclopedia of Biblical, Theological and Ecclesiastical Literature,* 10 vols. (Grand Rapids, MI: Baker Book House, 1981), III: 380. One of the greatest practical benefits of "internal apologetics" is the purity of the Church. Wong comments: "Some may complain that a firm stance against sin will turn people away from the church and God, and that we should concentrate on 'love' and 'tolerance'. But that would be the opposite of what God desires. Real love is truth and cannot tolerate sin (see 1 John 1:5-10; 4:8). In fact, a firm stand for personal purity was exactly what energized the early church into greater evangelism. They submitted to God and gave the devil no foothold in their lives (see James 4:7). This evident purity kept the fakes and phoneys outside because of their fear of God (Acts 5:13a) and prevented unbelievers from infiltrating the church like tares sown among the wheat (see Matt. 13:24-30). Only genuinely born-again Christians would be a part of such an assembly. This purity made even the outsiders hold them in 'high esteem' (Acts 5:13b) for their love of one another"; John-Michael Wong, *Opening Up Acts* (Leominster, England: Day One Publications, 2010), 51-52.

8. Greg Bahnsen, *Always Ready: Directions for Defending the Faith,* ed. Robert R. Booth (Texarkana: Covenant Media Foundation, 1996), 110.

9. D. Edmond Hiebert, *Second Peter and Jude: An Expositional Commentary* (Greenville, SC: Unusual Publications, 1989), 218.

10. Ralph Harris, Stanley Horton, Gayle Garrity, *The Complete Biblical Library: Hebrews—Jude,* (Springfield, Missouri: World Library Press, 1989), IX:457.

11. "Tares" or "darnel" from the Greek word *zizania*, Leon Morris, *The Gospel According to Matthew*, in *The Pillar New Testament Commentary* (Grand Rapids: Eerdmans Publishing Company, 1992), 349; see also Grant R. Osborne, *Matthew: Exegetical Commentary On the New Testament, Vol. 1*, ed. by Clinton E. Arnold (Grand Rapids: Zondervan, 2010), 521.

12. Bahnsen, *Always Ready*, 111. Tozer also recognized the desperate need to practice internal apologetics as a pastor and Bible teacher and he bemoaned the fact that it was woefully neglected in the church abroad during his lifetime. He wrote, "The fashion now is to tolerate anything lest we get the reputation of being intolerant. The tender-minded saints cannot bear to see Agag slain, so they choose rather to sacrifice the health of the Church for years to come by sparing error and evil; and this they do in the name of Christian love"; J. L. Snyder, *In Pursuit of God: The Life of A. W. Tozer* (Camp Hill, PA: Christian Publications, 1991), 128. Cornelius Van Til was a faithful practitioner of internal apologetics. He was not just an ivory tower, elitist philosopher, but was also committed to ministry in the local church. For decades he defended the Body of Christ from heretics and compromisers inside the church who threatened the sheep with their subtle, damning doctrines that were camouflaged in biblical and Christian nomenclature. For example, in exposing the neo-existentialism of Barth's deceptive attack on the authority and historicity of the Bible, Van Til said, "Now this is where we have to learn to be critical; that doesn't mean 'to be negative.' We would rather not be negative. But it is our task, our responsibility as defenders of the faith, of 'the once-for-all-delivered to the saints' and of the children of God, who cannot in general be expected...to understand it [Barth's esoteric compromise of Scripture]. Our task as ministers and as teachers is to alert the poor simple people against this sort of thing"; Cornelius Van Til, "Van Til on Karl Barth," part 1, 1968 lecture, www.watch?v=OE6KJbBTH2s>

13. Avery Dulles, *A History of Apologetics* (San Francisco: Ignatius Press, 2005), 23.

14. John Calvin, *Institutes of the Christian Religion*, translated by Henry Beveridge (Peabody, Massachusetts: Hendrickson Publishers, 2008), 725-726.

4

The Myth of Natural Theology

"Hot Potato! Hot Potato!"

Natural theology is like global warming: some apologists say it's the foundation for everything; others say it is all hot air.[1] Traditional apologetics stands on the foundation of natural theology. The problem is that, biblically speaking, there is no such thing as natural theology—there is only biblical theology. Natural theology is nothing more than a man-made imposter.

The topic of natural theology—its definition, origin, legitimacy, and relationship to general and special revelation—is a highly contentious issue in the realm of apologetics, philosophical religion and theology. This has been the case for a long time. To broach the topic is to risk the inevitable exchange of verbal and written fisticuffs with the proponents of contrarian views; all the contenders seem to agree. William Lane Craig, as a precursor to establishing his own view of apologetics, acknowledges the need to first "confront the difficult and controversial question of the relationship between general revelation and natural theology."[2] In like manner, R. C. Sproul admits that intellectual clashing over natural theology is a "perennial debate [that]...crosses ecclesiastical borders, inciting skirmishes not only among Protestant thinkers but among Roman Catholic scholars as well."[3] Sproul goes on to enter the ring himself and stoke up the skirmish.

Defining natural theology is not easy. It seems the topic is unfamiliar to most Christians. Simply stated, natural theology is doing theology without the Bible. Proponents of natural theology seek to understand God through venues of revelation apart from the Bible. When it comes to the topic of God's revelation and how humans come to know God, we can't be afraid of a skirmish—especially when the stakes are so high. The question of revelation and how people can come to know God is of the highest priority. A. C. Headlam poignantly observed, "the primary question in theology must be, what is the source of our knowledge of God?"[4] G. C. Berkouwer insightfully echoed the same sentiment when he wrote, "There is no more significant question in the whole of theology and in the whole of human life than that of the nature and reality of revelation."[5] Properly understanding what natural theology is in relation to general revelation and special revelation is one of the most important issues in the debate on Christian apologetics.

Defining Our Terms

Before embarking on this challenging task, key definitions need to be clearly established. Much of the contention over natural theology and its relationship to general revelation and special revelation is due in part to a lack of clearly delineated terms and phrases. Instead, convoluted assumptions often rule the day and confound the matter.[6] Many in the debate do not seem to agree on the meaning of basic terms and often fail to realize that they don't agree. This is particularly true among traditional apologists who frequently do not maintain homogeneity in how they define and utilize the three key phrases under consideration: natural theology, general revelation and special revelation. To clarify the matter, we will begin with summary definitions of each.

General revelation—also called *universal* or *natural* revelation, it is the self-revelation of God in nature, in providence, and in the moral law within the heart and conscience, whereby all persons at all times and places intuit a rudimentary understanding of the Creator and His moral demands. It is universally accessible to all and is not learned. It is external and internal and non-propositional. It was created by God and is given as a gift to humanity. It is perspicuous yet suppressed and denied by unbelievers. It is sufficient for providing culpability before God as Judge but insufficient to impart salvation. It complements, is propaedeutic to, and is in harmony with special revelation and needs to be clarified, explained and supplemented by special revelation. It is not natural theology. It has existed in all its forms, unchanged, since the beginning of creation at the time of the Fall. It is defined and explained in the Bible in at least seven hallmark texts.

Special revelation—also called *divine, particular, redemptive, direct, heavenly* or *supernatural* revelation. The supernatural self-disclosure of God and His will through special means, such as prophecy, visions, dreams, miraculous acts, prophets, angels, direct declarations from heaven, written Scripture and ultimately the incarnation of Jesus Himself. It is propositional, anthropic, personal and analogical in nature. For us today it is confined to the sixty-six books of the Bible. It produces faith needed for salvation. It is not accessible to all people everywhere at all times and needs to be propagated and preached. It corrects and clarifies the sinner's understanding of general revelation. It was created by God and given to humanity as a gift on His initiative. It was given progressively throughout history, beginning with the creation of Adam.

Natural theology—also called *philosophical* theology, *speculative* theology or *natural religion*, is the practice of philosophically reflecting on the existence and nature of God independent of divine revelation or Scripture; thoughts about God developed through discursive reasoning and ratiocination without the contribution of the Bible. It is not the same as general or natural revelation. It was created by man, not by God. It has changed throughout history and is defined in different ways by different philosophers. It was never used by the Old Testament prophets, Jesus or the apostles.

Having defined these three key phrases in a preliminary fashion, we will now look at each one in more depth, highlighting the implications relative to the current debate about the nature and methodology of Christian apologetics.

General Revelation

Richard Mayhue astutely observed, "one's view of general revelation will greatly influence one's apologetic system."[7] This being true, we will begin with an examination of *general revelation* and a summary of the historically accepted definition: the universal witness in nature, in providence, and in the moral law within the human heart, at all times and places to all people, about God's existence and nature. This definition actually is based upon and flows from the teaching of Scripture. In other words, the Bible contains a theology of general revelation. As such, the discussion of a legitimate concept of general revelation needs to be confined to and driven by Scripture. Richard Mayhue is right on as he buffers this indispensable truth: "whatever comprises our theology of general revelation as taught in Scripture must come from these sources. This demands that God's special revelation define God's natural revelation without contaminating the subject with man's philosophical reasoning."[8] Much contamination has been proliferated, hence the paramount need to clarify and recalibrate on the matter.

Although general revelation is defined by special revelation, it is not special revelation. Special revelation is supernatural revelation given by God through selectively special means including prophecy and Scripture (the Bible). General revelation refers to those truths that people know about God (*not* those things they can *progressively learn* about God!) in nature and in themselves apart from the Bible. For further clarification and development of general revelation it is imperative to briefly examine the seven non-disputed biblical passages that directly address the topic. They include Psalm 19:1-6; Ecclesiastes 3:11; Acts 14:17; Acts 17:22-31; Romans 1:18-25; Romans 2:14-15; and Romans 10:18.

Psalm 19:1-6
Several key truths about the nature of general revelation flow from this majestic psalm. It reads:

> [1]The heavens are telling of the glory of God; and their
>   expanse is declaring the work of His hands.
> [2]Day to day pours forth speech, and night to night reveals
>   knowledge.
> [3]There is no speech, nor are there words; their voice is not
>   heard.
> [4]Their line has gone out through all the earth, and their
>   utterances to the end of the world. In them He has
>   placed a tent for the sun,
> [5]which is as a bridegroom coming out of his chamber; it
>   rejoices as a strong man to run his course.
> [6]Its rising is from one end of the heavens, and its circuit to
>   the other end of them; and there is nothing hidden
>   from its heat.

The overriding theme in this passage is that truth about God is clearly displayed in a universal manner through the luminaries in the sky, the sun being the dominant voice in this created celestial choir's display of radiance and regularity. Verse one pinpoints what can be known about God from nature: His "glory" and the "work of His hands." God's "glory" in the Old Testament always refers to an outward, visible and resplendent manifestation of one or more of His divine perfections—any time the invisible God is made manifest for humanity to see and behold (cf. Exod 16:7, 10; 33:18-23; John 1:14).

The "work of His hands" (or "His handiwork", NKJV) at the end of verse 1 qualifies which of God's glorious perfections are put on display in the sky for the whole world to see. The context is clearly accentuating God's character as the mighty and majestic Creator. The theater of this display underscores that the audience is universal—all of humanity is exposed to God's nature as the mighty Creator, for all people everywhere are subject to the ever-present exposure of the billboard of the sky. It is immediately present to all. Verse four underscores this truth, saying it "has gone out through all the earth."

In addition to the universal reach, this natural revelation has universal permanence. It is continually on display—there are no intermissions of God's limitless power being arrayed in the sky, for the two Hebrew verbs, "telling" and "declaring," are participles, indicating that the action has been ceaseless, ever since the beginning of creation![9] The two verbs could be translated as "keep on telling" and "keep on declaring."[10] Hence, verse two's divine commentary on this reality: "Day to day...night to night."

Another key truth from this passage about the nature of general revelation is highlighted in verse three. It emphasizes that the truth about God in nature as seen in the splendor of the sky is not contingent upon one's literacy, academic sophistication, elitist social status, or intellectual discursive capabilities. The truth about God as a mighty Creator is immediately and intuitively apprehended. There is no *process* of discovery or toilsome learning procedure required. As one looks to the sky, the message is eidetically apparent, inescapable and understood. The truth of God is instantaneous and perspicuous. No elitist philosophical musings are required. This is what the psalmist meant when he said, "There is no speech, nor are there words." God communicates this basic truth about Himself in universally comprehended sign language. The curse of the Tower of Babel is bypassed.

Much more could be said about the inimitable features of Psalm 19 and its contribution to the realities of general revelation, but space limits doing so. Instead, we defer to Mayhue's unparalleled potent summary of the psalm's contribution to the discussion at hand:

> This grand psalm provides six major insights into general revelation. First, as to its *source*, the heavens comprise a significant element of general revelation (19:1). Second, in regard to its *message*, God's glory as the Creator of the heavens is unmistakable (19:1). Third, the never-ceasing cycle of day and night testify to its *permanency* so long as the created order exists (19:2). Fourth, as to its *character*, it is a silent witness comprised of phenomenological evidence (19:3). Fifth, its *extent* has no geographical limitations since the evidence can be observed everywhere (19:4a-b). Sixth, as to its *order* or *regulation*, the predictability of sunrise and sunset points to the precise order of the creation and thus the orderliness of the Creator (19:4c-6).[11]

In sum, Psalm 19:1-6 makes clear that God's nature as mighty Creator is apparent to all people despite historic time of life, native language or geographical location.[12]

Ecclesiastes 3:11

Being carried along by the Holy Spirit of God, King Solomon wrote the following inspired words 3,000 years ago about God: "He has made everything appropriate in its time. He has also set eternity in their heart." Whereas Psalm 19:1-6 addresses what can be known about God in the external world of nature, this passage addresses what can be known of God internally, within every human. Solomon says that God put an innate imprint in the soul of every human—He has "set eternity in their heart," guaranteeing an inescapable witness and reality of God's eternal existence and His rightful ownership on their very being. This passage is the Old Testament counterpart to Romans 1:18-25 which will be examined shortly. Regarding this internal witness that exists in every person, Mayhue aptly explains that, "It undoubtedly resulted from man being created in the image of God (Gen 1:27), which subsequently was distorted in the fall (Gen. 3:1-21), thus needing to be restored by God's gracious salvation (Rom 3:21-26)."[13] Calvin rightly acknowledged that every human was made in God's image. This reality is frequently referred to as the *imago Dei*. Because the *imago Dei* is an ontological reality, it is also perdurable and cannot be eradicated despite the fall of man and his resultant abiding sin nature (Gen 9:6; James 3:9).

God has left an irrefragable witness of Himself in the heart of every person who ever lived. That is what Solomon taught here. Every person has an inherent sense of the Divine and is by nature a religious being. Calvin ingeniously and accurately referred to this sense of the Divine as *sensus divinitatis*. Often called "the seed of religion," the *sensus divinitatis* "is not merely a capacity for the knowledge of God, nor is it the product of reflection upon natural revelation. It is an immediate intuition of the existence and majesty of the one true God."[14] In other words, it is an aprioristic knowledge of God in the soul and not one attained from ratiocination.

Amazingly, and disappointingly, William Lane Craig, who many claim to be the premiere Christian apologist of our time, rejects outright this basic fundamental Bible teaching. In defending his classical view of apologetics, which rests on the foundation of natural theology, discursive discovery of the knowledge of God and the priority of ratiocination, he categorically states, "I am very skeptical that any *sensus divinitatis* exists."[15] This is an outright rejection of the truth of Ecclesiastes 3:11, as well as Romans 1 and 2, as we will examine shortly. To reject the implications of the *imago Dei* is to have a severely defective biblical anthropology and hamartiology, and by direct implication, it will lead to a defective soteriology. Examples of Craig's heterodoxical and bizarre soteriology leak out here and there throughout his discussions in *Five Views*. One of the clearest examples is when he concurs with the idea that people can be wholly clean and acceptable to God and even be true disciples of Christ before they are actually born again of the Spirit![16]

Acts 14:17

The third passage addressing general revelation comes from Paul as he is preaching to the Gentiles in Lystra on his first missionary journey. After Paul healed a lame man the people began praising him, calling him Hermes (or Mercury, the god of dispensing food) and Barnabas his partner, Zeus (or Jupiter, the god of rain). Paul immediately admonished the people for their misplaced veneration and proceeded to correct their distorted view of God. To that end Paul asserted that God, "did not leave Himself without witness, in that He did good and gave you rains from heaven and fruitful seasons, satisfying your hearts with food and gladness." This verse is recognized as a standard text on the truth of general revelation because of the phrase, "He did not leave Himself without witness." Paul's point is that even the pagan Gentiles of Lystra did not need the special revelation of Scripture to know the basic truth revealed in nature that God is a good God who provides for all His creatures. It rains everywhere, and seasonally, in the world, enabling all to live off the land. God controls the rain and the weather. As such, the bounty that comes from God attests to His gracious provision for all who benefit, which includes all of humanity. The character of God highlighted in this passage is God's universal providence—He is the divine, good Provider.

Acts 17:22-31

This passage is one of the most controversial in the debate among apologists regarding the relation of general revelation to natural theology. Traditional apologists try to say that in his sermon to the wisdom-loving, pagan Athenians, Paul abandoned his practice of reasoning from the Scriptures (Acts 17:2) and went cold turkey with natural theology because he was addressing a Greek Gentile audience and not the Jews. Craig argues for the "legitimation of natural theology" when the apostles "confronted Gentile audiences who did not accept the Old Testament," and then he refers to Acts 17 as an example.[17] Kelly James Clark says that Paul's arguments were driven by "accommodations to Greek culture" in this passage.[18] Others invest this passage with more general revelation than actually exists. Bruce Demarest mistakenly says virtually the whole passage is laden with general revelation.[19] The truth of the matter is that Acts 17:22-31 contains no natural theology whatsoever and a minimal amount of general revelation, if any at all. The inspired passage reads as follows:

> [22]So Paul stood in the midst of the Areopagus and said, "Men of Athens, I observe that you are very religious in all respects. [23]For while I was passing through and examining the objects of your worship, I also found an altar with this inscription, 'TO AN UNKNOWN GOD.' Therefore what you worship in ignorance, this I proclaim to you. [24]The God who made the world and all things in it, since He is Lord of heaven and earth, does not dwell in temples made with hands; [25]nor is He served by human hands, as though He needed anything, since He Himself gives to all

people life and breath and all things; [26]and He made from one man every nation of mankind to live on all the face of the earth, having determined their appointed times and the boundaries of their habitation, [27]that they would seek God, if perhaps they might grope for Him and find Him, though He is not far from each one of us; [28]for in Him we live and move and exist, even as some of your own poets have said, 'For we also are His children.' [29]Being then the children of God, we ought not to think that the Divine Nature is like gold or silver or stone, an image formed by the art and thought of man. [30]Therefore having overlooked the times of ignorance, God is now declaring to men that all people everywhere should repent, [31]because He has fixed a day in which He will judge the world in righteousness through a Man whom He has appointed, having furnished proof to all men by raising Him from the dead."

Upon close examination this passage only makes two references to general revelation. The first is when Paul says God "Himself gives to all...all things" (25). Here Paul is saying that God is the good Provider, the very same truth mentioned previously in Acts 14:17. The second is when Paul says, "in Him we live and move and exist" (28), basically the same truth taught in Ecclesiastes 3:11 which we examined earlier, and also as taught in Romans 1-2.

So the two possible references to general revelation in this passage make no new contribution to the cumulative data of the content of general revelation, but simply confirm truths stated elsewhere. Mayhue is correct when he says of this passage's contribution to general revelation, "The minor and implicit emphasis is upon the most general of general revelation, which points to God as the source of the people's origin to which Paul alludes in his preaching. Of the seven hallmark texts on general revelation, this one makes the least contribution."[20]

Most of what Paul says in Acts 17:22-31 is actually special revelation, not general revelation; and none of it is natural theology like traditional apologists try to tell us. As he begins preaching, Paul says, "I proclaim to you" (23). "Proclaim" is the Greek word *katag-gelo*, and is used in 17:18 of Paul and is said to be synonymous with the act of "preaching Jesus and the resurrection." And that is exactly what Paul was doing here—he was preaching special, divine revelation, not making up natural, human, philosophical theology to accommodate and find common ground with the Epicurean and Stoic Greek thinkers.

Paul never resorted to rhetoric to convince anyone to believe. On the contrary he despised rhetoric and human wisdom. He told the believers at Corinth, Gentiles in a city immersed in Greek culture, "when I came to you, brethren, I did not come with superiority of speech or of wisdom, proclaiming to you the testimony of God. For I determined to know nothing among you except Jesus Christ, and Him crucified" (1 Cor 2:1-2). Paul was single-minded in the ministry: he preached Jesus and the cross, and only Jesus and the cross. "For Christ did not send me to baptize, but to preach the gospel, not in cleverness of speech, so that the cross of Christ would not be made void" (1 Cor 1:17). And again he declared, "But may it never be that I would boast, except in the cross of our Lord Jesus Christ" (Gal 6:14). Paul summarized his entire preaching ministry by saying that he routinely testified to the "Greeks of repentance toward God and faith in our Lord Jesus Christ" (Acts 20:21). Paul preached the gospel, not natural theology. The culmination of Paul's sermon in Acts 17:22-31 to the Greeks was a call to "repent" (30) and to believe in the resurrected Jesus Christ (31). His content was special revelation, not general revelation, nor natural theology based on general revelation.

Romans 10:18

In this passage Paul is talking about the need for special revelation to produce faith and salvation. In addition he speaks of the merits of general revelation: "But I say, surely they have never heard, have they? Indeed they have; *'Their voice has gone out into all the earth, and their words to the ends of the world.'*" This verse echoes the truth of Psalm 19. Mayhue gives a keen summary of its implications on general revelation:

> Paul quotes Psalm 19:4 in affirming that, even without a preacher, humans are not ignorant of God. They have known about God through general revelation (cf. Ps. 19:1-6). The general revelation of 10:18 is contrasted with the preaching of special revelation in 10:14-17. This…text on general revelation returns to the first text in Psalm 19. In context, the order is reversed (Ps. 19:1-6 on general

revelation and Ps. 19:7-11 on special revelation; Rom. 10:14-17 on special revelation and Rom. 10:18 on general revelation).[21]

Romans 1:18-25
This passage is the most specific and thorough text in the Bible regarding general revelation. It reads:

> [18]For the wrath of God is revealed from heaven against all ungodliness and unrighteousness of men who suppress the truth in unrighteousness, [19]because that which is known about God is evident within them; for God made it evident to them. [20]For since the creation of the world His invisible attributes, His eternal power and divine nature, have been clearly seen, being understood through what has been made, so that they are without excuse. [21]For even though they knew God, they did not honor Him as God or give thanks, but they became futile in their speculations, and their foolish heart was darkened. [22]Professing to be wise, they became fools, [23]and exchanged the glory of the incorruptible God for an image in the form of corruptible man and of birds and four-footed animals and crawling creatures. [24]Therefore God gave them over in the lusts of their hearts to impurity, so that their bodies would be dishonored among them. [25]For they exchanged the truth of God for a lie, and worshiped and served the creature rather than the Creator, who is blessed forever. Amen.

The thrust of this passage is that God is angry because sinful humans have spurned God's self-revelation in nature and they resort to idolatry by worshipping created things instead of God the Creator. God has a right to be angry because all people have the "truth," but they willfully "suppress" it or press against it in unrighteousness (1:18). George Zemek insightfully accentuates the drastic implications of this tragic suppression of truth:

> This is probably the key description of mankind in Romans 1:18-23. Humankind continuously incarcerates the truth about the Sovereign Creator so that natural revelation cannot convert them; it only condemns them.

> Because of their persistent refusal to accept the theology of this grand display of God's handiwork, they end up defenseless (cf. *anapologētous* at the end of v. 20).[22]

The "truth" that people suppress is the knowledge of God's existence which is innate and is "evident within them" (Rom 1:19). All people have an intuitive knowledge of God because all people were made in God's image (Gen 1:26) and as a result all people are inescapably religious, having in their very ontological composition the "seed of religion" or the "sense of the divine" within, which Calvin called *sensus divinitatis*. This validates the truth of Ecclesiastes 3:11 we examined earlier. Every human, without exception, knows in the soul that there is a God. There are no true atheists. Luther agreed with this based on the strict exegesis of Romans 1: "from the beginning of the world the invisible things of God have always been recognized through the rational perception of the (*divine*) operations (*in the world*). All men therefore, in particular all idolaters, had a clear knowledge of God, especially of His Godhead and His omnipotence...there was in their hearts a knowledge of a divine sovereign Being."[23]

Alvin Plantinga, considered by many, including William Lane Craig, to be the most brilliant philosopher and apologist in modern times, goes to great lengths to deconstruct Calvin's teaching of Romans 1 and his meaning assigned to the *sensus divinitatis*. Like a true postmodernist (or historical revisionist), Plantinga spins the original intent of the author, in this case Calvin who wrote in the 1500's, to conform to the meaning Plantinga wants to employ.[24] Plantinga accepts Calvin's phrase of *sensus divinitatis* but invests it with meaning Calvin never intended. Plantinga says the knowledge of God that all people seem to possess is not innate, intuitive and immediately apprehended. Rather, in contrast to what Calvin actually taught, he says it is knowledge that is not innate, but it matures over time, grows, develops, and is acquired and discursively discovered. That is not what Paul is saying in Romans 1. The apostle says categorically, "they knew God" (Rom 1:21) for they have the "Law written in their hearts" (2:15), for God, yea verily, engraved it indelibly on their "conscience" (2:15) from the point of conception (Ps 51:5). So this knowledge of God is intuitive—immediately apprehended, not learned over time.

Presuppositionalist, Greg Bahnsen, accurately comments on this in his examination of the epistemological implications in light of

Romans 1 when he writes: "Even without a discursive argument or a chain of inferences from elementary observations about experience, all men see and recognize the signature of their Creator in the world that He created and controls, as well as in themselves as His created image."[25]

In addition to Plantinga, Kelly James Clark also proves to be a postmodern, historical revisionist when it comes to Calvin's understanding of Romans 1. Clark claims kinship with Calvin,[26] then he goes on to allege that the knowledge of God that comes from general revelation is not perspicuous, but it is clouded by various barriers to religious belief like the problem of evil.[27] But Calvin, following Paul in Romans 1, taught that the knowledge of God gained by the unbeliever that comes from general revelation is perspicuous—crystal clear—"having been clearly seen, being understood" (Rom 1:20).[28] It is crystal clear intuitively, that is why Paul concludes in the same verse that every unbeliever is "without excuse." No one can claim ignorance based on the riddling problem of evil.

Paul goes further. Not only is the aprioristic knowledge of God internal, it is also external. He "made it evident to them" (Rom 1:19) in nature so that the knowledge of God is clearly "understood through what has been made" (1:20). This has been true "since the creation of the world" (1:20)—so it has applied to all people throughout all time. This corresponds to the truth seen in Psalm 19:1-6. Because God has given a perspicuous revelation of Himself internally in the heart and externally in creation to all people, Paul renders God's verdict that every soul is "without excuse" (Rom 1:20). No human can claim ignorance about the reality of God.

Not only does every person have the knowledge of God intuitively externally and internally in general revelation, but Paul also says that every person despises that knowledge of God because of sin. They "knew God" (1:21) existed but exchanged true knowledge of God for false religion (1:22-23). Because all sinners naturally resist the truth about God in general revelation, God judges them with His holy "wrath" (1:18) and by giving them over to their own sinful inclinations of perversion (1:24). In light of this reality, every human needs to be rescued from the damning prospects of their own sin by the redeeming power of the gospel (1:16; 3:23-24). Holloman elaborates on the soteriological implications here:

People naturally suppress and pervert the truth presented

in general revelation (Rom 1:18, 25: cf. Josh 24:14-15; Ac 14:15-17; 17:29; Rom 1:21-32; 2:12-15; 3:9-18, 23; 1 Thess 1:9), unless they are drawn by God to seek Christ (Jn 6:44, 65), for none seeks God (Rom 3:11). General revelation reveals enough that no one can plead ignorance (Rom 1:18-3:20). People are condemned by the light that they have unless that light is Christ (Jn 8:12).[29]

The specific intuitive knowledge people have about God is composed of "His invisible attributes" (1:20). God's invisible attributes or qualities that are known by man include "His eternal power and divine nature" (1:20). God's "eternal power" (*aidios dynamis*) refers to the eternity of God's person and His power.[30] God's "divine nature" (*theiotes*) refers to His deity. The Latin for this word is *divinitas*, from which Calvin got his *sensus divinitatis*. Keep in mind that William Lane Craig rejects the notion of all people having a *sensus divinitatis*.

Romans 2:14-15

The final text on general revelation says: "For when Gentiles who do not have the Law do instinctively the things of the Law, these, not having the Law, are a law to themselves, in that they show the work of the Law written in their hearts, their conscience bearing witness and their thoughts alternately accusing or else defending them." Here Paul explains that those who do not have the Law (here, the Old Testament Scriptures) still have an innate moral sensor imprinted on the inside through the "conscience" God gave them. The conscience is a gift from God to every human made in His image to serve as a moral barometer to distinguish between right and wrong. So even people who do not have the privilege of written special revelation still have an internal moral code of conduct to which they are accountable. As such, every person is morally accountable to God the Creator.

The Boundaries of General Revelation

God has limited the mediums of general revelation to two. From the above biblical texts it is clear that general revelation is a universal awareness of God made apparent (1) in God's creation (externally) and (2) in the heart and conscience (internally) of every person. To extend the reach of general revelation to include other extraneous information from other disciplines and theories about man, creation or anything else is biblically unwarranted. It is commonplace for theologians, traditional apologists and especially philosophers to smuggle alternate branches of learning under the umbrella of general revelation. Norman Geisler, one of the most respected Christian apologists of our generation, says the human arts and music constitute general revelation. About music he writes, "We learn something more about God's nature through the human voice."[31] He goes way afield from biblical warrant here. Thomas gives this helpful caution against such scriptural drifting:

> Kenneth Gangel includes science, mathematics, literature, music, and the like as parts of natural (i.e., general) revelation. He states that the humanities, as well as the hard sciences, are part of God's revelation. Both opinions are unwarranted. God's general revelation divulges information about God, but that is all.[32]

History is also routinely included in many definitions of what general revelation constitutes. But not one of the seven biblical texts above teaches that history is part of the rubric of general revelation. This is a particularly important point to keep in mind when scrutinizing the legitimacy of traditional apologetics, which presupposes history to be general revelation. Presuppositionalist, John Frame, confuses the issue here when he says, "God has revealed himself plainly in nature and historical events."[33] In context, he puts ordinary history on the same plane as general revelation. But history cannot be general revelation, for its contents are not universally available for all people for all time; nor is its truth immediately apprehended—history must be studied, discovered and it is routinely subjectively and selectively interpreted. Millard Erickson admits this shortcoming about history even though he includes it in his definition of general revelation:

> For one thing, history is less accessible than is nature. One must consult the historical record. Either he will be dependent upon secondhand materials, the records and reports of others, or he will have to work from his own experience from history, which will often be a very limited segment, perhaps too limited to enable him to detect the overall pattern or trend.[34]

History is not general revelation. I know nothing of the true nature of God from the brute facts of history. Yet my faith is based upon the true facts of history including creation, the Fall, and the birth, life, ministry, death and resurrection of Jesus Christ. But all these events were revealed to me through the Bible, special revelation. Mayhue is more biblically precise and sober-minded than most in his assessment of history and its relation to general revelation:

> To say that history is not part of general revelation is not to deny that Scripture speaks of God's providential hand in human history (cf. Job 12:23; Dan. 2:21, 4:17). However, what we know for certain about God's activities in history comes from the special revelation of Scripture, not from any human account of history itself treated as a distinct source of general revelation.[35]

Robert Reymond also underscores this basic observation made by Mayhue when he writes, "'mighty acts of God in history,' of course, required the propositional explanations that always accompanied them (Amos 3:7)."[36] Henry Holloman adds this helpful jewel: "Some theologians list history as another means of general revelation but history is really a work of providence."[37]

So it is paramount to honor the biblically established parameters of what constitutes general revelation—to extend it beyond truth about God is to "go beyond what is written" (1 Cor 4:6; NIV) which undermines the sufficiency of Scripture.

History is not revelation; history is discovery. Revelation is initiated by God alone. The study of history is initiated by man. Revelation unveils "truths" about God. History uncovers "theories" about the past of human activity. Revelation is objective. The study of history is subjective. God's revelation is impervious to error; man's study of history is prone to error. God's revelation is binding on man.

The study of history has no authority. The content of God's general revelation has been unveiled once for all. The content of history continues to grow and change.

Implications
Truths about general revelation gleaned from the above can be summed up as follows:

(1) General revelation is taught and clearly defined in the Bible, being most clearly explained and illustrated in seven hallmark Bible passages.

(2) General revelation is twofold: internal, in the conscience and heart, issuing from the *imago Dei,* and external, as seen in creation.

(3) The content and scope of general revelation is restricted to truths about God and various aspects of His being.[38] General revelation reveals God's glory, goodness, power, and justice but nothing of God's grace, mercy and Person which come only from special revelation.

(4) General revelation is available to all people, not just some with specialized training and privileged information.

(5) The content of general revelation has been the same since the beginning of creation.

(6) General revelation has been available for people of all time periods.

(7) The knowledge of God attained from general revelation is intuitive and immediately apprehended by all and does not result from a process of discovery. The study of history is not general revelation.

(8) General revelation is always rejected, or suppressed, by unbelieving sinners.

(9) General revelation provides a perspicuous knowledge of God's character and moral demands.

(10) General revelation is sufficient to condemn the sinner, but insufficient to save the soul.[39]

(11) General revelation is propaedeutic for the work of special revelation and God can use it to show a sinner his need for more revelation (Acts 17:24-29).

(12) General revelation was created by God and is a gift of God to humanity.

(13) General revelation is in harmony with special revelation.

(14) General revelation is inferior to special revelation; general revelation adds no new information about the character of God that is not already revealed in Scripture.

(15) General revelation needs to be interpreted by special revelation. General revelation is different in *content* than special revelation, not just in *degree*.

Special Revelation
Definition
Next we take up the definition of special revelation. Often called *divine, direct, redemptive* or *particular* revelation, it "refers to God's self-disclosure through signs and miracles, the utterances of prophets and apostles, and the deeds and words of Jesus Christ, whereby specific people at particular times and places gain further understanding of God's character and a knowledge of his saving purposes in his Son."[40] Stated another way, special revelation is, "God's disclosure of Himself in salvation history (revelation in reality) and in the interpretive word of Scripture (revelation in Word). Quantitatively this encompasses more than we have in Scripture...in this case the Scripture speaks of various modalities such as vision, dream, deep sleep, urim and thummim, the lot, theophanies, angels, divine speaking, historical event, and the incarnation resulting in *a product*, namely, the Word of God (the Bible)."[41] Distilling it down, we could say special revelation is when God reveals His character and will on a personal level, selectively, through words; it is propositional, redemptive truth. It should also be noted that the Holy Spirit frequently had a direct role in the agency of special revelation.

The Need for Special Revelation
The need for special revelation arose because of the Fall (Gen 3:6) and the resultant curse upon sinful humanity (3:14-19). Before Adam and Eve sinned, they enjoyed direct, immediate, ongoing personal intercourse with God (Gen 2:7-8, 15-17; 3:8-9). After they sinned God cursed them and their progeny as well as the natural world in which they lived (Gen 5:29; Rom 8:20-22). Sin had disrupted their

harmony with nature in creation, and worse, it separated them from a holy God (Gen 3:22-24).

From that point on, humans would have access to general revelation but would willfully suppress it because of sin (Rom 1:18-19). Hence there was the need for God to intervene with special revelation to redeem sinful humanity. The entire biblical account is the history of God intervening strategically and spontaneously through special acts of redemptive revelation to save sinful humanity from their self-inflicted alienation from God through disobedience. The climactic act of God intruding into human history for salvific purposes was through the incarnation of Jesus Christ, the God-Man (1 Tim 3:16).

The History of Special Revelation

God's special revelation was not dispersed in an ongoing fashion, but rather was sporadic and isolated throughout history, with occasional lengthy periods of time with "silence" from heaven when there were no words of God being revealed at all. Notable times of silence include 1,000 years between the time of Adam to Noah; 800 years between Noah and the Patriarchs; over 400 years between the Patriarchs and Moses; and 400 years from the close of the Old Testament until the New Testament.

It should not be regarded as significant then that there have been no notable acts of special revelation from the completion of the New Testament until today. With the coming of Christ came the fullest source of special revelation ever imparted to the world (John 1:14, 16; Col 1:19). As such, the New Testament stands as a living record, albeit written, of the fullness of God's personal, special revelation to man (Matt 5:18; Heb 4:12). Following is a summary of major time periods when God imparted special revelation:

(1) 4,000 BC [to Adam (Gen 2:16); to Cain (Gen 4:6-12)]
(2) 3,000 BC [to Noah (Gen 6:13) and his sons (9:1, 8)]
(3) 2,200-1,900 BC [Patriarchal period-Abram (Gen 12:1); Isaac (Gen 26:2); Jacob (Gen 28:13); Joseph (Gen 37:5)]
(4) 1,440-1,375 BC [to Moses (Deut 18:18); to Joshua (Josh 1:1)][42]
(5) 1,375-1075 BC [to the Judges and Ruth]
(6) 1,100 BC [to Samuel (1 Sam 3:4)]
(7) 1,000-850 BC [the period of the Kings-David (1 Sam 23:2-4); Solomon (1 Kgs 3:5);

> Asaph (Ps 73); Sons of Korah (Ps 84); Nathan (2 Sam 7:4-17); Ahijah (1 Kgs 11:29); Shemaiah (1 Kgs 12:22); Elijah (2 Chron 21:12); Micaiah (1 Kgs 22:17); Elisha (2 Kgs 2-13)]

(8) 800 BC [Obad, Joel]

(9) 700 BC [Jonah, Amos, Hos, Mic, Isa]

(10) 600 BC [Nah, Zeph, Hab, Jer]

(11) 500 BC [Dan, Ezek, Hag, Zech]

(12) 400 BC [Mal, Esth, Neh, Ezra]

(13) 4 BC [the birth of Christ (Luke 1-2; Matt 1-2)]

(14) AD 27 [John the Baptist (John 1)]

(15) AD 27-30 [Jesus' ministry]

(16) AD 30-95 [the Apostles and New Testament prophets]

(17) The Great Tribulation, yet future (Rev 11:3)

Special Revelation in Psalm 19

Earlier we looked at Psalm 19:1-6 relative to general revelation. Now it is imperative to examine the second part of the psalm as it addresses special revelation. By contrast the Psalmist shows clearly that special revelation, especially as it is found in Scripture, is superior to general revelation. Speaking of the exalted nature of the Old Testament Law the Psalmist writes:

> [7]The Law of the LORD is perfect, restoring the soul; the testimony of the LORD is sure, making wise the simple.
>
> [8]The precepts of the LORD are right, rejoicing the heart; the commandment of the LORD is pure, enlightening the eyes.
>
> [9]The fear of the LORD is clean, enduring forever; the judgments of the LORD are true; they are righteous altogether.
>
> [10]They are more desirable than gold, yes, than much fine gold; sweeter also than honey and the drippings of the honeycomb.
>
> [11]Moreover, by them Thy servant is warned; in keeping them there is great reward (19:7-11).

God's special revelation as found in written Scripture is described using six different monikers: "The Law," "the testimony," "The precepts," "the commandment," "The fear," and "the judgments."

Each specific name highlights a different efficacious element inherent in inspired Scripture.

The main truth in these verses is that special revelation is superior to general revelation, for only special revelation can spiritually transform the wicked. Scripture has the resident power for "restoring the soul" (Ps 19:7) of the sinner. This means God uses biblical truth to regenerate and save people. To acquire saving faith a sinner needs the input of special revelation. This was true of Abram the pagan, who when "the word of the LORD came to him" (Gen 15:4), he then "believed in the LORD; and He reckoned it to him as righteousness" (15:6). God saved Abram through the medium of special revelation. The New Testament teaches the same thing, declaring that, "you have been born again...through the living and enduring word of God" (1 Pet 1:23). God decreed that saving faith only comes from one source: special revelation. "Faith comes from hearing...the word of Christ" (Rom 10:17). Faith does not come from general revelation, not from natural theology, not from the laws of logic, rhetoric, archaeological findings, persuasive speech, human wisdom, theistic arguments, nor from philosophical syllogisms and theorems.

The above truth has dire implications for apologetics, as traditional apologetics says saving faith comes from other sources than just special revelation. For example, presuppositionalist John Frame, in answering the question, "Where does faith come from?" offers many options but not one of them is, "From special revelation."[43] He alleges faith comes from reality, truth, facts, the laws of thought and human logic, the Holy Spirit, rationality, evidences, natural revelation and history. But he never affirms the fundamental truth taught in Scripture that faith comes from the Word of God—special, divine, direct revelation. Faith does come from the Holy Spirit, but never apart from God's Word.

Kelly James Clark says saving faith comes from many sources: from maintaining humility, being on a mountain top, reading *The Chronicles of Narnia*, witnessing the birth of a child, watching a sunset, examining the beauty of a flower or walking through the woods.[44] But he never says faith comes from hearing the Word of God or from the Bible or from the gospel! Craig is similar. He says, "I and many others have seen people come to believe in God (and even Christ) on the basis of the *kalam* cosmological argument."[45] The *kalam* cosmological argument is sophisticated philosophical specu-lation that originates from Muslim dialectical theology and is not special revelation. It was not given by God. It does not refer to Christ or the gospel and cannot impart faith nor can it save anyone. Only the gospel can save a sinner (Rom 1:16). We need a revolution in Christian apologetics and it needs to start with putting the Word of God back in its rightful place. Like Peter, we need to declare that saving faith comes only from special revelation, the Word of God: "Simon Peter answered Him, 'Lord, to whom shall we go? You have words of eternal life'" (John 6:68).

Special and General Revelation Contrasted

Many distinctive features of special revelation follow when compared and contrasted with general revelation:

(1) Special revelation was given to a select few, often to just one individual (Gal 1:11-12), whereas general revelation was given by God to all humanity.

(2) Special revelation is propositional, whereas general revelation is wordless. Presuppositionalist John Frame is a bit confused here when he says that, "Natural revelation is every bit the word of God."[46] Natural or general revelation is not propositional and therefore is never called "the Word of God" in Scripture.

(3) Special revelation is personal and multi-dimensional; general revelation is generic and limited.

(4) Special revelation imparts faith; general revelation is suppressed by unbelievers and does not impart faith.

(5) Special revelation was intermittent; general revelation has been continual.

(6) Special revelation has been progressive and cumulative; general revelation has remained the same in content.

(7) Some occurences of special revelation were temporary and even private or secretive (2 Cor 12:2-4); general revelation is permanent and public.

(8) Special revelation was always sufficient salvifically at any point in the history of God's program; general revelation was sufficient to condemn but insufficient to save at all points in history.

(9) Special revelation has to be discursively processed, whereas general revelation is intuitively apprehended.

(10) Special revelation is superior, supplemental and corrective to general revelation; general revelation is prior and propaedeutic to special revelation.

(11) Special revelation as cotainted in Scripture is inherently "inspired" ("God-breathed"; 2 Tim 3:16-17); general revelation's veracity is derivative.

(12) Special revelation is autopistic; general revelation is not self-authenticating.

(13) The Word of special revelation endures forever; general revelation in nature will pass away.

Scripture as Special Revelation

A special word needs to be said about written special revelation. During the Mosaic Age God first commanded the inscripturation and preservation of select elements of special revelation, "possessing an organic character, that is, a perfection at every stage" of progressive revelation.[47] This fixed and literary corpus developed into a perennial, authoritative source of revelation called "the Law and the Prophets" (Luke 16:16) serving as God's preserved source of truth and authority governing the lives and practice of His people. Jesus and His apostles recognized these written Old Testament Scriptures as the very words of God (John 10:35; 2 Tim 3:16). Jesus commissioned His apostles to write a new corpus of special revelation that would be on par with the Old Testament in terms of authority and inspiration (John 14:26; 16:13; Mark 13:31). This became the New Testament. With the issuing of the last New Testament book, Christ's special revelation was complete as He intended for His church (Jude 3; Rev 22:18-19). Today He no longer speaks through the diverse manners He used all throughout history (Heb 1:1), but rather He speaks through the written Word of God as found in the Bible (2 Tim 3:16). In conjunction with the animating power of the Holy Spirit as He works on the minds, hearts and wills of people, Scripture truly does "speak," for it is living and active (Heb 4:12).

The Bible is special revelation, but historically special revelation included more than the Bible, for there were times when prophets, and Jesus Himself, spoke direct, special revelation that was never inscripturated (John 20:30-31; 21:25). Nevertheless, today the Bible defines for us what special revelation is and is itself a sufficient, though not an exhaustive, record of God's special revelation to us.

For 1,900 years the Church has recognized the Bible as the final, complete, fixed, sufficient, sole, authoritative source of special revelation for God's people. This is based on Jesus' own words, for He told His apostles that the Holy Spirit would bring to remembrance all that Jesus taught them (John 14:26), leading them into all the truth (John 16:13), so they could write it down (Rev 1:19) to be preserved as inspired Scripture (2 Tim 3:16; 2 Pet 3:15-16) to serve as the authoritative record of truth in the Church (Matt 5:17-18; Acts 2:42). There is no need for new revelation, ongoing visions, revelatory dreams, living prophets or the like (1 Cor 13:8). The Bible—God's Word—is sufficient.

Scripture's Sufficiency Challenged

The church's long-held sacred belief in the sufficiency of Scripture is being undermined by modern-day traditional apologists. Scripture itself attests that, as God's Word in written form, it is sufficient for all things relative to true spirituality, both for knowing God and for living: "All Scripture is given by inspiration of God, and is profitable for doctrine, for reproof, for correction, for instruction in righteousness, that the man of God may be complete, thoroughly equipped for every good work" (2 Tim 3:16-17; NKJV). God gave us Scripture to help people become "complete" and "thoroughly equipped." No one can improve upon "complete." This passage teaches the doctrine of the sufficiency of Scripture. The truth of Scripture is the sufficient tool for doing Christian apologetics. Scripture is what Jesus and Paul used when they did apologetics.

Kelly James Clark, modern apologist, disagrees and rejects the sufficiency of Scripture here. He alleges "Scripture woefully underdetermines...one's apologetic" because the Bible "was written to and for another culture." People are different today, he avers, and so, "How those people might best be approached, therefore, will require a great deal of human ingenuity and not merely reflection on how it was done in biblical times."[48] So for Clark, the Bible does not cut it—we need human ingenuity! Norman Geisler undermines biblical sufficiency as well when he asserts that without the theistic "arguments for the existence for God...there would be no basis for apologetics."[49] By "theistic arguments" Geisler means "natural theology." So according to Geisler, using just the Bible is not adequate to do the work of apologetics. R. C. Sproul also undermines biblical sufficiency. The starting point of his apologetics is natural theology, not the Bible. In defending his use of natural theology, he posits that "natural theology asserts that people can and do gain valid knowledge of God by means of natural reason."[50]

William Lane Craig embraces a classic neo-orthodox position of the Bible (which he inherited from Wolfhart Pannenberg) when it comes to apologetics. For him, the Word of God is not synonymous with the Bible. He supposes, "we cannot make a simplistic equation between God's Word and Scripture."[51] He equates the Word of God with anything spoken that the Holy Spirit might use, including his esoteric philosophical and theistic constructs.[52] He rejects the long-held orthodox view on bibliology that affirms the *inherent* authority of written Scripture in favor of his heterodoxical view that says "Scripture's authority is derivative in character."[53] In stark contrast to Craig's fallacious charge, 2 Timothy 3:16 says the *graphe* (and the *grammata* of 3:15) are "God-breathed," the very "writings" themselves are physical manifestations of God's thoughts.

Craig tries to dichotomize God and His Word, which is an illegitimate enterprise. God's Word is truth (John 17:17), Scripture is truth (Ps 19:9) and God Himself is truth (1 Thess 1:9)—truth cannot be divided into a taxonomy of varying hierarchies of authority. God cannot be pitted against His own Word. Jesus said His Word perfectly reflects who He is: "He who rejects Me and does not receive My sayings, has one who judges him; the word which I spoke will judge him at the last day" (John 12:48). And again Jesus said, "If anyone loves Me, he will keep My word" (John 14:23). In Revelation, John the apostle was commanded to "write" (19:9). What he wrote was Scripture. The verse goes on to comment on the divine quality of what he wrote by saying, "These are true words of God" (19:9). Scripture is God's Word, despite what Craig says. Jesus said, "Scripture cannot be broken" (John 10:35). That was His personal warning not to tamper with Scripture, God's sure Word.

Natural Theology

The Challenge

Having thus laid the groundwork by thoroughly defining general revelation and special revelation, we now turn to natural theology. Explaining natural theology is a challenge, for a specific, standardized definition does not exist. Year after year, I ask my seminary students what natural theology is and usually I just get panicked, befuddled, blank stares—even from some students who are experienced, well-educated pastors.

In my six-plus years of seminary training, I do not remember ever learning about natural theology. Most standard theological dictionaries and encyclopedias I own, as well as standard systematic theologies, do not even have a reference to the phrase "natural theology."

This is unfortunate because traditional apologetics is built on the foundation of natural theology. Since it is the monolithic rock of Gibraltar on which traditional apologists preach their man-made wisdom, it is imperative to have a clear grasp of what natural theology entails: its definition, origin, relationship to general and special revelation and its implications on Christian apologetics.

The Definition

One suggested definition is as follows: "Natural theology is the attempt to attain an understanding of God and his relationship with the universe by means of rational reflection, without appealing to special revelation such as the self-revelation of God in Christ and in Scripture."[54] Another source says it is "the practice of philosophically reflecting on the existence and nature of God independent of real or apparent divine revelation or scripture."[55] Another says it is "the favorite term in the 18th and 19th centuries designating the knowledge of God drawn from nature in distinction from the knowledge of God contained in revelation."[56] Cornelius Van Til scrutinized natural theology like few others and offered this insightful definition:

> This idea of natural theology assumes that without Scripture and the testimony of the Spirit men generally can have a measure of morally and spiritually acceptable knowledge of God. It assumes that there can be an interpretation of the natural revelation of God with which both believers and unbelievers are in basic agree-

ment…Thus the distinction between the revelation of God *to* man and the interpretation of this revelation *by* man is obscured. *Natural revelation* then tends to be identified with *natural theology*.[57]

Three Implications

Three key features about natural theology arise from these definitions. First, *the realm* of natural theology is philosophy, not theology; as such we are thrust into the unstable world of theoretical, metaphysical, ethereal and complex, multi-syllabled words. It is sometimes called the *philosophy of religion* or *philosophical theology*.

Second, *the source* of natural theology is finite (and fallen) human reason and wisdom apart from special revelation or the Spirit's intervention. The Bible and the Holy Spirit are banished from all dialogue and discussion in the pursuit of truths about God. A colossal assumption is being made by proponents of natural theology on this point that should not go unnoticed or unchecked. The presumptuous presupposition is that human reason alone can rightly appraise the infinite Creator of the universe by mere human, discursive ratiocination. "The claim of natural theology is that by the powers of reason and observation, the human mind can rise to an elementary knowledge of God, of the freedom and immortality of the soul, and of the basic demands of morality. The mind can reach these truths, it is claimed, unaided by revelation."[58] For example, traditional apologist, Kelly James Clark, dogmatically asserts "we can come to some moral and spiritual truths unaided by the Holy Spirit."[59] He says this because he believes truth can be attained from unaided reason. This is the very antithesis of Scripture that declares humans cannot attain any spiritual truth apart from the Holy Spirit's help in conjunction with special revelation (1 Cor 2).

Third, *the goal* of natural theology is the attempt to discover a few ambiguous realities about God, usually the probability of His existence and His role as Creator. It is admitted that neither God as a person, nor His essence, can be gained through natural theology. Traditional apologists differ over natural theology's efficacy in establishing the verifiability of God's existence, ranging from probable (Geisler), most plausible (Sproul), to certainty (Anselm).

The Content of Natural Theology

Beyond these proposed cursory and broad sweeping definitions, there is wide disparity of what actually constitutes natural theology. Many proponents say natural theology constitutes the philosophically constructed theistic arguments for God which include the following: the ontological, cosmological, teleological, and moral arguments.[60] To these Craig and Moreland add the arguments from consciousness, evil, reason, miracles, and religious experience.[61] Plantinga adds to these, the arguments from intentionality, collections, numbers, counterfactuals, physical constants, positive epistemic status, constancy, reliability, simplicity, induction, reference, intuition, colors, flavors, love, play, nostalgia, and the meaning of life.[62]

In addition to the theistic arguments, which are sometimes considered to be synonymous with natural theology, historical and archaeological evidences apart from Scripture are used as natural theology as well. Josh McDowell and John Warwick Montgomery are proponents of this approach.

Christian philosophers typically say the "Laws of Logic" also fall under the rubric of natural theology. For example, Geisler says essential to apologetics are the use of the Laws of Noncontradiction, Identity, the Excluded Middle as well as rules of Inductive and Deductive Logic.[63] To these, Moreland and Craig add several rules of inference of sentential logic including *modus ponens*, *modus tollens*, hypothetical syllogisms, conjunction, simplification, absorption, addition, disjunctive syllogisms and constructive dilemmas, to name a few.[64] Craig also includes theoretical calculus and secular astrophysics and cosmology in his definition of natural theology. In his apologetics presentations he frequently champions Bayes' Theorem with the same vigor and facility that the average Campus Crusader spouts *the Four Spiritual Laws.*[65] It is as follows:

$$\Pr(R/B\&E) = \frac{\Pr(R/B) \times \Pr(E/B\&R)}{\Pr(R/B) \times \Pr(E/B\&R) + \Sigma^n_{i=1} \Pr(A_i/B) \times \Pr(E/B\&A_i)}$$

I don't have a clue what it means or stands for, but I do know for a fact that Jesus and the apostles never referred to Bayes' Theorem when they were advancing and defending the gospel.

R. C. Sproul is an enigma in many respects as a classical apologist. He is Calvinistic, whereas many traditional apologists are Arminian. He touts *sola fide*, a refrain almost totally foreign to other traditional apologists' lexicon. And yet he undermines the very concept of *sola fide* in his apologetical methodology by utilizing natural theology instead of Scripture as his foundation and starting point. He even defines natural theology in a wholly different manner than all his classical apologist peers: "Natural theology refers to a knowledge of God acquired from God's revelation of Himself in nature."[66] That is not a definition of "natural theology," but rather the accepted definition of "natural revelation." And in his forty page explanation of natural theology, he continually makes general revelation interchangeable with natural theology.[67] At least Craig, a fellow classical apologist, is clear about this matter, unlike Sproul, when he says categorically "the arguments of natural theology are not identical with general revelation."[68] Sproul erroneously wants to seamlessly meld the two.

Another major blunder Sproul makes is when he says, "natural theology is *dependent* upon divine revelation"![69] Similarly, he repeats the idea: "Special revelation confirms natural theology."[70] Sproul is on his own here—no one agrees with that assertion. Remember our basic definitions above that said natural theology is gaining knowledge of God "without appealing to special revelation" and "independent of real or apparent divine revelation or scripture." For the record: natural theology is not general revelation and it is totally independent of special revelation in formulating its content. Sproul is woefully misguided here.

As for the content of his version of natural theology, Sproul is eclectic, but hard-line. He espouses the theistic arguments and the Laws of Logic as primary. As for the necessity and efficacy of the theistic arguments when it comes to apologetics, he peremptorily asserts that it is "logically impossible to avoid fideism without them."[71] "Fideism" for Sproul is a term of derision used against those who disagree with him and it means "those who don't use their brain." Fideists are radical skeptics who "detest natural theology," who take blind leaps of faith and who do not reason or think[72]—so he tells us. I am not a "skeptic" and I don't detest natural theology— I just don't believe it is warranted by Scripture.

Sproul, on the other hand posits that natural theology is allowed by Scripture and in addition to the theistic arguments it entails the following four ingredients: the law of noncontradiction; the law of causality; the basic reliability of sense perception; and the analogical use of language.[73] In his explanations of these terms Sproul routinely calls special revelation (passages in the Bible) natural theology. He carelessly says they are interchangeable. He equates John 2:22 with the law on noncontradiction;[74] he likens John 3:2 to the law of causality;[75] 2 Peter 1:16-18 and 1 Corinthians 15 are examples of sense perception;[76] and Genesis 1:26 is the analogical use of language.[77] Sproul avers, counter to almost every other theologian and philosopher who has written on the topic, that natural theology comes directly from God. He says, "Natural theology['s]...origin is divine."[78]

In addition to Sproul and the many other traditional apologists who base their apologetics scheme on the foundation of natural theology from the realm of philosophy, a recent trend finds natural theology now flowing from the fount of the natural and physical sciences. Hugh Ross is a self-proclaimed apologist of the Christian faith and is a purveyor of natural theology in the realm of astronomy. A trained astronomer and proponent of theistic evolution, Ross' writings have gained popularity among Christians interested in apologetics. He has a ministry of apologetics called *Reasons to Believe* and its goal is to integrate the Bible with "secular science," which is actually "scientism." The end result is a compromised version of theistic evolution that undermines the Bible. His website declares "an honest study of nature...can prove useful in a person's search for truth." Such an assertion denies the truth of Romans 1 where Paul declared that unbelievers always reject the truth about God found in natural revelation. Ross develops his own version of natural theology based on extrapolations deduced from wrong views of general revelation and then elevates that natural theology to an equal level of authority to that of Scripture. Ross goes on to call his view of natural theology the 67th book of the Bible.

More and more, classical apologists like William Lane Craig are following suit with Ross, venturing into the realm of astronomy and the hard sciences to buttress their own versions of philosophical natural theology. On *The Michael Coren Show* Craig denigrates Christians who believe the earth is only 6,000 years old and dogmatically asserts that the universe is about 13.7 billion years old. The bases of his assertions come from secular astronomy. He explains, "The arguments that I give are right in line with mainstream science. I'm not bucking up against mainstream science in presenting these arguments. I'm going with the flow of what contemporary cosmology and astrophysics supports." When questioned about what the Bible says regarding the age of the universe, he laughed and declared, "There's nothing in the Bible that says how old the universe is." So for Craig, defending the faith does not mean telling people what the Bible says, but rather it is about being in lock-step with secular, humanistic, atheistic, Darwinian cosmology and astrophysics.

The Origin of Natural Theology

The theistic arguments are most commonly equated with what constitutes natural theology. The four most prominent theistic arguments are (1) the cosmological (cosmos); (2) the teleological (design); (3) the ontological (necessary being); and (4) the moral argument (moral law). It is well established that the cosmological and the teleological arguments originate with the pagan Greek philosophers, Plato and Aristotle. "Plato (428-348 BCE), Aristotle (384-322 BCE), and their successors in ancient and medieval philosophy developed substantial arguments for the existence of god without relying on revelation."[79] One source says, "the teleological argument is said to be natural theology which Socrates and Cicero talked about."[80] Another asserts, "they go back to Aristotle who taught that God was the First Cause and the Last End of the world. Both arguments appeal to the observed features of human experience."[81] Apologist Norman Geisler admits, "Plato's proofs for God were a forerunner of later Christian forms of the cosmological argument" that would be further developed by Augustine (354-430), Anselm (1033-1109), and Thomas Aquinas (1225-1274).[82]

It needs to be noted that Geisler and many other traditional apologists frequently appeal to Augustine to justify their dependence on natural theology. But this is unwarranted. Although Augustine had some neo-Platonic tendencies, he did not view the theistic proofs with the same optimism as did Anselm, Aquinas or modern day traditional apologists. Demarest clarifies this oft-propagated misnomer:

> ...all the classical proofs of God's existence...were not intended by Augustine to prove formally the existence and character of God, as later scholastic theologians sought to do. Augustine did not deal with the data of the external world by means of inductive inference, concluding that God is, as in the case of Aquinas. Rather, Augustine

intended to show that finite man rebels against the truth of common grace if he fails to acknowledge the reality of an infinite and eternal God who undergirds the whole of life…Said Augustine, 'We were too weak by unaided reason to find out the truth, and for this cause needed the authority of the holy writings.' Through a supernatural working of the Holy Spirit, God set forth saving wisdom on the pages of the Old and New Testaments…Augustine is insistent that saving wisdom (*sapientia*) is not possible without faith, understood both as intellectual assent to truths mediated in Scripture and personal commitment to Christ. It is in this sense that Augustine writes of the priority of faith: 'If you will not believe, you will not understand' (*nisi credideritis, non intelligetis*). Again, 'If you cannot understand, believe in order to understand' (*si non potes intelligere, crede ut intelligas*)…In sum, then, God is redemptively known neither by induction from the data of the finite external world, nor by reflection on the internal data of experience. Augustine's distinctive Christian philosophy is succinctly stated thus: 'Faith is in some way the starting point of knowledge.'[83]

Anselm, another avowed Platonist, is a different story. He is credited as being the originator of the ontological argument. Anselm depended on the works of Augustine to formulate his doctrine of God, yet subtly drifted from the "faith-first" mantra of Augustine as he sought to develop a much more speculative and philosophically ambitious explication of theism. "Anselm thus represents a transitional link between the faith perspective of Augustine and the rationalism of the later Scholastic tradition championed by Aquinas."[84] Anselm posited that the "rational mind itself is most able to advance toward finding the Supreme Being."[85] He believed the theistic proofs and speculative argumentation (i.e. natural theology) could be coercive for the infidel who had no faith and facilitate his journey toward faith. Anselm also utilized a form of the cosmological argument and numerous other speculations to develop an extensive rational theology apart from Scripture.

Anselm sounds just like a modern-day traditional apologist when he wrote, "nothing in Scripture should be urged on the authority of Scripture itself, but that whatever the conclusion of independent investigation should declare to be true, should...with common proofs and with simple argument, be briefly enforced by the cogency of reason."[86] In other words, he was saying that our apologetics cannot start with Scripture, but must begin with natural theology! Sounds eerily familiar.

Natural theology came into its own with the Italian, Thomas Aquinas, the recognized formulator, systematizer and propagator of the Christianized version of the Greek philosophers' theistic proofs. Aquinas is the undisputed heavyweight father of Roman Catholic theology and apologetics. Although he rejected the ontological argument, he proposed five arguments of his own called "The Five Ways." As a Roman Catholic Dominican monk, he was enmeshed and worked within the framework of Aristotelian philosophy. Knowing no Greek and very little Hebrew, he was no biblical exegete, being incapable of interfacing with the original languages of God's Word. As such, he was content with philosophical and speculative theology, instead of biblical theology. Demarest summarizes Aristotle's influence on Aquinas's apologetic methodology:

> In the Aristotelian scheme, the intellect is the key that opens the door to the knowledge of God. By rational induction from temporal effects, Aristotle concluded the existence, intelligence, and providential care of the Prime Mover or Absolute Perfection, without uniting these characteristics in a single personal being. The Aristotelian tradition optimistically affirmed the ability of the human intellect to ascend to divine truth...Thomas' epistemological scheme was one with his vision of the apologetics task. When one communicates the faith to the Gentiles, appeal to biblical authority is of little value. 'We must,' Thomas argues, 'have recourse to the natural reason, to which all men are forced to give their assent.'...Thomas, with Aristotle, acknowledged...the finite creature can know in part the infinite Creator by virtue of the analogy that exists between God and all created things...Thomas' inflated emphasis on reason betrays a depreciation of the effects of the Fall on the human cognitive powers...Thomas, unlike Augustine, saw no need for a general illumination of reason as it evaluates

the data of the cosmic order...Given Thomas's vision of an untarnished *imago*, a self-sufficient natural theology is for the Christian and non-Christian alike a fruitful possibility....Hence Thomas affirms in the *Summa Theologica*, 'The existence of God can be proved in five ways.'...Virtually the entirety of Thomas's argumentation in the Five Ways was adopted from the formulations of Aristotle more than a millennium and a half earlier.[87]

Aquinas, more than any before him, argued for the legitimization of natural theology and the theistic proofs in the execution of Christian apologetics. As such, he is the true patriarch and exemplar of Roman Catholic apologetics and many modern-day Protestant apologists as well.

In addition to Aquinas, the Arminian Joseph Butler (1692-1752) deserves honorable mention for his part in bequeathing natural theology as foundational for modern-day Protestant apologetics. The once bishop of Durham is best known for his book on apologetics, *Analogy of Religion*, a defense of the plausibility of Christianity. Cornelius Van Til gives an astute summary of Butler's deleterious influence upon traditional Christian apologetics:

> The great textbook of Evangelical apologetics is Bishop Butler's famous *Analogy*...its argument is closely similar to that which is found, for instance, in the Summa Contra Gentiles of Thomas Aquinas. Butler holds to an Arminian view in theology. He therefore assumes that the natural man by 'a reasonable use of reason' can interpret aright 'the course and constitution of nature.' If only the natural man will continue to employ the same 'reasonable use of reason' with respect to the facts presented to him in Scripture about Christ and his work there is every likelihood that he will become a Christian.[88]

Butler was an advocate of the efficacy of unaided human reason. He said, "Reason can, and it ought to judge...the morality and the evidence, of revelation. First, it is the province of reason to judge of the morality of Scripture."[89]

The Great Compromise

What do we make of the notion of Christians depending upon the Greek pagan philosophers to build a foundation of natural theology? Traditional apologist Bernard Ramm suggested that Paul's writings were influenced by the Greek philosopher Zeno (335-263 BC) and that Plato and Aristotle were helpful allies in promoting a logical defense for Christianity.[90] Geisler says Aristotle is indispensible for Christian apologetics, for he "laid down the basic principles of reason used by most apologists" and apologists throughout church history were even "dependent on Aristotelian principles."[91] C. S. Lewis believed Plato and Aristotle, like Christianity and 'the Tao,' maintained the helpful teaching of "the doctrine of objective value, the belief that certain attitudes are really true, and others really false, to the kind of thing the universe is and the kind of things we are."[92] In his writings, R. C. Sproul bends over backwards to give Aristotle a pass against the criticism of discerning Christians throughout the ages.[93] He even credits Aristotle for fine-tuning the fundamental tools Christians need for doing apologetics: "Aristotle ascertained the necessary conditions for human beings to carry on meaningful conversations."[94] It is not as if Moses and all the prophets were handicapped in communication and conversation because they were without the benefit of Platonic and Aristotelian logic—they only had the Mind of the eternal God of the universe at their disposal (Moses talked with Him "face to face"), the One who invented the very Laws of Logic.

The fact of the matter is that Plato and Aristotle were unbelievers. We need to set the record straight here. One of the greatest philosophers of the 20th century was Cornelius Van Til. He studied Plato and the classics in the original Greek at Princeton where he earned his PhD in philosophy. While at Princeton he excelled in metaphysical analysis and mastered Hegelian philosophy. He went on to teach philosophy at Westminster Theological Seminary for forty-three years. He read and wrote extensively on Plato and Aristotle during the course of his life. He is more trustworthy than most in giving a biblical appraisal on the Greek philosophers. Van Til wrote, "The Greeks were among those of whom Paul speaks when he says that they hinder or repress the truth in unrighteousness. The significance of the fact that Greek speculation began with a definitely anti-theistic bias cannot be stressed too much because of the common misunderstanding on this score."[95] Further, he notes, "To the Greek mind the gospel was foolishness because it implied that the mind of the 'natural man' is radically corrupt."[96] He continues, "The Greek thinkers were as children who thought they could do everything…a striking manifestation of the pride, 'hubris' of the sinner who wishes to be as God"[97] In conclusion, he observes, "We hold that both Plato and Aristotle stood diametrically opposed to Christianity, and that it is out of the question to speak of Christianity as having developed out of either of their philosophies."[98]

Plato and Aristotle were both made in the image of God; they possessed the innate *sensus divinitatis*, as well as a conscience, and nature was continually at their disposal declaring the glory of God. Yet, history records they rejected God's general revelation, suppressed the truth in unrighteousness, refused to thank God, had their foolish minds darkened, and chose to worship the creature rather than the Creator. Practically speaking, the whole Greek culture of the time was morally and spiritually bankrupt. Historian Frederick Eby plainly notes, "The moral rottenness of their civilization is beyond description."[99] As such, their religion was corrupt, their thinking depraved and their souls were lost.

Plato invented his own god and said it was not personal nor the Creator, but was finite. He believed time and matter were eternal and that chance was ultimate. He erroneously postulated that evil always co-existed with good. Plato taught that matter is less real and less good than spirit. He propagated an anthropological dualism, asserting that the true nature of man is his soul, and not his body—as a matter of fact humans are imprisoned in their bodies. In contrast, ideal humanity in the Bible is physical resurrection man after the likeness of Christ's resurrection (1 Cor 15). The concept of resurrection humanity to the Greeks was "strange" and babbling nonsense (Acts 17:16-20). Plato ignored his own indwelling sin (1 Kgs 8:46) and arrogantly touted that man's mind was pristine and herculean in capabilities. Plato believed in the preincarnation of the soul as well as reincarnation; salvation came by education; humanity was perfectible in this life.

Aristotle fared no better. He made a god is his own likeness as well, and it mirrored a creature rather than the Creator. His god was not personal but a logical necessity. He said the universe was eternal. He did not believe that God created all things. He believed in the autonomy of human reason. And he denied the afterlife and the immortality of the soul (at least until he died in 322 BC, after which he faced YHWH as Judge; cf. Ezek 18:20; Heb 9:27; Phil 2:9-11).

Christ vs. Belial

The Bible is clear—there are only two kinds of people: believers and unbelievers; those who love God and those who hate God (Ps 83:2); sinners and saints—the saints and the ain'ts; those who walk in truth and light and those who walk in sin and darkness; those who are the sons of the King and those who are the pawns of the devil. Christians tend to forget this basic biblical teaching and instead create false categories and a sliding scale of unbelievers with "pre-believers," "seekers," and "good people" like Oprah on one end of the scale, and really bad, evil wicked people like Hitler and Charles Manson on the other end, men who really do deserve hell. But such is not the case. Scripture is categorical: "Who is the liar but the one who denies that Jesus is the Christ?...Whoever denies the Son does not have the Father" (1 John 2:22-23). John the apostle goes on, "the one who practices sin is of the devil...By this the children of God and the children of the devil are obvious" (1 John 3:8, 10).

Jesus said the same thing to the astute, pious, religiously respected leaders of His day who rejected biblical truth: "You are of *your* father the devil" (John 8:44). Paul said the same thing, affirming that all unbelievers are dead in "trespasses and sins" and walk "according to the prince of the power of the air, of the spirit that is now working in the sons of disobedience...indulging the desires of the flesh and of the mind, and were by nature children of wrath" (Eph 2:1-3). Paul goes on, saying unregenerate Greeks lived "in the futility of their mind, being darkened in their understanding, excluded from the life of God, because of the ignorance that is in them, because of the hardness of their heart; and they, having become callous, have given themselves over to sensuality, for the practice of every kind of impurity with greediness" (Eph 4:17-19). That is a more accurate portrait and biography of Plato and Aristotle from God's point of view.

That being the case, how can Christians continue to gaze on these pagans as paragons of wisdom and as icons of veritable virtue by which we model our apologetics? It is biblically inexcusable. Romans 1:25 says all unbelievers have "exchanged the truth of God for a lie." Believers cannot partner up with unbelievers in the pursuit and proclamation of the truth. "What partnership have righteousness and lawlessness, or what fellowship has light with darkness? Or what harmony has Christ with Belial, or what has a believer in common with an unbeliever? Or what agreement has the temple of God with idols?" (2 Cor 6:14-16). Notice here God calls Christians righteousness, light, Christ, believers and the temple of God, whereas he contrasts them with non-Christians who are labeled as lawlessness, darkness, Belial, unbelievers and idols.

Tertullian had it right back in the third century when he wrote:

> What indeed has Athens to do with Jerusalem? What concord is there between the Academy and the Church? What between heretics and Christians? Our instruction comes from "the porch of Solomon," who had himself taught that "the Lord should be sought in simplicity of heart." Away with all attempts to produce a mottled Christianity of Stoic, Platonic, and dialectic composition! We want no curious disputation after possessing Christ Jesus, no inquisition after enjoying the gospel! With our faith, we desire no further belief.[100]

Luther also had it right in diagnosing natural theology as counterfeit revelation. Packer and Johnston summarize Luther's indictment of man-made natural theology:

> His unflagging polemic against the abuse of reason has often been construed as an assault on the very idea of rational coherence in theology, whereas in fact it is aimed only at the ideal of rational autonomy and self-sufficiency in theology—the ideal of philosophers and Scholastic theologians, to find out and know God by the use of their own unaided reason. It was in her capacity as the prompter and agent of 'natural' theology that Mistress Reason was in Luther's eyes the Devil's whore; for natural theology is, he held, blasphemous in principle, and bankrupt in practice.[101]

Here's the point: there is no common ground for spiritual or theological enterprising together. The Apostle Paul concludes his argument by saying, "come out from their midst and be separate" (2

Cor 6:17). Indeed, Christians cannot accommodate or integrate the fallen, compromised, satanic wisdom of the world in any endeavor if they seek to please Christ, especially in the area of advancing and defending the faith through the work of biblical apologetics. And to accommodate and integrate the notions and methodologies of the Greek pagan philosophers into our apologetics by utilizing natural theology is to accommodate the wisdom of the world, which will ensure the undermining of biblical truth, circumventing the Spirit's intervention, the watering down of the gospel, and the short-circuiting of God's blessing.

Grand Presumptions

Traditional apologists who rely on natural theology as their foundation and starting point for implementing their methodology of apologetics presuppose countless assumptions that are unbiblical and fallacious. Following are a flurry of examples:

(1) Those who see a need for natural theology do so because they deny the perspicuity of general revelation, saying God's general revelation in nature and in man's makeup is not clearly understood by all.

(2) Proponents of natural theology assume atheists and agnostics are sincere and not culpable when they claim they do not know if there is a God, whereas the Bible says the one who says there is no God is a fool, a liar and a hater of God (Ps 14:1; Rom 1:30; 1 John 2:22).

(3) Proponents of natural theology assume unbelievers do not willfully suppress and reject the truth about God that can be known through general revelation, whereas the Bible says unbelievers always suppress the truth of general revelation (Rom 1:18-31).

(4) Proponents of natural theology assume efficacious faith can result from natural revelation, whereas the Bible says saving faith results only from special revelation (Rom 10:17; 1 Pet 1:21).

(5) Proponents of natural theology assume truth about God can be gained from the worldly wisdom of unbelievers like Plato, Aristotle and Muslim theology, whereas the Bible says unbelievers

do not have truth about God and they cannot discern spiritual truth apart from the indwelling Holy Spirit (1 Cor 2).

(6) Proponents of natural theology assume unaided human reason is the ultimate authority of determining what is true, whereas the Bible says God is the one who determines what is true (Rom 3:4).

(7) Proponents of natural theology assume that general revelation extends beyond the realms of the boundaries clearly laid down in Scripture: God's visible creation in nature and the *imago Dei*.

(8) Proponents of natural theology arrogantly assume that finite, fallen, physical man can attain truth about the metaphysical, infinite and invisible by pure deduction and inference.

(9) Proponents of natural theology assume unbelievers just need more information and more convincing arguments in order to believe.

(10) Proponents of natural theology reject the toal depravity of man and sin's deleterious impact on human reasoning; the Bible says unbelievers' capacity to reason about spiritual matters is "futile" and "darkened" (Rom 1:21), foolish (Rom 1:22), "depraved" (Rom 1:28), wicked (Rom 1:29), "untrustworthy" (Rom 1:31), "dead" (Eph 2:1), ignorant (Eph 4:18), and "callous" (Eph 4:19).

(11) Proponents of natural theology totally neglect any acknowledgement of the fact that all unbelievers suffer from supernatural, Satanic blindness that prohibits them from believing in spiritual truth (2 Cor 4:4).

(12) Proponents of natural theology do not acknowledge God's sovereignty in enabling unbelievers to believe (Acts 16:!4).

(13) Proponents of natural theology reject the sufficiency of Scripture and the efficacy of the gospel by insisting that the "Laws of Logic" and the theistic proofs must come prior to gospel proclamation.

(14) Proponents of natural theology undermine the sufficiency of Scripture claiming that the methodology of apologetics used by Jesus and the apostles is not adequate for us today.

(15) Proponents of natural theology assume there is epistemological common ground between totally depraved unbelievers and believers who are indwelt with the Holy Spirit.

(16) Proponents of natural theology fail to realize our common ground with unbelievers is ontological as all humans were made in God's image.

(17) Proponents of natural theology assume that using "reason" is mutually exclusive of reasoning from Scripture (Acts 17:2).

(18) Proponents of natural theology usually assume that those who reject natural theology are fideists.

(19) Proponents of natural theology often assume that those who reject natural theology also reject natural revelation.

(20) Proponents of natural theology assume the Bible is not self-authenticating.

(21) Proponents of natural theology fail to realize that seeking to establish God's existence as only "demonstrably plausible" instead of it being absolutely certain is actually blasphemy and an offense to God (Job 40:1-2; Heb 11:6).

Much more could be said about the pitfalls and utter folly of natural theology and how it compromises the very foundation of the work of Christian apologetics. Suffice it to say that natural theology needs to be categorically rejected, whereas biblical theology needs to assume sole position for all Christians as they seek to advance and defend the gospel of Christ in the midst of a lost and hostile world.

Summary

God can only be known by fallen, finite humanity through God's self-disclosure. God has revealed Himself to all people, in all time periods through general revelation in nature and in man's very personality. But as sinners, humans suppress this intuitive knowledge of God in unrighteousness. Because they know the truth about God they are culpable before Him. General revelation is not sufficient to save sinners because of man's self-inflicted rebellion, but it is sufficient to condemn man. Because of man's plight, God in His grace also decided to reveal Himself to sinful humanity through special revelation, by imparting to humanity propositional truths through selective and personal means for the purpose that sinners can be saved and come to know God personally and have their sins forgiven. The culmination of this special revelation was the incarnation of Jesus Christ as the God-Man. The necessary truth about Him has been preserved perpetually in Scripture, the Bible. The good news about Jesus as the Savior who died in the place of sinners and who rose from the dead is called the gospel. This special revelation of the gospel needs to be preached and taught to all unbelievers before they can be saved. As such, Christian mission to the world is imperative and a priority.

Natural theology was originally invented millennia ago by unbelievers who rejected God's general revelation. Instead of relying on God's revelation to learn about God, they depended solely on finite, fallen human reason to develop views about God. Natural theology was designed to supplant God's original purpose of general revelation. As such, natural theology is pseudo-revelation about God and is ineffectual in producing true saving faith. Unfortunately, Christians through the years have tried to integrate and adopt various features of natural theology with the goal of building an apologetical system that they think bridges the gap from unbelief to belief. Such an endeavor actually undermines biblical sufficiency.

God's Word is sufficient for defending the faith and advancing the gospel (2 Tim 3:16-17). Believers must resist the tremendous tide of pressure that is currently commonplace in the Christian world that says apologetics must begin with natural theology; and instead stand on the simplicity, power and efficacy of the gospel and the sufficiency of God's Word, the holy Scriptures.

Notes

1. For the truth about the myth of global warming read Genesis 8:22 and Brian Sussman's books *Climategate: A Veteran Meteorologist Exposes the Global Warming Scam* (Washington, D C: WorldNetDaily, 2010) and *Eco-Tyranny: How the Left's Green Agenda Will Dismantle America* (Washington, DC: WND Books, 2012), in addition to countless other recent scholarly resources such as *A Disgrace to the Profession*, ed. Mark Steyn (Woodsville, NH: Stockade Publishing, 2015) and *Climate Change: The Facts*, ed. Alan Moran (Woodsville, NH: Stockade Publishing, 2015).

2. William Lane Craig, "Classical Apologetics," *Five Views on Apologetics*, ed. Steven B. Cowan et al. (Grand Rapids: Zondervan, 2000), 39.

3. R. C. Sproul, John Gerstner and Arthur Lindsley, *Classical Apologetics: A Rational Defense of the Christian Faith and a Critique of Presuppositional Apologetics* (Grand Rapids: Zondervan, 1984), 24.

4. A. C. Headlam, *Christian Theology* (Oxford: Clarendon, 1934), 7.

5. G. C. Berkouwer, *Studies in Dogmatics: General Revelation* (Grand Rapids: Eerdmans, 1955), 17.

6. Michael J. Anthony and Warren S. Benson, *Exploring the History and Philosophy of Christian Education: Principles for the 21st Century* (Grand Rapids: Kregel Academic, 2003), 38. Anthony erroneously calls the Bible "general revelation" in contrast to miracles and Jesus, which he says constitute "special revelation." This is a basic error—the Bible is special revelation.

7. Richard Mayhue, "Is Nature the 67th Book of the Bible?" *Coming to Grips with Genesis: Biblical Authority and the Age of the Earth*, eds. Terry Mortenson and Thane H. Ury (Green Forest, AR: Master Books, 2008), 127.

8. Ibid., 112.

9. Bruce Demarest, *General Revelation* (Grand Rapids: Zondervan, 1982), 236.

10. Willem A. Van Gemeren, "Psalms," *The Expositor's Bible Commentary*, 12 vols. ed. Frank E. Gaebelein (Grand Rapids: Zondervan, 1991), V:179. See E. W. Bollinger, *The Witness of the Stars*, pp. 1-6 for a diagrammatical analysis based on the Hebrew text with lexical and syntactical observations that flesh out the first part of this Psalm.

11. Mayhue, *Genesis*, 112.

12. Robert L. Thomas, *Evangelical Hermeneutics: The New Versus the Old* (Grand Rapids: Kregel, 2002), 116.

13. Mayhue, *Genesis*, 113.

14. D. G. Dunbar, "Sensus Deitatis, Sensus Divinitatis," *Evangelical Dictionary of Theology*, ed. Walter Elwell (Grand Rapids: Baker, 1984), 1001.

15. Craig, "A Classical Apologist's Response," *Five Views*, 285.

16. Ibid., 286.

17. Ibid., 40-42.

18. Kelly James Clark, "Reformed Epistemology Apologetics," *Five Views*, 274.

19. Demarest, *General Revelation*, 242-43.

20. Mayhue, *Genesis*, 114.

21. Ibid., 115.

22. George J. Zemek, *A Biblical Theology of the Doctrines of Sovereign Grace: Exegetical Considerations of Key Anthropological, Hamartiological and Soteriological Terms and Motifs* (Little Rock, AR: B.T.D.S.G., 2002), 261 n. 85.

23. Martin Luther, *Commentary on Romans*, (Grand Rapids: Kregel, 1976, reprint), 43.

24. Alvin Plantinga, *Warranted Christian Belief* (New York, NY: Oxford University Press, 2000), 170-74. More recently, in 2015, Plantinga seems to have modified his views on faith and his understanding of Calvin's *testimonium*, moving closer to a biblical model where he acknowledges that God energizes faith when the Word works in conjunction with the Spirit on the human heart. He still falls short in his discussion, though, never acknowledging that saving faith is alien to us; *Knowledge and Christian Belief* (Grand Rapids: Eerdmans Publishing Company, 2015), 57-62.

25. Greg L. Bahnsen, *Van Til's Apologetic: Readings & Analysis* (Phillipsburg, NJ: P & R, 1998), 184.

26. Clark, *Five Views*, 267.

27. Ibid., 273.

28. Demarest, *General Revelation*, 51-53.

29. Henry Holloman, *Kregel Dictionary of the Bible and Theology* (Grand Rapids: Kregel, 2005), 467.

30. Demarest, *General Revelation*, 239.

31. Norman L. Geisler, *Systematic Theology*, 4 vols. (Minneapolis: Bethany House, 2002), I: 68.

32. Quoted in Thomas, *Hermeneutics*, 117. Gangel was at Dallas Seminary. Long ago, co-founder of Dallas Seminary, W. H. Griffith Thomas (1861-1924), taught the same thing about history. He said, "God has revealed himself in nature, in providence and in history"; cf. *How We Got Our Bible*, (Dallas, TX: Dallas Seminary Press, 1984), 15.

33. John Frame, "Presuppositional Apologetics," *Five Views*, 210.

34. Millard Erickson, *Christian Theology* (Grand Rapids: Baker, 1985), 154. Bookman accurately notes that general "revelation is by definition nondiscoverable by human investigation and cogitation." See Bookman's excellent full discussion on the matter in "The Scriptures and Biblical Counseling" in *Introduction to Biblical Counseling: a Basic Guide to the Principles and Practice of Counseling* by John MacArthur, Jr. and Wayne A. Mack, 71-97.

35. Mayhue, *Genesis*, 112. I don't know who the first person in Church history was that declared "history is general revelation," but today that is a *mantra* that is readily repeated without scrutiny or corroborating biblical support. History is not general revelation. History needs to be researched, discovered, taught and interpreted. History is not universally accessible, it is not immediately apprehended or intuitive to all, and the canon of its content is not fixed and unchanging like other real examples of general revelation. The Bible is the divine interpretation of true human history, and selective at that, in terms of the content addressed. Therefore, biblical history—as delineated and confined in Scripture—is special revelation. Yasser Arafat had a history textbook created for "Palestinians" in Israel. In it, he redefined, or revised history, by saying Israel never existed in the region historically. He also asserted that there never was a Jewish temple in the land of Israel! That is in their history book—so much for "universally" accepted historical truth. The Book of Mormon has created history by saying Native American Indians descended from the lost tribes of Israel. These two examples illustrate that non-biblical history is subject to interpretation and does not meet the basic requirements of what constitutes natural or general revelation.

36. Robert L. Reymond, *A New Systematic Theology of the Christian Faith*, (Nashville: Thomas Nelson, 1998), 5.

37. Hollomon, *Kregel Dictionary*, 465.

38. Thomas, *Hermeneutics*, 117.

39. Traditional apologist, Clark Pinnock, propagates the false notion that pagans can get saved by responding to general revelation; cf. *A Wideness in God's Mercy* (Grand Rapids: Zondervan, 1992), 163. But even Geisler disagrees, accurately pointing out, "While general revelation manifests God as Creator, it does not reveal Him as Redeemer," *Systematic Theology*, I:69.

40. Gordon R. Lewis and Bruce A. Demarest, *Integrative Theology*, (Grand Rapids: Zondervan, 1996), 61.

41. C. M. Horne, "Revelation," in *The Zondervan Pictorial Encyclopedia of the Bible*, 5 vols. ed. Merrill C. Tenney (Grand Rapids: Zondervan), V:88. Note Rigaux's keen insight: "The object of divine revelation is always something in the sphere of religion. It does not burden itself with cosmological data or metaphysical speculation, with which the sacred books of the majority of ancient religions were surfeited (for example, the Vedas of India, Gnostic works, or even certain Jewish apocrypha). God reveals His plans which trace the way of salvation for men. He reveals Himself so that man may be able to meet Him," Béda Rigaux,

"Revelation," in *Dictionary of Biblical Theology*, ed. Léon-Dufour (Ijamsville, MD: The Word Among Us Press, 2000), 500.

42. "The Jewish tradition associates Moses with the commencement of the Scripture, and there is no doubt of the essential truth of this position. Certainly there is no other tradition attached to the books; and in view of the tenacity with which the Jews kept their national traditions, this belief about Moses calls for adequate explanation. A careful study of passages should be noted: Exodus 17:14; Numbers 33:2; Deuteronomy 17:18; Joshua 1:8; 24:26; 1 Samuel 10:25; Isaiah 8:16, 20; Jeremiah 36:2; Daniel 9:2; Nehemiah 8:1. These references, taken from each period of the history, indicate a gradual growth of the Jewish Scriptures. The complete volume is associated by tradition with Ezra, and there are no valid reasons for doubting this, especially as it harmonizes with the testimony of the well-informed and representative Jew, Josephus, who, writing in the first century of the Christian Era, said that no book was added to the Jewish Scripture after the time of Malachi. As to the preservation of the gradually growing volume through the ages from Moses to Ezra, it has been pointed out by that eminent Egyptologist, Professor Naville, that it was the custom among Eastern nations to deposit their books in their sanctuaries, and there is every likelihood that the Jews did the same. The copy found by Hilkiah was probably this temple copy (2 Kings 22:8)"; W. H. Thomas, *How We Got Our Bible*, 3-4.

43. Frame, *Five Views*, 209-210; 215.

44. Clark, *Five Views*, 273, 279.

45. Craig, *Five Views*, 176.

46. John Frame, *Apologetics to the Glory of God* (Phillipsburg, NJ: P & R, 1994), 23.

47. Reymond, *Systematic Theology*, 9.

48. Clark, *Five Views*, 274-75.

49. Geisler, *Systematic Theology*, 65.

50. Sproul et al., *Classical Apologetics*, 27.

51. Craig, *Five Views*, 314.

52. Ibid., 314-15.

53. Ibid., 314, n. 1. In *Five Views*, Craig tries to make the Reformers his own, but that's not reality. Contrast Craig's Barthian view of Scripture with Calvin's, who said, "I take it for granted that the Word of God has such an inherent efficacy, that it quickens the souls of all whom He is pleased to favor with the communication of it"; *Institutes*, 277. Notice at least three glaring differences: (1) Calvin called Scripture "the Word of God," Craig denies that; (2) Calvin says Scripture's efficacy is "inherent," Craig says it's

"derivative"; and (3) Calvin assumes salvation results only from exposure to Scripture, Craig thinks people can get saved apart from the Bible.

54. C. Brown, "Natural Theology," in *New Dictionary of Theology*, ed. Sinclair B. Ferguson, David F. Wright and J. I. Packer (Downers Grove, IL: InterVarsity, 1988), 452.

55. J. P. Moreland and William Lane Craig, *The Blackwell Companion to Natural Theology* (West Sussex, UK: Blackwell, 2009), 1.

56. Samuel Macauley Jackson and Charles Colebrook Sherman, eds., *The New Schaff-Herzog Encyclopedia of Religious Knowledge*, (Grand Rapids: Baker, 1977), VIII:85. Recently, Alister McGrath has muddied the waters by convoluting the universally accepted definition of natural theology by inventing his own definition. Natural theology is doing theology without the Bible. McGrath is now proposing that natural theology is doing theology mostly without the Bible but using the biblical doctrine of creation as a foundation in lieu of "nature." So he mixes the Bible with man-made philosophy; kind of like mixing a little cyanide with your coffee, or a little hemlock with your tea, with 2 teaspoons of sugar of course. McGrath calls his version of natural theology "scientific theology." For further information see, James K. Dew, Jr.'s article, "The Future of Natural Theology: Exploring Alister McGrath's Natural Theology," in *Defending the Faith: Engaging the Culture; Essays Honoring L. Russ Bush*, eds. Bruce A. Little and Mark D. Liederbach (Nashville: B & H Publishing Group, 2011), 139-156. Also recently, MacArthur and Mayhue reestablish the correct traditional definition of natural theology in their systematic theology: "**natural theology.** Theology developed apart from the special revelation in Scripture; it attempts to demonstrate certain elements of theology from experience and reason alone"; John MacArthur and Richard Mayhue, *Biblical Doctrine: A Systematic Summary of Biblical Truth* (Wheaton: Crossway, 2017), 933.

57. Bahnsen, *Van Til's Apologetic*, 193-94.

58. William Gentz, ed., *The Dictionary of Bible and Religion* (Nashville: Abingdon Press, 1986), 729.

59. Clark, *Five Views*, 262.

60. Ferguson et al., *Dictionary of Theology*, 452-53.

61. Moreland and Craig, *Natural Theology*, "Table of Contents."

62. Alvin Plantinga, *www.splcs.com/ church/ Truth/ Lesson4/ two-dozen.pdf.*

63. Geisler, *Systematic Theology*, 81.

64. J. P. Moreland and William Lane Craig, *Philosophical Foundations for a Christian Worldview* (Downers Grove, IL: InterVarsity, 2003), 63-65.

65. Craig, *Five Views*, 125.

66. Sproul et al., *Classical Apologetics*, 26.

67. Ibid., 24 ff.

68. Craig, *Five Views*, 39.

69. Sproul et al., *Classical Apologetics*, 25.

70. Ibid., 36.

71. Ibid., 35.

72. R. C. Sproul, *Defending Your Faith: An Introduction to Apologetics* (Wheaton, IL: Crossway, 2003), 93.

73. Ibid., 30. Sproul here claims believers and the lost have common ground epistemologically in the intellect as well as the senses; listen to Calvin who adamantly disagrees: "Our minds are so blinded that they cannot perceive the truth, and all our senses are so corrupt that we wickedly rob God of his glory"; *Institutes*, 213. Sproul betrays his self-professed Calvinism in several ways with respect to his apologetical methodology: (1) he esteems the philosophers; (2) he prefers philosophy to exegetical theology; (3) functionally, he denies the totally depraved intellect of unbelievers; (4) he espouses natural theology; (5) he prefers to exegete Latin instead of the biblical languages; (6) he distorts the definition of general revelation; (7) he distorts Calvin's explanation of the Testimony; (8) on epistemology, he is in lock-step with the Arminian apologists and philosophers from Aristotle to William Lane Craig. Sproul needs a reformation in his apologetics and would be wise to heed Calvin's foundational warning: "never attempt to search after God anywhere but in his sacred word"; *Institutes*, 81.

74. Ibid.

75. Ibid., 31.

76. Ibid., 32.

77. Ibid., 33.

78. Ibid., 79.

79. Moreland and Craig, *Natural Theology*, 1.

80. John McClintock and James Strong, *Cyclopedia of Biblical, Theological, and Ecclesiastical Literature*, (Grand Rapids: Baker, 1969), VI:863.

81. Ferguson *et al.*, *Dictionary of Theology*, 452.

82. Norman L. Geisler, *Baker Encyclopedia of Christian Apologetics* (Grand Rapids: Baker Academic, 1999), 595.

83. Demarest, *General Revelation*, 28-29.; Groothuis makes this same mistake, as many traditional apologists do, over-generalizing and failing to discern the vast differences between Augustine's presuppositions pertaining to apologetical methodology versus those of Anselm and Aquinas; Douglas Groothuis, *Christian Apologetics: A Comprehensive Case for Biblical Faith*, (Downers Grove, IL: InterVarsity Press 2011), 68.

84. Ibid., 31.

85. Ibid.

86. Ibid., 33.

87. Ibid., 35-36.

88. Cornelius Van Til, *The Defense of the Faith* (Phillipsburg, NJ: P & R, 1967), 79.

89. Bahnsen, *Van Til's Apologetic*, 563.

90. Bernard Ramm, *A Christian Appeal to Reason* (Waco, TX: Word Books, 1977), 26.

91. Geilser, *Baker Encyclopedia*, 52.

92. C. S. Lewis, *The Abolition of Man* (London, 1947), 17.

93. Sproul *et al.*, *Classical Apologetics*, 28, 76, 110, 196-97, 264.

94. Sproul, *Defending the Faith*, 38. In contrast, Pearcey cuts to the chase by accurately observing, "the Greek thinkers were pagans, and many of their doctrines were incompatible with biblical truth"; Nancy Pearcey, *Total Truth: Liberating Christianity from Its Cultural Captivity* (Wheaton, IL: Crossway Books, 2004),74.

95. Bahnsen, *Van Til's Apologetic*, 48.

96. Ibid., 205.

97. Ibid., 258.

98. Ibid., 321.

99. Paul Kienel, *A History of Christian School Education* (Colorado Springs, CO: ACSI, 1998), 22.

100. Ibid., 5.

101. Martin Luther, *The Bondage of the Will*, trans. by J. I. Packer and O. R. Johnston (USA: Fleming H. Revell Company, 1957), 45-46. The authors continue explaining Luther's view: "It is blasphemous in principle, because it seeks to snatch from God a knowledge of Himself which is not His gift, but man's achievement—a triumph of human brain-power; thus it would feed man's pride, and exalt him above his Creator, as one who could know God at pleasure, whether or not God willed to be known by him. Thus natural theology appears as one more attempt on man's part to implement the programme which he espoused in his original sin—to deny his creaturehood, and deify himself, and deal with God henceforth on an independent footing. But natural theology is bankrupt in practice; for it never brings its devotees to God; instead it leaves them stranded in a quaking morass of insubstantial speculation. Natural theology leads men away from the Divine Christ, and from Scripture, the cradle in which He lies, and from the *theologia crucis*, the gospel doctrine which sets Christ forth. But it is only through Christ that God wills to be known, and gives saving knowledge of Himself. He who would know God, therefore, must seek Him through the Biblical gospel. We must not expect to understand

all that the gospel tells us, for the fact of Christ (that is, the achievement of our salvation by the death of the incarnate Son of God) is beyond man's rational comprehension. That is why the gospel has always seemed foolish to the wise men of this world. But we are not entitled to make rational comprehension the condition of credence, nor to edit and reduce God's Word...so as to make it square with our own preconceived ideas. That, again, is to try and make man into God, for to understand all things perfectly is the prerogative of the Creator alone. And it is also to exclude faith; for the very distinguishing mark of faith is that it takes God's word just because it is God's word, whether or not it can at present understand it. Man's part, therefore, is to humble his proud mind, to renounce the sinful self-sufficiency which prompts him to treat himself as the measure of all things, to confess the blindness of his corrupt heart, and thankfully to receive the enlightening Word of God. Man is by nature as completely unable to know God as to please God; let him face the fact and admit it! Let God be God! Let man be man! Let ruined sinners cease pretending to be something other than ruined sinners! Let them realise that they lie helpless in the hand of an angry Creator; let them seek Christ, and cry for mercy. This is the point of Luther's polemic against reason. It takes its place as a part of his all-embracing prophetic onslaught against the proud vainglory of helpless sinners who deny their own helplessness. But it has nothing to do with his conception of the theologian's business. Luther was no foe to the ideal of systematic consistency in formulating and organizing the contents of the *theologia crucis*; how could he be, when he found that ideal so clearly exemplified in Scripture itself, in the great dogmatic epistles of St. Paul? 'Reason in the sense of logic he employed to the uttermost limits,'" 46-47.

5

Truth: God's Wrecking Ball

Epistemology—the Theory of Knowledge

"What is truth?" That is what Pilate asked Jesus before he condemned the sinless Savior to death by crucifixion (John 18:38). Ironically, Pilate asked that question with pessimistic sarcasm, yet it is one of the most profound and poignant queries ever uttered! The formal intellectual pursuit to answer the above question is what philosophers call "epistemology." Geisler says, "*Epistemology* is the discipline that deals with the theory of knowledge. The term can be broken down into *episteme-ology* (Gk. *episteme*, 'to know'; *logos*, 'study'). It is the study of how we know."[1] Another definition says, "Religious epistemology is a sub-branch of epistemology concerned with the knowledge and verification of religious truth claims."[2]

Epistemology is the study of how we know *truth*, reality and all the related implications of attaining knowledge. Can we know truth with certainty? What is the standard or authority of truth? Where does truth come from? Is truth universal? Does it change? Is it objective or subjective? How does anyone know that they ever know anything at all? All these questions are answered under the umbrella of the discipline of "epistemology"—the theory of knowledge.

Mormons say they know the truth—how do they know they know the truth? Muslims say they know the Koran is true. How do they know that? World famous atheist and God-hater, Richard Dawkins, says he knows beyond a shadow of a doubt that evolution is true.[3] How did he determine that to be true? Christians say the Bible is God's Word. How do we know that to be true? How do we determine what is true and what we know?

Whether you like the philosophically heavy-laden six syllable word or not, if you want to study apologetics to any extent, inevitably you will come to a crossroads and have to make a decision and answer the question: "Where do I stand on epistemology?" It's unavoidable. Where you land in terms of your view about knowledge and truth regarding ultimate realities will determine your theology, philosophy and methodology about apologetics.

Epistemology Matters

The intramural debate about apologetics among Christians (which is what this whole book is about) is really a battle over epistemology.[4] Years ago traditional apologist Bernard Ramm alluded to this: "The apologist...proceeds to interpret the Christian faith from a per-spective which is cordial to his theory of knowledge."[5] Apologist Gordon Lewis used epistemology as the determining factor in cataloguing his taxonomy of the various apologetical methodologies.[6] More recently Steven Cowan asserts, "Religious epistemology can be the decisive factor in distinguishing one apologetic method from another."[7] I agree with Cowan, and in this chapter I will show why he is correct.

Not everyone agrees with Cowan though. For example, Paul Feinberg says, "Because a variety of epistemologies are compatible with the teaching of the Bible, a variety of apologetic approaches will have legitimacy."[8] In effect Feinberg is saying that there are many different ways to determine what is spiritually true and that there are many ways we can come to know ultimate truth. Feinberg could not be more wrong.

Traditional apologist, Kelly James Clark, is even more extreme than Feinberg. In *Five Views* he defends the novel and budding apologetical methodology called "Reformed Epistemology," but oddly he writes in his defense saying, "I am dubious, however, of finding any ultimate or coercive support for epistemology in Scripture"![9] He tries to defend Christian Reformed "Epistemology" by saying there is no biblical epistemology? This is frightening. That is akin to saying, "I can't find anything about knowing the truth of God in the Bible." Yet, the Bible is called "the truth" (John 17:17; Ps 19:9) and was inspired by the Holy Spirit, Who is the Truth (John 16:13), and it is about Jesus Who called Himself "the truth" (John 14:6). The whole Bible, from Genesis to Revelation, informs the discipline of epistemology or the theory of knowledge. Already we can see the intramural battle over epistemology brewing.

Presuppositional Epistemology

Cornelius Van Til was a godly man, faithful church minister, careful scholar, brilliant philosopher, competent theologian, prolific author, avid evangelist, and a beloved seminary professor who made monumental contributions to twentieth-century Christian apologetics by articulating, better than any before him, the foundations of a true biblical epistemology relative to apologetical methodology.[10] His protégé Greg Bahnsen later skillfully advanced Van Til's work in this area to an unmatched, systematized and comprehensive degree.[11] The solid scaffolding of a biblical epistemology is the greatest contribution made by presuppositional apologetics to the ongoing intramural debate over Christian apologetical methodology.

Sadly, most traditional apologists are ignorant of this great truth. Many even sneer and mock the presuppositionalist apologists for their epistemological prowess. For example, William Lane Craig demeans Van Til, condescendingly quipping, "Van Til, for all his insights, was not a philosopher"![12] Craig barks at Christian presuppositional apologetics in general calling it a "groping, implicit, inchoate."[13] With fangs exposed, Sproul, Gerstner and Lindsley accuse Van Til of "revolt[ing] against logic," and they say his apologetics was steeped in "agnosticism and in incoherence," and was "fatally ensnarled in self-referential absurdity."[14] Clark Pinnock accused Van Til of having an unbiblical epistemology that was characterized by "tragic irrelevance" and goes on the attack saying Christians are obligated to "dismantle his system,"[15] and "we must ...oppose Van Til."[16] After calling Van Til "pyrrhic," John Warwick Montgomery sarcastically refers to Van Til's epistemology as a two-tiered fairy tale after the likes of "*Alice in Wonderland*."[17] Kelly James Clark maligns presuppositionalists, calling them "arrogant."[18] Clark swipes at Bahnsen calling his arguments, "precious thin and his approach wearisome."[19] This is sad, unwarranted and a terrible testimony. Resorting to *ad hominem* attacks is not the solution when disagreeing with a fellow Christian scholar. The debate needs to stay up in the realm of ideas, not down in the slums of personal insults.

What is it about presuppositional apologists that makes traditional apologists squirm, mock and belittle them? It is their epistemology; their theory of knowledge and explanation of how we determine truth, how we know what is true, and how we can know ultimate realities with finality and certitude. The presuppositonalists assert that their epistemology is the biblical one and the correct one and it flows from two unassailable, rock-bed presuppositions: (1) the Christian apologist must begin apologetics with the presupposed existence of the triune God of the Bible; and (2) the Christian apologist must assume from the start the presupposed truth of the self-authenticating Christian Scriptures. These two virile assertions drive the traditionalists mad.

Van Til summarizes his apologetical epistemology this way:

> the central concern of a truly biblical apologetic method is...to show that without presupposing the Christian worldview, all of man's reasoning, experience, interpretation, etc., is unintelligible. Only the transcendent revelation of God can provide the philosophically necessary preconditions for logic, science, morality, etc., in which case those who oppose the faith are reduced to utter foolishness and intellectually have nowhere to stand in objecting to Christianity's truth-claims.[20]

It's his phrase, "presupposing the Christian worldview" that drives the traditional apologists bonkers, as they cry, "Foul!," accusing Van Til and like presuppositionalists of circular reasoning.[21] They allege you cannot say what God says or what the Bible teaches is the standard of determining what is true. "You can't use the Bible to prove the Bible!" they charge. You can't take at face value what God said in Scripture about what God is like or if He even exists.

Nevertheless, Van Til confidently affirms, "A truly Protestant view of the assertions of philosophy and science can be self-consciously true only if they are made in the light of Scripture. Scripture gives definite information of a most fundamental character about all the facts and principles with which philosophy and science deal. For philosophy or science to reject or even to ignore this information is to falsify the picture it gives of the field with which it deals."[22]

Greg Bahnsen is even more direct on the matter. His classic epistemological mantra for Christian apologetics says, "our defense must be rooted in the presupposed word of God."[23] Again, he says, "the Christian is obligated to presuppose the word of Christ in every area of knowledge; the alternative is delusion."[24] As Christian apologists, we are not to begin from autonomous human logic, but "the man of faith submits to the *a priori* dependability of God's word."[25] This is so because "God's word is its own authentication; it is self-attestingly authoritative."[26] For Bahnsen, "At bottom, the issue is always a matter of recognizing the sovereign Creator who has clearly revealed Himself, as well as your total dependence on Him even in the realm of thought and knowledge."[27] He continues:

> the fundamental principle which must guide all thinking: *the lordship of Christ in the realm of knowledge.* God speaks with self-attesting authority, and His revelation is the necessary foundation of man's knowledge…The Christian, then, is rescued from epistemic futility by presupposing God's word over all contrary claims….Since all argumentation over fundamental issues of life and belief reduce to a question of one's starting point, the Christian apologist must stand firmly on the word of God, setting forth its self-attesting nature over against the destructive assumptions of unbelief for epistemology.[28]

Presupposing the truth of God's Word or to say that God's Word is self-authenticating is no 20th century invention of the Van Tillian presuppositionalists. This was Calvin's teaching in the 1500's. He wrote, "Scripture bears upon the face of it as clear evidence of its truth, as white and black do of their color," and "Scripture carrying its own evidence along with it, deigns not to submit to proofs and arguments, but owes the full conviction with which we ought to receive it to the testimony of the Spirit."[29]

Traditional apologists say just the opposite. First they allege that the apologist's job is to begin by trying to prove that God probably exists, using unaided human logic. Second, the apologist is to prove that the Scriptures are worthy of being considered as a source of authority, once again relying on sheer autonomous human reason to do so. Then and only then can we begin talking about the Bible and the God of the Bible…that is, if the unbeliever even lets us get to this third stage. You can be sure that the world-class, popular, best-selling atheists, Christopher Hitchens[30] and Richard Dawkins, won't.

Here is the nexus of the issue then on the battle over epistemology in Christian apologetics: biblical apologetics says God and

His Bible are the standard of truth and the final determiners of what we know and what can be known. Traditional apologists say the ultimate standard of truth cannot be the Bible, so alternatives to the Bible must be the starting point for establishing a theory of knowledge.

Traditional Definitions for Truth

What is truth? How do we validate what is true? Virtually every Christian apologetics book written tries to establish early on a theory of knowledge, or epistemology, so that we can know what truth is, as well as determine the limits and boundaries of human knowledge. Before inspecting various tests of truth offered by traditional apologetics we will first examine their stated definitions of truth.

Geisler and Bocchino are representative when they say, "truth is an expression, symbol, or statement that matches or corresponds to its object or referent."[31] Geisler writes elsewhere, "Truth is that which corresponds to its object."[32] In his encyclopedia on apologetics he defines truth in the same manner.[33] Similar to Geisler, Craig and Moreland define truth as "a matter of a proposition...corresponding to reality."[34] They call the correspondence view the "classical theory of truth." Hardy agrees: "in order for something to be considered true, it must correspond to reality."[35]

The reader should notice that there are four glaring deficiencies in the typical traditionalists' definition of truth from a biblical point of view. First of all, they do not include God or the Bible in their definition of truth. They allege truth can be defined without reference to God. Their textbook definition of truth, therefore, is theologically sterile and *a*-theistic.[36]

Second, they think their definition of truth is neutral, assuming it will be accepted by and applied by believers and unbelievers alike. But Christians do not stand on epistemological neutral ground with unbelievers when defining truth or when determining what is true.[37] Unbelievers have darkened minds and their understanding of truth is distorted (Rom 1:21; Eph 4:18). In addition, satanic blindness doubly skews the epistemology of unbelievers (2 Cor 4:4). Believers and unbelievers do not stand on level ground when it comes to knowing truth. Scripture is clear on this: "The fear of the LORD is the beginning of knowledge; fools [unbelievers] despise wisdom [truth]" (Prov 1:7).

The third deficiency in the traditionalists' definition of truth is that

152

they fail to make a distinction between heavenly (spiritual) truth and earthly (temporal) truth. For them, and most traditional apologists, all truth is the same. In the words of Moreland and Craig, "there is no peculiarly Christian theory of truth."[38] But nothing could be further from the truth! Scripture clearly delineates two kinds of truth.

When talking with Nicodemus, Jesus referred to two kinds of truth, heavenly and earthly: "Jesus answered and said to him... 'If I told you earthly things and you do not believe, how will you believe if I tell you heavenly things?'" (John 3:12). Paul also made a distinction between earthly truth and heavenly or "spiritual" truth. Paul called spiritual truth "God's wisdom" (1 Cor 2:7). Unbelievers don't have access to spiritual truth apart from God's revelation appropriated by faith and the work of the Holy Spirit. Unbelievers' knowledge with respect to truth is inherently limited to the earthly realm. Paul explains:

> [6]Yet we do speak wisdom [i.e. *spiritual truth*] among those who are mature; a wisdom, however, not of this age, nor of the rulers of this age, who are passing away; [7]but we speak God's wisdom [*truth*] in a mystery, the hidden *wisdom,* which God predestined before the ages to our glory; [8]the wisdom [*truth*] which none of the rulers of this age has understood...[12]Now we have received, not the spirit of the world, but the Spirit who is from God, so that we may know the things freely given to us by God....[14]But a natural [*unbelieving*] man does not accept the things of the Spirit of God, for they are foolishness to him; and he cannot understand them, because they are spiritually appraised. But he who is spiritual [*a believer*] appraises all things...[16]For '*who has known the mind of the LORD, that he should instruct Him?*' But we [believers] have the mind of Christ (1 Cor 2:6-8, 12, 14-16).

Understanding this basic distinction between two kinds of truth, heavenly and earthly, explains why a pagan can be a brilliant mathematician when crunching the numbers and at the same time have a darkened mind about spiritual, revealed truths from God about ultimate realities like what heaven is like and how everything was created. The unbeliever knows some stuff yet does not know other things.

The fourth deficiency of the traditionalists' definition of truth flows from the third point above: traditionalists ignore the fact that heavenly or "spiritual" truth is sovereignly revealed by God at His discretion. The traditionalists assume that all that is required is for anyone to just engage the brain, honor the three laws of logic and, "*Eureka!*" they will find truth, all truth, even ultimate spiritual truths, like how all things came into being and the meaning of life.

While earthly truth is accessible to all God's creatures, Scripture is clear that spiritual truth is not. Jesus taught on this fundamental epistemological reality. Jesus taught spiritual truth through parables. When left unexplained the parables were meaningless and a mystery. When interpreted, the parables were vehicles of carrying the cargo of spiritual truth. Jesus at times chose to be discriminating, revealing parabolic spiritual truth only to His disciples while withholding the truth from unbelievers as an act of judgment. Read carefully Jesus' explanation to His disciples on this matter:

> [10] And the disciples came and said to Him, "Why do You speak to them in parables?" [11] Jesus answered them, "To you it has been granted to know the mysteries of the kingdom of heaven, but to them it has not been granted. [12] For whoever has, to him *more* shall be given, and he will have an abundance; but whoever does not have, even what he has shall be taken away from him. [13] Therefore I speak to them in parables; because while seeing they do not see, and while hearing they do not hear, nor do they understand. [14] In their case the prophecy of Isaiah is being fulfilled, which says,
>
> *'You will keep on hearing, but will not understand; You will keep on seeing, but will not perceive;* [15] *For the heart of this people has become dull, With their ears they scarcely hear, And they have closed their eyes, Otherwise they would see with their eyes, Hear with their ears, And understand with their heart and return, And I would heal them.'*
>
> [16] But blessed are your eyes, because they see; and your ears, because they hear. [17] For truly I say to you that many prophets and righteous men desired to see what you see,

and did not see *it*, and to hear what you hear, and did not hear *it* (Matt 13:10-17).

A key phrase in this passage is in verse eleven when Jesus said, "To you it has been granted to know...but to them it has not been granted." Jesus was saying that spiritual truth was given to some while it was withheld from others. This is a profound consideration to keep in mind when formulating a biblical epistemology and a God-honoring apologetical methodology.

Matthew thirteen is not the only occurrence of this reality. Examples abound. A popular one was when Jesus asked Peter, "who do you say that I am?" (Matt 16:15). Peter replied, "You are the Christ, the Son of the living God" (16:16). Jesus then answers with this categorical and fundamental epistemological pronouncement about heavenly or spiritual truth: "Blessed are you, Simon Barjona, because flesh and blood [i.e. human means; the laws of logic] did not reveal this to you, but My Father who is in heaven" (16:17).

A Biblical Definition of Truth

Truth is that which corresponds to reality as defined and determined by God. Notice this proposed definition includes God as the determining referent, unlike Geisler and Craig's earlier *a*-theistic definition. In simpler terms, truth is what God says it is. YHWH is the "God of truth" (Ps 31:5). Everything about truth issues from this reality. The Triune God of the universe defines truth. The Holy Spirit is "the Spirit of truth" (John 16:13). Jesus is the Incarnation of truth. He declared, "I am the...truth" (John 14:6). The statement that prompted Pilate's famous question, "What is truth?" was Jesus' proclamation to Pilate: "You say correctly that I am a king. For this I have been born, and for this I have come into the world, to testify to the truth. Everyone who is of the truth hears My voice" (John 18:37). Why was Jesus born? Why did He become a human? What was His mission? To save sinners? Yes. To conquer the devil? Yes. To overcome the world and evil? Yes. And also to bear witness to the truth! No epistemology is complete that neglects this greatest of all epistemological factors—generically a definition of truth must have God as its referent, and specifically it must be Christological.

The Bible is also truth—ultimate spiritual truth. Jesus said categorically as He prayed to God the Father, "Your word is truth" (John 17:17). The author of Psalm 119 said Scripture is "the word of truth"

(v. 43) and "Your law is truth" (v. 142). Psalm 119:160 declares autopistically: "The sum of Your word is truth." George Zemek comments on the uniquely inspired epistemological implications of this phrase regarding written Scripture:

> By juxtaposing the word *rōš*, literally "head," with *d'bār'kā*, "Your word," he draws attention to the "sum" of God's written communications to mankind, that is, the "totality" of the word. He associates with the "sum-total" of his LORD's inscripturated directives for life a primary attribute of (*'emeṯ*), "truth" (v. 160a; cf. v. 142 and John 17:17 again). Then he shifts his perspective slightly, moving to the various parts of the whole with the phrase *kol-mišpat sidqekā*, "(each and) every one of Your righteous judgments," the grateful child of God spotlights the Word's attribute of permanence (v. 160b; cf. Isa 40:6-8). Consequently, whether surveyed as one piece or as parts of a unit, God's Book has proven itself to be both dependable and imperishable. For needy pilgrims it exudes its never-failing reliability which enables them through a transcendent perspective to endure and persevere amidst the tempestuous tribulations of life in a hostile world.[39]

Scripture is here declared to be verbal and plenary truth. Traditional apologists will agree that the Bible is true, but they allege that such a claim is not a foundational, *a priori* reality. They say the Bible is true because it pans out to be logical after it is subjected to a battery of *a posteriori* tests for truth independent of God or what the Bible says. This avoids circular reasoning, they tell us.

To sum up, a biblical definition of truth should be defined according to the following parameters:

- Truth is what God says it is
- God is truth
- The Holy Spirit is truth
- Jesus is truth
- God's Word (Scripture) is propositional truth
- There are two kinds of truth: earthly and heavenly
- Earthly truth is accessible to believers and unbelievers alike

- Heavenly truth is accessible only by faith
- Heavenly truth is revealed discriminately at God's discretion[40]

Traditional Tests for Truth

Inextricably linked to a theory or definition of truth is the matter of "tests for truth." How do we determine what is true and what is false? Every apologist must deal with this topic. Traditional apologists are homogenous on this matter in three respects. First they say the Bible is not the test for truth, for the Bible is what is to be proven so the Bible has to pass the scrutiny of other so-called "ultimate" tests for truth.

Second they say that human logic or human wisdom is the ultimate determiner of truth. "God exists," they say, "because through our human logic we have deduced that probability." That is what Josh McDowell means when he says, "reason leads us to the inevitability of God's existence."[41] And again, "Before we place our trust in the ultimate absolute, reason should show us that it is a logical necessity with no rational alternative."[42] That is what Sproul means when he says, "we must start with ourselves rather than God...It is logically impossible for us to start with God for we cannot affirm God without assuming logic."[43] In other words, finite, fallen, autonomous human reason and logic are ultimate. Logic precedes God!

Geisler unequivocally says this very thing: "logic is prior to God *in the order of knowing* (epistemologically)."[44] But the Bible says just the opposite: God is prior to everything. He is preeminent in everything, including epistemology: "He is before all things" (Col 1:17); YHWH is "the first and...the last" (Isa 44:6). All reality is what God says it is. "In Your light we see light" (Ps 36:9). He is not true because the laws of logic validate Him to be so; God invented the laws of logic—they are limited, secondary and subject to Him. He is completely sovereign over all things (Ps 115:3). YHWH warns puffed-up, supposedly all-knowing, self-sufficient humans saying: "Remember this, and be assured; recall it to mind, you transgressors. Remember the former things long past, for I am God, and there is no other; I am God, and there is no one like Me, declaring the end from the beginning, and from ancient times things which have not been done, saying, 'My purpose will be established, and I will accomplish all My good pleasure'" (Isa 46:8-10).

The third invalid affirmation of traditional apologists regarding the test for truth is that they assert that all truth is subject to the same tests. They make no distinction between earthly and heavenly truth, so for them, even heavenly truths, like the most ultimate metaphysical and ontological realities, are subject to their epistemological gauntlet of Greek logic.

When it comes to tests for truth the traditionalists don't agree on everything though. They are all over the map when trying to delineate what the specific test or tests include. Note the following examples:

- E. J. Carnell says, "Consistency is our surest test for the absence of truth...The law of contradiction is so basic to meaningful thought...that nothing is meaningful without the law's validity being presupposed."[45] So for Carnell, it is not the Triune God or the Bible that is presupposed, but rather the laws of logic. Carnell concludes that the Bible is true because it is systematically consistent, and is therefore the Word of God.[46]

- Paul Feinberg gives eight tests for truth with a prescribed order of priority: "the most important test is...consistency...Correspondence or empirical fit is next, and comprehensiveness follows that."[47]

- For Moreland and Craig the three laws compose the litmus test for what is true: "truth conforms to the three fundamental laws of logic, which are themselves absolute truths...The law of identity...The law of noncontradiction...The law of the excluded middle." Note they say the laws of logic comprise "absolute truth," whereas we hold that only God is absolute.[48]

- For Sproul, there are four inviolable ultimate tests of truth, all driven by *a*-theistic, autonomous human reason: (1) the law of non-contradiction; (2) the law of causality; (3) the basic reliability of sense perception; and (4) the analogical use of language.[49]

- Apparently for the popular Josh McDowell the test of truth is unaided human reason, generally speaking, and the law of non-contradiction in particular: "reason leads us to the inevitability of God's existence";[50] "...no belief should be accepted without the full support of hard-nosed reason";[51] "...we cannot believe in an outright contradiction."[52]

- John Warwick Montgomery claims veridical productivity comes from historical inductivity: "everyone—non-Christian as well as Christian—employs and must employ inductive procedures to distinguish fact from fiction."[53]

- Hardy takes the easy way out by staying ambiguous and bypassing a clearly delineated commitment to any tests for truth: "we must take every situation, discover the appropriate tests to see if the belief corresponds to reality and use our minds and our senses to justify or even to disqualify the belief from being considered 'knowledge'."[54]

It is clear that the traditionalists can't agree among themselves as to what constitutes the ultimate test/s of truth. Some cannot even agree with their own writings on this matter. For example, Pinnock wrote dogmatically in the 1970's, asserting, "a biblical epistemology of religious knowledge...leans toward a correspondence view of truth, namely, that there exists a form of correspondence between belief and facts, against Van Til's idealist coherence theory that things are true if they hang together in a system."[55] Long ago Pinnock said the test for truth was "correspondence." But more recently Pinnock says just the opposite as he has defected against his own reasoning and apparently now sides with the once-despised Van Tillian "coherence" view. Pinnock more recently wrote, "I assume that the only way we can draw reliable conclusions from what we perceive is by thinking consistently and coherently about the data we encounter...We shall certainly try to observe the requirements of logic."[56]

Geisler is the most complex on this issue among the traditionalists and at times he's philosophically schizophrenic. Compare his many statements on the topic in some of the different writings he has produced:

- Early on Geisler summarized his tests for truth as follows: "We propose that *undeniability* is the test for the truth of a world view and *unaffirmability* is the test for the falsity of a world view."[57] He goes on to say, "...what is unaffirmably self-defeating is false. And, conversely, what is undeniable is true."[58] Furthermore, "...unaffirmability can falsify a world-view and undeniability can verify a world view."[59] Finally, he concludes, "As in almost everything else in life, probability is the guide. Whichever view *best* fits and is *most* consistent must suffice."[60]

- Later, he articulates the tests for truth this way: "All thinking...is governed by this foundational first principle of logic—the law of noncontradiction";[61] "...logic by itself will not help us find truth but will only help us detect error";[62] "...logic, by itself, can tell us what is false" (48);[63] "...coherence and correspondence will constitute our method of testing the truth claims of a particular worldview";[64] "Using logic and philosophy we have established the existence of a reality that is fixed and knowable."[65]

- Most recently, he put it this way: "...coherence is at best only a negative test for truth";[66] "Truth may be tested in many ways, but it should be understood in only one way, namely, as correspondence. There may be many different ways to *defend* different truth claims, but there is only one proper way to *define* truth."[67]

- Finally, Geisler makes this surprising statement that actually flies in the face of everything else he has said about the ultimate tests for truth: "the Bible and the Bible alone contains all doctrinal and ethical truth God has revealed to mankind. And the Bible alone is the canon or norm for all truth. All other alleged truth must be brought to the bar of Holy Scripture to be tested. The Bible and the Bible alone, all sixty-six books, has been confirmed by God through Christ to be his infallible Word."[68]

So for Geisler the tests for truth include undeniability plus unaffirmability, probability, consistency, the law of noncontradiction, coherence plus correspondence, logic and philosophy, and the Bible alone. Geisler does not want it both ways—he wants it all ways ...baffling, to say the least.

The common denominator for all the above traditional approaches to tests for truth is that unaided human reason is ultimate. Traditionalists say we determine something to be true or false by "thinking real hard." Such a proposition is futile and anemic. When it comes to the final authority on truth, God has spoken. He said, "rather, let God be found true, though every man be found a liar" (Rom 3:4).

The Missing Ingredient

The Christian theory of knowledge is rooted in the very character of God. God is, in the succinct words of Van Til, the infinite and eternal self-contained tri-personal Creator of the universe.[69] And this God has chosen of His own volition to sovereignly reveal Himself to His creation. The matter of epistemology cannot be discussed apart from addressing the matter of God's independent, divine "revelation," both the possibility and process by which they occur. This is really the same starting point as that of Van Til when he wrote, "We have constantly emphasized the concept of God as being basic to everything else a Christian believes"[70] And the same is true with regard to the question at hand, namely, true knowledge and the possibility of knowing.

I concede with Van Til's premise that the theory of knowledge cannot be addressed apart from the theory of being (ontology), for our knowledge will be true knowledge only to the extent that it corresponds to the character of God and the knowledge of God as revealed in the Scriptures. But let it be said first of all that the possibility for even grappling with the issues of reality and knowledge are rooted in the fact that God is a revealing God, and He has taken the initiative to reveal Himself to man. This is first seen in Genesis 1:28. After having created man in His own image (1:26-27), we read, "God said to them...." God could have created Adam and Eve and then left them helplessly to themselves without a divine interpretation of reality. But rather, as can be seen throughout Scripture, God's relationship with humanity is depicted as initiatory through the process of divine revelation, which amounts to divine interpretation. This is precisely the view of Calvin who wrote, "God himself must bear witness to himself from heaven...we are deficient in natural powers which might enable us to rise to a pure and clear knowledge of God...God himself being the only fit witness to himself."[71]

For us today, that divine revelation is in the Bible. It is the key to unlocking all the true knowledge with regard to God and man. It is the interpretive basis for the four key categories of epistemology. These are, according to Van Til, as follows: (1) God's knowledge of Himself; (2) God's knowledge of the world; (3) man's knowledge of God; (4) man's knowledge of the universe.[72]

The Bible is the record of God's revelations to man, the greatest of which came in the person of Jesus Christ. The question of epistemology is meaningless apart from Jesus, for in Him are hidden "all the treasures of wisdom and knowledge" (Col 2:3). Jesus is "the light of the world" (John 8:12). He is "the truth" (John 14:6), despite what Christian apologist, Hardy writes, when he asserts, "truth...is not a person; it is a property of sentences."[73] Jesus, the Truth, came that He might reveal and "explain" God (John 1:18), and hence interpret correctly "being" and "knowledge."

Ultimate Tests for Truth

We reject the traditional tests for truth, the laws of logic, as being ultimate for the reasons shown above. Instead we champion the biblical tests for truth as ultimate. These constitute the Christian apologist's epistemological arsenal and starting point for vetting truth from error. And they are the same tests of truth that Jesus wielded, along with His apostles and even the Old Testament spokesmen for God Almighty. They are as follows:

- God determines what is true (Rom 3:4).
- The Holy Spirit determines what is true (John 14:17; 16:13).
- Jesus determines what is true (John 14:6).
- The gospel determines what is true (2 Cor 4:3-6; Col 1:5).
- Scripture determines what is true (Ps 119:160; 2 Tim 3:16-17).

A couple observations are in order. First, these tests for truth parallel the earlier ingredients for a biblical definition of truth. This is intentional! Unlike traditional apologists who want to create a false dichotomy between a *definition* of truth and a *defense* of the truth,[74] the Bible and Jesus never allow such an artificial distinction. Van Til properly diagnosed a fatal flaw in the traditional model of apologetics in that it routinely made epistemology and ontology mutually exclusive and independent of one another. But they are not. Jesus identified Himself as, "I Am" (John 8:58). That is the most concise, yet potent and complete explication of an epistemological reality

(Jesus was self-consciously aware and knowledgeable of who He was; He had self-attesting knowledge of Himself as eternal God) ever articulated. And it was based on the greatest ontological reality in the universe—the very being and essence of the eternal God-man. With respect to truth, epistemology and ontology cannot be separated, but are inextricably united.

Second, the above tenets seem at first blush quite simplistic—not very highfalutin, academic, philosophical, profound, inaccessible or etymologically baggage-laden. That is a beautiful thing, not a weakness. It is a reminder that God communicates with His creatures in the "language of the people." God speaks with perspicuity and He gives His written revelation with clarity and simplicity as well. God wants us to understand. Contrary to what George Bush said in his pre-presidential debate, Jesus was not a philosopher—He was a theologian and exegete—a Hebrew rabbi (John 1:38) and a man of the people, a Friend of sinners (Luke 7:34). He spoke in language they could understand and obey (Matt 6:26; 7:28-29).

Jesus and Scriptural Apologetics

Jesus always used the above tenets as His tests for truth, without exception, when confronting unbelief. Most frequently He referred to the Scriptures as the final litmus test for truth and error. And not just strictly with believing audiences. Actually Jesus used the Scriptures just as frequently with unbelieving skeptics. Traditional apologists give the impression that the only unbelievers around were agnostics or full-blooded atheists. An unbeliever is an unbeliever, whether one is a theist, moralist, polytheist, agnostic or atheist. They are all on equal footing before God—lost in the blinding darkness of their own sin. That is why Jesus addressed them all in the same manner, by the same standard of authority for truth—God's Word, the Bible—written Scripture.

Jesus believed the Old Testament to be the authoritative Word of God. He was called Rabbi (John 3:2), and was therefore a master of the Old Testament, known in His day as the "Law and the Prophets" (Luke 16:16; cf. 24:27). Jesus believed the Scriptures, had Scripture memorized, taught the Scriptures, preached the Scriptures, obeyed the Scriptures, and fulfilled the Scriptures. They were the epicenter and circumference of His life, works, words and mission. One theologian rightly observes,

What role did the Bible have in the life of the Lord Jesus? He quoted Scripture from memory, argued from Scripture, taught from Scripture, chided his opponents for not reading or understanding the SCRIPTURE. He never appealed to (1) TRADITION, (2) EXPERIENCE, (3) or PHILOSOPHY. Time and time again Jesus explained why He was doing something by QUOTING SCRIPTURE and showing His life was in harmony with the WRITTEN WORD.[75]

One of Jesus' favorite statements was, "It is written...." It was a phrase He repeated so often (thirty times in the Gospels) that it was second nature to His teaching (cf. Matt 4:7, 10; 21:13; 26:31; John 6:31, 45; 10:34, etc.). For example, in Matthew 4:4 He rebuts the devil with the statement, "It is written," [Gk. *gegraptai*]; this is a perfect passive indicative and means, "it stands written and is still in force."[76] The perfect indicative emphasizes ongoing, continuous results. "There is a grand and solid objectivity about the perfect tense, *gegraptai*, 'It stands written'. 'Here,' Jesus was saying, 'is the permanent, unchangeable witness of the eternal God, committed to writing for our instruction.'"[77] What was written in the Old Testament has a past, completed action with ongoing, continuous results. In other words, Jesus was saying, "Even though the Scripture was written long ago, its truth is still absolutely binding, authoritative and sufficient for today." The Old Testament Scriptures, although written long before Jesus preached, still remained binding and authoritative. By this phrase, then, Jesus was making an appeal to the authority of the Hebrew Scriptures as God's authoritative word on any matter.

In Matthew 15:4 Jesus said, "For God said..." and then goes on to quote Exodus 20:12 and 21:17. Here is the most explicit statement of all showing that Jesus believed the Scriptures were the very words of God (cf. Mark 7:5-13). Other similarly emphatic statements that Jesus made regarding the authority of the written Hebrew Scriptures include John 10:35 ("the Scripture cannot be broken"), John 17:17 ("Your word is truth"), and when He said eleven times to His critics, "Have you not read..."—a phrase showing Jesus' commitment to Scriptural authority as well as its perspicuity.

Whether bantering with well-educated, erudite religious Jews (John 8:41-59), skeptical syncretistic Samaritans (John 4), a Gentile woman (Mark 7:24-30), or a pagan Roman soldier (Matt 8:5-13), Jesus never resorted to the Greek laws of logic or Aristotelian syllogisms to determine what was true or to seek common epistemological ground with unbelievers. His approach was always the same—He spoke spiritual truth—divine revelation—in an authoritative manner (John 4:19). He called people to believe in heavenly truth, which answered ultimate metaphysical questions, knowing that if they embraced His spiritual truth then it would set them free (John 8:32). In His apologetical and evangelistic altercation with the Samaritan woman, He did not say, "Now let's be purely logical here. For the sake of argument and neutrality, let's refrain from all allusion and innuendo to religious and spiritual matters." Not! Instead He gave her the gospel. He told her who He, Jesus the Savior, was; He exposed her sin; He showed her the need to be saved; He offered her eternal life based on grace through faith; He taught Scripture as authoritative and universally binding. Jesus is the Master apologist.

Sola Scriptura!

One of the main doctrines that traditional apologists undermine is the doctrine of "biblical sufficiency" or what the Reformers called *sola Scriptura*.[78] Grudem says,

> The sufficiency of Scripture means that Scripture contained all the words of God he intended his people to have at each stage of redemptive history, and that it now contains all the words of God we need for salvation, for trusting him perfectly, and for obeying him perfectly.[79]

The time-tested doctrine of biblical sufficiency says everything we need to know is in the Bible—not everything that can be known. The Bible is enough! The classic New Testament text on sufficiency is 2 Timothy 3:16-17: "All Scripture is inspired [God-breathed] by God and profitable for teaching, for reproof, for correction, for training in righteousness; so that the man of God may be adequate, equipped ["thoroughly equipped" NIV; "competent" ESV;] for every good work."

Notice the Bible is sufficient to equip or prepare every Christian "for every good work." "Every good work" includes the work of apologetics. Everything we need to know about defending the faith (1 Pet 3:15), for advancing and defending the gospel, is in Scripture.

Biblical apologetics entails "reproof," "correction," and "teaching." Second Timothy 3:16 says the Bible is "adequate" for such a task.

Traditional apologists tell us the Bible is not sufficient for the work of apologetics, and that we cannot even use the Bible when beginning apologetics with an unbeliever. They say we need to begin with human logic. They tell us we can't begin with gospel proclamation. We need to begin with philosophy and pre-evangelism. They say the Bible is not sufficient, for the Bible first has to be proven to be true in the mind of the unbeliever. Yet Jesus began His ministry from day one with gospel proclamation and the presupposed self-attesting authority of divine revelation: "Jesus came into Galilee, preaching the gospel of God, and saying, 'The time is fulfilled, and the kingdom of God is at hand; repent and believe in the gospel'" (Mark 1:14-15).

Scripture is Alive

Traditional apologists tell us the Bible must be tested to prove that it is true. Biblical apologetics says we use the Bible to test all things to see if they are true. Traditionalists tell us the laws of logic are absolute; God says His Word is absolute (Ps 119:89). Traditionalists tell us that we cannot know truth with certainty; God tells us we can know truth with certitude as we search the Scriptures (1 John 5:13). Sproul says logic is preeminent, God says His Word is preeminent (Ps 138:2). Craig says Scripture's authority is secondary and "derivative"; God says Scripture's authority is primary and inherent and that it is the very breath of God (2 Tim 3:16), the very incarnation of God's thoughts and will. Traditionalists tell us the Bible must pass the test of historiography; God says His Word determines history, and the future (Isa 46:8-11). Traditionalists tell us the Bible stands on equal footing with all other literature to be tested; God says His Word is eternal! (Ps 19:9)

Traditionalists tell us that unbelievers must first accept the Bible before it does its work; God says Scripture does its work despite human resistance and ignorance, for it is living and active. Scripture is dynamically creating (Ps 33:6), convicting (James 2:9), judging (Heb 4:12), piercing (Heb 4:12), being feared (Exod 9:20), being fulfilled (Isa 55:11), being obeyed (Ps 103:20), saving (1 Pet 1:23), sanctifying (Ps 105:19; 119:9), residing in believers (Ps 119:11), healing (Ps 107:20), illuminating (Ps 119:18), counseling (Ps 119:24), feeding (Isa 55:1-3), reviving (Ps 119:50), sustaining (Ps 119:116), guiding (Ps

119), consoling (Ps 119:28), imparting joy (Ps 119:35), and teaching (Ps 119:71). The Bible is alive!

God's Wrecking Ball

When the Bereans wanted to test Paul's words to see if they were true, they used the Bible as the grid—Scripture was the test of truth. They were "examining the Scriptures daily, to see whether these things were so" (Acts 17:11). When Paul reasoned with skeptics and unbelievers about religious truths and ultimate realities (Acts 17:17), he "reasoned with them from the Scriptures" (Acts 17:2). This is how we do apologetics: we filter everything through the grid of the Word of God, the Bible. We don't jettison "reason." Rather, we "reason with the Scriptures" or "reason from the Scriptures." Biblical apologetics is not mystical fideism; it uses the "reason" of God found in Scripture.

When confronted with antagonistic Muslims, atheists, humanists or Marxists, we expose their error using Scripture. When God commands us to "examine everything carefully; hold fast to that which is good; abstain from every form of evil" (1 Thess 5:21-22), we use Scripture to do so. False teaching, aberrant theology and humanistic ideologies are "evil" and need to be exposed. We do that with the searchlight of the Scriptures. We are obligated to scrutinize and discriminate everything coming down the pike in terms of philosophies, theologies, ideologies and worldviews.

One of the most important apologetics passages in the Bible, on a par with 1 Peter 3:15, is 2 Corinthians 10:3-6. Like the verses above, it is a call for all Christians to use the truth of God's Word, Scripture, as a test for truth. It reads as follows:

> ³For though we walk in the flesh, we do not war according to the flesh, ⁴for the weapons of our warfare are not of the flesh, but divinely powerful for the destruction of fortresses. ⁵We are destroying speculations and every lofty thing raised up against the knowledge of God, and we are taking every thought captive to the obedience of Christ, ⁶and we are ready to punish all disobedience, whenever your obedience is complete.

This passage is a complement to 1 Peter 3:15. Peter emphasizes evangelistic and responsive apologetics, whereas this passage emphasizes iconoclastic and aggressive apologetics. We need both. One is more offensive, the other defensive. One is positive, the other protective. Both are driven by the truth of Scripture.

Second Corinthians 10 exudes the theme of "warfare." Today it is politically uncouth to speak of Christianity in the terms of "Crusades," for that might offend the other religions of the world, or even the non-religious zealots. But there is no getting around the militaristic nature of this biblical imperative. Yet this is not temporal warfare, but rather spiritual warfare that transpires in the realm of ideas and ideologies, in the minds of people and in the invisible heavenlies where angels and demons roam and rampage (cf. Dan 10:10-20; Eph 1:20-21; 2:2). Notice the terms of warfare here: "war," "weapons," "warfare," "destruction," "fortresses," "taking...captive," "ready to punish." When it comes to antagonists to the faith, we are at war (2 Tim 2:3). And eternal souls are at stake.

The goal in apologetics according to this passage is taking our own thoughts captive while destroying the false thoughts and teachings of the enemy. Our thought life and what we believe is to be in subjection, or, "obedience to Christ." "Obedience to Christ" means "in accordance with the teachings of Christ, which are found in Scripture." The Bible is the test for truth. The "enemy" we are at war with is false teaching, false ideologies, errant theology, and humanistic philosophies which Paul calls "speculations." Modern day speculations would include evolution, naturalism, humanism, Islam, socialism, environmentalism, Marxism, materialism, postmodernism, progressivism, Hinduism, and Buddhism, to name a few.

The Christian is not supposed to accommodate, assimilate, contextualize, adapt, welcome or even tolerate these sinister ideologies. Rather, Paul says we are to demolish, eviscerate and smash them. Someone once said the purpose of war was, "to break and kill things." That is what we are supposed to do with false religion and anti-Christian worldviews—and we do this in the realm of ideas with preaching, teaching, admonishing, warning, rebuking and correcting...with the Scriptures. The Bible is God's wrecking-ball of truth against falsehood, deception and error. We need to tenaciously defend the gospel of Christ and intellectually smash and destroy all competitors—unlike traditional apologist Clark Pinnock, who wants Christians to embrace the "good" in all false religions, like Hinduism, Islam and Buddhism.[80] Ironically, Pinnock calls on Christians to "dismantle" the teachings of Christian presuppositionalists and to "oppose Van Til." Pinnock has his guns pointed in the wrong direction!

One pastor summarizes the implication of the battle well:

> The fortresses in view here are not demons, but ideologies…The battle is with the false ideologies men and demons propagate so that the world believes them. Doomed souls are inside their fortresses of ideas, which become their prisons and eventually their tombs—unless they are delivered from them by belief in the truth …Spiritual warfare is not a battle with demons. It is a battle for the minds of people who are captive to lies that are exalted in opposition to Scripture. In 1 Corinthians 3:20, he called them the useless reasonings of the worldy wise—all the anti-biblical ideologies, false religions, and pseudo gospels spawned by Satan…The objective of our warfare is to change how people think—taking every thought they have and making no longer captive to a damning ideology, but captive to the obedience of Christ.[81]

It's time to take the gloves off in the battle for truth and for the souls of men. Not only is Satan ceaselessly on the prowl, his minions on earth who are in blatant opposition to Christ are becoming more emboldened and vocal every day. There has been a flood of best-selling books on atheism and humanism in the past several years. Listen to the leader of the pack, Richard Dawkins, as he froths at the mouth in his animus toward God:

> The God of the Old Testament is arguably the most unpleasant character in all fiction: jealous and proud of it, a petty, unjust, unforgiving control-freak; a vindictive, bloodthirsty ethnic cleanser; a misogynistic, homophobic, racist, infanticidal, genocidal, filicidal, pestilential, megalomaniacal, sadomasochistic, capriciously malevolent bully.[82]

He takes blasphemy to unprecedented lows, and has now made them mainstream. Hence the need, more than ever, for a robust gospel-centered, Bible-driven, Christ-exalting, Spirit-charged, heresy-smashing reformation from the Church of Jesus Christ in biblical apologetics.

Summary

Epistemology is the study of truth and how we know truth. One's view of epistemology will influence and drive one's apologetical methodology. Traditional apologetics has a vastly different epistemology than biblical apologetics. The two disagree on a theory of truth, the tests of truth, the role of Scripture in determining ultimate truth and the role of Scripture in apologetics.

Cornelius Van Til popularized a form of presuppostional apologetics in the 20th century, its greatest contribution being a framework for a biblical epistemology and its unmasking of the follies of traditional apologetics' rationalistic approach to epistemology and the pursuit of truth. Traditional apologetics argues that human reason is ultimate; Van Til argued that God and Scripture are ultimate.

Traditionalists define "truth" irrespective of God. Biblical apologetics asserts that truth is that which corresponds to reality as defined and determined by God. God is truth and therefore truth cannot be defined irrespective of God and His revelation. Traditionalists cannot agree among themselves as to what the tests for truth entail. Biblical apologetics says the tests of truth are God Himself, the Holy Spirit, Jesus, Scripture and the gospel.

Jesus used divine revelation, and Scripture in particular, as the test for truth. His favorite saying when He taught was, "It stands written…." Jesus knew Scripture was sufficient for every human need, including the tasks of evangelism, apologetics, teaching and preaching. We need to follow Jesus' model in our bibliology and our apologetics. When we engage in the duty of apologetics, we need to reason "from the Scriptures." Part of that duty is defensive, aggressive apologetics. Second Corinthians 10:3-6 is paradigmatic in this regard. We are in the middle of an ongoing spiritual battle in the realm of ideas. How we think about truth is determinative of our eternal destiny. As such, the Christian is obligated to confront falsehood and all thinking and teaching contrary to the gospel of Christ with a relentless tenacity and precision, exposing and putting down error while exalting the truth of God in Scripture and in Christ.

Notes

1. Norman L. Geisler, *Baker Encyclopedia of Christian Apologetics* (Grand Rapids: Baker Academic, 2006), 214-15.

2. Steven B. Cowan, *Five Views on Apologetics* (Grand Rapids: Zondervan, 2000), 21.

3. Richard Dawkins, *The God Delusion* (New York: Houghton Mifflin, 2006), 282.

4. R. C. Sproul, *Defending Your Faith* (Wheaton, IL: Crossway, 2003), 29.

5. Bernard Ramm, *Varieties of Christian Apologetics* (Grand Rapids: Baker, 1962; 1976), 14.

6. Gordon Lewis, *Testing Christianity's Truth Claims: Approaches to Christian Apologetics* (Chicago: Moody, 1976).

7. Cowan, *Five Views*, 9.

8. Paul Feinberg, "A Cumulative Case Apologist's Response," *Five Views*, 249.

9. Kelly James Clark, "A Reformed Epistemologist's Response," Five Views, 256.

10. Greg L. Bahnsen, *Van Til's Apologetic: Readings & Analysis* (Phillipsburg, NJ: P & R, 1998), 144-404.

11. Greg L. Bahnsen, *Always Ready: Directions for Defending the Faith*, ed. Robert R. Booth (Texarkana, AR: Covenant Media Foundation, 1996), 3-106. This book was published posthumously as Bahnsen died in 1995 from complications after his third open-heart surgery; he was 47. Bahnsen earned his PhD is philosophy at USC in 1978. His dissertation was a masterful study in epistemology titled, "A Conditional Resolution of the Apparent Paradox of Self-Deception"; *The Standard Bearer: A Festschrift for Greg L. Bahnsen*, ed. Steven M. Schlissel (Nacogdoches, TX: Covenant Media Foundation, 2002), 17.

12. William Lane Craig, "A Classical Apologist's Response," *Five Views*, 235.

13. Ibid., 232.

14. R. C. Sproul, John Gerstner and Arthur Lindsley, *Classical Apologetics: A Rational Defense of the Christian Faith and a Critique of Presuppositional Apologetics* (Grand Rapids, MI: Zondervan Publishing House, 1984), 75. They utilize Plantinga's bombastic diatribe to concoct their caricature of Van Til. Overall, Geisler was more objective, fair and "Christian" in his critique of Van Til, acknowledging at length Van Til's positive contributions and, unlike Sproul's assessment, Geisler rightly says, "Van Til defended the formal laws of logic..." and concludes, "He was not an irrationalist," *Baker Encyclopedia*, 754.

15. Clark H. Pinnock, "The Philosophy of Christian Evidences," *Jerusalem and Athens: Critical Discussions on the Philosophy and Apologetics of Cornelius Van Til,* ed. E. R. Geehan (Phillipsburg, NJ: P & R, 1971), 423-24.

16. Ibid., 425.

17. John Warwick Montgomery, "Once Upon an *A Priori*," *Jerusalem and Athens*, 384.

18. Clark, *Five Views*, 256.

19. Ibid.

20. Bahnsen, *Van Til's Apologetic*, 676; similarly, Bahnsen declared, "God's revelation [i.e., Scripture] is more than the best foundation for Christian reasoning: it is the only philosophically sound foundation for any reasoning whatsoever," ibid, 4-5.

21. Cf. Craig, *Five Views*, 241-42; Clark, *Five Views*, 370-70; Norman L. Geisler, *Christian Apologetics* (Grand Rapids: Baker, 1999), 61; Sproul *et al*, *Classical Apologetics*, 212 ff.; Gordon R. Lewis, "Van Til and Carnell," *Jerusalem and Athens*, 359.

22. Bahnsen, *Van Til's Apologetic*, 65.

23. Bahnsen, *Always Ready*, 91.

24. Ibid., 5.

25. Ibid., 92.

26. Ibid. We saw earlier in chapter four that Craig rejects the Bible's self-authenticating nature. He believes the Bible has only "derivative" authority and not "inherent" authority; Craig's bibliology is neoorthodox. Reymond ably articulates the orthodox position on the Bible's self-authenticating nature: " 'the Holy Scripture…doth abundantly evidence itself to be the word of God'…(WCF, I/v)…This article asserts both the Bible's self-authenticating, self-evidencing, self-attesting, self-validating character as the Word of God and yet also the necessity of the Holy Spirit's saving work if one is to believe it savingly. It recognizes that the Word of God would, of necessity, have to be self-authenticating, self-attesting and self-validating, for if it needed anyone or anything else to authenticate and validate its divine character—based on the principle that the validating source is always the higher and final authority (see Heb. 6:13)—it would not be the Word of God…the Bible's ultimate attestation as God's Word does not derive from human or church testimony. Rather, the Bible carries within its own bosom, so to speak, its own divine *indicia*. John Calvin in the Latin version of his *Institutes* states (using Greek) that Scripture is *autopiston*, that is, "self-authenticating" (I.7.5). In the French version of the same work he affirms that the Scripture "carries with[in] itself its [own] credentials." He goes on to quote Berkhof: "The testimony of the Holy Spirit is therefore, strictly speaking, not so much the final

ground of faith, but rather the means of faith. The final ground of faith is Scripture only, or better still, the authority of God which is impressed upon the believer in the testimony of Scripture. The ground of faith is identical with its contents, and cannot be separated from it. But the testimony of the Holy Spirit is the moving cause of faith. We believe Scripture, not because of, but through the testimony of the Holy Spirit"; Robert L. Reymond, *A New Systematic Theology of the Christian Faith*, (Nashville, TN: Thomas Nelson, 1998), 79-80, 82.

27. Bahnsen, *Always Ready*, 104.

28. Ibid., 104-05 *Always Ready*; cf. Greg Bahnsen, *Presuppositional Apologetics: Stated and Defended*, ed. Joel McDurmon (Nacogdoches, TX: Covenant Media Press, 2008), 275-78.

29. John Calvin, *The Institutes of the Christian Religion*, trans. by Henry Beveridge (Peabody, Mass.: Hendrickson Publishers, 2009), 31, 33.

30. Cf. Christopher Hitchens, *God is Not Great: How Religion Poisons Everything* (New York: Hachette, 2007), 3. Hitchens writes with unmitigated, vitriolic blasphemy like few have, calling Jesus "sinister," among other countless irreverent, gushing virulent quips. Ironically he proves the Word of God to be true all the more, unknowingly fulfilling prophecy to a tee; Paul wrote of God-haters like Hitchens 2,000 years ago: "But realize this, that in the last days difficult times will come. For men will be lovers of self, lovers of money, boastful, arrogant, revilers...haters of good...reckless, conceited, lovers of pleasure rather than lovers of God" (2 Tim 3:1-4). Elsewhere Paul writes, "Their throat is an open grave, with their tongues they keep deceiving, the poison of asps is under their lips, whose mouth is full of cursing and bitterness...There is no fear of God before their eyes" (Rom 3:13-14, 18).

31. Norman L. Geisler and Peter Bocchino, *Unshakable Foundations: Contemporary Answers to Crucial Questions about the Christian Faith* (Minneapolis, MN: Bethany House, 2001), 33.

32. Norman L. Geisler, *Systematic Theology*, 4 vols. (Minneapolis, MN: Bethany House, 2002), I:114.

33. Geisler, *Baker Encyclopedia*, 745.

34. J. P. Moreland and William Lane Craig, *Philosophical Foundations for a Christian Worldview* (Downers Grove, IL: InterVarsity, 2003), 130.

35. Dean Hardy, *Stand Your Ground: An Introductory Text for Apologetics Students* (Eugene, OR: Wipf & Stock, 2007), 41.

36. Kruger exposes further examples of such *a*-theistic, relativistic and subjective views of truth in Evangelical circles. One example he exposes is in *Christian Apologetics in a Postmodern World* (1995), where one Christian apologist rejects objective truth outright. Kruger warns the reader, "A

specific instance of this is the article by Phillip D. Kenneson entitled, 'There's No Such Thing As Objective Truth, and It's a Good Thing Too.' As the title promises, Kenneson denies the concept of objective truth, and even suggests that such a concept is "corrupting the church." Kenneson also says, 'I realize there are plenty of Christians who think it makes good sense to say the proposition, "Jesus Christ is Lord of the universe" is objectively true; that is, our temptation is to insist that this is simply true whether we or anyone else believe it or not. But succumbing to such a temptation is deadly for the church. There is no place to stand and judge this statement as true per se'," Michael J. Kruger, "The Sufficiency of Scripture in Apologetics," *TMSJ*, 12/1, Spring 2001, 74. Potterie eloquently exposes such a sterile and biblically naïve definition of "truth" by noting the following: "Today's language calls a thought or word true when it conforms to the real. Something which has reality is itself called true when it reveals itself, when it is clear and evident to the intellect...This strictly intellectual Greek approach is ordinarily operative among us. But the Bible conceived truth differently. The biblical notion of truth is founded on the religious experience of encounter with God...in the NT truth will be the fullness of revelation hovering about the point of concentration, the person of Christ." Ignace de la Potterie, "Truth," *Dictionary of Biblical Theology*, ed. Xavier Leon-Dufour (Ijamsville, Maryland: The Word Among Us Press, 2000), 618.

37. Bahnsen, *Always Ready*, 3-13.

38. Moreland *et al.*, *Philosophical Foundations*, 131.

39. George J. Zemek, *The Word of God in the Child of God: Exegetical, Theological, and Homiletical Reflections from the 119th Psalm*, (Mango, FL: George J. Zemek, George Zemek, n.d.), 347-348.

40. Potterie gives a beautiful, compact summary of the fully-orbed biblical definition of truth: "The Christian meaning of *truth* therefore, is not the boundless area of being which we must conquer by the powers of the mind. It is the truth of the Gospel, the revealing Word of the Father, present in Jesus Christ and illuminated by the Spirit, which we must welcome in faith, so that it may transform our lives. This truth shines out for us in the person of Christ who is at once the mediator and the fullness of revelation; and it is in the sacred books that this truth of salvation is passed on to us authentically," *Biblical Theology*, 621. Similarly, Carver writes, "Truth is reality in relation to the vital interests of the soul. It is primarily something to be realized and done, rather than something to be learned or known. In the largest aspect it is God's nature finding expression in His creation, in revelation, in Jesus Christ in whom "grace and truth came" (Jn **1** 17), and finally in man apprehending, accepting and

practically realizing the essential values of life, which are the will of God (Jn **1** 14; **8** 32; **17** 19; **18** 37f; 1 Jn **2** 21; **3** 19). Truth is personalized in Jesus Christ. He truly expresses God, presents the true ideal of man, in Himself summarizes the harmony of existence and becomes the agent for unifying the disordered world. Hence He is the Truth (Jn **14** 6), the true expression ("Logos," Jn **1** 1), of God...Truth is presented in Scripture as a chief element in the nature of God (Ps **31** 5; Isa **65** 16. But this quality is never given as an abstract teaching but only as qualifying God in His relations and activities....It is always important to keep in mind that truth in religion is not primarily an intellectualistic affair, to be cognized, but is essentially a voluntaristic experience and duty to be done for the glory of God in the realization of the complete truth of God. Jesus Christ as the truth of God becomes the standard and test for truth in the religion of men," William Owen Carver, *The International Standard Bible Encyclopedia*, 5 Vols. ed. James Orr (Chicago: The Howard-Severance Company, 1930), V: 3026.

41. Josh McDowell and Thomas Williams, *In Search of Christianity* (Holiday, FL: Green Key, 2003), 134.

42. Ibid., 24.

43. Sproul *et al.*, *Classical Apologetics*, 223.

44. Geisler, *Systematic Theology*, I: 90. In contradistinction to Geisler, Guillet acutely notes, "Since 'the beginning' (Gn 1,1), God exists and His existence forces itself upon us as an initial fact which needs no other explanation. God had no origin, no becoming. The OT does not know those theogonies which, in the religions of the ancient East, explain the beginning of the world by the birth of the gods. Because He alone is 'the first and the last' (Is 41,4; 44,6; 48,12), the world is entirely His work, His creation. Because He is first, God does not have to introduce Himself. He demands recognition by man's spirit through the sole fact that He is God. In no way should there be the thought of a discovery of God, a graduated approach of man resulting in the acknowledgement of His existence. To know Him is to be known (cf Am 3, 2) and to discover Him at the source of one's own existence...Because God is first, as soon as he makes Himself known His personality, His reactions, His plans are sharply defined...This absolute priority of God is expressed in the traditions of the Pentateuch...," Jacques Guillet, *Dictionary of Biblical Theology*, 206.

45. Edward John Carnell, *An Introduction to Christian Apologetics: A Philosophical Defense of the Trinitarian-Theistic Faith* (Grand Rapids: Eerdmans, 1956), 57.

46. Ibid., 63.

47. Feinberg, *Five Views*, 156.

48. Moreland *et al.*, *Philosophical Foundations*, 132.

49. Sproul, *Defending the Faith*, 30.

50. McDowell *et al.*, *In Search of,* 134.

51. Ibid., 25.

52. Ibid., 41.

53. Montgomery, *Jerusalem and Athens*, 390.

54. Hardy, *Stand Your Ground*, 52.

55. Pinnock, *Jerusalem and Athens*, 421.

56. Clark H. Pinnock, *Reason Enough: A Case for the Christian Faith*, (Eugene, OR: Wipf and Stock, 1997), 17.

57. Geisler, *Christian Apologetics*, 141.

58. Ibid., 143.

59. Ibid., 145.

60. Ibid., 146.

61. Geisler *et al.*, *Unshakable Foundations*, 23.

62. Ibid., 28.

63. Ibid., 48.

64. Ibid., 49.

65. Ibid., 52.

66. Geisler, *Systematic Theology*, I:111.

67. Ibid., 118.

68. Geisler, *Christian Apologetics*, 376-77. Geisler arrives at this assertion in an *a posteriori* manner, for it is at the conclusion of his book. The Bible is said to be God's Word because it passed the tests of undeniability and unaffirmability.

69. Cornelius Van Til, *The Defense of the Faith* (Phillipsburg, NJ: P & R, 1967), 9-13.

70. Ibid., 42-43. In a weak moment, Geisler briefly slips into a presuppositional mode, conceding to Van Til, saying, "Unless God sovereignly wills to reveal himself, we would be in complete ignorance. Revelation, whether general or special, is the source of all truth," *Baker Encyclopedia*, 754. This is just one example of Geisler's philosophical schizophrenia we re-ferred to earlier.

71. Calvin, *Institutes*, 24-25, 50.

72. Van Til, 35-46.

73. Hardy, *Stand Your Ground*, 32.

74. Geisler, *Baker Encyclopedia*, 746; cf. Craig, *Five Views*, 54.

75. Marc T. Mueller, "Bibliology: The Doctrine of Authority" (*The Master's Seminary*, class syllabus, 1989), 5; Jesus referred to the OT at least 64 times in the Gospels, and always as authoritative truth.

76. A. T. Robertson, *Word Pictures in the New Testament*, 6 vols. (Grand Rapids: Baker, 1930), I:31.

77. John W. Wenham, *Inerrancy*, ed. Norman L. Geisler (Grand Rapids: Zondervan, 1980), 15.

78. The phrase *sola Scriptura* is a by-product of the Reformation, but the truth of it comes from the Bible, both the Old and New Testaments. *Sola Scriptura* means "by Scripture alone" and when used by the Reformers it meant that the Bible was the sole authority, and was sufficient, for religious and spiritual truth for the church, over against the Pope, church councils or the traditions of men. When the Scripture spoke, God spoke.

79. Wayne Grudem, *Systematic Theology: An Introduction to Biblical Doctrine* (Grand Rapids: Zondervan, 1994), 127. Another simple way of explaining the sufficiency of Scripture is to say, "Between the Scriptures and the indwelling Holy Spirit, the believer needs no additional revelation to be informed on how to live the Christian life," John MacArthur and Richard Mayhue, *Biblical Doctrine: A Systematic Summary of Bible Truth* (Wheaton: Crossway, 2017), 105. Kruger writes, "as the church has slowly abandoned its commitment to the sufficiency of Scripture, nowhere has it been more evident than in the area of apologetics," Michael J. Kruger, "The Sufficiency of Scripture in Apologetics," *TMSJ*, 12/1, Spring 2001, 70.

80. Clark H. Pinnock, "An Inclusivist View," *Four Views on Salvation in a Pluralistic World*, ed. Dennis L. Okholm and Timothy R. Phillips (Grand Rapids: Zondervan, 1996), 110.

81. John MacArthur, *2 Corinthians: The MacArthur New Testament Commentary* (Chicago: Moody, 2003), 329-30.

82. Dawkins, *Delusion*, 31.

6

Hamartiological Hangovers: Barriers to Belief

Why do critics of Christianity reject the Bible and the faith? Why won't they believe? Traditional evangelical apologists have a few answers. They will typically say something like, "What unbelievers need is a little more information, or a tighter logical argument, or a few more archaeological discoveries, or an iron-clad, high-resolution theistic argument, or a symphony of scientific theorems, theories and discoveries. If they have more of this then maybe they will believe." These suggestions all have one thing in common—it is assumed that the greatest roadblock preventing a non-Christian from believing is ignorance. And the remedy for removing ignorance is persuasive or coercive information. It is that simple, so we are told.

But that does not reflect reality. The Bible gives a radically different reason for explaining why antagonists don't believe in Christianity or the Bible. They don't believe because of two spiritual realities: (1) personal sinfulness and (2) satanic blindness.

Note an example of the typical approach and explanation of why a non-Christian will not believe the truth:

> It goes without saying that unbelievers are opposed to the gospel. For a multitude of reasons, they simply will not accept its truth. They have convinced themselves that it is something not worth believing—for them, it lacks plausibility. So, part of what we want to do in our discussion is to take what we can of what they do believe, and incorporate that into the truth of the gospel. In that

way we join together what they think is completely separate.

If you just present valid Christian arguments to the
non-Christian, you will be met by stark disagreement. But
if you adopt in your argumentation something that your
opponent has agreed is true, then your other points may
sound more credible.[1]

There are many things wrong with this diagnosis of why non-
Christians don't believe; and his advice on how to overcome the
problem of unbelief is riddled with faulty assumptions as well. But a
couple points will suffice to highlight the main point.

First, there are NOT "a multitude of reasons" why unbelievers
oppose the gospel—only two: a darkened mind from personal sinfulness and satanic blindness. This author refers to neither in the greater
context of his discussion.

Second, this scholarly Christian apologist suggests that if we just
come across arguing with more "plausibility" and make our arguments "sound more credible" then belief may result. Such a notion is
shallow and truncates the Bible's heavenly diagnosis of the true problem of unbelief.

Similarly, in the popular book, *Five Views on Apologetics*, four of the
authors hardly mention sin as an issue to be discussed in the study,
methodology and implications of apologetics and all five authors fail
to mention anything at all about the reality of satanic blindness that
darkens the mind and heart of the unbeliever. Christian philosopher
Kelly James Clark does not refer to "satanic blindness" that inhibits
the unbeliever's ability to understand spiritual truths because he does
not believe Satan is real.[2] John Frame, who represents the presuppositional view in the book, aditted to me in a class discussion that he
had never thought much about satanic blindness with respect to
epistemology and its noetic implications on the unbeliever's ability to
think about spiritual truths. His comment was a result of me pointing
him to the reality of 2 Corinthians 4:4, which explicitly teaches that
Satan blinds unbelievers, inhibiting their ability to reason properly
about gospel truths apart from the intervention of the Holy Spirit.
See the following chart which clearly shows the utter disregard that
the five authors have regarding sinful and satanic blindness:

Five Views on Apologetics: Indifference to Spiritual Blindness

Author	Length of article	References to "sin"	References to "satanic blindness"
W. L. Craig (classical)	30 pp.	3	0
G. Habermas (evidentialist)	30 pp.	1	0
P. Feinberg (cumulative)	25 pp.	2	0
J. Frame (presuppositionalist)	24 pp.	Dozens	0
K. J. Clark (Reformed)	19 pp.	0	0

A rare breath of fresh air over the years on this topic has been John Whitcomb, who concisely summed it up this way:

> In our efforts to make the Bible and Christianity attractive and acceptable to men we find ourselves immediately confronted with two stupendous obstacles: man's fallen nature and the Satanic forces which surround him. Though these facts should come as no great surprise to one who is even superficially acquainted with Biblical Christianity, it is astonishing to me how few of the better known evangelical works on Christian apologetics today give them serious consideration. One is almost led to believe, when reading such books, that what we really need to win intellectuals to Christ (in addition to the Gospel) is an arsenal of carefully developed arguments against the

various false religious and philosophical systems we may confront today and/or an impressive array of evidences from, say, archaeology and history, that the Bible and Christianity are true. If this were really so, one might be pardoned for wondering why Christianity has not long since made a clean sweep of the religious world, since it is uniquely possessed of infallible proofs of its claims (cf. Acts 1:3; 26:26).[3]

In keeping with Whitcomb, we will see from Scripture that the main reason critics do not believe in Christianity and the Bible is because of personal sin and satanic blindness, not mere ignorance.

Personal Sin

The study of sin in the Bible is called "hamartiology" from the New Testament Greek word, *hamartia*, which means "to miss the mark, to fall short of the target."[4] It was an archery term. God is perfect and requires perfection from His creatures—anything short of perfection is *hamartia*, or sin. God is the One who defines sin, and a systematic summary of sin as given by God in Scripture is any thought, deed or word that violates God's will or character. Or as 1 John 3:4 aptly summarizes, "sin is lawlessness." The Bible also calls sin *evil* (Prov 8:13), *wickedness* (Gen 6:5), *corruption* (Gen 6:12), *iniquity* (Ps 51:2, 9), *transgression* (Ps 32:1, 5), *impurity* (Lev 16:16), *rebellion, ungodliness, unholiness,* and *profanity* (1 Tim 1:9), *disobedience* (Eph 2:2), *error* (Ps 19:12), *unrighteousness* (Ps 119:3), and *wrongdoing* (Ps 37:1).[5] Beginning with the first man Adam, sin has separated humankind from God who is holy (Isa 59:1-2). As a result, every human needs to be reconciled to God the Creator.

The doctrine of sin rests on the foundation of the disobedience of our first parents, Adam and Eve (Gen 3). Paul says that sin entered the world through Adam (Rom 5:12-14). Adam was a real person. Unfortunately it is becoming commonplace for evangelical theologians, philosophers, apologists and pastors, and as a result, Christian colleges, seminaries and churches, to question or blatantly reject the historicity of Adam.[6] So we need to set the record straight: Adam was a real man, sin entered our world through him, and that is why there is sin in the world today.

Inherent Sin

Much can be said about sin, but three corollary truths will be highlighted that are relevant to apologetics and include the following: inherent sin, total depravity and the progression of sin. First we address the issue of inherent sin, sometimes called innate or original sin. "Inherent sin is the original corruption and disposition to sin that all people inherit from Adam through natural generation and have from conception throughout their earthly lives (Ps 51:5; Mt 7:11; Rom 5:19; 7:18)."[7] In other words, every person ever born inherits a sin nature at conception. David, speaking as a prophet of God, exclaimed this truth saying, "in sin my mother conceived me" (Ps 51:5). Similarly, Psalm 58:3 says, "Even from birth the wicked go astray: from the womb they are wayward and speak lies" (NIV). Only Jesus bypassed the curse of original sin by being born of a virgin (Luke 1:35). Unlike many religions that teach people "become" sinners later in life (like Mormonism that says one becomes a culpable sinner at age eight), the Bible says that people do not become sinners when they begin to sin. Rather, they do acts of sin because they are sinners by nature, from birth.

Because of original sin inherited from Adam (Rom 5:18) all people are born sinners (Rom 3:23) and are "by nature children of wrath" (Eph 2:3), separated from God (Eph 2:12), His avowed "enemy" (Rom 5:10), and need to be born again (John 3:3). By nature, before redemption by belief in the gospel, all people are spiritually "dead in...transgressions" (Eph 2:5). They are of their father, the devil (John 8:44; 1 John 3:8). Apologist Clark Pinnock is wrong when he says that all people are basically good.[8] And so is Craig when he says that unbelievers can "enjoy a veridical experience of God...as the loving Father of mankind."[9] God is not the Father of unbelievers and Craig gives no Bible verse to validate his erroneous claim. Original sin separates all people from God.

Total Depravity

The second important truth about sin, or hamartiology, is the truth of "total depravity." Because every person is born with a sin nature, they are in turn totally depraved from birth. There is much confusion and debate over the doctrine of total depravity, almost always resulting from wrong definitions of the phrase. So it is imperative to define the doctrine biblically. First we need to state what it is not:

• Total depravity was not invented by John Calvin.[10]

• Total depravity does not mean that all people are as bad as they can be.[11]

• Christians are not totally depraved.[12]

• Total depravity does not mean that people cannot do anything good.[13]

• Total depravity did not eradicate the *imago Dei* or conscience in any person.[14]

What is total depravity? Reymond accurately summarizes it as follows:

> Every part of his being—his mind, his will, his emotions, his affections, his conscience, his body—has been affected by sin...His understanding is darkened, his mind is at enmity with God, his will to act is slave to his darkened understanding and rebellious mind, his heart is corrupt, his emotions are perverted, his affections naturally gravitate to that which is evil and ungodly, his conscience is untrustworthy, and his body is subject to mortality.[15]

In a similar vein, Holloman says, "'Total depravity' means that people are so corrupted by sin that of themselves they can do nothing good or right to gain saving merit in their relation to God...Fallen humans are unable to do anything good or right to gain saving merit before God."[16]

There are countless verses that speak to total depravity, but a few representative ones make the case. The first is in Genesis 6:5 where God gives His binding hamartiological diagnosis of the human condition apart from redemption through Christ. The Holy Spirit declared: "Then the LORD saw that the wickedness of man was great on the earth, and that every intent of the thoughts of his heart was only evil continually." This verse like no other delineates the depth and the breadth of human depravity. Note the resultant implications:

(1) **Every** human is subject to total depravity, for it includes every person "on the earth."

(2) The **actions** of all people are sinful for God saw their deeds of "wickedness."

(3) All humans' **attitudes** and **motives** became depraved for God diagnosed "every intent" of their thoughts to be corrupt.

(4) Every human's **inner nature** is depraved for "his heart" was evil; this would include the will, the emotions, and all that constitutes the inner man.[17]

(5) The **extent** of human depravity is all encompassing, or "total," for the disease of sin is "only evil" and spreads to "every" intent.

(6) Total depravity is **permanent**[18] for man is sinful "continually."

Another key representative verse exposing the hamartiological fallout of the human heart is Jeremiah 17:9: "The heart is more deceitful than all else and is desperately sick; who can understand it?" Humans are inescapably self-deceived by nature. Apart from God's supernatural intervention through a work of His grace, natural man is beyond cure. Ecclesiastes 9:3 says, "The hearts of the sons of men are full of evil and insanity is in their hearts throughout their lives."

The above three verses all mention that the human heart is corrupt from sin. In the Old Testament, the heart referred to the inner man and all related capacities. So the teaching of the Bible is that sin has tainted every faculty of human composition—his will, mind, emotions, motives, desires, spirit, soul, and conscience. And sinful man's nature is now naturally bent toward self and away from God. Natural, fallen, unredeemed man is totally depraved.

Because the effects of sin are pervasive and comprehensive on a personal level, man's ability to think has been affected. Because of sin, unredeemed people suffer from devastating noetic implications. Their ability to think, reason, speculate, and meditate on the things of God, spiritual truths and ultimate metaphysical realities are warped and skewed. The Bible says they are spiritually blind, "their foolish heart was darkened" (Rom 1:21), and they have "exchanged the truth of God for a lie" (Rom 1:25). It is impossible for unbelievers to perceive spiritual truth from mere human logic, reason and observation, for sin has caused an unbridgeable chasm between the human realm and the spiritual realm. Paul states plainly that "a natural man does not accept the things of the Spirit of God, for they are foolishness to him; and he cannot understand them, because they are spiritually appraised" (1 Cor 2:14). In short, unbelievers have been intellectually and spiritually blinded by sin. Mayhue gives an excellent summary of the comprehensive hamartiological-hangover that plagues unbelievers' ability to think accurately about spiritual truth:

> When the human race fell in Genesis 3, one of the terrible consequences included the spiritual debilitation of the mind. The New Testament uses 12 different negative Greek words to describe the ruin on man's intellectual capacity.

1. Debased—Rom 1:28	7. Deluded—Col 2:4
2. Hardened—2 Cor 3:14	8. Deceived—Col 2:8
3. Blinded—2 Cor 4:4	9. Sensuous—Col 2:18
4. Futile—Eph 4:17	10. Depraved—1 Tim 6:5
5. Darkened—Eph 4:18	11. Corrupted—2 Tim 3:8
6. Hostile—Col 1:21	12. Defiled—Titus 1:15

> As a result of this mental mayhem people are "always learning and never able to come to the knowledge of the truth" (2 Tim. 3:7), and some even "have a zeal for God, but not in accordance with knowledge" (Rom. 10:2).[19]

The implications of total depravity on apologetics are monumental. Because the unbeliever's thinking is darkened by sin and skewed in any attempt to understand spiritual truth apart from supernatural intervention, there is no epistemological neutral ground between Christians and non-Christians. This is where traditional apologists make a fatal flaw in methodology. Their doctrine of sin is compromised and they attribute too much intellectual capability and virtue to the unbeliever's thoughts about God and ultimate reality. In terms of capability, most traditional apologists insist that unbelievers stand on equal footing with Christians when it comes to knowing, thinking and reasoning in pursuit of spiritual truth. This is specifically manifested when they say our common ground with the unbeliever is in the area of logic and sense perception. They reject the clear biblical teaching that says unbelievers' reasoning and volitional capacities are fallen, darkened, warped and inept, thus rendering them incapable of attaining truth about ultimate reality apart from supernatural intervention and revelation.

Traditional apologist Groothuis, is a typical example here. He says categorically, "reason is not fallen...sound reasoning is the norm for people willing to follow truth wherever it leads."[20] To say that "sound reasoning is the norm" for unbelievers, as he does here, is blatantly unbiblical. The Bible says the norm for unbelievers is that "they are corrupt, their deeds are vile; there is no one who does good" and none of them understands spiritual truth nor do they seek after God...not even one! (Ps 14:1-3; NIV).

In terms of virtue, traditional apologists grant that the average atheist or agnostic is sincere when they claim, "I don't believe in God" or "I'm not sure God exists." Scripture says the atheist is an informed liar and clever rebel about such claims: "The fool has said in his heart, 'There is no God'" (Ps 14:1). Atheists are not sincere. Every person knows God exists through internal (conscience) and external (creation) general revelation. The reality of God's existence has "been clearly seen" (Rom 1:20), therefore "they are without excuse."

The problem with the atheist, the agnostic and the skeptic is that they love their sin. That is what Jesus said (John 3:20). And when someone loves their sin they hate the light of truth (Prov 1:22; John 7:7). Therefore they will deliberately suppress the innate truth of God they possess with a vengeance. The end result is that they will make up excuses and justify their rebellion by pleading ignorance: "I don't know if there is a God" or even worse they will demand that God prove Himself to them on a personal level on their terms. In essence

187

they say, "If God exists, then let Him reveal Himself!" That sounds eerily familiar…like the mockers at Jesus' cross, who demanded that He prove Himself to be the Messiah by coming down off the cross: "the chief priests also, along with the scribes and elders, were mocking Him, saying, 'He saved others; He cannot save Himself. He is the King of Israel; let Him now come down from the cross, and we will believe in Him'" (Matt 27:41-42).

So when we are dealing with all unbelievers, we need to be consciously aware of what is really under the veil, in the human heart—whether it's a Mormon, Muslim, Moonie or mailman. God has declared in His Word that all unbelievers have a serious "hamartiological-hangover" from inherent sin that has separated them from God, darkened their understanding about spiritual truth, warped their thinking about metaphysical realities, and is the catalyst to their persistent suppression of God's truth revealed in general revelation.

Scripture says the logic of unbelievers is defective and unreliable as a source of truth. Paul declared categorically, "Where is the wise man? Where is the scribe? Where is the debater of this age? Has not God made foolish the wisdom of the world?" (1 Cor 1:20). When it comes to knowing metaphysical realities and spiritual truth, there is no epistemological common ground between believer and unbeliever. Again Paul states, "what fellowship has light with darkness? Or what harmony has Christ with Belial, or what has a believer in common with an unbeliever?" (2 Cor 6:14-15).

Augustine vs. Aquinas on Total Depravity

With respect to apologetics during the Church Age, two figures stand out historically as paradigmatic for variant schools of thought regarding hamartiological implications on man's noetic capabilities: Augustine (AD 354-430) and Aquinas (AD 1224?-1274). Augustine had a balanced, biblical view of total depravity—unredeemed man's mind was darkened yet the image of God was still intact and common grace ameliorated man's noetic devastation from the Fall. Aquinas, on the other hand, downplayed the effects of the Fall and sin's deleterious impact on human reasoning. Demarest gives a cogent summary of Augustine's take on man's inherited hamartiological-hangover:

The bishop insisted that natural man's cognitive powers

have been crippled by the effects of sin. In matters pertaining to the eternal realm, the sinner is unable to intuit eternal, changeless truths, whereas in the temporal realm man's knowledge of changing things is distorted. The mind of natural man has been darkened and weakened by original sin. As Augustine argues, 'Every man is born mentally blind.' In addition, the will is not free but is bound by the power of reigning sin. Only what is loved and embraced by the will is known. But the fact is that the unregenerate will is perverse and corrupt. Fallen man's proclivity to self-love and pride compels him to turn aside from God. With Paul, Augustine insists that autonomous man holds down or suppresses God's presentation of Himself to the soul. God must heal, perfect, and free the will to make it willing to respond positively to Him. It is only when faith is established and sinful pride is routed that the intellect is enabled and the will freed to receive wisdom. Plainly, Augustine upheld a total moral depravity affecting every part of man's nature.[21]

For Augustine, man cannot reach God by unaided reason, but needs the supernatural intervention of God through His Holy Spirit and Scripture to attain a true knowledge of God. Yet, faith and reason were not at odds either. What sinners need is "redeemed" reasoning capabilities, which come only from God's special intervention. God's Spirit and Word efficaciously and concomitantly impart such capabilities. As a result Augustine could say both of the following statements that at first blush seem contradictory: "Reasoning does not create truth but discovers it"[22] and, "Faith is in some way the starting point of knowledge."[23]

In stark contrast to Augustine, Aquinas said that man is not totally depraved. Aquinas affirmed, "that natural man can, by the ordinary use of his reason, do justice to the natural revelation that surrounds him."[24] Aquinas rejected the biblical teaching of total depravity and sin's noetic effects on unredeemed humanity. Demarest notes the fallout of Aquinas' anemic view of the Fall:

> Furthermore, it is clear that Thomas's inflated emphasis on reason betrays a depreciation of the effects of the Fall on the human cognitive powers. Whereas man lost his

ethical likeness to God in his reckless quest for autonomy, his natural likeness to God remained untarnished by the Fall. Hence Thomas, unlike Augustine, saw no need for general illumination of reason as it evaluates the data of the cosmic order. Burtt thus concludes correctly that in Thomas 'human reason is metaphysically competent…to attain absolute truth concerning God's existence and attributes.' Given Thomas's vision of an untarnished *imago*, a self-sufficient natural theology is for the Christian and non-Christian alike a fruitful possibility.[25]

In sum, Augustine and Aquinas held polar opposite views regarding the natural man's ability to reason.

> Augustine argued that man's understanding and reasoning function only upon the foundation of faith in God. Reason has no self-sufficient ability to interpret experience and no true authority to judge the veracity of Christian faith…Understanding (reason) presupposes faith (the truth of the Christian message). Augustine repudiated any autonomous philosophy or use of any human intellect.[26]

Aquinas believed just the opposite:

> The Thomistic approach assumes that fallen man is capable of reasoning in a proper way (prior to repenting of sin and submitting to the Savior) and that knowledge and intelligible interpretation of experience are philosophically possible apart from God's revelation (i.e., possible in terms of a basic perspective different from the Christian worldview. Man's own intellect, when used at its best, is thus granted the ability and the right to pass judgment on the credibility of God's word (its worthiness of faith). Reason—set up as a judge, not simply used as a tool—takes a privileged position alongside faith.[27]

The theological noetic disparity between Augustine and Aquinas did not end in the thirteenth century, but rather is a perennial conflict in every era. Aquinas' view was adopted by the Roman Catholic Church and remains their formal position to this day.[28] During the Reformation, Luther (1483-1546) and Calvin (1509-1564) reiterated the Augustinian view. Calvin said, "Man is blind and intoxicated with self-love…man, being immured in the darkness of error, is scarcely able, by means of that natural law, to form any tolerable idea of the worship which is acceptable to God. At all events, he is very far from forming any correct knowledge of it."[29]

Jacobus Arminius (1560-1609) rejected the theology of Calvin he was taught, and preferred an inflated view of human freedom—his overemphasis of human free will became popularly known as Arminianism, and reigns supreme in modern, traditional evangelical apologetics.

John Wesley (1703-1791) did not outright reject original sin but did make it practically null and void with his concocted "preventing" grace doctrine.[30] In the twentieth century the Augustinian position of the sinfulness of sin was championed in the field of apologetics by Cornelius Van Til (1895-1987). He drew a clear line in the sand on this issue, stirred up the pot that the hegemonic death-grip of Thomisitc ideology had long held on apologetics, and gave birth to a reinvigorated approach to biblical apologetics that came to be called "presuppositionalism."

On the question of epistemology, and the effects of sin on the natural man's ability to reason about spiritual truths and come to a knowledge of metaphysical realities, every Christian must decide which apologetical camp they belong to: Augustinian or Thomisitc.

And the choice is not between the allegiance held to a preferred apologist of one's liking, but is rather a commitment to clear biblical teaching (inherent sin and total depravity) or the compromise and rejection thereof. Van Til, and his protégé, Greg Bahnsen (1948-1995), led the way to recovering and revitalizing a fresh Augustinian biblical approach to understanding epistemology relative to apologetics.

When evaluating any apologist or any apologetical methodology, it is always helpful to first look at the hamartiology that undergirds the system. Do they hold to a biblical view of sin or not? Do they believe in total depravity or reject it? Is the system Augustinian or Thomistic? One's view of sin directly affects epistemology. Following is a selective summary of various "apologists" regarding their epistemological underpinnings and lineage evidenced in their methodological approach:

Hamartiology and Epistemology in Apologetics

Augustinian	Thomistic
1. Martin Luther	1. B. B. Warfield
2. John Calvin	2. Gordon Clark
3. Abraham Kuyper	3. E. J. Carnell
4. Cornelius Van Til	4. C. S. Lewis
5. Greg Bahnsen	5. Francis Schaeffer
6. Walter Martin	6. R. C. Sproul
7. Albert Martin	7. Norman Geisler
8. Richard Mayhue	8. William Lane Craig
9. George Zemek	9. Josh McDowell
10. Kirk Cameron	10. Gary Habermas
11. John Whitcomb	11. Alvin Plantinga
12. John MacArthur	12. Catholic Theology
13. John Piper	13. Arminian Theology

The Axiological Factor of Sin

The third corollary truth about sin, aside from the ontological reality of inherent sin and the epistemological reality of total depravity, there is also the axiological reality of the progression of sin in the unbeliever. Romans one teaches that sinners who resist God go from bad to worse in the progress of their depravity. As a sinner hardens his heart toward the things of God, then his heart becomes more hardened (Heb 3:13). As an unbeliever stiffens his neck when he hears biblical truth, then his neck becomes even more stiffened (Prov 29:1). As a rebel sears his conscience one choice at a time to pursue the pleasures of sin, then with each rebellious, self-centered choice, his conscience becomes even more seared (1 Tim 4:2). This is the progression of the hardening effects of sin. These kinds of calculated rebels "proceed from bad to worse, deceiving and being deceived" (2 Tim 3:13). Because sinners by nature suppress the truth of God within them through natural revelation, unless they repent when confronted with truth, they will be given over into a spiral of judgment by God who will relinquish sinners to their own devices, and they will become steeped even deeper in depravity and hardness of heart.

This progressive spiral of sin is described by Paul as a "giving over" to judgment by God as a natural consequence of the sinner's deliberate choice to reject truth: "Therefore God gave them over in the lusts of their hearts to impurity...For this reason God gave them over to degrading passions...God gave them over to a depraved mind" (Rom 1:24, 26, 28). Notice the tri-fold progression—"God gave them over," "God gave them over," "God gave them over." This is the downward spiral of an ever-increasing and accelerating hardened heart and seared conscience that leads to a thoroughly "depraved mind." This is the inviolable spiritual law of sowing and reaping: "Do not be deceived, God is not mocked; for whatever a man sows, this he will also reap. For the one who sows to his own flesh will from the flesh reap corruption" (Gal 6:7-8).

The apologetical implications from this hamartiological progression towards hardening are telling. When dealing with critics of the faith like world-renowned, seasoned, brazen atheists like Christopher Hitchens,[31] Richard Dawkins,[32] and Victor Stenger,[33] we are not dealing with innocent seekers who just need a little more information or surer logic in order to be won over to theism. These men have hearts as hard as flint. "There is no fear of God before their eyes" (Ps 36:1; cf. Rom 3:18). No amount of archaeological proof, no amount of amassing historical evidences, no amount of iron-clad theistic arguments or elitist theorems from astrophysical cosmology[34] will convince or persuade recalcitrant antagonists like these. Only the sovereign, supernatural power of God's Holy Spirit working through His life-changing Word can soften and change such hardened, unbelieving hearts. This was God's promise in Ezekiel:

> I will sprinkle clean water on you, and you will be clean; I will cleanse you from all your filthiness and from all your idols. Moreover, I will give you a new heart and put a new spirit within you; and I will remove the heart of stone from your flesh and give you a heart of flesh. I will put My Spirit within you and cause you to walk in My statutes, and you will be careful to observe My ordinances (Ezek 36:25-27).

For a hardened heart to be softened it takes a sovereign work of God

(God says "I will" five times—softening and salvation are by His initiative), through the working of His Holy Spirit and His Word in Scripture ("statutes" and "ordinances" refer to God's Word and they have inherent, efficacious power). What an unbelieving rebel needs is not more logic but more Spirit-empowered biblical truth. As when Paul spoke Scriptural truth of the gospel to Lydia, the byproduct was that "the Lord opened her heart to respond to the things spoken by Paul" (Acts 16:14). What an amazing statement! This is the most vital truth we need to recognize, master and integrate into our approach to apologetics: because of the deceitfulness of sin and its devastating compounding and enslaving tendencies, we must depend upon and use God's truth in His Word as we talk with unbelievers so that He might open sinners' hearts to respond to that truth.

On this most basic matter of sin's stifling impact on sinners, Whitcomb is profoundly insightful:

> Christian apologetics has been traditionally concerned with giving rational answers to the challenges of unbelievers concerning God's special revelation in Scripture. But what kind of minds are we appealing to? To what extent have sin and spiritual rebellion against God affected man's rational capacities? Ponder these statements: "You were dead in your trespasses and sins, in which you formerly walked according to the course of this world . . . indulging the desires of the flesh and of the mind, and were by nature children of wrath, even as the rest" (Eph. 2:1-3). "The Gentiles . . . walk in the futility of their mind, being darkened in their understanding, excluded from the life of God, because of the ignorance that is in them, because of the hardness of their heart" (Eph. 4:17-18).
>
> But is the human "mind" not capable of detaching itself from the so-called "heart" and of drawing its own conclusions about God independent of the downward direction of the fallen nature? The answer is no. Mark our Lord's explanation of the unbreakable relationship between the mind and the heart: "out of the heart come evil thoughts" (Matt. 15:19; cf. Mark 7:31). He later asked his disciples: "why do doubts arise in your hearts?" (Luke 24:38). The Scriptures offer us no hope of bringing about a fundamental change in a man's thinking about God apart

from a profound change in his "heart," the moral/spiritual center of his personal being. This is a basic reality that no Christian apologist can afford to ignore.[35]

Satanic Blindness

Know the Enemy

When I was a new Christian in college I attended a Sunday night vespers service led by a team of college students. The student leaders always prayed as a team prior to the service. One night, as they were holding hands, eyes closed, taking turns praying for the impending fellowship time, one of the student leaders prayed a prayer I will never forget. This student was a recent convert and had an unusually sweet disposition. She prayed, "Dear God, please soften Satan's heart and draw him to Yourself so that he might repent and be saved." At that moment all the others in the group opened their eyes as wide as saucers—panicked, embarrassed and a little shocked...then there was a moment of strange silence. The other students were right to feel shocked. Despite the naïve desire of the student's prayer, Satan will not repent or be saved. Scripture is clear about Satan's totally corrupt nature, incorrigible will and assured eternal doom in the lake of fire. The devil is evil to the core.

Unfortunately, newly saved, naïve college students are not the only Christians who have an unbiblical view of Satan, underestimating the paramount danger he poses. Too many are ignorant of his true evil nature, supernatural powers and ongoing havoc he wreaks on humanity. This is all too true among evangelical apologists as evidenced by their writings. Christian apologist Dean Hardy says in his book, *Stand Your Ground: An Introductory Text for Apologetics Students*, "you cannot have a fully evil entity. Even Satan is not completely evil! He does have a few good qualities."[36] Hardy does not tell the reader what Satan's good qualities are. He can't, because there are none—according to Scripture Satan is one hundred percent, unmitigated, incarnate evil. Worse than this is the growing trend of evangelicals saying that Satan is not even real. Earlier we noted that all five authors of *Five Views on Apologetics* failed to mention the implications of satanic blindness in the work of apologetics. This is typical of most books about apologetics. Apologetics is supposed to deal with questions like, "Why don't skeptics believe the truth? Why do they reject Christianity?" According to the Bible, the first answer is because of personal sinfulness. The other key factor is the reality of satanic blindness.

The Biblical Assertion

The clearest passage on this matter is 2 Corinthians 4:3-4: "And even if our gospel is veiled, it is veiled to those who are perishing, in whose case the god of this world has blinded the minds of the unbelieving, so that they might not see the light of the gospel of the glory of Christ, who is the image of God." Several relevant truths issue from this passage.

First, the Apostle Paul assumes Satan is a real person or being. That cannot be ignored. A countless pod of professing evangelical scholars today reject the idea of a real spiritual being named Satan. To reject the idea of a real Satan is to reject the Bible.

Second, Paul designates Satan as the "god of this world." That means Satan has delegated authority and supernatural power over the entire world's system, including its ideologies as well as its occupants, which entails fallen angels and unbelieving people. Similarly John said, "the whole world lies in *the power* of the evil one" (1 John 5:19). Unbelievers belong to Satan and his jurisdiction—he owns them, and most of them don't even know it. Paul says further in Ephesians that unbelievers actually have a satanic lineage by birth, practice and allegiance, for all unbelievers walk or live "according to the course of this world, according to the prince of the power of the air, of the spirit that is now working in the sons of disobedience" (Eph 2:2-3). Paul here calls Satan "the prince of the power of the air"—he rules over unbelievers from the spiritual domain like a puppet-master manipulating his marionettes. Jesus similarly told unbelievers that they belonged to the family of Satan by virtue of their unbelief: "You are of your father the devil" (John 8:44). John said the same thing in his epistle: "the one who practices sin is of the devil...By this the children of God and the children of the devil are obvious: anyone who does not practice righteousness is not of God" (1 John 3:8, 10). The Bible is clear—there are only two categories of people: (1) the children of God; and (2) the children of Satan, the god of this wicked world, the prince of the power of the air.

Third, 2 Corinthians 4:4 says Satan has "blinded" unbelievers. This refers to spiritual blindness and blindness of their "minds." Their ability to think and reason and discern spiritual truth is doubly darkened, first from personal sinfulness and now satanic blindness.

The blinding force is external to them and prevents them from believing the truth of the gospel. Why do skeptics reject the gospel? Why do atheists say they don't believe in God? Why do agnostics claim ignorance? Because Satan has supernaturally blinded them with spiritual blinders that prevent them from accepting the truth of Jesus Christ and His gospel. They are ontologically deceived, for the devil is their arch-deceiver. They are epistemologically darkened because the god of this world has veiled the truth from them. They are volitionally powerless for the prince of the power of the air is a stakeholder of their wills (John 8:44). They are morally bankrupt because Satan has corrupted their hearts (Acts 5:3).

Fourth, this epistemological and intellectual satanic blindness is a supernatural blindness, a blindness that cannot be overcome on the human level. The origin of this mental blindness is in the spiritual realm. That is why in the same book, six chapters later Paul reminds Christians that the true spiritual battle with unbelievers is not on the physical, fleshly realm, but in the spiritual domain. "For though we walk in the flesh, we do not war according to the flesh, for the weapons of our warfare are not of the flesh, but divinely powerful for the destruction of fortresses" (2 Cor 10:3-4). In a parallel passage Paul says, "Put on the full armor of God, so that you will be able to stand firm against the schemes of the devil. For our struggle is not against flesh and blood, but against the rulers, against the powers, against the world forces of this darkness, against the spiritual forces of wickedness in the heavenly places" (Eph 6:11-12). Zemek hones in on the significance of this truth relative to the work of apologetics:

> Negatively, our struggle is not *pros heima kai sarka*, "not against blood and flesh." The apologetical implications of this compound prepositional phrase are great—we are not engaged in a finite battle. In our own strength we are astronomically out-matched, because these variously designated opponents are all related to *ta pneumatika tes ponerias ev tois epouranios*. Consequently, the burden of the context is an appeal for a total dependence upon God and His gracious provisions...We especially need His help in the area of truth dissemination. We are in desperate need not only of God's enablement but also His prevailing methodology.[37]

The only way to counteract and overcome supernatural satanic blindness is with heavenly weapons, not human ones. Anemic human weaponry includes persuasive speech (1 Cor 2:1), clever rhetoric (1 Cor 1:17), man-made philosophy (Col 2:8), so-called convincing human arguments (1 Cor 2:6), the wisdom of the world in the trappings of the laws of logic (1 Cor 1:21) and under the guise of what is falsely called science and true knowledge (1 Tim 6:20-21), all originating from autonomous, anthropocentric human reason (Prov 14:12; Rom 3:4).

All of these tactics are impotent against the spiritual deceptions of our nefarious enemy, Satan. Apart from divine intervention by God's saving grace through the power of His Spirit working through the truth of His Word, supernatural, spiritual satanic blindness cannot be overcome.

The Indispensability of Efficacious Prayer

We would be remiss if we failed to mention the need for biblical prayer in the work of apologetics and especially in our evangelistic endeavors. Lost souls are naturally hardened against the gospel because of their own personal sin and they are supernaturally blinded from the deceitfulness of Satan. God has ordained prayer to help overcome these damning spiritual hurdles.

Prayer is a gift from God to believers to enable personal communion and communication with Him as Creator, Savior and Father. The act of prayer is an inherent work of dependence upon God. Praying to a God we cannot see is a manifestation of walking by faith and not by sight, as Scripture mandates (2 Cor 5:7). And sincere, biblical prayer in the Spirit unleashes supernatural power from heaven itself. James reminds believers of the supernatural effects of fervent prayer:

> The effective prayer of a righteous man can accomplish much. Elijah was a man with a nature like ours, and he prayed earnestly that it would not rain, and it did not rain on the earth for three years and six months. Then he prayed again, and the sky poured rain and the earth produced its fruit (James 5:16-18).

John the Apostle reminds believers as well of the inestimable efficacy of prayer:

This is the confidence which we have before Him, that, if we ask anything according to His will, He hears us. And if we know that He hears us in whatever we ask, we know that we have the requests which we have asked from Him (1 John 5:14-15).

Not only is prayer a gift from God; prayer is also a weapon. It is one of the "spiritual" weapons that Paul refers to when he writes to believers reminding them that we are at war with spiritual demonic forces that warrant spiritual weapons (Eph 6:12; 2 Cor 10:4). Paul said, "Put on the full armor of God, so that you will be able to stand firm against the schemes of the devil" (Eph 6:11). He goes on to say that prayer is part of the believer's armor and a vital weapon (Eph 6:18). Mere feeble, earthly, human weapons won't suffice when it comes to spiritual warfare.

In light of this great truth, believers should bathe all the pertinent areas of apologetics in fervent prayer. A few priority areas come to mind. First, Christians should pray against the work of Satan as he seeks to continually deceive unbelievers and blind them. Peter the apologist knew this truth, for in the same book that he penned 3:15, he also wrote: "casting all your anxiety on Him, because He cares for you. Be of sober spirit; be on the alert. Your adversary, the devil, prowls around like a roaring lion, seeking someone to devour" (1 Pet 5:7-8). Prayer is inseparable from the believer's ongoing battle and resistance against the work of Satan.

Second, believers should pray for boldness in the work of apologetics. Defending the faith in the face of opposition requires supernatural courage. That heavenly courage can result from prayer. The apostle Paul asked believers to pray for boldness as he preached the gospel to unbelievers: "With all prayer and petition pray at all times in the Spirit, and with this in view, be on the alert with all perseverance and petition for all the saints, and pray on my behalf, that utterance may be given to me in the opening of my mouth, to make known with boldness the mystery of the gospel" (Eph 6:18-19). If Paul needed prayer in the work of apologetics, how much more all other believers?

Third, not only do we need prayer for courage, we also need prayer for wisdom. Defending the faith in certain circumstances and especially with difficult people requires heavenly insight—and that only comes from God. "But if any of you lacks wisdom, let him ask of God, who gives to all generously and without reproach, and it will be given to him. But he must ask in faith without any doubting, for the one who doubts is like the surf of the sea, driven and tossed by the wind" (James 1:5-6).

Fourth, pray specifically for the lost people with whom you are engaged. Pray that God's Spirit would soften their hearts and remove their satanic blindness. Pray that God's Word would penetrate the conscience. Pray that the seed of the gospel would take root in their soul. Pray that they would repent and believe. Paul is exemplary here. He did not disdain unbelievers. He loved them and had great compassion for their lost souls (Rom 9:1-5).

Listen to his longing for their salvation: "Brethren, my heart's desire and my prayer to God for them is for their salvation. For I testify about them that they have a zeal for God, but not in accordance with knowledge (Rom 10:1-2). Notice carefully his words, "my prayer to God for them is for their salvation"! Like Paul, we need to pray for the lost. Paul believed in election, taught and preached on election, was himself elected by God sovereignly before the foundation of the world—and yet prayed for their salvation. A mystery resolved only in the mind of the Eternal God (cf. Rom 11:33; Acts 13:48).

Implications

Traditional Christian apologetics typically fails to account for the epistemologically blinding effects on the unbeliever that result from personal sinfulness and satanic blindness. The Bible, on the other hand, shows that these two spiritual ailments are first order concerns for the Christian apologist to consider. Internally speaking, original sin and total depravity render the unbeliever spiritually blind from birth. The progression of sin through ongoing resistance to truth exacerbates the unbeliever's spiritual blindness, propelling the skeptic's darkened mind from bad to worse.

Externally, the unbeliever's spiritual bankruptcy is compounded from the supernatural blinding power of Satan. The end result is that the unredeemed person is completely spiritually dead in trespasses and sins (Eph 2:1). It is in this area of how hamartiology affects epistemology that Cornelius Van Til made one of the most significant contributions to the field of Christian apologetics. Here's a typical classic Vantilian statement about the debilitating noetic effects of sin on the unbeliever:

Man by his sinful nature hates the revelation of God. Therefore every concrete expression that any sinner makes about God will have in it the poisoning effect of this hatred of God. His epistemological reaction will invariably be negative, and negative along the whole line of his interpretative endeavor. There are no general principles or truths about the true God—and that is the only God with whom any man actually deals—which he does not falsify. The very idea of the existence of abstract truth is a falsification of the knowledge of the true God that every sinner involuntarily finds within himself.[38]

Van Til concluded correctly that the unbeliever has logic, but because of sin and satanic blindness, it's a warped, darkened logic. Van Til believed unbelievers have a conscience, but it was a self-serving, twisted conscience. Van Til believed non-Christians have real sense perception, but because of hamartiological hangovers, their inter-pretive gauge for the senses is jaded and jilted. Following suit, Bahnsen similarly believed that the Christian had no epistemological neutral ground in the domain of reason with the darkened and warped unbeliever:

...the Christian who strives for neutrality in the world of thought is (1) not neutral after all, and thus (2) in danger of unwittingly endorsing assumptions that are hostile to his Christian faith. While imagining that his intellectual neutrality is compatible with a Christian profession, such a believer is actually operating in terms of unbelief! If he refuses to presuppose the truth of Christ, he invariably ends up presupposing the outlook of the world instead. All men have their presuppositions; none is neutral. Shall your presuppositions be the teachings of Christ or the vain deception against which Paul warns? Choose this day whom ye shall serve![39]

In stark contrast to this biblical view of no neutrality in thinking with the unbeliever, most traditional apologists think just the opposite. When it comes to establishing a starting point or basis by which to dialogue with the unbeliever, traditionalists assume we have neutral or even common ground with non-Christians in the intellectual/reasoning realm. They propose that the neutral ground is with the laws of logic, sense perception and common sense. They tell us that fallen, darkened, satanically blind sinners can think aright in the realm of logic when opining about ultimate reality and even spiritual truth.

For example, R. C. Sproul argues that our starting point with unbelievers is the domain of reasoning in at least a three-fold manner, for Sproul claims believers have neutral ground with unbelievers (1) in the laws of logic as defined by Aristotle; (2) in the basic reliability of sense perception; and (3) in the analogical use of language.[40] Craig says believers and unbelievers have epistemological common ground in the areas of "sense perception, rational self-evidence, and common modes of reasoning."[41] John Frame betrays his presuppositional commitments when he admits he also agrees there is epistemological common ground in the areas of rational self-evidence and common modes of reasoning.[42] He even makes the drastic claim that "everyone has the intellectual knowledge required for faith," including depraved unbelievers![43] Habermas affirms epistemological common ground in the areas of sensory data, scientific theories and the general rules and application of inference.[44] Feinberg believed in common ground in the areas of sense perception, scientific theories, the laws of logic, law, history and literature.[45] Geisler, who alleges "that depraved human beings have the power of free will,"[46] is another proponent of perceived epistemological common ground between believer and unbeliever. Then there is apologist Kelly James Clark of Calvin College, who is in a camp by himself when it comes to the biblical teaching of the noetic effects of sin on the unbeliever. He writes, "I am dubious, however, of finding any ultimate or coercive support for epistemology in Scripture."[47] He further states, "I also think a serious reader of Scripture can doubt that God's Word plays a determinative role in the human knowledge of God"[48] This is a startling claim—he suggests that the Bible has nothing to say about knowledge, knowing truth or what truth is![49] So on this matter, ironically, he is an unbelieving agnostic.

Because the above traditional apologists believe the unregenerate person has intact reasoning capabilities with respect to spiritual truth, they believe through sheer human reason they can get the skeptic to believe in God if they can establish a consistent, logical, theistic argument. The second admitted step of the traditional apologist is then to prove from logic, archaeology and human arguments that the Bible should be given consideration as a "generally reliable" document. If they can just get the lost, Christ-hating, spiritually dead unbeliever to believe in some of the Bible through certain proofs, then maybe the skeptic will fall for the rest of the Bible. The whole notion is futile and preposterous. We agree with Calvin's biblically informed axiom on the matter: "it is foolish to attempt to prove to infidels that the Scripture is the Word of God."[50]

Many more examples could be multiplied to illustrate this fundamental compromise that runs rampant in evangelical apologetical theory. The utter disregard for the biblical doctrines of original sin, total depravity and satanic blindness relative to the unbeliever, is a fatal flaw. We need to get back to biblical basics in diagnosing man's true spiritual bankruptcy and helplessness as well as the only remedy for that bankruptcy found solely in the life-changing power of the gospel of Jesus Christ that comes from Scripture, which is the living, active and abiding Word of God. As for man's true plight, Scripture declares:

> Transgression speaks to the ungodly within his heart;
> There is no fear of God before his eyes.
> For it flatters him in his *own* eyes
> Concerning the discovery of his iniquity *and* the hatred
>   *of it.*
> The words of his mouth are wickedness and deceit;
> He has ceased to be wise *and* to do good.
> He plans wickedness upon his bed;
> He sets himself on a path that is not good;
> He does not despise evil (Ps 36:1-4).

And as for God's only solution to sinful humanity's spiritual demise, Scripture celebrates:

> But God, being rich in mercy, because of His great love with which He loved us, even when we were dead in our transgressions, made us alive together with Christ (by grace you have been saved), and raised us up with Him, and seated us with Him in the heavenly places in Christ Jesus, so that in the ages to come He might show the

surpassing riches of His grace in kindness toward us in Christ Jesus (Eph 2:4-7).

Summary

Apologetics deals with the questions, "Why do unbelievers reject the gospel? Why won't they believe?" Traditional apologists say it is primarily because they lack information, evidence, or a lucid presentation. In contrast, the Bible says they don't believe because they are dead in sin. Genesis 6:5, among other key passages, gives a heavenly diagnosis of the depth and breadth of man's comprehensive fallen status. Unbelievers are also supernaturally blinded by Satan, which doubly compounds their inability to perceive spiritual truth with unaided reason. Few Christian apologists acknowledge the significance of the noetic effects of sin on epistemology and even fewer ever hint at the reality of Satan's blinding influence on unbelievers. Augustine had a proper view on this matter. Thomas Aquinas did not. Both men have been highly influential throughout Church history and most Christian apologists identify with one camp or the other.

Prayer is a gift from God given to men. The fervent prayer of righteous believers is used in conjunction with God's Word, His gospel and the Holy Spirit to work in the hearts of sinners, enabling a supernatural override with respect to their personal sinfulness and satanic blindness.

Cornelius Van Til and Greg Bahnsen were two rare exceptions among the traditional apologists who preserved a biblical perspective on this matter of hamartiological hangovers in the hearts of unbelievers that was integrated practically into their apologetical methodology. From all the above, resultant implications can be drawn:

- Christians need to have an accurate appraisal of every unbeliever as diagnosed by God in the Bible.

- Christians need to remember that unbelievers have darkened minds and cannot understand spiritual truth apart from God's Spirit and His Word.

- Christians always need to be cognizant of the blinding work of Satan on unbelievers.

- When doing the work of apologetics Christians need to

employ God's methods, not commonly accepted counterfeits modeled after worldly wisdom, philosophy and secular science.

• Christians need to realize there is no neutral ground with unbelievers in epistemology.

• Christians need to appeal to unbelievers based on their ontological common ground of internal and external general revelation.

• Christians need to call all unbelievers to repent, for unbelief is in itself sinful rebellion (Acts 17:30-31).

• Christians need to trust God for the results of their work in apologetics, for only God can change a hardened, unbelieving heart.

• Christians need to bathe all of their apologetics work in prayer, asking God for protection against Satan, supernatural courage, heavenly wisdom and the conviction of sinners.

The only starting point for witnessing to unbelievers and for defending the faith is on the sure foundation of the Word of God, which is Scripture. Only the gospel has the supernatural power capable of overriding the damning effects of personal sin and the supernatural death-grip of Satan, the prince of the power of the air and the god of this wicked world. Paul rightly declared, "For I am not ashamed of the gospel, for it is the power of God for salvation to everyone who believes" (Rom 1:16).

Notes

1. K. Scott Oliphint, *The Battle Belongs to the Lord: The Power of Scripture for Defending Our Faith* (Phillipsburg, NJ: P & R Publishing, 2003), 151-52. Groothuis also says the greatest roadblock to belief for the unbeliever is ignorance when he quotes Machen: "False ideas are the greatest obstacles to the reception of the gospel," Douglas Groothuis, *Christian Apologetics: A Comprehensive Case for Biblical Faith* (InterVarsity Press, Downers Grove IL, 2011), 28. Wrong information is not man's greatest impediment to embracing the saving gospel—it is personal sin, satanic blindness and rebellion against God. As such, God needs to take the initiative in the salvation process—He is the One Who seeks and saves sinners. "Salvation is from the LORD" (Jonah 2:9).

2. *The Cornerstone Seminary*, Vallejo, CA, class discussion, May 2015.

3. John C. Whitcomb, "Defending the Bible: Contemporary Apologetics and the Christian Faith," the W. H. Griffith Thomas Lectures, *Dallas Theological Seminary*, February 8-11, 1977.

4. Robert Duncan Culver, *Systematic Theology: Biblical & Historical* (Great Britain: Christian Focus Publications, Ltd., 2005), 339.

5. Henry Holloman, *Kregel Dictionary of the Bible and Theology* (Grand Rapids: Kregel, 2005), 501.

6. For example, the highly popular theologian and prolific writer, Tremper Longman, who taught for many years at Westminster Seminary and is currently at Westmont College in Santa Barbara, denies the reality of a historical Adam; see www.youtube.com/watch?v=I8Pk1vXL1WE; many others follow suit like Peter Enns, Kenton Sparks, Denis Lamoureux, John Walton, the BIOLOGOS blog, and many more.

7. Holloman, *Kregel Dictionary*, 503.

8. Clark H. Pinnock, *A Wideness in God's Mercy: The Finality of Jesus Christ in a World of Religions* (Grand Rapids: Zondervan, 1992).

9. William Lane Craig, "Classical Apologetics," *Five Views on Apologetics*, ed. Steven B. Cowan (Grand Rapids: Zondervan, 2000), 365.

10. Calvin himself admits this: "the doctrine which I deliver [i.e., 'total depravity'] is not new, but the doctrine which of old Augustine delivered with the consent of all the godly, and which was afterward shut up in the cloisters of monks for almost a thousand years." And Calvin shows how Augustine got this doctrine from the Bible; *Institutes*, 180-181.

11. Calvin showed how Scripture clearly teaches total depravity of the human nature. He explains from Ephesians 4, "that there is no part in which it is not perverted and corrupted" and concludes that "it cannot be denied that the hydra lurks in every breast." But at the same time he acknowledges that all possible vices of evil do not manifest themselves equally in an

unbridled manner with all people: "I confess, indeed, that all the iniquities do not break out in every individual." In other words, people are not as bad as they could be because God in His grace and mercy provides a general "divine grace" for all humanity (i.e., common grace) to ensure a modicum of restraint for "the preservation of the established order of things"; *Institutes*, 178-179.

12. Calvin taught that God makes believers radically new creatures through salvation by the work of Christ's atonement; Christians are no longer lost and totally depraved, but have become the beloved children of God: "in order that all ground of offense may be removed, and He may completely reconcile us to Himself, He, by means of the expiation set forth in the death of Christ, abolishes all the evil that is in us, so that we, formerly impure and unclean, now appear in His sight just and holy"; *Institutes*, 326.

13. Horton makes an important distinction here: "First, human beings—including unbelievers—are credited in Scripture with good actions, just as they are credited with knowledge and wisdom in human affairs. Nevertheless, it is with respect to the righteousness of God's own character, which he has revealed in his law, that God judges all mortals. While we have abundant evidence of knowledge and wisdom in ordinary human affairs, the gospel—identified by the apostle Paul as the heavenly wisdom that confounds us—is a mystery apart from the Spirit's regenerating work. Second, related to the first, human beings have a *natural* ability to fulfill God's commands, but lack the *moral* ability to love God and neighbor so as to fulfill those commands. Human beings have all of the requisite faculties and abilities with which God endowed them in creation. The fall did not destroy these characteristics of covenantal identity, but twisted and de-formed them. Therefore, all human beings are by definition covenantal creatures and image-bearers; being a human person is not dependent on being related to God in rectitude. The problem is that the human will is in moral bondage to sin"; Michael Horton, *The Christian Faith: A Systematic Theology for Pilgrims on the Way* (Grand Rapids: Zondervan, 2011), 431.

14. R. C. Sproul, John Gerstner and Arthur Lindsley, *Classical Apologetics: A Rational Defense of the Christian Faith and a Critique of Presuppositional Apologetics* (Grand Rapids: Zondervan, 1984), 213. Sproul, Gerstner and Lindsley falsely accuse presuppositionalists of teaching that total depravity has eradicated the *imago dei*. Similarly, Kelly James Clark, and a host of others accuse Van Til of teaching that "unbelievers can't know anything," which is patently false and a gross misrepresentation of what Van Til actually taught. Clark leaks in the same article that he actually has not read much of Van Til. That is obvious by the fallacious straw man he has

created for the sole purpose of then tearing Van Til down. See Kelly James Clark, *Five Views*, 255-57. Geisler has recently gone on a crusade, declaring war on the five points of Calvinism, including total depravity. He attacks and rejects total depravity by first misrepresenting what it is—he creates a straw man and then burns it. In the end, Geisler says that Calvinists believe total depravity teaches that unbelievers are so spiritually dead that "they cannot even understand the gospel or receive the gospel" [www.youtube.com/ watch?v= OFs64zcTCYc&NR=1]. But that is a wrong definition of total depravity. Unbelievers understand the gospel, and many reject it categorically because they love their sin more than they love God. That is what Jesus said in John 3:19-20. For a correct understanding of total depravity, as opposed to Geisler's caricature, see *The Five Points of Calvinism: Defined, Defended and Documented*, pp. 18-27; David N. Steele, Curtis C. Thomas and S. Lance Quinn (Phillipsburg, NJ: P & R Publishing, 2004) and Edwin H. Palmer's, *The Five Points of Calvinism*, where he says, "total depravity is not the same as absolute depravity"; (Grand Rapids, MI: Baker Book House, 1972), 9-23.

15. Robert L. Reymond, *A New Systematic Theology of the Christian Faith* (Nashville: Thomas Nelson, 1998), 450.

16. Holloman, *Kregel Dictionary*, 109. MacArthur expounds further on the implications of total depravity and why it is the most despised biblical doctrine of all among unbelievers and even among many professing believers: "Sin is a cruel tyrant. It is the most devastating and degenerating power ever to afflict the human race, such that the entire creation 'groans and suffers the pains of childbirth together until now' (Rom. 8:22). It corrupts the entire person—infecting the soul, polluting the mind, defiling the conscience, contaminating the affections, and poisoning the will. It is the life-destroying, soul-condemning cancer that festers and grows in every unredeemed human heart like an incurable gangrene...Not surprisingly, the very notion of such absolute enslavement (a doctrine commonly known as 'total depravity' or 'total inability') is repugnant to the fallen human heart. In fact, no doctrine is more hated by unbelievers than this one, and even some Christians find it so offensive that they zealously attack it. Though the doctrine of total depravity is often the most attacked and minimized of the doctrines of grace, it is the most distinctly Christian doctrine because it is foundational to a right understanding of the gospel (in which God initiates everything and receives all the glory). The neglect of this doctrine within American evangelicalism has resulted in all kinds of errors, including both the watered-down gospel and the seeker-driven pragmatism of the church growth movement. But the Scripture is clear: unless the Spirit of God

gives spiritual life, all sinners are completely unable to change their fallen nature or to rescue themselves from sin and divine judgment. They can neither initiate nor accomplish any aspect of their redemption. Even the supposed 'good things' that unbelievers do are like filthy rags before a holy God (Isa. 64:6). Contrast that with every other religious system, in which people are told that through their own efforts they can achieve some level of righteousness, thereby contributing to their salvation. Nothing could be further from the truth"; John MacArthur, *Slave: The Hidden Truth about Your Identity in Christ* (Nashville, Tennessee: Thomas Nelson, 2010), 121-22. Cf. MacArthur's excellent exposition on total depravity in *Proclaiming a Cross-Centered Theology*, eds. Mark Dever, J. Ligon Duncan III, R. Albert Mohler Jr., C. J. Mahaney (Wheaton, IL: Crossway, 2009), 81-98.

17. O. R. Brandon, "Heart," *Evangelical Dictionary of Theology*, ed. Walter A. Elwell (Grand Rapids: Baker Book House, 1984), 499. Brandon well notes the significance of "heart," *lēb* in Hebrew: "in the OT, heart is also used very frequently in a psychological sense, as the center or focus of man's inner personal life. The heart is the source, or spring, of motives; the seat of the passions; the center of the thought processes; the spring of conscience. Heart, in fact, is associated with what is now meant by the cognitive, affective, and volitional elements of personal life." Horton well notes that, "Sin is first of all a *condition* that is simultaneously judicial and moral, legal and relational. Accordingly, we sin because we are sinners rather than vice versa"; Horton, *The Christian Faith*, 427. Being a 'relational' offense, sin is primarily vertical in perspective as it is first and foremost a transgression against God.

18. Total depravity is permanent in the unbeliever until it is overcome by personal salvation in Jesus Christ through belief in His gospel (cf. 2 Cor 5:17).

19. Richard Mayhue, "Is Nature the 67th Book of the Bible?" in *Coming to Grips with Genesis: Biblical Authority and the Age of the Earth*, ed. Terry Mortenson and Thane H. Ury (Green Forest, AR: Master Books, 2008), 119-20.

20. Groothuis, *Christian Apologetics*, 177.

21. Bruce Demarest, *General Revelation: Historical Views and Contemporary Issues* (Grand Rapids: Zondervan, 1982), 27.

22. Ibid., 28.

23. Ibid., 29.

24. Cornelius Van Til, *The Defense of the Faith* (Phillipsburg, NJ: P & R, 1867), 87.

25. Demarest, *General Revelation*, 35-36.

26. Greg L. Bahnsen, *Van Til's Apologetic: Readings & Analysis* (Phillipsburg, NJ: P & R, 1998), 46.

27. Ibid., 47.

28. Culver, *Systematic Theology*, 381. Culver notes, "Roman Catholic theology…regards man's rational faculties as not vitiated by the fall of Adam."

29. John Calvin, *Institutes*, 234.

30. Culver, 353-54.

31. Christopher Hitchens is not just an atheist, but a self-proclaimed "antitheist"—purposefully hostile to theism. His hostile posture is obvious from the title of his book, *God is Not Great: How Religion Poisons Everything*, 2007.

32. Dawkins is the atheistic best-selling author of *The God Delusion*. He gloats, "to be an atheist is a realistic aspiration, and a brave and splendid one. You can be an atheist who is happy, balanced, moral, and intellectually fulfilled…atheism nearly always indicates a healthy independence of mind and, indeed, a healthy mind"; (New York: Houghton Mifflin Company, 2006), 1, 3.

33. Like Hitchens and Dawkins, Stenger is also sarcastic and snobbishly condescending. He writes, "We have no evidence for Bigfoot, the Abominable Snowman, and the Loch Ness Monster, so we do not believe they exist. If we have no evidence or other reason for believing in God, then we can be pretty sure that God does not exist." Victor J. Stenger, *God, The Failed Hypothesis: How Science Shows That God Does Not Exist* (Amherst, NY: Prometheus Books, 2008), 18. Hitchens, Dawkins and Stenger are not victims of innocent ignorance, but rather are in willful revolt against the Creator. Horton says it well: "Apart from the gospel we flee from God's self-revelation, dressing folly in the robe of wisdom and ungodliness in the garments of virtue. It is ultimately an ethical revolt against the God who made us," 53.

34. Craig, *Five Views*, 50.

35. Whitcomb, "Defending the Bible."

36. Dean Hardy, *Stand Your Ground: An Introductory Text for Apologetics Students* (Eugene, Oregon: Wipf & Stock Publishers, 2007), 106.

37. George J. Zemek, "Exegetical and Theological Bases for a Consistently Presuppositional Approach to Apologetics," Unpublished Th.D. dissertation (Winona Lake: Grace Theological Seminary, May 1982), 139.

38. Bahnsen, *Van Til's Apologetic*, 292.

39. Greg L. Bahnsen, *Always Ready: Directions for Defending the Faith*, ed. Robert R. Booth (Texarkana: Covenant Media Foundation, 1996), 7.

40. R. C. Sproul, *Defending Your Faith: An Introduction to Apologetics* (Wheaton, IL: Crossway, 2003), 30, 36. We need to be clear about what we mean by "common ground." Van Til, Bahnsen, true presuppositionalism and biblical apologetics say that between believers and unbelievers, there is (1) no neutral ground; (2) no epistemological common ground; but (3) there is ontological common ground. It is on this topic that Van Til is most misunderstood and misrepresented by classical apologists who repeatedly accuse him of denying any common ground between a Christian and an unbeliever. House and Holden are typical here, falsely alleging that presuppositionalists recognize "no common ground with the unbeliever" and they also falsely allege that presups say there is no value whatever in the use of apologetics when talking with unbelievers; see H. Wayne House and Joseph M. Holden in *Charts of Apologetics and Christian Evidences* (Grand Rapids, MI: Zondervan, 2006), chart 9. It is interesting to note that traditional apologist Pinnock once rejected the notion of epistemological common ground. He wrote in 1967, "Psychologically there is no common ground between Christian and non-Christian, in that the latter will not yield to the force of the evidence for the gospel, but will seek to equivocate its thrust. This fact does not relieve us of the duty of presenting it to him prayerfully"; Clark Pinnock, *Set Forth Your Case: An Examination of Christianity's Credentials* (Chicago: Moody Press, 1974), 16. He has long since abandoned this position and continues to radically morph in all of his views.

41. Craig, *Five Views*, 44.

42. John Frame, *Five Views*, 80, 130.

43. Ibid., 219. In a personal conversation I had with Frame in my apologetics class (The Cornerstone Seminary, Vallejo CA, May, 2015) he admitted he had never thought about the implications of satanic blindness on the unbeliever relative to apologetics and he admitted he was not too familiar with the implications of 2 Corinthians 4:4. This is evidenced by the lack of his addressing this truth in all of his books written the past several decades.

44. Habermas, *Five Views*, 97.

45. Feinberg, *Five Views*, 130, 149.

46. Norman Geisler, *Systematic Theology*, 4 vols. (Minneapolis: Bethany House, 2004), III:128.

47. Kelly James Clark, *Five Views*, 256.

48. Ibid., 371.

49. For Clark, a Christian philosophy and apologetics scholar, to claim ignorance about epistemological principles being taught in the Bible is inexcusable. It undermines the doctrine of the sufficiency of Scripture

among other things. Entire books have been written on biblical epistemology and resultant apologetical implications. Three popular works by Greg Bahnsen are monumental treatises on biblical epistemology: *Always Ready, Presuppostional Apologetics: Stated and Defended* and *Van Til's Apologetic: Readings and Analysis*. In addition there is his Ph.D. dissertation at the University of Southern California, which was on the very topic. Other excellent works on biblical epistemology relative to apologetics include Cornelius Van Til, *A Christian Theory of Knowledge* (Phillipsburg, N.J.: P&R, 1969); Robert L. Reymond's, *The Justification of Knowledge* (Phillipsburg, NJ: P & R, 1979), and Bruce Demarest's, *General Revelation: Historical Views and Contemporary Issues.*

50. Calvin, *Institutes*, 42.

7

Philosophy: The Love of Big Words

Good Old Fashioned School Daze

Philosophy has hijacked apologetics. The biblical and theological task of defending the faith has been co-opted and commandeered by the professional metaphysicists. The New Testament practice of all Christians aggressively and confidently defending their faith with Scripture on a personal level has been abdicated. It has been supplanted by the subtle takeover of elitist scholars with their knack for obfuscation and purported profundity with all things ontological and theoretical. The evidence is ubiquitous. I own countless books on Christian apologetics. Not one was authored by a non-philosopher. The understood pre-requisite for having a worthy say about anything related to apologetics in today's Christian world is a PhD in philosophy. We noted earlier that all the authors chosen to represent the various Christian approaches to apologetics in the *Five Views* book were selected because of their expertise in philosophy and logic, not because of their role as church men or acumen to exegete the Scriptures.

When I was a sophomore at Westmont College and a brand new, zealous, excited sponge-of-a baby Christian, I took a class called "Christian Theology." It was an entry-level doctrine class. The teacher was William Lane Craig, the now famous world-class evangelical philosopher/apologist. I did not know who he was at the time but I enjoyed the class and learned much about Christianity. I had lots of remedial catching up to do as I was an unbeliever for the first nineteen years of my life and had never studied the Bible up to that point. Our textbook was the helpful little theology book by Bruce Milne called, *Know the Truth*.

Dr. Craig was an engaging instructor and he taught with enthusiasm and authority and he was delighted to be imparting basic Bible theology to all us naïve, idealistic collegiates with young skulls full of mush. I don't remember any weird or esoteric stuff being taught. Craig even seemed to embrace inerrancy—which was in question by many professors at Westmont at the time. As the semester went on I came to realize that Dr. Craig was highly esteemed in the academic world for his advanced intellectual achievements at such a young age—thirty-six years young or so—and already had a doctorate in theology and philosophy at apparently quite prestigious institutions. My more seasoned and experienced fellow classmates assured me that this was a rare treat to have Dr. Craig as a professor and that I should be appreciative and impressed—so I was. Dr. Craig was at Westmont for one year as a visiting professor. I was in the right place at the right time...providential.

I enjoyed Christian Theology 101 so much I signed up for another class with Dr. Craig the next semester—"The Doctrine of the Knowledge of God." I was looking forward to digging deeper into God's Word to study about the Father, the Son and the Holy Spirit. The first day of class arrived and proved to make an indelible impression on me for a few reasons. The first was that this class had way fewer students in it and I did not know anyone. None of my friends were in the class. This obviously was not a general education class—I was among the elites. Second, I noticed that they were all much older than me—like juniors and seniors—very intimidating upper classmen, who all shaved and used big words during class discussion. Something was wrong but I could not put my finger on it initially. Third and finally, there was the initial lecture. After an hour and a half of Craig waxing eloquent, I was stunned. He never used the Bible. "Why did I bring my Bible to class?" I asked myself later that day.

By the third week I began to see the real picture. Three entire class periods of talking about God's knowledge, but no one was referring to the Bible—not even the professor. And the words—so many words and phrases were being used that I did not understand...it was making me dizzy: epistemology, cosmological, metaphysical, ontological, teleological, *a priori*, *posteriori*, rationalism, empiricism, transcendentalism, contingent, veridical, axiological, existential, predication, hylomorphism, dialectical, demiurges, acts of predication, the law of the excluded middle, innate ideas, eternal forms, noumenal causes, necessary postulates. "I already met my foreign language requirements when I took Spanish one," I thought to myself.

In addition to the multi-syllabled, incomprehensible vernacular, there was the main topic of discussion. Dr. Craig spent a great portion of the time talking about God's "middle knowledge." That was baffling because even though I was a relatively new Christian I knew that the phrase "middle knowledge" was not in the Bible—as a matter of fact I had never heard anyone talk about that concept. To me, the novice believer, the notion that God had middle knowledge was weird...a canard. It turns out I had unwittingly enrolled in an upper division philosophy elective course, not a Bible class. It took me three weeks to figure it out. By that time I was lost in a sea of confusion and dropped the class. It was a memorable experience, even though I was disillusioned by the notion that the doctrine of God could be investigated and explored by Christians without using the Bible. At that point I was only interested in what the Bible had to say. What I did not realize then that I realize now is that at some point in Christian history philosophy had hijacked apologetics.

A few years later I enrolled in seminary. In my last year I took apologetics since it was a required course. Going in, I naively thought, "Cool! We are going to learn how to witness to Mormons, new-agers—do some street evangelism and study the doctrines of the faith." That never happened. Once again I was confronted with those big, scary words and concepts: epistemology, metaphysics, ontology, cosmological and new ones—autopistic, transcendental presuppositionalism and the impossibility to the contrary. This time around I was not quite as disillusioned. I even found some of the metaphysical musings intriguing. Here I was introduced to the works of Cornelius Van Til, and twenty-five years later, with my two mammoth Christian apologetics encyclopedias at my side, I am finally beginning to understand what he was talking about.

Fast-forward fifteen years and it was now my turn to be an apologetics professor at the seminary level. As I prepared the curriculum and my lectures, the reservoir of data and resources available in the Christian world on the topic of apologetics was heavy-laden with philosophy and logic. There did not seem to be a biblically-driven, comprehensive, practical, non-philosophy-major friendly approach to apologetics at the popular level suited for training seminary students to be pastors in the local church.

It seemed to me that philosophy had hijacked biblical apologetics. With that in mind, the goal of this chapter will be to expose the philosophical approach to Christian apologetics as an anemic counterfeit, show from Scripture why it's misguided and give practical, biblical alternatives.

Historical Landmarks of Intrusion and Allusion

God spoke through the Apostle Paul when he warned the church of his day with these timeless words: "See to it that no one takes you captive by philosophy and empty deceit, according to human tradition, according to the elemental spirits of the world, and not according to Christ" (Col 2:8; ESV). Watch out for Greek philosophy! That's exactly what he was saying. His face-value meaning in this verse cannot be ignored and should not be historically revised.

Paul spoke Greek, he ministered in a Greek culture, and he interacted with the Greek philosophers of all the dominant schools (cf. Acts 17) in his day. When he sounded the alarm against "philosophy," pagan Greek philosophy[1] was in the forefront of his mind, not just some generic idea of philosophy or an inane undefined concept.

The new church in Colossae resided in the middle of the pagan Greek world,[2] surrounded on every side by centuries-old Gnostic, Platonic, Aristotelian, Stoic and Epicurean philosophy. Paul knew the church, and Christians, would be vulnerable to the influences of their immediate culture. The church needed to be discerning and take safeguards against such an imminent and dominant competing worldview.

But the inevitable happened—Greek philosophy penetrated and made inroads into the Christian church within decades of Paul's warning, and its insipid influences have been plaguing the church for two millennia.

Philosophy's usurpation of apologetics happened subtly, little by little, incrementally over the course of church history. No one period or person can be called out as the culprit, for there were many culpable contributors. But major landmarks can be identified that set the course steering apologetics away from being theologically, biblically and practically driven toward being philosophically, theoretically and formally oriented.

Justin Martyr (100-165)

"However, the religions of the nations are regarded as idolatrous throughout this [Old Testament] history. Ever since Justin Martyr, some Christians have claimed that the pagan philosophers prepared the way for Christ among the Gentiles as Moses and the prophets prepared the Jews. But this is to confuse general revelation with special revelation and the law with the gospel."[3] So says Michael Horton, who identifies Justin Martyr as a key historical flashpoint who spawned the ensuing Hellenistic philosophical juggernaut that would infect the Church for years to come.

Justin is considered by historians as one of the first "apologists," but as we saw in chapter 2, all believers are to do the work of *apologia* (1 Pet 3:15). It just so happens that some of his writings entitled *First Apology* and *Second Apology*, were preserved and found.[4] There were probably plenty of other unknown Christians during his day who wrote tracts defending the faith, or who defended their faith orally day to day.

Little is known about his personal life. Greek in culture and education, he was born in Flavia Neapolis in Samaria and was drawn to Platonism, but finally found true philosophy in the wisdom of the prophets and embraced Christianity in 130. A full-blown Greek Stoic philosopher prior to salvation, Justin never abandoned the system upon becoming a Christian. Instead of purging pagan paradigms, he integrated them with his newfound biblicism. He "regarded Christianity as a philosophy, and continued to wear the philosopher's gown."[5] Justin went so far as to say that Christ "is the Word of whom every race of men were partakers; and those who lived reasonably (*meta logou*) are Christians, even though they have been thought atheists."[6] The Apostle Paul called the Stoics to repentance (Acts 17:18, 30), whereas Justin welcomed and tried to commandeer their metaphysical underpinnings. Horton notes the following:

> The ancient Greek school of Stoicism (founded by Zeno in the third century BC) taught that divinity permeates nature with its seminal reason (the *logos spermatikos*). The apologist Justin Martyr (AD 100-165) adapted this Stoic idea to Christianity by arguing that the divine spark or seed of rationality (the *logos spermatikos*) emanates from Christ throughout the world and can be found in the best philosophies of noble pagans. Just as Moses and the

prophets prepared the Jews for Jesus Christ, Socrates, Plato and Stoicism prepared the Gentiles for the gospel. Here we discover the seeds of the later Roman Catholic tendency to treat general and special revelation as different in *degree* rather than in *content*. Medieval theology increasingly developed a dualistic approach in which what we might call *secular* knowledge was attributed to nature, and *spiritual* knowledge to grace. Even in spiritual matters, however, the natural mind (weakened but not depraved from the fall) could discover truth. Consequently, medieval theology affirmed not only *natural revelation* but *natural theology*, on whose foundations the supernatural theology based on special revelation was erected.[7]

So Justin paved the way for intellectual accommodation and theological integration of pagan Greek philosophy with Christian thought and hermeneutics that many would later mimic.

Clement of Alexandria (AD 150-215)

Titus Flavius Clemens, Greek theologian and writer, was one of the first key representatives of the Alexandrian theological tradition.[8] Like Justin, historians in hindsight refer to him as one of the first official "apologists" of the church. Born of pagan parents in Athens, he went to Alexandria where he succeeded his teacher Pantaenus as head of the Catechetical School. Gonzalez summarizes his influence:

> Clement was convinced that philosophy had been given to the Gentiles to lead them to Christ, just as the Law had been given to the Jews for the same purpose. Therefore, a great deal of his theology is in truth an interpretation of Christianity from the perspective of middle Platonism. This he did by means of allegorical interpretations of Scripture and on the basis of the doctrine of the Logos, which inspired both Scripture and philosophy, and which was incarnate in Jesus...he was influential in the later course of theology through his disciple Origen and may be said to be the first great teacher of the Alexandrian school.[9]

Like Justin, Clement had an inflated view of the pagan Greek philosophers, and instead of eschewing their unredeemed humanistic thinking as Paul commanded in Colossians 2:8, Clement gave it credence and tried to assimilate their thinking with the Bible:

> Clement affirmed that "before the advent of our Lord, philosophy was necessary to the Greeks for righteousness...Perchance, too, philosophy was given to the Greeks directly and primarily, till the Lord should call the Greeks. For this was their schoolmaster to bring 'the Hellenic mind' as the law, the Hebrews, 'to Christ'" (*Stromata* 1.5). He also spoke of the inspiration of Greek poets (*Exhortation to the Heathen* 8), and went so far as to declare that 'by reflection and direct vision, those among the Greeks who have philosophized accurately, saw God' (*Stromata* 1.19)...From mastery of the prevailing philosophy, he defended the superiority of the Christian revelation. While non-Christian philosophers possessed some truth, it too came from God, either by general or special revelation.[10]

Horton observes that Clement's compromise with Greek philosophy became a legacy for other Christians who in turn created an extreme dichotomy in treating the relationship between faith and reason, which amounted to a strict rationalism that attempted to base theological beliefs on universal principles of innate reason.[11] Similarly, Weinrich observes:

> Clement is important for his positive approach to philosophy which laid the foundations for Christian humanism and for the idea of philosophy as 'handmaid' to theology. The idea of the Logos dominates his thinking. The divine Logos, creator of all things, guides all good men and causes all right thought. Greek philosophy was therefore, a partial revelation and prepared the Greeks for Christ just as the law prepared the Hebrews. Christ is the Logos incarnate through whom man attains to perfection and true *gnōsis*...Through self-control and love man rids himself of passions, reaching finally the state of impassibility wherein he attains to the likeness of God. With this

idea Clement profoundly influenced Greek Christian spirituality.[12]

Notably, Greek philosophy also influenced Clement's[13] hermeneutics, even after he came to faith. Instead of reading Scripture in the grammatical-historical sense as the apostles and first Christians did, Clement utilized the Greek allegorical method of interpretation. Clement found five possible meanings to a passage in Scripture: historical, doctrinal, prophetic, philosophical, and mystical (a deeper moral, spiritual and religious truth symbolized by events or persons).[14] History is riddled with those who followed suit with Clement, freely employing his fanciful Scriptural analysis.

Origen (AD 185-254)

Born of Christian parents and a keen mind, Origen is regarded as one of the great "apologists" of the early church. His father, Leonides, was beheaded in 202 during the persecution under Roman emperor Lucius Septimus Severus (A.D. 193-211) when Origen was about twelve.[15] Fastidiously religious from a young age, he practiced a rigorous asceticism; possessed one coat and no shoes; rarely ate meat and refrained from wine; castrated himself based on a literal reading of Matthew 19:12; deprived himself of sleep in favor of late night prayer vigils and slept on the bare floor; memorized vast portions of Scripture; mastered Hebrew; traveled broadly and wrote voluminously.[16] Considered by some to be the greatest theologian of the early Greek Church and a paragon of apologetical potency,[17] he is considered by others as a rank heretic.[18] Ordained in Palestine in 228, he was defrocked four years later for violation of various theological church laws.[19] Despite his heretical propensities, he was nonetheless one of the most learned men and profound thinkers in the ancient Church and probably exerted more influence on the systematic doctrinal development of the Church than any other man.[20] Nevertheless, his compromise with Greek philosophy virtually undermined all good intents he had as a professed convert to Christianity. Horton justly describes Origen as "the church father most enthralled by Greek philosophy."[21]

Origen took integration of pagan Greek philosophy and biblical theology to extreme, unparalleled levels. As a result, he convoluted many of the most basic doctrines of the Christian faith. Origen promoted an inchoate version of purgatory that he inherited from

Plato.[22] "The influence of Platonism on the church Father Origen (AD 185-254) was so thorough that the early Greek theologian taught not only that the soul was the immortal part of human beings that preexisted eternally but also that this soul was often reincarnated in different bodies."[23] Practically, it was a reincarnation of sorts—all, including Satan, will be reunited with God. In other words, Origen believed, and even declared that "even the devil could be saved."[24] "Officially condemned in the sixth century, Origen's theory of universal restoration (*apokatastasis*) held that all spirits (though not bodies), including Lucifer, would be reunited in heavenly bliss."[25] Horton further comments on this harbinger to Hinduism: "the pedagogical ascent of mind in Origen, where purgatory is regarded as a process of spiritual education and enlightenment through various reincarnations until finally every soul (including the devil) is united with God. Origen's teachings were rejected by the church."[26] This pre-medieval view of spiritual purgatory Origen called *apokotastasis*: the concept of the universal restoration (universal salvation) for all of creation, humanity, and fallen angels alike. This teaching was condemned at the Fifth Council of Constantinople in 553.[27]

As to sanctification, Origen went way afield. He held to the Platonic or Neoplatonic notion of ontological participation (*methexis*—the Platonic term for participation) or ontic union of the soul with the divinity or literally a fusion with the deity (where God's essence is literally communicated to His creatures), on an ever-ascending ladder of being, instead of the biblical concept of covenantal union (*koinōnia*) with Christ. This violates the biblical reality whereby God always remains transcendent from His creation ontologically so our participation with Him is analogical. "Thus, union with God-in-Christ is not the goal to which the soul aspires in its striving ascent, but the freely-given communion that every believer enjoys from the very beginning. Believers live *from* this union, not *toward* it, and it is a forensic and relational reality: a communion of persons and their gifts rather than an exchange (much less fusion) of essences."[28] For Origen, the believer becomes more and more a part of God. But the Bible does not teach "a fusion of essences...but of a communion of persons."[29]

Worst of all, Origen had a mangled Christology. He rejected the literal, bodily resurrection and ascension of Christ: "the ascension of Jesus Christ in the flesh most radically challenges the Platonist/

Neoplatonist ontology. Origen said that this event was 'more an ascension of mind than of body.'"[30] Again, for such a view Origen is indebted to Plato: "Christ's ascension was 'more an ascent of mind than body,' blazing the trail for contemplative disciples. Echoing Plato, much of ancient and medieval Christian spirituality was characterized by this contemplative ascent toward the 'beatific vision'—the direct sight of the Good in itself."[31]

In addition, his view of the Atonement was distorted:

> One view, called the 'classical' or ransom theory—formulated by Origen—regarded the atonement as a ransom paid to Satan. Assuming that the devil was the rightful owner of sinners, Origen taught that Christ was a trap: his humanity was the necessary bait for luring Satan into thinking that he had at least won out over Yahweh, and then he conquered the devil by his deity. Although attracted to aspects of the theory, Gregory of Nanzianzus challenged the idea of God conquering through deception, but the more basic question is whether it can be said in any sense that Satan was the rightful owner of human beings. Theologians throughout the centuries have pointed out the speculative character of this idea. Furthermore, it contradicts several lines of biblical teaching on this subject.[32]

And he promulgated an indefensible, extreme ontological subordinationism of the Son from the influence of Philo.[33]

Christian historian, C. C. Kroeger concluded that, "Origen must chiefly be remembered for the power and understanding with which he developed, propounded, and defended the major doctrines of the Bible."[34] We could not disagree more. We conclude that based on Origen's wholesale compromise with pagan Greek philosophy through the process of integration, he taught that all people would eventually be saved (including Satan!), that we become part of God and that Jesus did not in fact physically rise from the dead.[35] We echo with the Apostle Paul, "But if there is no resurrection of the dead, not even Christ has been raised...and if Christ has not been raised, your faith is worthless; you are still in your sins" (1 Cor 15:13, 17). The bodily resurrection of Christ is at the heart of the gospel (1 Cor 15:1-4). Paul said, "believe in your heart that God raised Him from the dead, [*and*] you will be saved" (Rom 10:9). No resurrection, then no gospel; no gospel, then no salvation. Origen rejected the resurrection of Jesus. He should have rejected Greek philosophy instead, as Paul had commanded (Col 2:8).

Augustine of Hippo (AD 354-430)

Living seventy-six years, the first thirty-three as an unbeliever, Augustine's mark on the Church is unparalleled as his influence has boldly reverberated for fifteen hundred years. He is truly unique among the early Church fathers as the Catholic Church,[36] Protestants of every ilk,[37] and even the great modern philosophers[38] have all claimed him as their own and are marked by his insights. Dulles correctly observes, "Thanks to his rare combination of speculative power, erudition, and literary eloquence, Aurelius Augustine (354-430) occupies a place of unique eminence in the story of patristic apologetics."[39] He is still considered to be the principal theologian of the Latin church, the father of all Western Christianity after him,[40] as well as the greatest Western preacher of the early church.[41] His shadow looms large down the corridors of Church history.

Despite his legacy of greatness and the overly idealistic, forgiving nature of the winds of time, Augustine was not flawless nor was he made of marble. He was a sinner saved by grace and his life was one of dynamic complexity—progress amidst struggles, evidenced by the walk of a pilgrim with feet of clay, longing ever onward toward heaven's glory. As one of the most important fathers of the early Church, we know much about his personal life through a variety of especially full and useful sources. He was one of the most fertile writers of the early period. His *Confessions* (written between 397 and 400) tell us much about the formative events of his first thirty-three years leading up to his salvation.[42]

Augustine was born at Thagaste (the present Algeria) North Africa, on November 13, 354. His father Patricius, was a lively, sensual, hot-tempered person, and unfriendly to Christianity until the close of his life. His mother, Monnica, was a believer and was influential in Augustine's mid-life conversion. He received his first education at Thagaste, learning reading and writing, as well as the rudiments of Greek[43] and Latin literature, from teachers who followed the old traditional pagan methods. In his youth his education was void of any systematic instruction in the Christian faith. At sixteen he moved to Carthage where he would study and then teach rhetoric. He relates that a personal turning point in his early career was when he took up philosophy with great zeal at age nineteen.[44] From an early age, beginning in his teens, he acknowledges the widespread exposure he had to immorality and profligate living. That lifestyle would haunt and shame him all of his days. He also had an insatiable desire to learn and his first three decades were a relentless, futile, pursuit of wisdom, which he sought in classical education, Cicero, Manichaeism, Platonism and Neoplatonism. Eventually unfulfilled and disillusioned with much of the world's philosophy, Augustine embraced the truth of Christianity in response to his mother's prayers, the preaching of the Italian bishop, Ambrose of Milan, and through a direct confrontation with Scripture, the living Word of God. Evans relays his oft-repeated salvation testimony:

> In late August 386, still in this period of spiritual turmoil, Augustine sat down one day in a garden with the book of Romans in his hands. He wept with frustration and pain, 'in the bitterness of my heart' as he describes it....'I read in silence the first thing my eye fell on,' he says. This was the passage in Romans 13.13-4, which he quotes. It calls on the reader to turn away from a life of sexual indulgence and to 'put on the Lord Jesus Christ'. 'I did not need to read further,' he says. 'As soon as I came to the end of that sentence it was as though the light of security flooded me and all my doubts fell away.' His life was transformed. Everything fell into place; the strain and anxiety left him and from that time on he was a committed Christian.[45]

After his dramatic conversion, Augustine went on to be ordained as a priest and found the first monastery in Africa in 391, became co-bishop of Hippo from 391-395, and in 395 became the permanent bishop until his death in 430.

During his thirty-five-plus ministry years as a churchman, he proved to be a prolific and indefatigable writer, teacher and preacher of theology. The breadth of material he issued is almost incomparable for someone of that time period. Summarizing his beliefs remains a challenge in light of the sheer amount as well as the vast span of time he actively wrote. Demarest says, "Augustine's thought is rendered more difficult by the voluminous and unsystematic character of his writings."[46] When analyzing Augustine, one-dimensional, static, and anachronistic conclusions need to be avoided.

Viewing the whole corpus of his theological writings, Augustine clearly had biblical interests in mind. And there is clear evidence that he grew and matured as a biblical thinker and writer as the years progressed. This is most evident in his *Retractions* at the end of his life. The biblical and ecclesiastical coloring of his thoughts becomes more and more visible and even vivid. He affirmed a triune God, the depravity of man, the priority of faith, the authority of Scripture, the primacy of the Church and salvation by grace. He had a strong view of God's sovereignty. There are indeed many jewels to be mined by any believer from the treasury of the writings and reflections of the great bishop.

Nevertheless, Augustine was plagued in his thinking his whole Christian life from the hang-over of the man-made philosophies in which he was awash for the first three decades of his unredeemed life. They seemed to reside residually in his very DNA and could never be leached from his life. Here's where Augustine becomes the quintessential example of why Paul warned Christians not to be taken "captive through philosophy and empty deception, according to the tradition of men...rather than according to Christ" (Col 2:8). The dominant man-made philosophies that left an indelible impact on Augustine included Manichaeism, Platonism,[47] and Neoplatonism.[48]

Manichaeism (also Manicheeism)

At age nineteen Augustine embraced Manichaeism and remained an avid devotee for the ensuing nine years. Mani (c. 216-276), born in southern Mesopotamia, was the leader of this heretical sect that spread to Asia Minor and the Roman Empire. Manichaeism was rehashed Gnostic dualism. Dualism "is the belief that there are two coeternal principles in conflict with each other, such as matter and form (or spirit) or of good and evil. Platonism is an example of the former and Zoroastrianism, Gnosticism, and Manichaeism are examples of the latter. Dualists believe in creation *ex materia*, that is, out of preexisting matter or stuff."[49] A few things especially attracted young Augustine to Manichaeism: the liberty to criticize the OT; also, they held to an ascetic chastity and self-denial; and its dualistic view of the world provided a mechanism by which to explain evil in the world—two powers in the universe, two "first principles," good and evil, eternally at war. He also welcomed the notion of a mistrust of the body and the whole material world: the evil god was regarded by Gnostics and Manichees as the creator of matter, the good god as the creator of spirit.[50] A human being is an intellectual and spiritual being which finds itself thrust into the world of mater as a stranger, longing to return to the regions whence it came. Augustine strove later in life rather painfully for celibacy.[51]

Although Augustine would lose enthusiasm for Manichaeism after nine years, he never freed himself of its fundamental dualism. With its built-in dualities, it is an obvious source for his "two cities," but the concept is also found in Platonism, Stoicism and in Philo, influences that also impressed him.[52] Evans says about Manichaeism's long hold on Augustine: "this system he found it impossible ever to quite shake off after he became a Christian."[53] After becoming a Christian he would integrate this pagan philosophy with his biblical theology. "It was dangerously easy for Christians to feel sympathy with Manichean talk of a war of good and evil, for Christians too had deep within their tradition the consciousness that they were inwardly at war (Galatians 5.16-24)."[54]

Platonism

Platonism also held sway over Augustine. Long before there was *The Matrix*, there was Plato who believed in two worlds: this one—the physical, made of matter, deficient in reality, revealed by perception—and the real world, which was the invisible, eternal, divine realm of immutable, mind-independent Forms that are proper objects of knowledge.[55] Plato championed "Forms" as the building blocks to reality. Forms were eternal, invisible templates of the thoughts of god in the spiritual realm that corresponded to and issued in lesser objects in the lower, physical realm. Forms included the good, truth, beauty, justice, courage, wisdom and other virtues. Instead of jettisoning Plato's pagan worldview of "Forms" in obedience to Colossians 2:8 as Paul commanded, Augustine assimilated this notion, along with other Platonisms, into his Christian worldview after his salvation. The by-product was a compromised hermeneutic and theological system. Horton notes, "Augustine certainly believed in *ex nihilo* creation over Platonism's emanation of the world from the divine One. However, he still had trouble accepting that creation was spoken into existence rather than coming into being silently from the forms in the divine mind."[56] Even after becoming a bishop, Augustine maintained an inflated view of the pagan philosopher:

> Because Plato so acutely perceived the necessity of rising above matter and the sense he was, according to Augustine, very close to Christ. If Plato were to return to life, Augustine assures us, he would be delighted to find the churches full of men seeking spiritual and intelligible goods, animated by hope of eternal blessedness. Augustine is confident that Socrates and Plato, if they lived today, would become Christians "as so many Platonists of recent times have done."[57]

Demarest diagnoses the same trend:

> With his emphasis on the ascent of the soul to God, Augustine is the Christian Platonist *par excellence*... Augustine acknowledged in Greek philosophy the presence of considerable truth...of all the Gentile philosophers, Plato attained the highest level of truth. Said Augustine, "It is evident that none came nearer to us than the Platonists." Moreover, "their gold and silver [were] dug out of the mines of God's providence which are everywhere scattered abroad"...Through the pursuit of reason, the Platonists constructed a comprehensive natural theology. They believed that the invisible things of God are known through the things that are made. Plato and his school reasoned that God is the cause of all existence, the ultimate good, the ground of understanding and knowledge, the end to which life is to be regulated, and the bountiful bestower of blessedness.[58]

Horton shows how Platonism even hampered Augustine's Christology:

> Based on its view of human beings as composed of three parts—body, soul, and spirit (trichotomy), Apollinarianism taught that Jesus' human spirit was replaced with the divine Logos. Charles Hodge explains that Apollinarianism was motivated by "the doctrine then held by many at least of the Platonizing fathers, that reason in man is part of the divine Logos or universal reason." In this way, the soul-

body dualism was the conceptual corollary to Christ's deity and humanity. Even some of the orthodox theologians such as Athanasius and Augustine could speak as if the Logos "wielded" a human body, almost the way one might drive a car. A marked discomfort with the idea of the genuine humiliation, suffering, temptation, and anguish of the incarnate Son was often expressed.[59]

Neoplatonism

As a believer, Augustine was plagued by Neoplatonism as well. Neoplatonism was the revival and recasting of Platonism in the third century mainly through writers such as Plotinus and Porphyry, which influenced theologians such as Origen, Augustine, Boethius, and Bonaventure.[60] At age thirty-one, two years before his conversion, Augustine became strongly attracted to Neoplatonism—the idealistic character of this philosophy awoke unbounded enthusiasm, and he was attracted to it also by its exposition of pure intellectual being and the origin of evil.[61] Loofs says, "Full as the writings of this epoch are, however, of Biblical phrases and terms—grace and the law, predestination, vocation, justification, regeneration—a reader who is thoroughly acquainted with Neoplatonism will detect Augustine's old love of it in a Christian dress in not a few places."[62] So once again, as with Manichaeism and Platonism, Augustine does not abandon pagan philosophy as a Christian, but tries to integrate it with the Bible. This theological alchemy left him with a quasi-Christian epistemology: "Neoplatonic philosophy, championed by Plotinus (d. 270) and Porphyry (d. 305), exercised considerable influence on Augustine's religious thought, including an emphasis on self-transcending contemplation of truth, the primacy of cognitive intuition over sense perception, and the direct union of the soul with God."[63] Augustine relates in his *Confessions* that the books of the Neoplatonists that he read prior to his conversion to Christianity affirmed the existence of the infinite God and His Word, the creation of the world, and the inner presence of the divine light. "Their juster thoughts concerning the one God who made heaven and earth, have made them illustrious among philosophers."[64]

Integrating Greek pagan philosophies with biblical theology was not considered a compromise in Augustine's mind though—he saw it as baptizing or hallowing their rudimentary insights and raising them to a higher, truer level of spirituality:

In depicting the effort of the mind to reach upward beyond all material and changeable things to the eternal, invisible Godhead, Augustine relies heavily on his Neoplatonic philosophic heritage. But he finds numerous Scripture texts in his favor. He is fond of quoting from Paul: "We look not to the things that are seen but to the things that are unseen; for the things that are seen are transient, but the things that are unseen are eternal (2 Cor 4:18)."[65]

Augustine, like many Church fathers before him, opted for a synthesis or melding of biblical faith with classical culture, while correcting the errors of the pagans in the light of biblical revelation. They meet adversaries such as Galen and Celsus, Porphyry and Julian the Apostate on their own ground, accepting certain elements of the dominant forms of Platonism and rejecting others.[66] Similarly, Gonzalez appraises:

Augustine's theology is a combination of the earlier teachings of the church with Neoplatonism…From Neoplatonism Augustine derived his doctrine of God, whom he conceived in terms of the Neoplatonic "ineffable One," as well as his theory of the incorporeity of the soul. This latter view, which later became commonplace among Christians, was at first rejected by many as an unbiblical innovation. Also from the Neoplatonists, he derived his view of evil as not a substance but rather a deprivation of good. Every creature is in itself good, for it is made by God. But the corruption of the goodness of a creature is what we call evil.[67]

In hindsight, integration hindered rather than heightened Augustine's work as a biblical theologian and Christian teacher. Augustine was strong in all areas where he remained true to Scripture. He was aberrant at every point he attempted to assimilate and mix Greek philosophy with biblical truth. Cyanide and coffee don't mix well.

Anselm of Canterbury (AD 1033-1109)
Seven centuries after Augustine, another prominent Christian thinker came on the world scene, leaving a vast and indelible legacy in the

realm of metaphysics, philosophy, and theology. "The father of medieval scholasticism[68] and one of the most eminent of English prelates,"[69] *Anselmus Candiae Genavae*, or Anselm, was born in Aosta by the Italian Alps in Northern Italy in 1033. He was born to wealthy parents—a harsh father and a prudent mother. As a teenager he tried to enter the monastery but was rejected. That desire was later realized when he became a Benedictine monk at age twenty-seven (c. 1060). In 1063 he became prior; abbot in 1078; and the archbishop of Canterbury in 1093.[70] He was later canonized in 1494 and proclaimed Doctor of the Church in 1720 by Pope Clement XI.[71]

He was a preeminent scholar and effective teacher, who was humble in disposition and worked well with people. Admired for his keen intellect, Anselm is best known for his development of the ontological argument[72]—God is the perfect being "than which greater nothing can be thought"—and a unique version of the satisfaction theory of the atonement.[73] As a theologian he is called by many "the second Augustine." Beckwith summarizes Anselm's unique standing: "his writings display profundity, originality, and masterly grasp of intellect."[74]

Anselm was also known for being a philosopher. Two of his most noted works, *Monologion* and *Proslogion*, are more philosophical than theological or biblical. Both aim to prove the existence and nature of God from human reason apart from Scripture.[75] "Philosophically, Anselm's ideas were molded by Plato (428-348 B.C.) ...Anselm was a child of his day, which was dominated by platonic philosophy."[76] Charlesworth says Anselm's worldview was broadly that of Neoplatonism, which he inherited from his primary influence, Augustine, as well as Pseudo-Dionysius the Areopagite. He also inherited a rationalist way of thinking from Aristotle and Boethius.[77] Anselm's philosophical approach would impact others who followed including Rene Descartes, Benedict Spinoza, Georg Hegel, Charles Hartshorne, Norman Malcolm, along with most contemporary traditionalist Christian apologists including Alvin Plantinga, Clark Pinnock, Norm Geisler, William Craig, etc.[78] "Anselm is a model of traditional or classical apologetics. He believed in offering proofs for the existence of God...Anselm is the antithesis of...presuppositional apologetics."[79]

As a theologian, Anselm gave lip service to "faith that leads to reason"[80] but practically, and at the end of the day, he sounded more like an Aristotelian rationalist. Dulles observes:

> In the *Monologion* he agrees to write in such wise "that nothing from Scripture should be urged on the authority of Scripture itself, but that whatever the conclusion of independent investigation should declare to be true, should, in an unadorned style, with common proofs and with a simple argument, be briefly enforced by the cogency of reason, and plainly expounded in the light of truth."[81]

Although he was not as dependent upon pagan Greek philosophy to the degree that Justin, Clement or Origen were, he nevertheless made considerable use of Platonism and Neo-platonism. And once again, we see that this practice of integration of secular Greek philosophy with biblical truth always leads to compromise, to whatever degree, with respect to the truth. For example, regarding evangelism and apologetics, "Anselm is concerned to speak in terms meaningful to the nonbeliever. The common ground between them and believers is not faith but reason. 'For although they appeal to reason because they do not believe [and thus have no alternative], and we, on the other hand, because we do believe, nevertheless, the thing sought is one and the same.'"[82] Herein, in seminal form, is the precursor of the 20th century notion of "pre-evangelism" and the common practice of most apologists today who say believers can't approach unbelievers with biblical truth first, but rather we need to find common ground in reason and the laws of logic. The understood or unstated premise for such an approach is an utter disregard for the biblical teaching on the blinding effects of personal sin and Satanic deception (see chapter 6).

Demarest highlights other theological shortfalls of Anselm relative to apologetics due to his integrationist model. Anselm subtly departed from Augustine by attempting a more extensive philosophical explication of theism than Augustine. He thus "represents a transitional link between the faith perspective of Augustine and the rationalism of the later Scholastic tradition championed by Aquinas."[83] With Augustine he postulated the primacy of faith for the saving knowledge of God, but unlike Augustine, Anselm argued that reasons unaided by revelation must be adduced in support of the Christian faith.[84] He said, "The rational mind itself is most able to advance toward finding the Supreme Being."[85] In the case of the Christian, Anselm said rational demonstration [without special revelation] heightens faith's understanding of the gospel. Anselm believed in the Fall, but not in total depravity: "the corrupting influence of sin is not such that it can prevent the natural man's reason from assenting to the 'necessities' of the Christian faith once these have been presented to him."[86]

Demarest concludes that Anselm drew too heavily from Platonic idealism, arguing from the realm of rational thought, thus betraying his Augustinian and biblical commitments. In the end then, Anselm "demanded more of the innate God-idea and general revelation than they are capable of delivering."[87] Needless to say, Anselm's apologetic was not scripturally-driven nor gospel-centered. He also paved the way for the onset of wholesale Scholasticism that would reach its zenith under Thomas Aquinas. Anselm would have done well to disown the influences of pagan Greek philosophy, as Paul warned in Colossians 2:8, rather than integrating them into his reservoir of faith.

Thomas Aquinas (AD 1224-1274)[88]

We come now to the Prince of the Scholastics, the master of medieval Latin theology, the don of Rome's sacerdotal system and the patron Saint of the traditional and classical apologists—Thomas Aquinas. Born in Italy near Naples, he was placed in the monastery of Montecassino when he was five. At fourteen, he went to the University of Naples where he first came in contact with the Aristotelian philosophy.[89] In 1244 he joined the Dominican Order of Preachers. The Dominicans' practice of living on alms was deplored by many, thus, fearing that Thomas would ruin his career, his family kidnapped him and kept him a prisoner for over a year. They wanted him to join the Benedictine order. During this time they tried to dissuade him from joining the Dominicans, even resorting to the most manipulative antics. He escaped, became a Dominican, and was sent to study at Cologne in 1244, where Albertus Magnus was teaching. From Magnus he learned the Aristotelian method which would become the permanent template for his *Weltanschauung.*[90] Initially his genius was not apparent to his classmates, who called him "the dumb ox" because of his size and paucity of speech. On the personal side Thomas was refined, affable and lovable; he was content with the simple life.[91] Eventually, Magnus and his peers recognized his inimitable abilities and his mentor directed him toward an academic career. In 1252 he went to Paris for more formal education, and began teaching in 1257. His memory was a steel trap. He proved to be an analytical and authoritative teacher. He spent most of his career at the University of Paris as a university professor of philosophy and wrote commentaries on Aristotle[92] and theology. His *magnum opus* was the *Summa Theologica* which he composed for ten years at the end of his life.

> The great challenge to theology in Thomas' time was the philosophy of Aristotle, which was being brought into western Europe by means of new Latin translations. Many philosophers, particularly at the University of Paris, claimed that on the basis of the newly translated works, philosophy must come to a number of conclusions that contradicted generally accepted doctrine—conclusions such as matter has always existed, and that all souls are one. In reaction, many church leaders declared that the traditional Platonic and Augustinian philosophy was the only true one, and banned the study and discussion of certain elements of Aristotelian philosophy. Thomas took up the challenge, and set out to show that Christian faith is compatible with Aristotelian philosophy, as long as one understands the proper field and methodology of both theology and philosophy.[93]

Aquinas was considered innovative by many in his day, and not a few regarded his innovations dangerous. Thomism—the name given to his system—came under attack from both extreme Aristotelians and traditional theologians. There were repeated charges against his metaphysical novelties. In 1277, three years after the death of Thomas, the bishop of Paris issued a condemnation of 219 Aristotelian propositions, several of which had been held by Thomas. Similar steps were taken at Oxford. But slowly, with the staunch defense of many Dominicans, and the backing of the Roman Catholic Church, Thomism forever gained a foothold in Western Christianity. In 1323 John XXII canonized Thomas, and in 1567 Pius V declared him a "Universal Doctor of the Church."[94]

Aquinas is best known for integrating Aristotle with the Bible[95]—a clear violation of Colossians 2:8. Instead of watching out for pagan, humanistic philosophy, he co-opted it. "Next his decided Aristotelianism, not without an admixture of Neoplatonic elements, must be noted. He owed not only his philosophical thoughts and world-conception to Aristotle, but he also took from him the frame for his theological system; Aristotle's metaphysics and ethics furnished the trend of his system."[96] Vos further explains:

> Thomas Aquinas...embraced Aristotle's thought whole-heartedly as a philosophy...For him this philosophy became the basic tool for his theology; in his famous phrase, philosophy is the handmaid of theology. In almost every discussion—God's nature, the Trinity, the human soul, grace, faith, etc. —one finds Aquinas using distinct-ions developed by philosophers, especially Aristotle, to explain the meaning of faith.[97]

The practice of integrating human philosophy with God's Word directly undermines the doctrine of the sufficiency of Scripture. The Bible alone speaking to pertinent issues of the day was not adequate or sufficient for Thomas—Scripture needed to be bolstered with "other" truth to establish it as thorough and convincing. And Thomas did not stop at using just Aristotle in his theo-philosophical integrationism. Brown notes:

> Aquinas would start with a problem. He then would quote his authority. This could be a text of Scripture, a passage from one of the early Christian writers or a quotation from 'the philosopher'. The latter was never named; he did not need to be. It was Aristotle, the Greek philosopher from the fourth century BC, whose writings had been redis-covered and translated into Latin in the twelfth century. From now on his ideas set the tone. The Islamic philosophies of Avicenna and Averroes, as well as con-temporary Jewish thinkers, were also taken into account. Only when he had taken note of all the relevant points both for and against would Aquinas give his own answer.[98]

Although Aquinas was a believer, his compromise with pagan Greek philosophy wrought dramatic ramifications for the Church. His writings do not reflect biblical theology, but rather natural theology, rational theology and philosophical theology. This resulted from his integrationist approach and unbiblical view of exalted, unaided human reason. He says many good things in his theological writings, but it's all smothered in philosophical trappings and sophistry.

This is most evident in his view of the sacraments, especially Communion. For Aquinas, transubstantiation was at the heart of Communion or the Lord's Supper. His sophisticated and highly nuanced interpretation of transubstantiation issued from his Aristotelian worldview. Schaff notes, "Scholasticism gave the doctrine of transubstantiation the final form...the body and blood of Christ, and therefore their real presence under the accidents and elements, have their inception in the elements...The effect of the form upon the matter is to change it in the Aristotelian sense into the new, for which it possesses an inherent capability."[99] When the priest "consecrates" the wafer or host, a miracle supposedly takes places, whereby the bread in its very elements becomes Jesus' literal body—although not visibly, but in substance. And at that moment a real "immolation" takes place, whereby Jesus is crucified anew, His sacrifice then atoning for a new allotment of accrued sins that were not covered by His original death 2,000 years ago at Calvary. At the "sacrifice of the Mass," through the act of transubstantiation, Jesus is crucified time and time again. Aquinas taught that "the sacraments 'cause grace'...the effect of the sacraments is to infuse justifying grace into men."[100]

The backbone, the heart, and the very life-blood of true biblical Christianity centers on the reality of Christ's death, as well as its meaning and application on a personal level. Communion, or the Lord's Supper, is the tangible picture given by Christ to His Church by which to understand and even participate in the benefits of His atoning death for sinners. To convolute, distort or tamper with its true, original meaning is the gravest violation. Aquinas was guilty here. And it was because of his compromised accommodation of pagan Greek philosophy in utter disregard to Paul's warning in Colossians 2:8. Horton explains,

> Aquinas spends eight articles in his *Summa Theologica* providing a series of philosophical arguments for 'the way in which Christ is in the sacrament.' Yet again, this is consistent with his treatment of grace as a metaphysical substance whose infusion is caused by baptism and subsequent sacraments. However...sacraments involve a

giving of gifts from one person to another, not an exchange of substances. Its interest is not in what happens *to the signs* but in what happens *between persons through them*, not *how* Christ is present in the sacraments, but *that he is present in saving action toward us*...I am inclined to believe that such an account...could evolve only within the onto-theological discourse. Even when Thomas engages in proof texts from scripture, Aristotle is everywhere in the treatment of the sacraments the dominant voice.[101]

There is great fall-out from Thomas' paganized version of Jesus' death and the ordinance of Communion that Christ bequeathed to His Church. With transubstantiation, it is supposed that the "priest,"[102] a mere man, turns bread into Jesus' literal body, although it looks unchanged, and that His real body is eaten, which amounts to cannibalism, and that with this act Jesus is crucified anew, time and time again, because His death 2,000 years ago was not sufficient for all sin, and that by merely partaking in the act of "the Eucharist" grace is merited by works through an act of infusion [versus imputation by faith].[103] That is an all-out frontal assault on the heart of the saving gospel. When Jesus was crucified, just before He gave up His spirit, He declared to all, for all time: "It is finished!" (John 19:30). In Greek it was just one word, "*tetelestai*," a verb used in the perfect tense. As a perfect tense indicative it means his death was a past completed action with ongoing, continuous results[104]—the blood of His one-time death is fully efficacious, and still flowing for all sin, in all sinners, for all time for those who come to Christ in faith and repentance. He died once—He does not need to be "immolated" again and again. Scripture is emphatic here: "For Christ also died for sins once for all" (1 Pet 3:18). Hebrews prophetically and preemptively spoke to this line of attack that would be waged against the all-sufficiency of Christ's death and the simplicity of the gospel.

> [24]For Christ did not enter a holy place made with hands, a mere copy of the true one, but into heaven itself, now to appear in the presence of God for us; [25]nor was it that He should offer Himself often, as the high priest enters the holy place year by year with blood that is not his own. [26]Otherwise, He would have needed to suffer often since the foundation of the world; but now once at the con-

236

summation of the ages He has been manifested to put away sin by the sacrifice of Himself...[28]so Christ also, having been offered once to bear the sins of many (Heb 9:24-26, 28).

Aquinas tried to mix the truth of Scripture (Communion) with the tradition or teaching of man (Aristotelian philosophy) and ended up with transubstantiation. Religionists in Jesus' day tried the same thing—integrating Old Testament Scripture with human teaching. Jesus condemned the net result of their religious alchemy, saying, "You are experts at setting aside the commandment of God in order to keep your tradition...thus invalidating the word of God by your tradition which you have handed down" (Mark 7:9, 13). Aquinas would have been better served had he rejected human philosophy as Paul warned (Col 2:8) and instead embraced the sufficiency of Scripture, knowing that the Word of God is "more desirable than gold, yes, than much fine gold; sweeter also than honey and the drippings of the honeycomb" (Ps 19:10).

The Reformation Reaction

Not every prominent theologian in church history ignored the warning of Colossians 2:8. Some took it quite seriously. Two paramount examples include the great Reformers, Martin Luther and John Calvin.

Martin Luther (AD 1483-1546)

Martin Luther, the father of the Reformation, was born at Eisleben in Germany on November 10, 1483 and died there on February 18, 1546.[105] He was 62. His parents were strict, honest, middleclass Catholics. He began formal study in Latin at age thirteen in Magdeburg and then in 1498 at Eisenbach. "There, with other poor students, he was obliged to sing in the streets begging for bread."[106] Luther would go on to be an accomplished musician, playing the lute, the flute, singing, and even composing hymn books in German for the common man. At eighteen he went to the University of Erfurt and studied under the nominalists, Trutvetter and Arnoldi, and earned a bachelor degree in 1502 and his Master of Arts in 1505, next destined for a law career. Instead, he entered the Augustinian monastery at Erfurt in 1505, and although religious, he had minimal Bible training or knowledge to date. In 1507 he was ordained a priest and in 1508 he was appointed as the "Chair of Philosophy" at Wittenberg.[107] He received the doctorate of theology on October 18, 1512 and three years later was appointed vicar.

While at the monastery in Wittenberg, between 1515 and 1517, Luther gave himself to studying the Scriptures voraciously for the first time. The mere study of the Word of God began to transform him: "Turning from philosophy, he sought the kernel of the trust of salvation in the Bible, especially in the Epistle to the Romans and in the Psalms, which he interpreted entirely from the New Testament."[108] He immersed himself in the study and preaching of Galatians, Hebrews and Titus next. Although still devoted to the Catholic Church, his mind had been steeped in gospel truth, and the living Word continued its transforming work from the inside out. By age thirty-two the simple truth of salvation by grace apart from works had gripped the budding Reformer—there would be no turning back. He began viewing the work of the ministry through the lens of Scripture, which would pit him more and more head-on against the established institution that employed his services.

His growing scriptural knowledge increased his discernment and intolerance for religious compromise among the leaders of the established Church. And fueled by a righteous zeal and inestimable personal courage, it all providentially came to a head with one event that would open the floodgates of the historic Protestant Reformation. While rector (president) of Wittenberg University, at about noon, Luther made public his grievances with his hand-written Ninety-five Theses:

> The sale of indulgences by Johann Tetzel near Wittenberg incited Luther to a polemic attitude...He began assailing the misuse of indulgences, while his dogmatic views concerning them gradually developed out of the cardinal principles of his belief. On Oct. 31, 1517, he nailed his ninety-five theses on the castle church at Wittenberg, though he had no intention of making a decisive attack nor did he wish them to be generally circulated.[109]

The content of his theses caught on and spread like wild fire, creating angst within the ranks of the established Church and fascination and loyalty among the people and his colleagues. His theses spread throughout Germany within two weeks and over the next two years his teachings would spread to France, England, and Italy. In the ensuing ten years his preaching and writing would transform the entire nation, disrupt over 1,000 years of Roman Catholic tradition and dogma, render him an official heretic by the Church of Rome, and pave the way for a simpler, more scriptural brand of Christianity for the next five hundred years.

In the last thirty years of Luther's life there was a discernible, incremental shedding of Roman Catholic dogma, which he exchanged in favor for biblically-driven convictions and practices. Salvation was wholly the work of God; human works could not merit God's favor. Bishops were to be given to preaching the Word, not maintaining the status quo of ecclesiastical compromise. There were only two sacraments instituted by Christ, not seven as the Catholic Church maintained. Every believer was a priest and a king, not just the professional clergy. He rejected transubstantiation and the sacrifice of the Mass. With time, and exposure to deep Bible study, his ecclesiology changed. He came to reject the old view that said the Church was fundamentally a sacramental agent, but instead it was a community of believers. He put Scripture in the language of the common man for all to read and learn, in contrast to the Catholic Church which outlawed Bible reading.[110] He completed his German translation of the Bible in 1531. He rejected the role of the Pope as the Vicar of Christ, and championed the binding authority of Scripture. Further, after living a celibate life for forty-one years, he realized from Scripture that the practice was baseless and then married a wife, the ex-nun, Katharina von Bora, on June 13, 1525.[111] They had six children together.

Another by-product of his biblical transformation was Luther's growing love and allegiance to Scripture and a disdain for the counterfeit as found in human tradition, human wisdom and human philosophy. He rightly understood the implications of Colossians 2:8. Once a trained philosophy professor, he became philosophy's biggest critic. On June 23, 1520, Luther wrote a letter to Nicholas von Amsdorf saying,

> What are the universities, as at present ordered...[but] schools of Greek fashion and heathenish manners, full of dissolute living, where very little is taught of the Holy Scriptures and of the Christian faith, and the blind heathen teacher, Aristotle, rules even further than Christ. Now my

advice would be that the books of Aristotle, the 'Physics,' the 'Metaphysics,' 'Of the Soul,' and 'Ethics,' which have hitherto been considered the best, be altogether abolished, with all others that profess to treat of nature, though nothing can be learned from them, either of natural or spiritual things. Besides, no one has been able to understand his meaning, and much time has been wasted, and many vexed with much useless labor, study, and expense.[112]

On another occasion he wrote, "How I regret that I did not read more poetry and history, and that no one taught me in these branches. Instead of these I was obliged with great cost, labor, and injury, to read Satanic filth, the Aristotelian and Scholastic philosophy, so that I have enough to do to get rid of it."[113] In contrast to Justin, Clement, Augustine, Anselm and Aquinas, there would be no integration of biblical truth with pagan Greek philosophy for Luther.[114] He correctly understood Scripture that says the wisdom of the world is foolishness before God (1 Cor 3:19). The wisdom of the world is "Satanic filth"! Paul called it something similar: *scubala!* (Phil 3:8)[115] For Luther, Aristotle was not to be emulated, but rather excoriated:

> Why, this wretched fellow...teaches...As though we did not have the Holy Scriptures, in which we are fully instructed about all things, things about which Aristotle has not the faintest clue! And yet this dead heathen has conquered, obstructed, and almost succeeded in suppressing the books of the living God. When I think of this miserable business I can only believe that the devil has introduced this study.[116]

Many traditional apologists attempt historical revisionism with Luther's diatribes against Aristotle in order to preserve the long practiced ploy of religious alchemy of integrating pagan Greek philosophy with the Bible. An example is when Sproul *et al* fallaciously assert that the reason Luther disparaged Aristotle is because Luther was ignorant of his writings and was not formally trained in Aristotelian philosophy.[117] But Luther had an answer for his naïve critics about his criticisms toward "the philosopher":

[Aristotle's] book on ethics is the worst of all books. It flatly opposes divine grace and all Christian virtues, and yet it is considered one of his best works. Away with such books! Keep them away from Christians. No one can accuse me of overstating the case, or of condemning what I do not understand. Dear friend, I know what I am talking about. I know my Aristotle as well as you or the likes of you. I have lectured on him and been lectured on him, and I understand him better than St. Thomas or Duns Scotus did. I can boast about this with pride and if necessary, I can prove it.[118]

Sproul even goes on to accuse Luther of being opposed to reason! Sproul writes, "Luther is notorious for his opposition to reason."[119] But nothing could be further from the truth. Luther was not opposed to reason—he was opposed to worldly, finite, fallen, darkened, human, unbiblical reason. Unsanctified reason was to be condemned:

Reason is the Devil's greatest whore; by nature and manner of being she is a noxious whore; she is a prostitute, the Devil's appointed whore; whore eaten by scab and leprosy who ought to be trodden under foot and destroyed, she and her wisdom...Throw dung in her face to make her ugly. She is and she ought to be drowned in baptism...She would deserve, the wretch, to be banished to the filthiest place in the house, to the closets.[120]

On the other hand, divine reason gleaned from Scripture is to be embraced. Luther exalted heavenly reason; reason and wisdom that came from God, from above, from the Scriptures—supernatural truth that was living and active, that never returned to God void. That's why he could look back in hindsight at the avalanche of the Reformation and realize it all happened not because of his own doing through human ingenuity, finite learning or fallen reason, but because of the supernatural efficacy of God's reason—God's truth as found in the Bible:

In short, I will preach it, teach it, write it, but I will constrain no man by force, for faith must come freely without compulsion. Take myself as an example. I opposed indulgences and all the papists, but never with force. I simply taught, preached, and wrote God's Word; otherwise I did nothing. And while I slept, or drank Wittenberg beer with my friends Philips and Amsdorf, the Word so greatly weakened the papacy that no prince or emperor ever inflicted such losses upon it. I did nothing; the Word did everything.[121]

John Calvin (AD 1509-1564)

Lastly, we come to the second great father of the Reformation, John Calvin. He was born one of five sons in Noyon, Picardy, France, sixty miles north of Paris. He spent much of his ministry life in Geneva, Switzerland, where he died May 27, 1564.[122] His parents were devout Catholics. His father, Gerard, was a notary public for the Catholic bishop of Noyon and an attorney of the cathedral chapter.[123] His mother, Jeanne, was remembered for her personal beauty, great religious fervor and strictness. She died when Calvin was a child.[124] At age twelve Calvin was given the chaplaincy of Noyon, a duty for which he was paid.

In 1523, at age fourteen, he was enrolled in the University of Paris to study for the priesthood. Here he earned a masters by age seventeen while studying the basics of classical education, Latin, logic, and philosophy.[125] Frustrated with the Church, his father ordered him to change his studies to law in 1528 at Orléans and Bourges. After his father died in 1531, Calvin left Bourges and returned to Paris to study the classics, Greek, Hebrew and Reformation ideas.[126] Upon completing his studies he proved to be officially a humanist in the Romanist tradition.[127] In 1533 he received his Doctor of Law degree. That same year, as he was exposed more and more to Reformation teaching, especially the writings of Luther, the doctrines of grace took root in his heart. He experienced a sudden conversion that inflamed his soul with the insatiable desire to know the Scriptures more and more.[128]

His newfound faith was not welcomed in the city of Paris, so in 1534 he fled, living in several cities over the next two years. Having enemies and hostile critics because of his biblical beliefs would prove to be his lot in life. "His life was at times in danger. Some showed their terrified contempt for him by naming their dogs after him."[129] While a wanderer, he began writing his *Institutes of the Christian Religion*.[130] In 1536, at age twenty-six, he ended up at Basel where he officially issued the *Institutes*. He would continue working on his classic *magnum opus* for the next twenty-three years until his death, never having to retract his beliefs as much as refine and expand them.[131] In July, 1536, he made a providential visit to Geneva, Switzerland, intending to stay just one day. But God had other plans, for Geneva would be the hub of Calvin's highly productive, and at times intensely tempestuous, ministry for the next twenty-eight years. In 1540 he married Idelette de Bure and had one son together who died in infancy. Idelette died just nine years later, and Calvin never remarried. Calvin himself died young at age fifty-five, after living much of his life as a chronic invalid. Despite his many foibles, he was a man of faith and integrity: "He was refined, conscientious, pure, faithful, honest, humble, pious. He attracted men by the strength of his character, the loftiness of his aims, and the directness of his efforts. He had the common human affections."[132]

Calvin's accomplishments and influence are breathtaking. He transformed an entire city in his day. He studied constantly, preached daily, wrote voluminously, and travelled broadly. He established the Genevan Academy to train pastors; he wrote exegetical commentaries on almost the whole Bible; he was an influential citizen among Geneva's city council. His *Institutes* is still in demand and his name is invoked ceaselessly by pastors everywhere in sermons today. He reigns as one of the greatest systematic theologians and exegetical expositors in Church history.

As for Calvin's influence in apologetics, the great Reformer spurned human reason as folly and gave precedence to God's divinely given reason revealed in Scripture. He exclaimed, "We are deficient in natural powers which might enable us to rise to a pure and clear knowledge of God...It is necessary to begin with heavenly teaching...if we aspire in earnest to a genuine contemplation of God—we must go, I say, to the Word...Never attempt to search after God anywhere but in His sacred Word"[133] Trained and groomed in law and literature, following his conversion in about 1530, "he renounced all secular pursuits and devoted himself entirely to the service of God."[134] He understood the teaching of total depravity, and as a result he broke dramatically from Aquinas and like classical apologists who practiced theological integrationism. Geisler is in gross error when he says of Calvin: "He falls into the general category of classical apologetics."[135] Commenting on Colossians 2:8, Calvin wrote: "philosophy is nothing else than a persuasive speech, which insinuates itself into the minds of men by elegant and plausible arguments. Of such nature, I acknowledge, with all subtleties of philosophers be, if they are inclined to add anything of their own to the pure word of God. Hence philosophy will be nothing else than a corruption of spiritual doctrine, if it is mixed up with Christ."[136] In other words, Calvin rightly concluded that Colossians 2:8 condemned integrating human wisdom with the pure Word of God found in Scripture. Calvin was not a classical apologist. He was a biblical apologist!

Calvin was not impressed with the learned Greek philosophers. He considered them "puffed up with pride."[137] Commenting on 1 Corinthians 1:18-20, Calvin castigates Greek learning and their so-called wisdom: "a knowledge of all the sciences is mere smoke, where the heavenly science of Christ is wanting; and man, with all his acuteness, is as stupid for obtaining of himself a knowledge of the mysteries of God, as an ass is unqualified for understanding musical harmonies."[138] Regarding the Epicurean and Stoic philosophers Paul met in Acts 17, Calvin calls them "enemies" of the truth who were "born only to brawl and cavil,"; "stubborn and importunate men"; deluders of men, full of vices; "bent to pamper the flesh"; "filthy surmisers"; corrupt in their thinking; "they knew not what true virtue was, and they did puff men up with pride"; they were filled with a "certain rash and immoderate fierceness."[139] Calvin refers to the musings of Plato and the greatest of philosophers as "obtuse ...vulgar...stupidity...absurdities" and "hallucinations" when it comes to their speculations about spiritual and metaphysical realities apart from Scripture.[140] Greek philosophy had nothing to offer Calvin when it came to spirituality or truth.

Calvin's belief in the complete sufficiency of Scripture and the complete sufficiency of salvation in Christ made it unthinkable for him to even consider integrating human philosophy with biblical truth. He states further,

> Without Christ sciences in every department are vain, and that the man who knows not God is vain, though he should be conversant with every branch of learning. Nay more, we may affirm this, too, with truth, that these choice gifts of God—expertness of mind, acuteness of judgment, liberal sciences, and acquaintance with languages, are in a

manner profaned in every instance in which they fall to the lot of wicked men.[141]

Examples abound of Calvin's disdain for fallen human reason and vain philosophy. Suffice it to say, that, along with Luther, Calvin's exegesis, preaching, writing and theology, complied with the divine imperative of Colossians 2:8: "See to it that no one takes you captive through philosophy and empty deception, according to the tradition of men, according to the elementary principles of the world, rather than according to Christ."

Apologetical Gleanings

There is much to learn from those who have gone before us with respect to biblical teaching, philosophy and apologetics. Here are some highlights to glean from Justin, Clement, Origen, Augustine, Anselm, Aquinas, Luther and Calvin.

(1) As the Church fathers accommodated pagan Greek philosophy, at the same time they compromised their hermeneutics; they supplanted the grammatical-historical with an allegorical approach that came from the Greeks by way of Philo the Jew.[142] Allegorical hermeneutics has plagued the Church ever since. The Church needs to return to a pure, normal, literal, unfanciful, non-subjective and non-esoteric manner of interpreting the Bible.

(2) The early Church fathers too often had an inflated view of human wisdom and thus approached Scripture in a rationalistic[143] manner. Instead, in developing our apologetical methodology, we need to approach Scripture with inductive exegesis and humble deference.

(3) The early Church fathers practiced "integration," mixing the Bible with pagan Greek philosophy; the end result was the despoliation of the truth. Integration also directly undermines the sufficiency of Scripture. As apologists we need to reject integration[144] and renew our commitment to the sufficiency of Scripture, knowing God's Word addresses every issue pertaining to this life and godliness (2 Pet 1:3).

(4) As the early Church fathers assimilated pagan philosophy into their worldview, they effectively gave preeminence to the metaphysical, which smothered out the soteriological. Their writings are not strongly cross-centered or gospel-centered. We need to be like Paul and the rest of the Apostles who were cross-centered in their apologetics. As Paul said, "But may it never be that I would boast, except in the cross of our Lord Jesus Christ, through which the world has been crucified to me, and I to the world" (Gal 6:14).

(5) In integrating pagan philosophy, the early Church fathers diluted the language of the Bible, infusing secular and non-specific terms and concepts into religious and spiritual conversation. Compromising the language of the Bible with alien terminology always creates an artificial barrier separating the mind of the reader from the direct thoughts of God which are found in Scripture—for the writings themselves are "God-breathed" (2 Tim 3:16; NIV), having inherent authority. Biblical parlance needs to be safeguarded and preserved:

> Biblically sensitive church leaders will insist that the terminology they use represents, as accurately as possible, the original biblical terms and concepts of [the] New Testament. False teachers have had their greatest triumphs when they redefine biblical words in a way that is contrary to the original meaning...Much of our church vocabulary is unscriptural and terribly misleading...Such terminology misrepresents the true nature of apostolic Christianity and makes it difficult, if not impossible, to recapture it. As a result, most of our churches are in desperate need of language reform.[145]

In our apologetics we need to resist the temptation toward the draw for the love of big words and instead preserve the purity of biblical vocabulary and concepts.[146]

(6) Luther and Calvin brought welcomed, redeeming reform that counteracted the pitfalls of accommodation and integration mentioned above. The Reformers returned to exegesis and a literal hermeneutic; they exalted Scriptural authority and not finite human reason; they rejected the so-called wisdom of the world and the polluting practice of integration; they were cross-centered and gospel-centered, knowing that in the pure, simple gospel is the only power for salvation to all who believe; and they tore away the philosophical trappings that smothered the fidelity of pure biblical words. Following the Reformers we need another modern day reformation in our Christian apologetics.

Mumbo Jumbo and Biblical Simplicity

After seminary I went back to school for graduate work in English. One of the required classes was called "Ethnic Literature," and I had to read a bunch of weird books. One was called *Mumbo Jumbo* by Ishmael Reed. An avant-garde novel written in 1972, *Mumbo Jumbo* employed several typographic and stylistic conventions not normally used in novels. I thought it was bizarre. Without the professor's specialized training I never would have understood the book as I read it. Whenever I read a typical modern day traditional Christian apologetics book, I immediately think of *Mumbo Jumbo*. Instead of writing in clear, perspicuous, practical, accessible language, they opt for specialized, highfalutin, oft incomprehensible metaphysical terminology that the average Christian does not understand.

Consider just a few examples of smatterings from pop evangelical apologists. In the first pages of the first chapter of his popular book on Christian apologetics, J. P. Moreland writes:

> Before we attempt to establish these premises, it is important to distinguish between two kinds of infinity—a potential infinite and an actual infinite. The distinction goes back to Aristotle...A *set* refers to a collection of objects called the members or elements of the set. For example, the set A, composed of my two children, Ashley and Allison, would be represented as follows:
>
> $$A = \{\text{Ashley, Allison}\}$$
>
> Similarly, the set B, composed of all the even integers from one to ten, would look like this:

$$B = \{2, 4, 6, 8, 10\}$$

Now we need to define the notion of a *proper subset*. A set C is a proper subset of a set D if and only if there is no member of C that is not a member of D, but there is a member of D that is not a member of C. Thus the following set $A1$ is a proper subset of A:

$$A1 = \{\text{Ashley}\}$$

And $B1$ is a proper subset of B:

$$B1 = \{2, 4\}$$

If a set C is a proper subset of a set D, then C is a part of D or is contained in D, but not vice versa.[147]

If the above makes you dizzy, you're normal. Norman Geisler is also dizzying in his basic introductory book on Christian apologetics with this brain-twister:

> My nonexistence is logically possible; it is not inconceivable that I exist not. No logical necessity is grounding my existence. Even if I cannot affirm that I *do* not exist, I can nonetheless meaningfully think that I *might* not exist. Of course, I must exist in order to conceive of my nonexistence. But the "must exist" does not mean "*logically* must" but only "*actually* must." For unless I actually exist I cannot conceive of anything, for there is no "I" or "me" there at all. But this does not mean that my existence in the first place is based on logical necessity.[148]

R. C. Sproul can also go adrift into the obscure realm of metaphysical nomenclature when he writes on Christian apologetics:

> We are convinced that an epistemology established upon naked empiricism is doomed to travel the road to the graveyard of Hume. If the axiom *nihil est in intellectu quod non fuerit in sensu* is accepted in an absolute sense, skepticism is unavoidable. That is, if all a prioris, either of principles or abilities or categories, are excluded, we see no way to progress beyond an inchoate blob of sensations. Not a single datum can be discovered without an a priori making discrimination and individuation possible.[149]

We saw earlier in chapter four William Lane Craig's incomprehensible Baye's Theorem, which he says constitutes Christian apologetics and a logical corollary to 1 Peter 3:15. But it isn't. Nor is his stated definition of faith: "The biblical notion of faith includes three components: *notitia* (understanding the content of the Christian faith), *fiducia* (trust) and *assensus* (the assent of the intellect to the truth of some proposition)."[150] Craig says three different Latin terms define biblical faith—but he gives no Bible verses to support the notion. Because he can't—since Latin is not the language of the Bible. This tripartite delineation of faith is "mumbo jumbo," undermines the true definition of biblical faith and unfortunately is frequently wielded by traditional apologists, creating confusion, not clarity, in the apologetics task.

Alvin Plantinga, in his basic apologetics book on belief in God says the following:

> Let us say further that a belief is *0ᵗʰ level in* N if it is basic in N, *1ˢᵗ level in* N if it is immediately based on some belief that is 0th level in N, and, in general, *n + 1ˢᵗ level in* N if it is immediately based upon at least one belief that is nᵗʰ level in N. In a rational noetic structure N.[151]

Presuppositionalist, Cornelius Van Til, had many good things to say about Christian apologetics, but frequently got sucked into the metaphysical malaise of esoteric, specialized jargon. In his classic introductory book to apologetics, he writes,

> At the same time phenominalism is still rationalistic in that whatever unity it thinks it finds in this atomistically conceived reality virtually proceeds from the human mind. At least this rationality is not taken as proceeding from the mind of God. The rationalizing effort that is inherent in phenominalism would, if successful, destroy all individuality. Its rationalizing effort is admittedly a step-by-step affair. *That this is so is evident from the fact that its rationalizations are rationalizations of admittedly non-rational material.*[152]

One final example is from traditional apologist, William P. Alston—it's a doozy:

Now back to our initial question about the justifiability of CP. We have seen that J_{nw} is the most we can have for PP and for our other commonly accepted, basic epistemic practices. How does CP stand in this regard? As for J_{ns}, I shall just assume without argument that we no more have an adequate noncircular reason for supposing CP to be reliable than we have in the case of PP. Here, too, although the practice may well be reliable, and so be J_e, we have no sufficient *reason* for judging this to be the case. And so CP is not J_{ns}, and we lack sufficient basis for supposing it to be J_e. If, then, CP is J_{nw}, it will be in just the same epistemic position as PP and other commonly accepted, basic epistemic practices; and it will be just as rational to take Christian experience to provide prima facia justification for M-beliefs as it is to take sense experience to provide prima facia justification for perceptual beliefs.[153]

All the above excerpts supposedly are examples of giving an account to the unbeliever of the hope that is in the believer (1 Pet 3:15). But I would suggest that neither Peter nor God ever intended the Christian hope to be so complicated, ethereal, theoretical or inaccessible to the average person.

In contrast, the language of the Bible is simple—it is written in the language of the people; newspaper vernacular. God intended His people to understand His revelation. The Scriptures have a beautiful simplicity about them. This truth is known as the doctrine of the perspicuity of the Scriptures or the clarity of Scripture. Obfuscation is the opposite of clarity, and that is what the philosophers major in.

Jesus was the wisest person in history (and He still is). But listen to the way He spoke in contrast to the philosophizing of the modern-day Christian apologists:

Look at the birds of the air, that they do not sow, nor do they reap nor gather into barns, and yet your heavenly Father feeds them. Are you not worth much more than they?...Observe how the lilies of the field grow; they do not toil nor do they spin, yet I say to you that not even Solomon in all his glory clothed himself like one of these (Matt 6:26, 28-29).

A young child can understand Jesus here, in His most famous sermon, preached on the mount. Jesus never utilized specialized, elitist, metaphysical vocabulary and concepts when He taught and preached. He taught in the language of the people—readily accessible and easily understood. He regularly spoke to large, mixed crowds of people—and all could comprehend the message. And even though His language and illustrations were simple, the truth communicated was profound, authoritative and life-changing. So much so, that "when Jesus had finished these words, the crowds were amazed at His teaching; for He was teaching them as one having authority" (Matt 7:28-29).

In our apologetics we need to be like Jesus—simple, clear and biblical. We need to resist mumbo jumbo and the love of big words that so often puffs up—even though it might win the approval of the elites in academia. We need to discerningly and courageously reject the integration of human wisdom with biblical theology. And we need to stand firmly committed to obeying the heavenly mandate and warning of Colossians 2:8 which states: "See to it that no one takes you captive through philosophy and empty deception, according to the tradition of men, according to the elementary principles of the world, rather than according to Christ." Then and only then can we rescue biblical apologetics that has been hijacked by philosophy.

Notes

1. "The term *philosophia*, or 'love of wisdom,' as well as much of the substance behind that term is an invention...of Pythagoras (fl. c. 520) and his followers in southern Italy, around the end of the sixth century B.C. The significance of this neologism, in Pythagoras's mind, was that he felt, in contrast to the early physicists and other contemporary experts (who would have called themselves *sophoi*) that wisdom (*sophia*) properly belonged to God alone, and that humans could only aspire to being seekers after wisdom (*philosophos*)"; J. M. Dillon, "Philosophy" in *The IVP Dictionary of the NT*, ed. Daniel G. Reid (Downers Grove, IL: Inter-Varsity Press, 2004), 877.

2. Modern scholars attempt to say that the philosophy Paul was condemning was strictly a Jewish heresy, confined to a narrow Hebrew cul-de-sac in upscale, kosher Colossae. But that is mere conjecture and historical revisionism totally unfounded based on the large Gentile population that existed in that city for centuries up until Paul's day. "Colossae's population consisted mainly of indigenous Phrygian and Greek settlers ...the Colossae of Paul's day seems to have been a cosmopolitan place in which differing cultural and religious elements mingled"; P. T. O'Brien, "Colossians, Letter to the" in *The IVP Dictionary of The New Testament*, 210. Further, Paul explicitly intended Colossians to be a cyclical letter which he commanded to be read in other churches in cities outside Colossae (cf. 4:16), so the intended audience of the epistle cannot be restricted to a mere sub-group within the isolated Jewish district of Colossae. The content of the book was written to a broader audience in a Gentile, Hellenized culture. Paul's main point is that humanistic 'love of wisdom' is to be rejected, not accommodated and assimilated into the Christian worldview. Pagan Greek philosophy was Christ-less to the core and void of the gospel—it was not divine revelation, and as such it is to be assertively discarded as a human counterfeit to God's true, spiritual, heavenly revealed wisdom that comes plenarily from the Scriptures and specifically from the gospel. Cf. Carson's helpful summary here; Herbert M. Carson, *The Epistles of Paul to the Colossians and Philemon: An Introduction and Commentary*, Tyndale New Testament Commentaries (Grand Rapids: Eerdmans, 1960), 61-62.

3. Michael Horton, *The Christian Faith: A Systematic Theology for Pilgrims on the Way* (Grand Rapids, MI: Zondervan, 2011), 982.

4. Norman L. Geisler, *Baker Encyclopedia of Christian Apologetics* (Grand Rapids: Baker Academic, 2006), 395.

5. Clyde Manschreck, "Justin Martyr" in *The Dictionary of Bible and Religion*, ed. William H. Gentz (Nashville, Tennessee: Abingdon Press, 1986), 569.

6. Geisler, *Baker Encyclopedia*, 395.

7. Horton, *The Christian Faith*, 140. Calvin exposed the integration of the many church fathers who melded pagan philosophy with biblical truth. "Among ecclesiastical writers (i.e., Chrysostom, Jerome)…many of them made too near an approach to the philosophers. Some of the most ancient writers appear to me to have exalted human strengths from a fear that a distinct acknowledgment of its impotence might expose them to the jeers of the philosophers with whom they were disputing…Therefore, to avoid teaching anything which the majority of mankind might deem absurd, they made it their study, in some measure, to reconcile the doctrine of Scripture with the dogmas of philosophy…they have bestowed on man more than he possesses for the study of virtue…the Greek fathers, above others…have exceeded due bounds in extolling the powers of the human will, yet all ancient theologians, with the exception of Augustine, are so confused, vacillating, and contradictory on this subject, that no certainty can be obtained from their writings….Succeeding writers (every one courting applause for his acuteness in the defense of human nature) have uniformly, one after the other, gone more widely astray, until the common dogma came to be, that man was corrupted only in the sensual part of his nature, that reason remained entire, and will was scarcely impaired ….Persons professing to be the disciples of Christ have spoken too much like the philosophers on this subject"; *Institutes*, 159-160.

8. "Alexandria at the beginning of the Christian era was the most cosmopolitan city in the world. Oriental and Occidental culture met and blended there as nowhere else. The Jewish-Alexandrian philosophy, as seen most fully developed in the writings of Philo, was one of the most noteworthy products of the eclecticism that there prevailed…The Alexandrian theologians with whom the scientific spirit had its birth, were *Platonists* (with a strong admixture of Pythagoreanism and Stoicism)…after they adopted Christianity…they remained Platonists, and sought to explain Christianity according to the Platonic categories, in somewhat the same way in which Philo had, two centuries earlier, attempted to explain Judaism…Heretofore, the allegorical interpretation had been applied to the Scriptures, whenever it suited a writer's purpose. Allegorizing was now reduced to a system"; A. H. Newman, *A Manual of Church History*, 2 vols. (Philadelphia: American Baptist Publication Society, 1912), I: 272.

9. Justo Gonzalez, *The Dictionary of Bible and Religion*, 208.

10. Geisler, *Baker Encyclopedia*, 156-57

11. Horton, *The Christian Faith*, 100.

12. W. C. Weinrich, "Clement of Alexandria" in *Evangelical Dictionary of Theology*, ed. Walter A. Elwell (Grand Rapids, MI: Baker Book House,

1987), 253. Pearcy notes, "Many of the church fathers were deeply influenced by Platonism, including Clement of Alexandria, Origen, Jerome, and Augustine...most of them absorbed at least some of the Greeks' negative attitude toward the material world"; Nancy Pearcey, *Total Truth: Liberating Christianity from Its Cultural Captivity* (Wheaton, IL: Crossway Books, 2005), 76-77.

13. "No survey will be attempted concerning early Jewish apologetical methodology (e.g. Philo; s.v. ISBE, "Philo, Judaeus," by R. M. Wenley, 4:2380-83). However, it must be noted that both early Jewish and Christian apologetics were generally steeped in Greek humanistic philosophy. This was the assumed sphere of common ground wherein they fought their word-wars. Furthermore, this Alexandrian mindset has greatly affected not only 'classical apologetics' and polemics but also hermeneutics and theology ever since those early days"; George J. Zemek, "Christian Apologetical Methodology" unpublished syllabus (Sun Valley, CA: The Master's Seminary, 1992), 1.

14. Bernard Ramm, *Protestant Biblical Interpretation* (Grand Rapids, MI: Baker Book House, 1978), 31.

15. Charles S. McCoy, "Origen" in *The Dictionary of Bible and Religion*, 759. Septimus Severus was one in a string of ten brutal Roman emperors who inflicted horrendous persecution on early Christians over a 250-year period (A.D. 64-313). Marcus Aurelius was another of the ten murderous thugs, contrary to the distorted Hollywood portrayal of him as a sober-minded nice guy in the movie "Gladiator." Persecuted Christians in the early Church did not resort to philosophy in their defense of the faith. Rather, they relied on God, His Word and practical tactics to defend themselves. Kienel delineates some of the basic apologetical priorities in the "martyrs' school" that existed for persecuted believers in the second and third centuries during the Roman persecution: "Spense-Jones says the martyr's school even had training manuals, which stressed the following: (1) How to answer judges when brought into a Roman court. (2) How to focus on heaven and the eternal reward of being a martyr for Christ. (3) How to rehearse the heroism of earlier martyrs. (4) How to prepare the body through physical exercise to endure public flogging, all forms of torture, long periods in prison and even death by hanging, crucifixion, sword, fire, and possibly by the fangs and claws of beasts in the Roman Colosseum before forty-five thousand spectators. (5) How to prepare heart and mind through memorization of such Scriptures as, 'Therefore whosoever confesses me before men, him will I also confess before my Father who is in heaven' (Matt. 10:32) and 'Blessed are those who are persecuted for righteousness' sake, for theirs is the kingdom of heaven'

(Matt. 5:10)"; Paul A. Kienel, *A History of Christian School Education* (Colorado Springs, CO: The Association of Christian Schools International, 1998), 38.

16. Newman, *Church History*, I: 280.

17. Catherine C. Kroeger, "Origen" in *Evangelical Dictionary*, 803.

18. Geisler says, "Origen was at best a mixed blessing for Christian apologetics. He did defend the basic inspiration and historicity of the Bible. He stressed the use of reason in defending early Christianity against the attacks of paganism and other false teachings. He was a textual scholar. However, Origen's negatives seem to far outweigh the positives. He denied the inerrancy of the Bible, at least in practice. He taught universalism contrary to both Scripture and orthodox creeds. He taught the preexistence of the soul in contrast to the orthodox teaching of creation. He engaged in highly allegorical interpretation of Scripture, undermining important literal truths. He held an aberrant view on the nature of Christ, which gave rise later to the Arian heresy. He denied the tangible, physical nature of the resurrection body"; Geisler, *Baker Encyclopedia*, 567.

19. Newman, Church History, I: 281.

20. Ibid., 281.

21. Horton, *The Christian Faith*, 842.

22. Ibid., 914.

23. Ibid., 48.

24. Ibid., 977.

25. Ibid., 516.

26. Ibid., 83.

27. Ibid., 991.

28. Ibid., 603.

29. Ibid., 910.

30. Ibid., 842.

31. Ibid., 48-49.

32. Ibid., 501.

33. Ibid., 279.

34. Kroeger, *Evangelical Dictionary*, 803.

35. "Origen's philosophical assumptions about the preexistence of souls, eternality of worlds, spiritual resurrection, universalism, and recurrence of the Fall caused extensive controversies that have not been resolved fully to this day. Origen's 'errors' were declared heretical at Constantinople in 543 and 553"; McCoy, *The Dictionary of Bible and Religion*, 760.

36. "Augustine is practically the father of all western Christianity after his time...there is scarcely a single Roman Catholic dogma which is histor-

ically intelligible without reference to his writing"; F. Loofs, "Augustine" in *The New Schaff-Herzog Encyclopedia of Religious Thought,* ed. Samuel Macauley Jackson and Charles Colebrook Sherman (New York: Funk & Wagnalls Company, 1908), I: 368.

37. Bruce A. Demarest, *General Revelation: Historical Views and Contemporary Issues* (Grand Rapids, MI: Zondervan, 1982), 25.

38. "In the history of philosophy, too, he has been a force far beyond the Middle Ages; in both Descartes and Spinoza his voice may be distinctly heard"; *Schaff-Herzog Encyclopedia,* I: 369.

39. Avery Dulles, *A History of Apologetics* (Eugene, OR: Wipf and Stock Publishers, 1999), 73. Cf. Pearcey, *Total Truth,* 74-83.

40. Loofs, *Schaff-Herzog Encyclopedia,* I: 368.

41. Ibid., 371

42. Ibid., 365.

43. Horton notes the shortcomings in Augustine's non-mastery of the Greek New Testament. He was dependent on Latin, which handicapped his ability to be precise as a systematic theologian: "Augustine...[had] a lack of fluency in reading Greek"; Horton, *The Christian Faith,* 284-285.

44. *Schaff-Herzog Encyclopedia,* I: 365.

45. G. R. Evans, "Introduction" in *Saint Augustine City of God* (London, England: Penguin Books, 2003), xxvii.

46. Demarest, *General Revelation,* 27. Calvin was a master of Augustine's writings and theology as is evident from Calvin's interactions with him in *The Institutes.* Calvin treats him fairly—often agreeing with him and sometimes showing where he drifts from Scripture. Calvin specifically notes that with time Augustine matured and "made greater progress in the knowledge of Scripture"; 620.

47. "Plato/Platonism. Probably the most influential philosopher who has ever lived (428-348 B.C.)...His philosophical work survives in the form of about thirty dialogues, distinguished not only for their contributions to epistemology, ethics, metaphysics, aesthetics, politics, and the philosophy of religion but also, in many cases, for their dramatic and literary power...Plato's earlier dialogues are still strongly under the influence of Socrates, who appears as the principal spokesman...The Apology contains Socrates' defense, made before the magistrates of Athens, concluding with the dramatic words: 'The hour of departure has arrived and we go our ways—I to die, and you to live. Which is better is known to God, and *only to him.*' ...the belief in the reality, importance, and immortality of the soul, together with the duty of tending and cultivating the soul, becomes a major tenet in the philosophy of Plato himself and in subsequent Platonism...the individual...[is]...tripartite. On the one hand, the human

soul has three parts or levels. The highest of these is reason, the faculty by which we can know the eternal Ideas; below that is the 'spirited' part, characterized by courage and enterprise; below that again lies a multitude of passions and desires, clamoring for gratification. In the soul of the just person, these three parts are in harmony. The ideal life is that in which rational judgment prevails. It is therefore a life of intellectual contemplation, directed upon the Forms or Ideas, and especially on the Form of the Good, which stands at the apex of the hierarchy of Forms...Full reality belongs only to the eternal world of ideas, and the physical world is only a copy of it...He offers arguments for the existence of God and claims that God is wise and righteous. Here we seem to have reached a fully theistic position. Plato criticizes the unworthy and sometimes immoral myths that were told about the gods, it does not seem that he denied their existences...As early as the first and second centuries A.D., Platonism was combining with Jewish and Christian theology (Philo, Justin Martyr, Clement of Alexandria, Origen, and many others). From the third century onwards, Platonism was being superseded by the related Neoplatonism, which strongly influenced Christian theology from Augustine until the Middle Ages"; John Macquarrie, *The Dictionary of Bible and Religion*, 822-823.

48. "The philosophy originating in Alexandria, developed by Plotinus (205-270), and continued by such figures as Origen (about 182-251)...Drawing on Pythagorean, Aristotelian, and Stoic sources more than on Plato, Neoplatonism...continued as a major influence in Western thought mainly through its impact on Augustine (354-430) and through him to subsequent Christian theology and philosophy. In Neoplatonic thought, being emanates from the One or the Good. From the One comes the realms of Nous, of Soul, and then of Matter, which represents a falling away toward nonbeing or nothingness. Some souls remain unembodied and are not contaminated by incarnation; human souls exist as embodied and are called to turn away from Matter as evil and ascend toward knowledge of and ecstatic union with the One"; Clyde Manschreck, *The Dictionary of Bible and Religion*, 734.

49. Geisler, *Baker Encyclopedia*, 206.

50. Evans, *City of God*, xxiv.

51. Ibid., xxv.

52. Ibid., xlvii.

53. Ibid., xxiii.

54. Ibid., xxii. Philosophical dualism is alive and lurking in today's church. Traditional apologist Carnell suffered from an infection of dualism as evidenced in his introduction to apologetics, where he pit the soul against

the body: "The fact that man is both soul and body makes for happiness and misery. On the one hand there are pleasures. Those of the body come from proper emotions, while those of the mind come from reflection, memory, and anticipation. Plato rightly names the latter set as better...*Qua* body man is animal, while *qua* body spirit he is a celestial being. As a creature of time and space, man is limited by death, while as a creation of spirit, man is able to live eternally." In other words, spirit good, body bad—invisible holy, matter evil; E. J. Carnell, *An Introduction to Christian Apologetics: A Philosophical Defense of the Trinitarian-Theistic Faith* (Grand Rapids, MI: Eerdmans Publishing, 1956), 19-20.

55. *The Harper Collins Dictionary of Religion*, ed. Jonathan Z. Smith (New York, NY: HarperCollins Publishers, 1995), 848.

56. Horton, *The Christian Faith*, 388.

57. Dulles, *A History*, 75-76.

58. Demarest, *General Revelation*, 25-26.

59. Horton, *The Christian Faith*, 472.

60. Ibid., 997.

61. Loofs, *Schaff-Herzog*, 367.

62. Ibid., 368.

63. Demarest, *General Revelation*, 26.

64. Ibid., 26.

65. Dulles, *A History*, 75. Augustine's practice of integration is actually dangerous and is practiced routinely by evangelicals today, usually resulting in dire consequences. We need to heed Barrick's warning here: "Evangelicals too often attempt to baptize secular and humanistic theories in evangelical waters without realizing that those theories and their methodologies have never been converted. While there are valuable kernels of truth buried within contemporary critical and so-called 'scientific' studies, evangelicals must take great care to irradiate the material with the Word of God so as not to unknowingly and unin-tentionally introduce secularized thinking into the Church"; William D. Barrick, "Noah's Flood and Its Geological Implications," *Coming to Grips with Genesis: Biblical Authority and the Age of the Earth*, eds. Terry Mortenson and Thane H. Ury (Green Forest, AR: Master Books, 2009), 252.

66. Dulles, *A History*, 88-89.

67. Gonzalez, *The Dictionary of Bible and Religion*, 91.

68. Scholasticism was the attempt to make faith and human reason compatible—to literally make Catholic dogma blend [integration] with the pagan philosophy of the Greek philosopher Aristotle. "The tool that Christian [Catholic] Scholasticism used to reestablish unity was of pagan origin, the philosophy of Aristotle. Understandably, in the beginning the

Church protested against the rapidly increasing interest in the works of the heathen, newly translated from Greek and Arabic; and conservative churchmen condemned the doctrines of Thomas Aquinas with their Aristotelian logic so that Albertus Magnus had to go to Paris in his defense"; cited by Paul A. Kienel, *A History of Christian School Education* (Colorado Springs, CO: ACSI, 1998), 93. Kienel goes on to observe, "Scholasticism was 'a kind of rationalization of the Gospel [that] placed Aristotle, called "the Teacher" or "the Philosopher" beside Jesus as the supreme authority.' This, of course, is the essence of humanism, in which man is elevated to a level equal to, or above, Christ. In contrast, Ephesians 1:22 says (referring to Christ), 'And He put all things under His feet, and gave Him to be the head over all things to the church'; and Colossians 1:18, '...that in all things He [Christ] may have the preeminence' (NKJ)."

69. C. A. Beckwith, *Schaff-Herzog*, I: 188.
70. Ibid., 189.
71. Ibid.
72. Geisler, *Baker Encyclopedia*, 25.
73. Beckwith, *Schaff-Herzog*, I: 189.
74. Ibid.
75. Ibid.; cf. Demarest, *General Revelation*, 32.
76. Geisler, *Baker Encyclopedia*, 25-26.
77. M. J. Charlesworth trans. and ed. *St. Anselm's Proslogion* (Notre Dame, Indiana: University of Notre Dame Press, 2003), 23-24.
78. Geisler, *Baker Encyclopedia*, 26; cf. Beckwith, *Schaff-Herzog*, I: 189; Horton, *The Christian Faith*, 508.
79. Geisler, *Baker Encyclopedia*, 26.
80. He prayed, "I do not seek to understand that I may believe, but I believe in order to understand"; Anselm, "Proslogion," in *St. Anselm, Proslogium and Monologium*, trans. Sidney Norton Deane (Chicago: Open Court, 1935), 6. For Anselm, when he said, "I believe in order to understand," he does not mean, "I believe **in the Scripture** in order to understand." Anselm put traditional church dogma on the same par as Scripture and even considered it revelation. Beckwith says, "The dogmas of the Church are to him identical with revelation itself"; *Schaff-Herzog*, I: 189. So faith does not come from the divine revelation of Scripture alone (as Romans 10:17 says), but faith could result from "truth" whatever its source. This is the exact same position of modern day traditional apologists (Craig, Kelly James Clark, etc.) who believe faith can be created from other sources and experiences apart from Scripture.
81. Dulles, *A History*, 101.

82. Ibid., 102.

83. Demarest, *General Revelation*, 31.

84. Ibid., 31-32

85. Anselm, *Monologion*, LXVI, in *Anselm of Canterbury*, ed. And trans. J. Hopkins and H. Richardson, 4 vols. (Toronto and New York: Edwin Mellen, 1975-76), vol. I, 76.

86. Jasper Hopkins, *A Companion to the Study of St. Anselm* (Minneapolis: University of Minnesota Press, 1972), 52.

87. Demarest, *General Revelation*, 33-34.

88. The year of his birth is disputed; see Reinhold Seeberg, "Thomas Aquinas," in *The New Schaff-Herzog Encyclopedia of Religious Thought*, XI: 422.

89. Gonzalez, *The Dictionary of Bible and Religion*, 62-63.

90. One of William Craig's favorite terms he uses when speaking and writing which he acquired while studying theology in Germany under Wolfhart Pannenberg.

91. Seeberg, *The New Schaff-Herzog Encyclopedia*, XI: 423.

92. "He judged that the errors of Aristotelianism could best be met by erecting a Christian Aritotelianism that incorporated the best insights of the Stagirite. To this end St. Thomas wrote a series of philosophical commentaries on Aristotle, seeking to interpret the master in a way more favorable to Christianity than his Arabic commentators had done. On certain points, he conceded, Christian revelation had corrected and completed what Aristotle had seen in a deficient manner"; Dulles, *A History*, 113.

93. Gonzalez, *The Dictionary of Bible and Religion*, 62-63.

94. Ibid.

95. Like Augustine, he integrated Greek philosophy with the Bible. Distinct from Augustine he preferred Aristotle over Plato: "Where Augustine used Neoplatonism, Thomas has recourse to Aristotle. Where Augustine argued through the interpretation of history, Thomas depends primarily on metaphysics. Where Augustine uses the persuasion of rhetoric, Thomas uses careful and dispassionate reasoning"; Dulles, *A History*, 120.

96. Seeberg, *The New Schaff-Herzog Encyclopedia*, XI: 427.

97. A. Vos, "Aristotelianism" in *New Dictionary of Theology*, eds. Sinclair B. Ferguson, David F. Wright, J. I. Packer (Downers Grove, IL: InterVarsity Press, 1988), 44-45.

98. Colin Brown, "Scholasticism," in *Introduction to the History of Christianity*, Tim Dowley, ed. (Minneapolis: Fortress Press, 1995), 286.

99. D. S. Schaff, "Transubstantiation," in *The New Schaff-Herzog Encyclopedia of Religious Thought*, 496.

100. Seeberg, *Schaff-Herzog*, XI: 426.

101. Horton, *The Christian Faith*, 784.

102. The idea that some Christians are priests and others are not is another heretical distortion of clear New Testament teaching—all Christians are priests—having direct access to God by virtue of Christ's atoning work (Hebrews 4:14-16; Revelation 1:6).

103. According to Aquinas a sacrament "makes people holy"...by causing grace to be infused into the recipient; Horton, *The Christian Faith*, 765.

104. Cleon L. Rogers, Jr. and Cleon L. Rogers III, *The New Linguistic and Exegetical Key to the Greek New Testament* (Grand Rapids, MI: Zondervan, 1998), 224-25.

105. "Luther, Martin" in *The New Schaff-Herzog Encyclopedia of Religious Thought: Liutprand-Moralities*, vol. VII (New York and London: Funk and Wagnalls, 1910).

106. Ibid.

107. Kienel, *A History*, 192.

108. "Luther" in *Schaff-Herzog*, VII, np.

109. Ibid.

110. "At the Council of Valencia, Spain, in 1229, the Bible was placed on 'The Index of Forbidden Books' with the following decree: 'We prohibit the permitting of the laity to have the books of the Old and New Testament, unless any one should wish, from a feeling of devotion, to have a psalter or breviary for divine service, or the hours of the blessed Mary. But we strictly forbid them to have the above-mentioned books in the vulgar tongue'"; Kienel, *A History*, 59.

111. "Luther" in *Schaff-Herzog*, VII, np.

112. Martin Luther, *Three Treatises* (Philadelphia: Fortress Press, 1970), 4, 92-93.

113. Kienel, *A History*, 202.

114. Luther disagreed with his friend Melanchthon on this matter; cf. Kienel, 246.

115. All of Paul's human achievements as an unbeliever—his education, training, reputation, amassed worldly wisdom—he considered to be *skubala* after he came to know Christ. *Skulaba* is from the Greek *skubalon*, meaning "human excrement" or "rubbish, dung"; Arndt, William F., and Gingrich, F. Wilbur, *A Greek-English Lexicon of the New Testament and Other Early Christian Literature*, second edition. Revised by F. Wilbur Gingrich and Fredrick W. Danker (Chicago and London: The University of Chicago Press, 1979), 758; Max Zerwick and Mary Grosvenor, *A Grammatical Analysis of the Greek New Testament* (Rome: Biblical Institute Press, 1981), 599.

116. Luther, *Three Treatises*, 93.

117. R. C. Sproul, John Gerstner and Arthur Lindsley, *Classical Apologetics: A Rational Defense of the Christian Faith and a Critique of Presuppositional Apologetics* (Grand Rapids, MI: Zondervan, 1984), 197.

118. Luther, *Three Treatises*, 93-94.

119. Sproul *et al*, *Classical Apologetics*, 196.

120. Martin Luther, *Works*, Erlangen Edition v. 16, pp. 142-148; "Again, his unflagging polemic against the abuse of reason has often been construed

as an assault on the very idea of rational coherence in theology, whereas in fact it is aimed only at the ideal of rational autonomy and self sufficiency in theology—the ideal of philosophers and Scholastic theologians, to find out and know God by the use of their own unaided reason. It was in her capacity as the prompter and agent of 'natural' theology that Mistress Reason was in Luther's eyes the Devil's whore; for natural theology is, he held, blasphemous in principle, and bankrupt in practice....natural theology is bankrupt in practice; for it never brings its devotees to God; instead it leaves them stranded in a quaking morass of insubstantial speculation ....Luther was no foe to the ideal of systematic consistency in formulating and organizing the contents of the *theolgia crucis*; how could he be, when he found that ideal so clearly exemplified in Scripture itself, in the great dogmatic epistles of St. Paul? 'Reason in the sense of logic he employed to the uttermost limits,' says Dr. Bainton"; Martin Luther, *The Bondage of the Will*, trans. by J. I. Packer and O. R. Johnston (Fleming H. Revell Company, 1957), 45-47. In light of the above, it is very disappointing to see how such an admired "Reformed" evangelical, R. C. Sproul, could misrepresent Luther so terribly on this issue—but it makes sense. Remember, Sproul is first and foremost a philosopher, and second a theologian, and hardly a biblical exegete.

121. *Luther's Works*, vol 51; Martin Luther's basic theological writings, "The Second Sermon, March, 1522, Monday after Invocavit" by Martin Luther, Timothy F. Lull, William R. Russell (Fortress Press, 2005), 287.
122. Geisler, *Baker Encyclopedia*, 111.
123. *The New Schaff-Herzog Encyclopedia*, II: 353.
124. 123. Ibid., 354.
125. Ibid.
126. Clyde L. Manschreck, *The Dictionary of Bible and Religion*, 173; and Steven J. Lawson, *The Expository Genius of Calvin* (Lake Mary, FL: Reformation Trust, 2007), 6.
127. *The New Schaff-Herzog Encyclopedia*, II:354.
128. Ibid., 354.
129. Ibid., 356.
130. Ibid.
131. Ibid., 355.
132. Ibid., 358.
133. Ibid., 358.
134. Calvin, *Institutes*, 23, 28, 81.
135. Geisler, *Baker Encyclopedia*, 113. Calvin was not a classical apologist—not even close. Geisler is not the only one who misrepresents Calvin's position in this area. Sproul and a host of others claim Calvin explained faith with three Latin terms, which he did not. Sproul also says Calvin used natural theology—another bogus assertion. Plantinga distorts Calvin's view of the *sensus divinitatis*. Kelly James Clark, the liberal theologian and philosopher, also tries to claim Calvin as his own in the area of apologetics. Many traditional apologists re-write Calvin's views in order to gain the Reformer's endorsement posthumously. Packer noted

this trend half a century ago when he wrote, "In each century from his day to ours, self-styled 'Calvinists' have claimed him as their patron. But it would not always be safe to judge of his theology by theirs....If we would know Calvin the theologian, we must do more than study the 'Calvinists'; we must go to the man himself"; J. I. Packer, *John Calvin: A Collection of Distinguished Essays*, ed., G. E. Duffield (Grand Rapids: Eerdmans Publishing Company, 1966), 150-151. Hall makes a similar pertinent observation: "Too often we look back to Calvin through the distorting lens of our own Protestant religious history, which, however admirable and original in its aims and achievements, is not Calvin's Calvinism 'englished'"; Basil Hall, "The Calvin Legend," in *John Calvin: A Collection of Distinguished Essays*, 4.

136. John Calvin, *Commentaries on the Epistles of Paul the Apostle to the Philippians, Colossians, and Thessalonians*, ed. John Pringle (Grand Rapids, MI: Baker Book House, 2003), 180-81. Lawson makes it clear that Calvin believed in the sufficiency of Scripture, and as a result he rejected any kind of natural theology, human philosophy or appealing to human reason void of divine revelation. "He wrote. 'their [ministers'] whole task is limited to the ministry of God's Word; their whole wisdom to the knowledge of His Word; their whole eloquence, to its proclamation.'...He knew that 'as soon as men depart, even in the smallest degree from God's Word, they cannot preach anything but falsehoods, vanities, impostures, errors, and deceits....A rule is prescribed to all God's servants that they bring not their own inventions, but simply deliver, as from hand to hand, what they have received from God'....For Calvin, any Bible teachers, small or great, who decide to 'mingle their own inventions with the Word of God, or advance anything does not belong to it, must be rejected, how honourable soever may be their rank'"; Lawson, *The Expository Genius of Calvin*, 25-26.

137. John Calvin, *The First Epistle of Paul the Apostle to the Corinthians* (Grand Rapids, MI: Baker Book House, 2003), 87.

138. Ibid., 82.

139. John Calvin, *Calvin's New Testament Commentaries: Acts of the Apostles*, vol II. Grand Rapids, MI: Baker Book House, 2003), 149-150.

140. John Calvin, *Institutes of the Christian Religion*, trans. by Henry Beveridge (Peabody, Massachusetts: Hendrickson Publishers, 2009), 18, 22-23, 48, 66, 97, 450.

141. Calvin, *First Corinthians*, 83.

142. Horton, *The Christian Faith*, 473-74; "Alexandria had been the seat of Philo, the Jewish philosopher who attempted to blend Judaism with Platonism. The catechetical school in Alexandria (under Origen and his successors, Clement and Cyril) followed a similar course with Christianity. For them, Christianity is the true gnosis, the higher enlightenment that Greek philosophy anticipated but could not fully know apart from Christ. Presupposing intellectual ascent from the realm of appearances to the contemplation of eternal Truth, Alexandrian theology frequently displays a tendency toward allegorical (spiritualizing) exegesis. Historical, temporal, and sensual reality serves merely as a stepping-stone to ever-higher,

eternal, and intellectual realities. The tendency to assimilate history (the realm of appearances) to eternity and matter to spirit prejudiced Alexandrian theology toward assimilating Christ's humanity to his deity. Just as the Platonizing tendency led Apollinarianism to replace Christ's human mind with the Logos, Cyril (early on at least) tended to collapse Christ's humanity into his deity." Ramm shows how much of modern day evangelicals inherited their quasi-allegorical hermeneutic from Augustine: "Augustine was driven to the allegorical interpretation of Scripture by his own spiritual plight. It was the allegorical interpretation of Scripture by Ambrose which illuminated much of the Old Testament to him when he was struggling with the crass literalism of the Manicheans. He justified allegorical interpretation by a gross misinterpretation of 2 Cor. 3:6. He made it mean that the *spiritual* or *allegorical* interpretation was the real meaning of the Bible; the *literal* interpretation kills. For this experimental reason Augustine could hardly part with the allegorical method"; Ramm, *Biblical Interpretation*, 35.

143. By "rationalistic" I do not mean "rational," but rather I mean they ascribed to varying degrees of human autonomy in their thinking.

144. Modern day traditional apologists put a premium on integration. For example, listen to Stanley Obitts, philosophy professor at Westmont College, and his frightening recommendation: "In order to encompass as much of God's truth as possible from natural revelation within a comprehensive view of the universe created and sustained by the...God of Scripture, the Christian must engage in philosophical speculation....All that a Christian must do to pursue philosophy properly is critically to scrutinize the discoveries, insights, and theories that have increased our knowledge of God's universe, and coherently to weave this knowledge into an adequate whole consistent with Scripture"; Stanley R. Obitts, "Philosophy, Christian View of," in *Evangelical Dictionary of Theology*, edited by Walter A. Elwell (Grand Rapids, MI: Baker Book House, 1987), 853.

145. Alexander Strauch, *Biblical Eldership: An Urgent Call to Restore Biblical Church Leadership* (Colorado Springs, CO: Lewis and Roth Publishers, 2005), 33-34.

146. J. I. Packer, writes, "Nor, again, may we present the faith as a philosophy, to be accepted (if at all) on grounds of rational demonstration; we must always declare it as revealed truth, divinely mysterious and transcending reason's power to verify, to be received humbly on the authority of God. Faith involves the renunciation of intellectual self-sufficiency; we must always proclaim the gospel in a way that makes this clear"; J. I. Packer, *'Fundamentalism' and the Word of God* (Grand Rapids, MI: Eerdmans, 1958), 136.

147. J. P. Moreland, *Scaling the Secular City: A Defense of Christianity* (Grand Rapids, MI: Baker Book House, 1987), 19-20.

148. Norman L. Geisler, *Christian Apologetics* (Grand Rapids, MI: Baker Book House, 1976), 144.

149. Sproul *et al, Classical Apologetics*, 85.

three parts to it, which were described by three Latin words: *notitia, assensus* and *fiducia*."[6] Traditional apologist Kenneth Boa mimics the same: "There are three Latin words that can all mean *faith: noticia, assentia, fiducia*."[7] J. I. Packer whistled this tune as well:

> Older Reformed theology analyzed faith as *notitia* ("knowledge," i.e., acquaintance with the content of the gospel), plus *assensus* ("agreement," i.e., recognition that the gospel is true), plus *fiducia* ("trust and reliance," i.e., personal dependence on the grace of Father, Son, and Spirit for salvation, with thankful cessation of all attempts to save oneself by establishing one's own righteousness: Rom. 4:5; 10:3). Without *fiducia* there is no faith, but without *notitia* and *assensus* there can be no *fiducia* (Rom. 10:14).[8]

A glaring red flag regarding the above trichotomization of faith repeated by the traditional apologists is that they all say this supposed trilogy of belief comes as a legacy from the Reformers, but nowhere do they quote from the Reformers to prove the point. They assume it comes from the Reformers. I could not find Calvin defining faith like this in the *Institutes*. Luther used the various Latin terms but was not dependent on them for his full understanding of biblical faith. After 1517 he is not found waxing eloquent about a Latinized, splintered faith. On the contrary, Luther was all about preserving the biblical languages:

> Experience too has proved this and still gives evidence of it. For as soon as the languages declined to the vanishing point, after the apostolic age, the gospel and faith and Christianity itself declined more and more...On the other hand, now that the languages have been revived, they are bringing with them so bright a light and accomplishing such great things that the whole world stands amazed and has to acknowledge that we have the gospel just as pure and undefiled as the apostles had it, that it has been wholly restored to its original purity, far beyond what it was in the days of St. Jerome and St. Augustine.[9]

Luther points out that preserving the original languages of the Bible (not Latin) provides a beautiful simplicity. Even if the Reformers did somewhere dissect faith in a three-fold manner, it does not make it right—they are not the authority. Scripture is. Jesus never delineated a three-headed Roman cognate of "believe." The Apostles did not talk of faith in three tones of Latin—neither should we. This common trichotomization of faith, typical of so many evangelical writers, is a fabricated canard. The traditional apologists do this in an attempt to by-pass the effects of total depravity on the unbeliever's ability to "reason" about God, illegitimately granting them a dose of the so-called *noticia* kind of faith, while depriving them of the imaginary *fiducia* brand. The whole notion is quite sophisticated, elitist and misleading. The Bible knows of only one kind of true faith, not three.

The above examples clearly illustrate that a true biblical definition of faith is not being well publicized in Christian literature at present. Parks is correct when he laments,

> The concept of faith has been radically redefined in some philosophical and theological circles during the past century. Those definitions rarely address the complexities of the biblical concept, a concept in which the whole person, the physical world, God's Word, and God Himself play crucial roles. Those alternative definitions often do not grasp the objective and subjective characteristics of biblical faith.[10]

An Excursus on the Supposed Nobility of the Priority of Latin in Religious Studies

I know Christians who believe that Latin is a more spiritual and religious language than other languages, and therefore think that if they know Latin, then they will have special insight into the "true, deeper" and even more scholarly meaning of the Bible. This is particularly true of many professional philosophers of religion and traditional apologists. They'll even quote Calvin, who they say wrote in Latin, to make their point. Calvin wrote in French and Latin, but he did not do exegesis in Latin; he did exegesis of Scripture from Hebrew and Greek, as is evident from his *Institutes* and commentaries. So knowing Latin does not give one the upper hand in religious and biblical studies. As a matter of fact, knowing Latin will be inherently no more beneficial in understanding the Bible than knowing English, Spanish, Chinese or Telugu.

you, he who hears My word, and *believes* [*pisteuōn*] Him who sent Me, has eternal life, and does not come into judgment, but has passed out of death into life."

One dominant characteristic construction in the New Testament for saving faith is the verb *pisteuō* followed by the preposition *eis*. Frequently this construction can literally mean to believe "into." It denotes a faith, which, so to speak, takes a man out of himself, and puts him into Christ. This is parallel in meaning to Paul's assigning the believer as "in Christ," a phrase that occurs over twenty times in Ephesians. It denotes not simply a belief that carries an intellectual assent, but one wherein the believer cleaves to his Savior with all his heart, and shares the very identity of Christ.[25] The man who believes in this sense abides in Christ and Christ in him (John 15:4). Faith is not only accepting certain things as true, but includes trusting a Person, and that Person Christ.

Sometimes *pisteuō* is followed by *epi*, "upon." Faith has a firm basis. We see this construction in Acts 9:42, where, when the raising of Tabitha was known, "many believed on [*epi*] the Lord." The people had seen what Christ could do, and they rested their faith "on" Him. Sometimes faith rests on the Father, as when Paul speaks of "those who believe in Him who raised Jesus our Lord from the dead" (Rom 4:24). Prominent in the New Testament is the absolute use of the verb. When Jesus stayed with the Samaritans many of them "believed because of His word" (John 4:41).

The different tenses of *pisteuō* are also important to note. Morris summarizes:

> The aorist tense points to a single act in past time and indicates the determinative character of faith. When a man comes to believe he commits himself decisively to Christ. The present tense has the idea of continuity. Faith is not a passing phase. It is a continuing attitude. The perfect tense combines both ideas. It speaks of a present faith which is continuous with a past act of belief. The man who believes enters a permanent state.[26]

Much more could be said about the true meaning of biblical faith from an Old Testament and New Testament perspective. Notice the vast array of variables contributing to its meaning, usage, application and development—a conglomeration of differing words, the proximity of multiple prepositions, differing cases, varying verb tenses, verb and noun cognates, Hebrew and Greek origins, countless individual contexts, all producing an organic, dynamic and thematic unity that defines and illustrates the supernatural gift from God bequeathed to sinful humanity providing the means whereby sinners can be in covenant relationship with the Creator. How majestic!

In light of the above, Zemek is correct when he says, "From the array of data previously surveyed, it should be obvious that it is difficult to synthesize a comprehensive definition of faith."[27] But it's not impossible. Zemek continues, "Having recognized the limitations of all simple definitions, does not mean, however, that descriptive attempts at summarizing the basics of biblical faith should be abandoned.

Some of these attempts, as a matter of fact, put an illuminating spotlight on the various characteristics and associations of faith in the Bible."[28] With that said, we highlight Morris' skillful summary definition:

> Faith is clearly one of the most important concepts in the whole NT. Everywhere it is required and its importance insisted upon. Faith means abandoning all trust in one's own resources. Faith means casting oneself unreservedly on the mercy of God. Faith means laying hold on the promises of God in Christ, relying entirely on the finished work of Christ for salvation, and on the power of the indwelling Holy Spirit of God for daily strength. Faith implies complete reliance on God and full obedience to God.[29]

Hopefully one thing is readily apparent from the above survey. Categorically defining faith myopically in a simple half sentence as *fiducia, notitia* and *assensus,* exposes such a definition for what it really is: a superficial inane and hackneyed counterfeit. Words matter. With Luther, let us take pains to preserve the original sheath in which God gave us the sword of His Word, along with the original vocabulary. Thus we will ensure the original intent and meaning in which God first gave His Word, including the God-given attitude and virtue of divine faith.

are preaching" (Rom 10:8). So the source of supernatural, saving faith is in the content or substance of Scripture and specifically the gospel, which is a heavenly message outside of ourselves—it is alien to us. It is not intuitive or innate. In other words, saving faith is a gift from God. Faith that saves is a gift from God; we can't earn it; we don't deserve it; we can't conjure it up on our own. It's inaccessible apart from God's intervention through the revelation of Scripture; and it's a gift that He initiates by His grace.[46] This is in contrast to our ability to believe in God, which according to Romans 1 and 2 is inherent in us as a result of general revelation from the *imago dei* and our conscience.

All people have the needed (innate) faith to believe in God; no one has faith to believe in Jesus until they hear the gospel and the Holy Spirit enables the sinner to believe. This is why we don't need to labor with unbelievers trying to prove to them that God "probably" exists; they already know He exists and they are suppressing that truth willfully because of their love for their sin (John 3:19). In contrast, we must labor with unbelievers to explain the gospel from Scripture, since believing in Jesus does not come naturally for them and they don't have the necessary content of information to believe in Him until we impart the full gospel from the Bible through preaching and teaching so they can "hear" and assimilate the truth that is outside themselves.

To sum up this phrase, "faith comes from hearing," Paul means "the only source of saving faith is in the preached message of the gospel." So saving faith comes from no other source. Richards is right when he says, "Faith is not some response to evidence, even when that evidence is clearly miraculous. Abraham believed *God*."[47] Traditional apologists say faith comes from mere "evidence," usually the so-called evidence produced by human logic apart from special revelation.

For example, Carnell says the Christian should not begin with the gospel when talking with the unbeliever, for that "is to cast pearls before swine"! Rather we are to begin with unaided reason (or "philosophy"), logic and human arguments which "may serve to prepare the way for the display of those objective evidences" which may "effect regeneration."[48] The "evidences" are not gospel truths for Carnell, but rather the Laws of Logic and natural theology. So Carnell says saving faith is produced and has its source in unaided human logic. Craig says the same thing. He purports that Christians can present "rational self-evidence" to woo someone to belief apart from Scripture.[49] Likewise, Plantinga says, "natural theology could be useful in helping someone move from unbelief to belief."[50] They say, "faith cometh from the Laws of Logic," or "faith comes from human reason in the form of evidences and natural theology." In stark contrast, Paul, inspired by the Spirit of God, says, "faith comes from hearing" the preached message of the gospel.

The Medium of Faith

In the last part of 10:17 Paul specifies what he means by "hearing" or the published message that produces faith—specifically it is "hearing by the word of Christ." The preposition "by" is *dia* with the genitive here it is instrumental, "by means of."[51] Faith comes "by means of" the word of Christ. Lange notes, "the thing heard is through or by means of the revelation of God."[52] Lenski comments, "what the gospel heralds make men to hear is not their own so that men might be justified if they were disbelieving; it is mediated by nothing less than 'Christ's own utterance.' Now the preposition is *dia* and not *ek*."[53] And Alford highlights as well the inseparable link showing *dia* connects saving faith with its ultimate and only origin, the word of Christ: "the report (the publication of the Gospel) is by means of...'by,' as its instrument and vehicle the word of Christ."[54]

The Origin of Faith

Finally we examine the ultimate origin of saving faith—divine, special revelation about Christ, "the word of Christ." Where does faith come from? Saving faith comes from the "word of Christ," and only "the word of Christ." Here "word" is not the usual *logos* but *rhema* (cf. Rom 10:8).[55] *Rhema* refers to uttered and spoken words, and in the New Testament specifically in relation to special revelation uttered, spoken, proclaimed and preached[56] by Jesus and the apostles, usually revolving around the good news of the gospel.[57] The gospel must be verbalized so people can hear its propositional truth! We don't "live" the gospel for unbelievers; we "proclaim" it in propositional verbal speech. We are not the "good news"; Jesus is. Lange nails it here. He says the *rhema* of Christ is "the revealed word with which prophets and apostles were entrusted. The Divine message... denotes the Divine sources of revelation, on whose effluence the authority and effect of every message depend."[58] Again, the very important point is reiterated: efficacious faith comes only from divine or special revelation. Or as Luther said 500 years ago in his commentary on this verse: "Hearing indeed comes only through the Word of Christ."[59]

In the phrase, "hearing by the word of Christ," Christ is an objective genitive or a genitive of content. As such, that which is spoken (*rhema*), is "the message which has Christ as its object or content."[60] Faith results only after an unbeliever has been exposed to special revelation from God's Word that is Christo-centric as it is preached and taught. This is what Peter meant in his apologetics passage. He said we begin by "setting apart Christ as Lord in our hearts" (1 Pet 3:15). We begin with the gospel. We station ourselves, pivoted on Scripture. All our conversation is Christ-centered, cross-centered and Scripturally-driven, because we know the unbeliever needs the supernatural gift of faith. And faith comes only from hearing about Christ in Scripture. Calvin knew this. In his commentary on Romans 10:17 from 500 years ago he wrote:

> And this is a remarkable passage with regard to the efficacy of preaching; for he testifies, that by it faith is produced....

> It must be further noticed, that faith is grounded on nothing else but the truth of God; for Paul does not teach us that faith springs from any other kind of doctrine, but he expressly restricts it to the word of God; and this restriction would have been improper if faith could rest on the decrees of men. Away then with all the devices of men...because it tears away faith from the word....[61]

Similarly, addressing the practical implications for Christians as they practice apologetics defensively and evangelistically while interacting with unbelievers, MacArthur says this about Romans 10:17:

> Salvation does not come by intuition, mystical experience, meditation, speculation, philosophizing, or consensus but by hearing and having faith in the word of Christ. To proclaim the saving word of Christ is therefore the central and essential purpose in evangelism...

> The purpose of evangelism is not to use human persuasion and clever devises to manipulate confessions of

faith in Christ but to faithfully proclaim the gospel of Christ, through which the Holy Spirit will bring conviction and salvation to those who hear and accept the word of Christ. It is tragic that many appeals to salvation are a call for trust in someone and something they know nothing about.[62]

The Gift of Faith

Romans 10:17 makes it clear that faith comes only from special revelation. And that special revelation concerns the gospel truths of Jesus Christ: who He is and what He did. Faith comes from no other source. Faith is a divine gift given by God. That is what Paul meant when he said, "For by grace you have been saved through faith, and that not of yourselves, it is the gift of God" (Eph 2:8). Faith is not the by-product of clever rational arguments. Faith does not result from impressively amassed, indisputable archaeological evidences. Faith does not come from life-changing personal encounters and experiences. Faith is a supernatural gift from God. Faith is of a distinctly heavenly origin. This is what Calvin meant when he spoke of "the conviction which revelation from heaven alone can produce," and he also noted that, "faith depends upon the Word of God alone."[63] In Ephesians 2:8 Paul is actually saying that everything about salvation is a gift from God: the grace, the faith and the justification that is concomitant with it. Zemek explains:

> The antecedent of the pronoun "that" in this verse is not "faith" alone. Buswell handles the syntax of this verse very credibly when he says, "The word 'that' refers not only to the 'grace' and not only to the 'faith' but to the whole manner expressed in these words. Both grace and faith are feminine nouns, but the word 'that,' *touto*, is neuter showing that it is not merely grace, and not merely faith, but the entire concept of grace accepted by faith, which must be regarded as the gift of God."[64]

To summarize our commentary on the truth of Romans 10:17 thus far: "faith *comes* from hearing, and hearing by the word of Christ." We noted that "faith" here entails certainty, not probability. We also highlighted that Paul said the origin or source of this supernatural faith is found only in God's special revelation which for us today is the gospel message as found in the Bible. There is no other source for life-changing faith.

Aberrant Views for the Origin of Faith

Notwithstanding all the above about faith's true and only origin, many Christian apologists allege that faith comes from other sources than just the special revelation of "the word of Christ" as Romans teaches. This amounts to saying that we can preach the gospel without the Bible or without the truth and revelation of Scripture. For example, Evangelical Kelly James Clark says God "causes faith in a variety of ways."[65] He is talking about "saving faith" here. He says God uses non-scriptural human "evidence as a means to bring about faith." Notice Clark's phrase here, "as a means." Earlier it was noted that the preposition *dia* in 10:17 means "as a means," describing where faith comes from. Little prepositions are important. Paul limited "the means" by which faith comes to "the word of Christ" and only "the word of Christ." So Clark is wrong. Unaided human logic, human wisdom and man-made evidences apart from the special revelation of Scripture are not "a means" for producing faith. Calvin highlighted that point for us as well. In contrast to Calvin, and the Bible, Clark thinks any person can muster up faith simply from their own volition or will power. He says, "We, in most cases, must rely on our God-given intellectual equipment to produce beliefs."[66] Elsewhere he says, "One's properly functioning cognitive faculties can produce belief in God."[67] This is startling. Scripture says, "faith comes...by hearing the word of Christ." In contrast Clark proposes, "faith cometh by our own reasoning capabilities." The Bible teaches that saving faith is alien to us;[68] Clark teaches saving faith is inherent in us. He also suggests many other ways faith is created apart from Scripture, including "the birth of one's child, watching the sunset on the mountains or the ocean, examining the beauty of a flower, noting that we are 'fearfully and wonderfully made,' or walking through the woods in a time of quiet reflection." He literally suggests that saving faith "is quickened, enlivened" in such circumstances.[69]

He does not stop there. He says that "by reading the *Chronicles of Narnia*" the scales can be removed and faith can be evoked thus bringing salvation.[70] But *The Chronicles of Narnia* never mentions the gospel nor the name of Jesus and has no ability to evoke saving faith and has zero power for imparting salvation to anyone. Only the gospel has the power to create faith and impart salvation: "For I am not ashamed of the gospel, for it is the power of God for salvation to everyone who believes" (Rom 1:16). Putting faith in Jesus means salvation. Putting faith in Aslan the fictitious lion is silly.

Presuppositionalist John Frame says faith can come from many non-scriptural sources and occasions as well. Saving faith is not limited to divine revelation found in Scripture. He asserts that the unbeliever is not in need of "more information" to attain faith; for "everyone has the intellectual knowledge required for faith."[71] I could not disagree more. Every unbeliever needs more information to attain faith and salvation. The needed information is the objective contents of the saving gospel. That is why in Romans Paul asks, "How shall they believe in Him whom they have not heard? And how shall they hear without a preacher?" (Rom 10:14). They cannot believe without the needed information of the gospel, which is special revelation. That unique, life-changing information is not inherent in the individual.

What does the unbeliever need in order to be saved? He needs more information—the message of the gospel. And he also needs the supernatural ability to believe it—faith. Frame goes on to say that we can "persuade" unbelievers and advance them toward faith or belief through, or "by means of" [dia], various arguments, evidences and natural theology apart from Scripture, including the cosmological argument.[72]

Sola Holy Ruach, Nada Logos
An important related matter to the traditional apologists' assumption that saving faith can arise apart from special revelation, is their belief that the Holy Spirit simply creates faith in people apart from the truth of the Word of God found in Scripture generally, and in the gospel specifically. This is a quasi neo-orthodox, semi-existentialist notion that crops up everywhere in traditional apologetics. They affirm the indispensability of the Holy Spirit's role in salvation, which is a good thing. But then they undermine the indispensability of Scripture's role in generating faith by dichotomizing the synergistic function of Spirit and Word, by isolating the work of the Spirit from the Word. In other words, they surmise that the Holy Spirit does His work routinely while being indifferent to Scripture.

For example, Craig summarizes his view saying, "Conversion is exclusively the role of the Holy Spirit."[73] He actually argues that conversion can happen without the Bible as long as the Spirit is active, because the Spirit can do anything...even save people apart from special revelation. Evidentialist Gary Habermas writes, "Without the interceding of the Holy Spirit, no one comes to God."[74] On the face that statement is true. The problem is that Habermas does not believe the Word of God always needs to be working in conjunction with the Holy Spirit to produce saving faith. Stackhouse says the same thing: "Conversion is a divine work only, effected by the Holy Spirit of God (1 Corinthians 3:5-7)."[75] The problem in the preceding statements is not what these men say; the problem is in what they don't say, or what they refuse to say. They will not say that God's Spirit uses only, and always, the Word of God found in Scripture and the gospel to convert sinners. They won't say this because they believe saving faith can come from other sources apart from Scripture. They maintain that God's Spirit can just create faith in a vacuum, out of thin air, without the truth-reservoir of Scripture.

Frame is typical here. In *Five Views*, answering the question, "Where does faith come from?" he says, "the answer is that God causes faith by his own free grace. This is the regenerating work of the Holy Spirit."[76] He never says the Holy Spirit causes faith by using "the word of Christ" (Rom 10:17) or Scripture. Instead, he says, "The Spirit creates faith in the heart, as we have seen, and that faith may or may not arise through an argumentative process."[77] So instead of faith coming from hearing the word about Christ as Romans 10:17 says, Frame claims the Spirit of God can simply say, "Poof!" and behold, a person has faith in the heart. But it does not work that way. Again, Paul asks, "How shall they believe if they have not heard" the gospel message found in the Word of God? Answer: They won't believe, because they can't believe, because saving faith is alien to the sinner.

Craig's writings are replete with this *Sola* Holy Spirit approach that neglects Scripture's role in conversion and salvation. In his short chapter in the *Five Views* book, eighty times Craig refers to the Holy Spirit doing His regenerating work apart from Scripture! Here's a sample: "Belief in the Christian God is properly basic when formed in the circumstances of the witness of the Holy Spirit."[78] Holy Spirit, yes; Word of God needed, no. Here's another one: "The truth of the Christian faith is grounded in the witness of the Holy Spirit."[79] The "witness of the Spirit" is a subjective reality, often hard to discern; the Scriptures provide the Christian with an objective "ground" for faith that Craig wholly ignores. But he goes on: "A believer…is rational in believing on the grounds of the witness of the Spirit in his heart even in the face of such unrefuted objections."[80] Again, he claims all Spirit, but no Word. "The Christian will…rely primarily …on the gracious witness of God himself given to all his children by the indwelling Holy Spirit."[81] But in contrast to Craig's claims, the Christian should equally rely on the objective truth revealed in Scripture as a witness for personal faith. Again he asserts: "God has not left us to our own devices to determine whether Christianity is true but has given us the testimony of his own Spirit."[82] And again, "Surely faith is available to everyone who, in response to the Spirit's drawing, calls upon the name of the Lord."[83]

Scripture says faith is available to everyone who responds to the gospel as found in Scripture. Responding to the Spirit's drawing is a passive action for the sinner; responding to the objective contents of the gospel is a required and active action on the part of the sinner. Craig neglects this objective component of salvation. Craig just cannot bring himself to recognize the dual role of the Holy Spirit in conjunction with the Word of God in Scripture by which God accomplishes salvation. Nowhere does Craig acknowledge the reality of 1 Peter 1:23 which says, "for you have been born again not of seed which is perishable but imperishable, that is, through the living and abiding word of God."

Is the Holy Spirit prominent in the work of regeneration? Yes! Titus 3:5 makes that clear. But the Word of God is equally prominent and indispensible in the work of salvation. We saw that in 1 Peter 1:23 and Romans 1:16. That has always been true, for Psalm 19:7 teaches that God saves human souls with His written Word. Calvin said it best when he wrote, "the Word is the instrument by which the illumination of the Spirit is dispensed" and he also wrote, "Scripture is the school of the Holy Spirit."[84]

The Reformers on the Spirit and the Word—the Testimony

In contradistinction to the traditional apologists, who routinely accentuate the role of the Spirit apart from Scripture when it comes to generating faith and affecting an inner testimony to the truthfulness of Christianity, the Reformers taught differently. In particular, Luther and Calvin taught that the Spirit and the Word of Scripture were inseparable in working on the hearts of sinners, as they jointly labor together yielding conviction, faith and an inner testimony of witness. This biblical teaching of the Spirit working with the Word in the hearts of people came to be known as the doctrine of "the Testimony" (also referred to as the *testimonium,* another snazzy Latin word; the actual Greek word Jesus used was *martūreō*). The doctrine of the Testimony is based on the promise given by Jesus to His disciples just before His death. He told them He would send the Holy Spirit in His place and the Spirit will "bear witness to" or "testify to" the truthfulness of His ministry, particularly His teaching (John 15:26). Luther affirmed the basic components of the doctrine and Calvin systematized it with an inimitable theological and exegetical precision. On the import of the doctrine of "the Testimony," Zemek reminds us as follows:

> Sometimes we forget that alongside of the grand *Solas* of the Reformation stood another crucial watchword, the *testimonium,* i.e., the internal testimony of the Holy Spirit. It should not surprise us that the Divine Author of the Word is furthermore its effectual Applier. In salvation He attests to it as being God's own Word and then applies it to the heart. He is also the Agent who uses His written instrument in and throughout the process of sanctification. He wields the sword of His own fabrication mightily (Eph 6:17).[85]

Here Zemek reminds us that the Spirit works in conjunction with Scripture, not independent of it. Traditional apologists like Craig, K. J. Clark, Frame and even Sproul, try to invoke the Reformers' doctrine of the Testimony, but in a historically revisionist manner. They say the Spirit creates faith and gives a subjective inner witness of truth apart from the objective revelation of Scripture.[86] To assert such, turns the Reformers' Testimony doctrine on its ear.

Note some of Luther's comments on the efficacy of the Spirit working necessarily in conjunction with the Word of Scripture: "These things, I say, being temporal, may be endured with less harm than inveterate evil ways, which will inevitably ruin all souls that are not changed by the Word of God. If the Word were removed, eternal good, God, Christ, and the Spirit, would be removed with it."[87] And again, in refuting the rationalist tendencies of Erasmus, Luther wrote:

This is our contention: that spirits must be detected and tried by a double judgment. The first is internal. By it, through the enlightening of the Holy Ghost, the special gift of God, one enjoys complete certainty in judging of and deciding between the doctrines and opinions of all men as they affect oneself and one's own personal salvation....This is what we earlier spoke of as the *internal perspicuity of Holy Scripture*....

The second is an external judgment. By it, we judge the spirits and doctrines of all men, also with the greatest certainty, and not now for ourselves only, but also for the benefit and salvation of others. This judgment is the province of the public ministry of the Word and the external office, and is the special concern of teachers and preachers of the Word.... We spoke of this earlier as the *external perspicuity of the Holy Scripture*. We hold that all spirits should be proved in the sight of the church by the judgment of Scripture. For it should be settled as fundamental, and most firmly fixed in the minds of Christians, that the Holy Scriptures are a spiritual light far brighter even than the sun, especially in what relates to salvation and all essential matters.[88]

In assailing those who would try to extricate the work of the Spirit from Scripture, Luther had this rebuke: "The Psalmist does not say: 'thy Spirit alone is a lamp unto my feet,' though he assigns to the Spirit His part when he says: 'thy good spirit shall lead me into the land of uprightness' (Ps. 143.10). Thus Scripture is called a *way* and a *path*, doubtless by reason of its certainty."[89] And finally, Luther says, "It has pleased God not to give the Spirit without the Word, but through the Word; that He might have us as workers together with Him, we sounding forth without what He alone breathes within wheresoever He will. This He could do without the Word; but He will not."[90]

Calvin is more exhaustive on this matter of the Spirit working in conjunction with Scripture; he formally referred to the Testimony as "the secret testimony of the Spirit"[91] and the "inward persuasion of the Holy Spirit."[92] Calvin's doctrine of *the Testimony* was based on five inviolable presuppositions he slavishly posited: (1) the Holy Spirit is superior to the best of unaided human reason; (2) only God the Spirit can properly bear witness to His own words found in Scripture; (3) the Spirit does not work in conjunction with natural theology to create faith or conviction; (4) the Spirit always bears witness to the Word to create faith and conviction; and (5) the Spirit does not create saving faith apart from the Word.[93] Following is a vintage statement by Calvin on the Testimony, taken from his commentary on the Psalms:

> God deals bountifully with men, when he invites them to himself by his word and doctrine; and, secondly, that still all this is lifeless and unprofitable, until he govern by his Spirit those whom he has already taught by his word. As the Psalmist desires not simply to have his steps directed, but to have them directed to God's word, we may learn that he did not hunt after secret revelations, and set the word at naught, as many fanatics do, but connected the external doctrine with the inward grace of the Holy Spirit; and herein consists the completeness of the faithful, in that God engraves on their hearts what he shows by his word to be right.[94]

Notice Calvin says Word and Spirit work together—both are present. There is not one without the other. The Spirit does not trump or work independently of Scripture as many traditional apologists allege. Also note that Calvin here, along with Luther earlier, equates the "word" with "Scripture"—a truth categorically denied by William Lane Craig and others. In his writings Craig claims Calvin as his own, but nothing could be further from the truth, especially regarding bibliology where Calvin's view is the polar opposite of Craig's.

For example, regarding Calvin, Dakin notes, "the modern distinction between the Bible and the Word of God in the Bible is one that he did not make."[95] Craig says the Bible and the Word of God are not synonymous. Calvin and Luther taught, "No Spirit, no Word, then no witness." Craig believes the Testimony entails only the Spirit and no Scripture needed. He writes,

> Notice that if we restricted the Spirit's witness to the Scriptures, we should have to say that believers who have not yet heard or read the Scriptures . . . have no experience of the witness of the Spirit. But even believers without the

Scriptures surely do know on the basis of the Spirit's witness that they are God's children. I therefore appeal to the witness of the Holy Spirit himself rather than Scripture in explaining how it is that we *know* Christianity is true.[96]

Contrast that with a synopsis of Calvin's view:

> Calvin taught "that the same Spirit who speaks to us in the Scriptures speaks also in our hearts. The exterior testimony which we read in black and white is confirmed to us and sealed in our hearts by the secret testimony of the Spirit. And the secret testimony of the Holy Spirit does not lift us proudly above the letter of the Word, but, on the contrary, having made us understand it a little, it stimulates us to submit ourselves to it further in order to know it better. The inner testimony then sends the believer back to the external testimony, which alone is normative. It adds nothing to the written revelation. *Extra eam nulla revelatio*, said Calvin of Scripture. The Spirit only attests, seals, and confirms to the heart of man that such and such a page in the act of being read or explained in public worship or in private is truly the Word of God. The work of the Spirit then consists in making the exterior testimony speak in the inner testimony. . . . On the part of Calvin the inner testimony of the Holy Spirit occurred at two points: it made the believer know, on the one hand, the authority of Scripture, and on the other hand the certainty of his own personal salvation...."[97]

As shown above the doctrine of the Testimony for Calvin was the Spirit working with the truth of Scripture, "the Word," on the hearts of people. Calvin did not apply the Testimony of the Spirit to natural theology, the Laws of Logic, human reason independent of special revelation, or in reference to the truth of general revelation. The Testimony is reserved for the Spirit's attestation of the truth of Scripture. Sproul, Gerstner and Lindsley misrepresent Calvin here. They say Calvin's Testimony applied to the Spirit working in conjunction with natural theology and human reason apart from special revelation. Like Craig, they turn Calvin's Testimony on its ear through selective historical revisionism. They write,

Calvin regarded evidence as a foundation for faith. Evidences "open the door" to or "commence" a process which is continued by instruction in the truth and by the internal testimony of the Holy Spirit. In light of these passages, it is difficult to say that for Calvin testimony of the Holy Spirit was apart from or opposed to evidence.[98]

The fatal flaw in Sproul's thinking here is that he equates "evidences" with natural theology. Calvin never did that. When Calvin referred to "evidences" he was referring to miracles contained in Scripture, which is special revelation.[99] Sproul *et al*, try to conflate divine evidences contained in Scripture with humanly fabricated evidences that are the byproduct of natural theology. As a result, like Craig, Sproul *et al*, misconstrue and misapply Calvin's teaching on the Testimony.

Luther and Calvin were justified in their teaching that the Holy Spirit and the Word of God go together. That is what Paul meant when he said the sword of the Holy Spirit "is the word of God" (Eph 6:17). The Spirit and the truth of Scripture must be preserved in tandem for only the Holy Spirit and the Word of God are capable of penetrating the deepest inner recesses of the human heart, weather hardened or redeemed. Regarding the Holy Spirit's interpenetrating ministry into the deepest hollows of the human soul, the Psalmist acknowledged,

> Where can I go from Thy Spirit?
> Or where can I flee from Thy presence?
> If I ascend into heaven, Thou art there;
> If I make my bed in Sheol, behold Thou art there....
> Search me, O God, and know my heart (Ps 139:7-8, 23).

A century after Luther and Calvin, the historic and unparalleled *Westminster Confession of Faith* was penned and distributed to the public in 1647. This monumental statement of faith was the by-product of 121 of the ablest Bible scholars of the day, carefully composed over the course of five years, and to this day is one of the strongest articulations of the infallibility and efficacy of Holy Scripture ever composed in the English language. The divines of that day clearly understood the reality and the importance of the doctrine of the Testimony, for they preserved it with precision in their document.

They affirmed the synergistic work of the Holy Spirit and Scripture when they wrote, "our full persuasion and assurance of the infallible truth, and divine authority thereof, is from the inward work of the Holy Spirit, bearing witness by and with the Word in our hearts."[100]

The Reformers and Westminster divines were merely echoing what the Bible clearly teaches about the Holy Spirit's cooperation with the Word on the souls of men. The New Testament affirms this unique ministry of the Holy Spirit. Paul said, "for the Spirit searches all things, even the depths of God" (1 Cor 2:10).

In like manner, the divine revelation of the truth found in Scripture can penetrate into the deepest inner recesses of the human soul. "For the word of God is living and active and sharper than any two-edged sword, and piercing as far as the division, of soul and spirit, of both joints and marrow, and able to judge the thoughts and intentions of the heart" (Heb 4:12).

So contrary to the Reformers and the Bible, traditional apologists go adrift on the doctrine of the Testimony—the timeless truth whereby the Spirit works necessarily and always interdependently with the divine revelation of the Word of God. Beware of this oft occurring idiosyncrasy of many traditional Christian apologetics who champion the role of the Holy Spirit in salvation and apologetics while at the same time minimize or dismiss altogether the indispensable role of the special revelation of Scripture which God uses to produce faith in the sinner, which alone imparts salvation.

Faith vs. Reason or Faith with Reason?

One more issue needs to be addressed in our discussion on faith. Not long ago a fellow Christian made the following remark that is commonly stated and believed: "Religion is a matter of faith, and since we believe our religious teachings based on faith, there is no evidence for what we believe; it just comes down to personal, subjective faith, and all religions believe what they believe based on faith, not on any objective evidence."

It sounds like this believer is saying that there is no evidence for the truth of Christianity and that we don't need any evidence either. I would say just the opposite—there is evidence for the truth of Christianity and in fact Christianity is based on true historical events that are corroborated by evidence. I agree with the late eminent Christian apologist, Greg Bahnsen, in his famous debate with the atheist Gordon Stein in 1985, when Bahnsen said, "I believe in the truth of Christianity because of the evidence; if there were no evidence for it, then I would not believe it."

Let me explore this matter further with four main points. The first point is that faith and reason are not incompatible or mutually exclusive. Actually, true faith is the perfect complement to legitimate reason. Logic compliments belief. Intelligible thinking enhances sound believing. Faith is a necessity resulting from the fact that humans are finite—we don't know and can't know everything there is to know in this life. Faith is inescapable. And our ability to think comes from God. God is the greatest intellect in the universe—He has a perfect and infinite mind. The ability to think, be rational, use logic, and reason all came from God as a gift. Long before Descartes declared, "I think, therefore I am," God declared, "I Am that I AM," (Exod 3:14), a statement infinitely more profound than that of the 17th century French philosopher. So faith and reason, by God's design, complement one another.

The second point is that every worldview, religion, or ideology has at its ultimate foundation basic presuppositions that can be labeled as "faith-based" assumptions. Atheistic evolution, for example, claims to have objective evidence for the "process" of how life developed, but no atheist can tell us how everything began in the first place, or what started the Big Bang. Through "faith," based on no objective evidence whatsoever, the atheist believes the Big Bang happened billions of years ago, but cannot explain how. As a matter of fact, every worldview in existence, apart from biblical Christianity, fails to explain how everything began in the first place. They have no objective evidence to explain ultimate origins. The question of origins lies outside the domain of the scientific method; it's a metaphysical question. They hold to their views based on subjective personal faith.

The third point is that biblical Christianity is not founded upon a sheer "leap of faith" that is lacking evidence or objective historical foundations. There is a popular aberrational strain of Christianity that is based upon a mere "leap of faith," but it is a counterfeit of true Christianity. It is not based on clear biblical teaching. The idea that Christianity is based on a "leap of faith" and not on evidence is usually attributed to Soren Kierkegaard, the 19th century Danish philosopher. He argued that subjectivity reigned supreme and that objective truth was over-rated.

His view also came to be known as existentialism—defining life and reality first through the lens of self and subjective experience. Kierkegaard's definition of Christianity and faith is unbiblical and should be categorically rejected. It was his distorted view of Christianity that actually led to the idea that Christians don't care about facts, evidence, true science, studying, attaining knowledge or even thinking logically. Even today Christians are stigmatized as ignorant, uneducated buffoons who are not up to speed on modern science or logic—to believe in the Bible is to check your brain at the door. Nothing could be further from the truth. Faith does not disparage knowledge, but is inseparable from it. Calvin rightly maintained that "Faith consists not in ignorance, but in knowledge—knowledge not of God merely, but of the divine will....Faith consists in the knowledge of God and Christ (John 17:3)."[101]

The fourth point is that Christianity is based upon evidence. Or another way of saying it is that Christianity is based on real, historical events and people. For example, Jesus really lived, He truly died on a cross, He actually had Apostles and they really wrote down what happened. Moses was real. The Exodus was real. Adam and Eve were actual historical individuals. Noah was a real man, and so was his wife, Mrs. Noah. Those who say that none of these people were historical simply refuse to look at the available evidence, or worse, they misinterpret and distort the evidence. Sinners misinterpret, deny and reject cold hard facts every day in courtrooms across the world.

The Bible explicitly teaches that there is "evidence" for what it asserts to be true. A couple examples will suffice. In Romans 1, the Apostle Paul explains that there are no real agnostics—no one can sincerely say, "I don't know if God exits." In verse 19 he plainly states through the Holy Spirit, "that which is known about God is **evident** within them." The word "evident" is related to the word "evidence." So this passage explains that God has given evidence to every human establishing that God exists.

Paul explains what that evidence is. First he says the evidence is "within them," which he goes on to explain is the human conscience, which every person has from birth resulting from being made in God's image (Gen 1:26). And in the next verse he goes on even further laying out the incontestable evidence: "for God made it evident to them; for since the creation of the world His invisible attributes, His eternal power and divine nature, have been clearly seen, being understood through what has been made, so they are without excuse" (Rom 1:20). So this passage says all people have internal "evidence" (a conscience) and external "evidence" of God's existence and that evidence is clearly understood and undeniable. In view of this biblical fact, no one actually needs faith to believe in God! Belief in God is innate and inherent from birth. The problem is that over time sinners resist and mangle the self-evident revelation of God's existence contained in their own constitution until they develop a self-inflicted seared conscience about the truth of God. To over-ride this spiritual self-destruction, God offers supernatural faith in the life-changing good news of the gospel that comes only from His living Word, the Holy Scriptures.

Another example that Christianity is based on evidence is when Paul said that there were over 500 eyewitnesses who saw first-hand the bodily resurrection of Jesus (1 Cor 15:6-8). Paul himself was one of those eyewitnesses. Eyewitness testimony is accepted in courtrooms today. Paul was trained as a Jewish rabbi and was a scholar of the Torah, the Law of Moses. In the legal community of Paul's day truth had to be verified by eyewitness testimony. People could not make hapless assertions on a whim without corroborating support or validation. Truth assertions could only be established "on the evidence of two witnesses or three witnesses" (Deut 17:6). Paul had 497 witnesses in addition to the required three to validate the truth of Jesus' resurrection from the dead! We know Jesus rose from the dead because of the reliable evidence of the overwhelming eyewitness testimony.

Faith is not incompatible with evidence. Actually, true faith demands evidence and is based on evidence. That is why Hebrews 11:1 says, "faith...is the evidence" for things, or biblical spiritual truths, not seen. Faith that saves is a gift from God, it issues from exposure to Scripture, is the fruit of a rational enterprise, and is itself "evidence" for the truth of Christianity.

Summary

In this chapter we reviewed four important issues about faith relative to apologetics: (1) the definition of faith; (2) the source of saving faith; (3) the role of the Holy Spirit in conjunction with special revelation (i.e., the Bible) in producing faith that leads to salvation; and (4) the relationship between faith and reason.

First we asked the question, "What does the unbeliever need in order to be saved?" Among other things, the believer needs faith to be saved.[102] Paul said, "By grace you have been saved through faith" (Eph 2:8). We showed how traditional apologists typically define faith, inappropriately, with the three Latin terms, *notitia* (knowledge), *assensus* (assent), and *fiducia* (trust). Biblical faith needs to be defined with biblical terms from the Hebrew Old Testament and the Greek New Testament. One of the common Hebrew Old Testament words we know for faith is "amen" and is a word that speaks of certitude and assurance. Jesus used it often in His teaching (Matt 5:18, 26; 6:2, 5, 16; 8:10). The main word in the Greek New Testament for faith is the noun *pistis* and the verb *pisteuō*. We also noted that mere word studies are not sufficient to define faith. All the other literary variables of syntax, grammar, usage and context also have to be considered. Doing so gives the true picture of the richness, versatility and depth of what constitutes biblical faith or belief in God—the supernatural ability to respond to God and His promises as revealed in special revelation, fulfilled in the person of Christ.

Second we answered the question, "Where does faith come from?" Paul answered that question for us in Romans 10:17: "So faith comes from hearing, and hearing by the word of Christ." The sole origin of saving faith is found in the supernatural special revelation of God, found for us today in Scripture generally, and specifically in the gospel of Jesus Christ. Many traditional Christian apologists wrongly believe faith can originate from various sources, experiences and means apart from Scripture. Such a notion undermines the entire apologetical enterprise, short-circuiting the very power supply provided by God to accomplish salvation through the truth of His Word.

Third we examined the role of the Word of God in relation to the Holy Spirit to bring salvation to sinners. Traditional apologists say the Holy Spirit works independently from God's Word in Scripture to produce faith. To do this, they often misinterpret the Reformers' doctrine of the Testimony. Luther and Calvin taught that the Spirit always works on people's hearts in conjunction with the Word of God contained in Scripture, not independent of it. True biblical apologetics teaches the Spirit of God always uses the truth of God's Word to create faith and to effect salvation. Traditional apologists say the Holy Spirit is indispensible to conversion, but Scripture is not.

We say the Holy Spirit and the Word of God are equally indispensible to conversion. This is a direct implication of Romans 10:17: "So faith comes from hearing, and hearing by the word of Christ."

And the fourth question we looked at was, "How does faith relate to reason?" We determined that faith and reason are not mutually exclusive, that faith entails reasoning and thinking entails believing and volition. Biblical faith and accurate thinking don't contradict each other.

One of the basic essentials an unbeliever needs to be saved is faith—supernatural, heavenly, alien faith that comes only from hearing the gospel of Jesus Christ found in Scripture along with the concomitant work of the Holy Spirit who enables the spiritually dead sinner to believe unto newness of life. And this kind of saving faith is solely the gracious, gratuitous gift of God. In the words of Calvin, "Faith is the special gift of God."[103]

Notes

1. E. J. Carnell, *An Introduction to Christian Apologetics: A Philospohic Defense of the Trinitarian-Theistic Faith* (Grand Rapids, MI: Eerdmans Publishing, 1956), 65-88. Carnell writes an entire chapter titled "What is Faith?" Unfortunately he does not answer the question from a biblical point of view, but rather from a philosophical one. He never refers to any of the Hebrew words for faith and never makes mention of *pistis* or *pisteuō*. He says, "faith is a resting of the soul in the sufficiency of the evidence" (p. 82). The truthfulness of any evidence is to be measured by the burning in the bosom (p. 69), the law of contradiction (p. 70), "Aristotle's fourth book of the *Metaphysics*" (p. 78), and human reason (72-73). "Reason is the test for truth" (p. 86). "Logic can be the means by which the Spirit leads a man into faith" (70). Aside from the title of his book, Carnell's discussion is nothing close to "Christian."

2. Bernard Ramm, *A Christian Appeal to Reason* (Waco, TX: Word Books, 1977), 107.

3. J. P. Moreland and William Lane Craig, *Philosophical Foundations for a Christian Worldview* (Downers Grove, IL: InterVarsity Press, 2003), 18. Craig's mentor, Panneberg, defines faith the same way: "faith in the Reformation sense is above all trust (*fiducia*). A more exact look shows that this does not rule out the elements of knowledge (*notitia*) and assent (*assensus*) but instead presupposes them"; Wolfhart Pannenberg, *Systematic Theology*, 3 vols. trans. by Geoffrey W. Bromiley (Grand Rapids, MI: Eerdmans Publishing, 1997), III:138.

4. R. C. Sproul, *Defending Your Faith: An Introduction to Apologetics* (Wheaton, IL: Crossway, 2003), 22. In another book Sproul asserts, "Early Reformed theologians customarily distinguished among various elements or aspects of saving faith. For the most part they discerned three chief aspects known as *notitia*, *assensus*, and *fiducia*"; typically, Sproul in his discussion does not name the Reformed theologians he's referring to nor does he give any quote or reference to validate his allegation; he just asserts it to be so; see, R. C. Sproul, *What Is Reformed Theology? Understanding the Basics* (Grand Rapids: Baker Books, 1997), 71.

5. Gregory Koukl, "Knowledge, Assent and Trust" <http://www.str.org/site/News2? page =NewsArticle &id= 5391>; also, see Groothuis, who calls himself a Reformed Calvinist apologist (633-34). In his mammoth tome on apologetics he does not define faith from a biblical perspective (nor a Calvinistic one), but instead resorts to the popularly concocted tri-fold Latin *mantra* of *fiducia*, *notitia*, etc. 39-40.

6.

7. Kenneth Boa, "A Tale of Twin Sisters," www.kenboa.org.

8. J. I. Packer, *Concise Theology: A Guide to Historic Christian Belief* (Tyndale House Publishers, 1993), 159-160; John Frame is another solid Reformed theologian, like Packer, who missteps here, espousing the Latin trilogy of faith, suggesting it is the historic position of the Church, yet he gives no reference of any one of the Reformers ascribing to it; see *Apologetics: A Justification of Christian Belief*, 261.

9. Martin Luther, "To the Councilmen of All Cities in Germany That They Establish and Maintain Christian Schools" cited by in *Basics of Biblical Hebrew Grammar*, Gary D. Pratico and Miles V. Van Pelt (Grand Rapids, MI: Zondervan, 2007), 120. Even Pannenberg, who defines faith with the three Latin terms, admits that Luther changed his view about faith after 1510, and it evolved even more during the course of his life as he got leeched by Scripture, bleeding out old, pre-conversion, Scholastic notions he was brainwashed with in his early education; Pannenberg, *Systematic Theology*, III: 3, 139-143. Those who want to know what Calvin the Reformer really taught about faith can read his masterful 31 page exegetical exposition in his *Institutes* called "Of Faith: the Definition of it; its Peculiar Properties." In his discussion you won't find a hint of a Latinized triad, but rather Bible verses everywhere and a supremely lucid, yet weighty, distillation being a byproduct of his careful exegesis of the Hebrew and Greek text of Scripture; *Institutes*, 352-383. Calvin believed the same as Luther, namely that to preserve integrity and exactitude in theology, one must go back to the biblical languages and furthermore use only biblical words and terminology; to introduce non-biblical words only invites ambiguity, obfuscation and confusion. Listen to Calvin: "I willingly abstain from disputes about words, but I could wish that Christian writers had always observed this soberness—that when there was no occasion for it, they had never thought of using terms foreign to Scripture—terms which might produce much offense, but very little fruit"; *Institutes*, 517. As to the benefit of knowing the original languages, Calvin says, "Those acquainted with Hebrew understand the meaning better"; 476; cf. 482.

10. D. Mark Parks, "Faith, Faithfulness" in *Holman Illustrated Bible Dictionary*, eds. Chad Brand, Charles Draper and Archie England (Nashville, Tennessee: Holman Bible Publishers, 1998), 547. I don't know who first proposed that faith is a tri-fold combination of *notitia*, *assensus*, and *fiducia*, but it is surprising how widespread the notion is among evangelicals and it is considered to be the authoritative, *de facto* definition of biblical faith in popular Christian literature—it seems to be ubiquitous. For example, Pazmiño is typical when he says without any biblical justification, "Faith can be viewed as including the dimensions of *notitia* (intellectual

affirmation), *assensus* (affective affirmation), and *fiducia* (intentional affirmation) as persons respond to God's activities and revelation in Jesus Christ"; Robert W. Pazmiño, *Foundational Issues in Christian Education: An Introduction in Evangelical Perspective* (Grand Rapids, MI: Baker Academic, 2008), 47.

11. Renowned historian, Will Durant, rightly noted that "in the fourth century, the Latin language as the noble and enduring vehicle of Catholic ritual" had been co-opted right out of the ash heap of Roman paganism, along with many other syncretistic Catholic rituals including "the title of Pontifex Maximus for the Supreme Pontiff [i.e. 'Pope']"; *Caesar and Christ* (New York: Simon and Schuster, 1944), 618-619. Calvin, who wrote in Latin and French, gave precedence to the Greek text over the later "corrupted" Latin version when it came to biblical exegesis and exposition; see his *Institutes*, 518.

12. Henry M. Shires, "Faith" in *Hastings Dictionary of the Bible*, ed. James Hastings (New York: Charles Scribner's Sons, 1963), 288.

13. William D. Barrick, "Noah's Flood and Its Geological Implications," in *Coming to Grips with Genesis: Biblical Authority and the Age of the Earth*, eds. Terry Mortenson and Thane H. Ury (Green Forest, AR: Master Books, 2009), 260. Noted Princeton grammarian and New Testament scholar William Hendriksen said the same thing more concisely: "the meaning of a word is not determined first of all by its etymology but by its use in given contexts"; *Romans: New Testament Commentary* (Grand Rapids: Baker Book House, 1981), 402.

14. Shires, *Hastings Dictionary*, 288.

15. J. I. Packer, "Faith" in *Evangelical Dictionary of Theology*, ed. Walter A. Elwell (Grand Rapids, MI: Baker Book House, 1987), 399.

16. Shires, 288.

17. Parks, *Holman Dictionary*, 548.

18. R. E. Nixon, "Faith, Faithfulness" in *The Zondervan Pictorial Encyclopedia of the Bible* 5 vols. ed. Merrill C. Tenney (Grand Rapids, MI: Zondervan, 1976), II: 480.

19. Shires, 288.

20. Ibid.

21. George J. Zemek, *A Biblical Theology of the Doctrines of Sovereign Grace: Exegetical Considerations of Key Anthropological, Hamartilogical and Soteriological Terms and Motifs* (Littlerock, Arkansas: George Zemek, 2002), 181.

22. Parks, *Holman Dictionary*, 547. Faith is personal knowledge of God and supernatural belief that results from hearing His revelation and taking God at His Word. Faith is a gift from God (Eph 2:8-9). Faith is alien to our own nature and being; it is not innate or inherent. Faith is

soteriological to the core. Compare these biblical elements to a typical philosophical definition proposed by respected "apologists" as delineated by Lewis: "FAITH. (1) Whole soul trust in an unseen reality on the ground of sufficient (seen) evidence (Carnell). (2) Assent to the truth of an unprovable presupposition (Clark and Van Til). (3) A passionate leap into the dark (Kierkegaard)"; Gordon R. Lewis, *Testing Christianity's Truth Claims: Approaches to Christian Apologetics* (Chicago, IL: Moody Press, 1976), 342. Notice in the preceding three definitions of faith there is no reference to God, the Word, Christ or the gospel, but rather they are patently godless, Christ-less and scripturally sterile.

23. Packer, *Evangelical Dictionary*, 399.

24. Leon Morris, "Faith" in *The Illustrated Bible Dictionary, Part 1 Aaron-Golan*, ed. J. D. Douglas (Wheaton, IL: Tyndale House Publishers, 1980), 496.

25. Ibid., 497; or as Van Drunen aptly notes, "Scripture emphasizes again and again that true faith is faith *in Christ*" David Van Drunen, "The Nature of Justifying Faith" in *Justified: Modern Reformation Essays on the Doctrine of Justification* (Escondido: Modern Reformation, 2010), 49.

26. Morris, 497.

27. Zemek, *A Biblical Theology*, 182.

28. Ibid.

29. Morris, *Illustrated Bible Dictionary*, 498.

30. John Frame, *Five Views On Apologetics* ed. Steven B. Cowan, (Grand Rapids, MI: Zondervan, 2000), 219.

31. William Lane Craig, *Five Views*, 54-55.

32. Gary Habermas, *Five Views*, 97.

33. Norman Geisler, *Christian Apologetics* (Grand Rapids: Baker Books, 1976), 146.

34. Dennis McCallum, *Christianity: The Faith that Makes Sense, Solid Evidence for Belief in Christ* (Wheaton, IL: Tyndale House Publishers, 1997), 12.

35. J. P. Moreland, *Scaling the Secular City* (Grand Rapids, MI: Baker Book House, 1987), 13.

36. Sproul, *Defending Your Faith*, 50.

37. Craig, *Five Views*, 53.

38. Frame, *Five Views*, 224.

39. Kell James Clark, *Five Views*, 277.

40. Lawrence O. Richards, "Belief/Faith" in *New International Encyclopedia of Bible Words*, (Grand Rapids, MI: 1991), 113.

41. Ibid. 113.

42. Cleon L. Rogers, Jr. and Cleon L. Rogers, III, *The New Linguistic and Exegetical Key to the Greek New Testament* (Grand Rapids, MI: Zondervan, 1998), 542. In the 1500's Calvin exposed the "probability" mantra that

slithered into the ranks by Christian philosophers and theologians and he would have none of it. Instead, he argued the opposite: "We ask not for proofs or probabilities on which to rest our judgment, but we subject our intellect and judgment to it as too transcendent for us to estimate …because we have a thorough conviction that, in holding it, we hold unassailable truth"; John Calvin, *Institutes of the Christian Religion*, trans, by Henry Beveridge (Peabody, Massachusetts: Hendrickson Publishers, 2009), 34.

43. W. Bauer, W. F. Arndt, F. W. Gingrich, and F. W. Danker, *A Geek-English Lexicon of the New Testament* (Chicago and London: The University of Chicago Press, 1979), 234.

44. R. C. H. Lenski, *Interpretation of Saint Paul's Epistle to the Romans 8-16* (Minneapolis, MN: Augsburg Fortress, 2008), 667-668.

45. Cf. 10:16 where NASB translates the dative of *akoā* as "report"; McKenzie gives an accurate summary of the implications here: "Faith, for Paul, is not only faith in Christ Jesus (Gal 2:16; Eph 1:15; Col 1:4), but in the specifically Christian sense it is faith in the preaching, 'the word of faith' (Rm 10:8). No one can be saved unless he invokes the name of the Lord, but no one can invoke His name unless he believes in Him; and how is one to believe in Him unless one has heard of Him through the preaching (Rm 10:13-15)? Hence faith comes through the preaching of those who are witnesses of the life, death, and resurrection of Jesus Christ. The content of the Christian faith is summed up briefly in Rm 10:9: Jesus is Lord and God has raised Him from the dead. It is faith in Him who raised the Lord Jesus from the dead, who was delivered to death for our sins and raised for our righteousness (Rm 4:24 ff)"; John L. McKenzie, "Faith" in *Dictionary of the Bible*, (New York: Macmillan Publishing Company, 1965), 268-69. Girdlestone is succinct and on target as well: "Faith is taking God at His word….Faith, according to Scripture, seems to imply a word, message, or revelation"; Robert Baker Girdlestone, *Girdlestone's Synonyms of the Old Testament: Their Bearing on Christian Doctrine*, ed. by Donald R. White (Grand Rapids, MI: Baker Book House, 1991), 122.

46. This is no novel idea; this is the historic position of the Church. Canon 5 from the Council of Orange in 529 said the following: "If anyone says that not only the increase of faith but also its beginning and the very desire for faith, by which we believe in Him who justifies the ungodly and comes to the regeneration of holy baptism—if anyone says that this belongs to us by nature and not by a gift of grace, that is, by the inspiration of the Holy Spirit amending our will and turning it from unbelief to faith and from godlessness to godliness, it is proof that he is

opposed to the teaching of the Apostles, for blessed Paul says, 'And I am sure that he who began a good work in you will bring it to completion at the day of Jesus Christ' (Phil. 1:6). And again, 'For by grace you have been saved through faith; and this is not your own doing, it is the gift of God' (Eph. 2:8). For those who state that the faith by which we believe in God is natural make all who are separated from the Church of Christ by definition in some measure believers"; cited by Michael Horton, *For Calvinism* (Grand Rapids: Zondervan, 2011), 31-32. Also see Schreiner's fine biblical and historical exposition of saving faith where he clearly establishes that Luther taught "that faith is God's gift to us"; Thomas Schreiner, *Faith Alone: The Doctrine of Justification* (Grand Rapids: Zondervan, 2015), 44. Contrary to Luther and Calvin, Jonathan Edwards actually deviated from the two great Reformers on this matter, arguing that saving faith is not alien, but inherent and served as a secondary ground for justification. Hunsinger summarizes Edwards' heterodoxical view thusly: "faith is that condition 'in us' that makes it fitting for us to be justified. Edwards is quite explicit. Faith, along with all it entails, is described as 'that in us by which we are justified.'² In short, justification finds its primary ground 'in Christ,' in his negative and positive righteousness, and its secondary or derivative ground 'in us,' that is, in faith, defined as a disposition, as a 'habit and principle in the heart'"; George Hunsinger, "An American Tragedy: Jonathan Edwards on Justification," in *Justified: Modern Reformation Essays on the Doctrine of Justification*, eds. Ryan Glomsrud and Michael S. Horton (Escondido, CA: Modern Reformation, 2010), 53.

47. Richards, *New International Encyclopedia*, 115.

48. Carnell, *Christian Apologetics*, 41.

49. Craig, *Five Views*, 44. Groothuis argues that saving faith can come "through rational arguments" (i.e., "philosophy") apart from special revelation and he goes on to say that "we come to faith partially through recognizing good apologetic arguments" (30, 62). This view then believes that salvation is, at least in part, the result of human effort through sheer intellectual prowess, whereas Scripture says salvation is a "right" given by God and does not result from sheer human decision (John 1:13).

50. Alvin Plantinga, quoted in *Five Views* by Craig, 45.

51. Bauer *et al*, *Greek-English Lexicon*, 180.

52. John Peter Lange, *Commentary on the Holy Scriptures: Critical, Doctrinal and Homiletical* vol. V, trans. Philip Schaff (Grand Rapids, MI: Zondervan, 1960), 349. Cf. Lenski, *Romans*, 667.

53. Lenski, *Romans*, 668.

54. Henry Alford, *Alford's Greek Testament* (London: Gilbert and Rivington Printers, 1861), II: 422.

55. The Greek *rhematos* genitive singular from *rhema*

56. Notice all the terms emphasizing verbal proclamation in this passage: *legei* in 10:6 and 10:11; *kerūssomen* in 10:8; *homologesēs* in 10:9; *kērūssontos* in 10:14; *euangelizomenōn* in 10:15.

57. Bauer *et al*, *Greek-English Lexicon*, 735.

58. Lange, *Commentary on the Holy Scriptures*, 349.

59. Martin Luther, *Commentary on Romans* trans. J. Theodore Mueller (Grand Rapids, MI: Kregel Publications, 1976), 152.

60. Rogers, *Linguistic and Exegetical Key*, 335. Cf. A. T. Robertson, *Word Pictures in the New Testament: Epistles of Paul* (Grand Rapids, MI: Baker Book House, 1931), IV: 390.

61. John Calvin, *Commentaries on the Epistle of Paul the Apostle to the Romans* trans. and ed. by John Owen (Grand Rapids, MI: Baker Book House, 2003), XIX: 401. When Calvin says the "word of God" what he is referring to is Scripture. That is important to point out, since several traditional apologists do not confine the phrase "the word of God" to Scripture. For example, Craig equates the *kalam* cosmological argument, and anything else he might say, to "the word of God." This flows from his existentialist proclivities regarding bibliology. He quips: "we cannot make a simplistic equation between God's Word and Scripture"; *Five Views*, 314.

62. John MacArthur, *Commentary on Romans 9-16* (Chicago: Moody Press, 1994), 86-87.

63. Calvin, *Institutes*, 34, 765.

64. Zemek, *A Biblical Theology*, 184.

65. Clark, *Five Views*, 250.

66. Ibid., 271

67. Ibid., 284

68. Interestingly, Sproul speaks much of "alien-righteousness" when talking about justification, [see *Faith Alone: The Evangelical Doctrine of Justification* (Grand Rapids, MI: Baker Books, 1995), 107], but he does not believe in the biblical concept of "alien saving faith" that brings that "alien righteousness" of justification. With respect to apologetics, he is a proponent of "inherent faith" just as Clark the Arminian is.

69. Clark, *Five Views*, 279.

70. Ibid., 273.

71. Frame, *Five Views*, 219. Coleman makes the same mistake when he implies that faith can come from other sources apart from the special revelation of the Word of Christ, for he purports that faith can also come from the testimony of church history, church history not even being general

revelation as the Bible describes it; see Robert E. Coleman, *The Heart of the Gospel: The Theology Behind the Master Plan of Evangelism* (Grand Rapids, MI: Baker Books, 2011), 161.

72. Ibid., 219-223.

73. Craig, *Five Views*, 55.

74. Habermas, *Five Views*, 97.

75. John G. Stackhouse, Jr., *Humble Apologetics: Defending the Faith Today* (New York, NY: Oxford University Press, 2002), 82.

76. Frame, *Five Views*, 209.

77. Ibid., 215.

78. Craig, *Five Views*, 32.

79. Ibid.

80. Ibid., 35.

81. Ibid., 36.

82. Ibid., 37.

83. Ibid. Cf. his statement again: "The proper basis of faith is the witness of the Holy Spirit..." (38).

84. Calvin, *Institutes*, 4, 608. On this topic, Calvin went on to caution believers telling them, "whenever the Lord shuts His sacred mouth" we humans should desist from inquiry—in other words, don't try to find spiritual truth if God did not reveal it in the Bible, or, today the Holy Spirit does not reveal truth apart from the Bible.

85. George Zemek, *Testimonium Spiritus Sancti*, unpublished class syllabus, nd., 1.

86. John Calvin, *Commentaries on the Epistle of Paul the Apostle to the Hebrews*, trans. by John Owen (Grand Rapids, MI: Baker Books Grand Rapids MI, 1999), XXII: 94. See R. C. Sproul's chapter, "The Testimony of the Holy Spirit" in *Defending Your Faith*, 189-93, for his confused explanation of Calvin's *testimonium*. Cf. R. C. Sproul, John Gerstner and Arthur Lindsley, *Classical Apologetics: A Rational Defense of the Christian Faith and a Critique of Presuppositional Apologetics*, (Grand Rapids, MI: Zondervan, 1984), 206.

87. Martin Luther, *The Bondage of the Will*, trans. by J. I. Packer and O. R. Johnston (U. S. A.: Fleming H. Revell Company, 1957), 92.

88. Ibid., 124-125.

89. Ibid., 126.

90. Ibid., 184.

91. John Calvin, *Institutes of the Christian Religion*, trans, by Henry Beveridge (Peabody, Massachusetts: Hendrickson Publishers, 2009), 4.

92. Ibid., 13.

93. Calvin clearly lays these out in the *Institutes*: (1) "the testimony of the Spirit is superior to reason"; (2) "God alone can properly bear witness to his

own words"; (3) "the truth of Scripture must be derived from a higher authority than human conjectures"; (4) "The same Spirit...must penetrate our hearts to convince us...Let it therefore be held as fixed, that those who are inwardly taught by the Holy Spirit acquiesce implicitly in Scripture; that Scripture carrying its own evidence along with it, deigns not to submit to proofs and arguments, but owes the full conviction with which we ought to receive it to the testimony of the Spirit"; (5) "But what kind of Spirit did our Savior promise to send? One who should not speak of himself (John 16:13), but suggest and instill the truths which he himself had delivered through the word"; and Calvin quotes Isaiah 59:21 to show how the Spirit and Word always work inseparably. Those who elevate the Spirit's work over the Word or extricate the Spirit's work from the Word, (as traditional apologists and neo-orthodox Barthians are prone to do) Calvin called "miscreants guilty of fearful sacrilege" and men who have "an infatuation with the devil"—strong language indeed, especially to the soft, desensitized, and wimpified, politically correct ears of the modern day; see *Institutes*, 33, 44.

94. John Calvin, *Commentary on the Book of Psalms*, trans. by James Anderson (Grand Rapids, MI: Baker Book House, 2003), V: 14.

95. Arthur Dakin, *Calvinism*, (Duckworth, London: Kemp Hall Press, 1941), 190. Robert Coleman seems to accommodate this modern error of dichotomizing Word and Spirit when he writes, "Though the Bible is the most authoritative source of truth, the Spirit can bring conviction through any number of other means (1 Thess. 1:5). Often he speaks through the counsel of Christian loved ones and friends or through our reading a book, seeing a display of power in nature, or meditating on some providence of deliverance. Usually these varied influences accumulate over a period of time, one experience building on another. As the awareness of need dawns on the consciousness, one begins to feel a discomforting awareness of spiritual truth"; Coleman, *The Heart of the Gospel*, 155.

96. Craig, *Five Views*, 315. R. C. Sproul teaches a revisionist understanding of Calvin's *testimonium* as well. Sproul says the Holy Spirit uses natural theology (in the form of the laws of logic, sense perception and the analogical use of language) to prepare the hearts of unbelievers so they will then accept the Word: "the Word will not find acceptance in the hearts of people before they are sealed by the inward testimony of the Holy Spirit. The first move for us, then, in this apologetics endeavor, is to present persuasive arguments for the existence of God"; *Defending Your Faith*, 193. But contrary to Sproul, Calvin said the Holy Spirit uses the Word itself to prepare the hearts of unbelievers.

97. Theo Preiss, "The Inner Witness of the Spirit" in *Interpretation*, trans. by Donald G. Miller, VII: 260-264.

98. Sproul *et al*, *Classical Apologetics*, 206.

99. Ibid., 202-207.

100. The *Westminster Confession of Faith*, 1. V, 1646.

101. Calvin, *Institutes*, 101.

102. Geisler accuses Calvinists, falsely, of teaching that faith is not required to be saved. He says that Calvinists teach that one first must be saved and then after having salvation one can then exercise faith for the first time. He says this in the context of his convoluted explanation and understanding of "total depravity"—a concept he categorically rejects. He says Calvinists teach that "faith follows salvation; faith is NOT the condition by which we get salvation. Salvation is the means by which we get faith" <www.youtube.com/ watch?v=OFs64zcTCYc &NR=1> Geisler's distortion of such a basic concept is very disappointing, especially in light of the influence he wields among evangelicals and the scholarly world. Biblical Calvinists believe faith is required to have salvation, and contrary to Geisler's view, faith is not the "condition" for salvation; faith is the "means" for salvation. God's grace and Christ's atoning death are the "conditions" for salvation.

103. Calvin, *Institutes*, 377.

9

The Verdict on "Evidences"

"You Fideist!"

I remember when someone once called me a "fideist." My reaction? First, my feelings were hurt. Second, after I recovered emotionally, I then hunted for a dictionary to look up the word "fideist." I did not find it because I did not know how to spell it. Eventually, over the years, I finally learned what a "fideist" was. Am I a "fideist"? Yes, and no, depending upon how you define it.

In the realm of apologetics there are basically two different understandings or definitions proposed for the word "fideist" or "fideism," one positive and one negative. First there is the negative definition used as a term of derision, usually in the form of a straw man or "caricature." A caricature is "a picture, description, etc., **ludicrously exaggerating** the peculiarities or defects of persons or things." Those who resort to ludicrous exaggerations when misrepresenting Christian fideism say that fideists are people who believe something solely on faith apart from any facts, evidence, reason, data, or objective justification. This rendition says fideists are opposed to logic and bask in the subjective realm of irrationality—what fideists believe is not even based in reality.

Straw-Man Fideism

Let's look at some ludicrously exaggerated examples of caricatures given by those who distort the true meaning of evangelical biblical fideism. Sproul, Gerstner and Lindsley lead the pack here. They unleash a flurry of dogmatic, unfounded assertions like when they say all fideism is "radical" and upholds "in practice an irrational faith—a faith without reason—and rejecting any natural knowledge of God."[1] They allege here that fideists don't believe in natural revelation (i.e. "natural knowledge of God"). That is categorically false. Next they say that fideism is not based on any reason, logic or fact, but instead "denies man's ability to know God except by faith."[2] Here Sproul *et al* make their classic, ubiquitous false dichotomy between faith and reason. True biblical faith results from reasoning, thinking, and meditating upon the objective data of divine revelation revealed in Scripture, in a logical manner. The human brain must be fully engaged throughout the entire process. Sproul *et al* say fideists believe that faith results apart from reason, logic, intellect or processing any objective data but is rather a subjective "leap," a pure anti-rationalist mystical enterprise. Not true though—another false caricature... heaped upon a previous caricature.

They don't relent. They allege fideists say "no cogent proof for God's existence could be given; the question of the existence of God had to be relegated to the sphere of faith."[3] They accuse fideists of being advocates of "nominalism,"[4] paranoid "skeptics,"[5] proponents of "dialectical metaphysics,"[6] heirs of "the Enlightenment,"[7] Kantian "agnostics,"[8] adherents of "*ad hominem*" methodology,[9] "neoortho-dox"[10] and being allies with "Nietzsche, and Kierkegaard," "Marx" and "Barth"![11] They conclude their cacophonous crescendo of ludicrous and exaggerated monikers of derision toward fideists, which bleed with guilt-by-association techniques, by writing the following:

> Here is unalloyed fideism, fideism in its pure state. Faith is a decision—it requires resting in contradiction. Faith is more a matter of will (choice) than of mind. This is the leap-of-faith syndrome which refuses to ground faith in any rational proof or evidence. Not only is rational evidence unnecessary to the fideist, it is undesirable as well, signaling a kind of intrusion of pagan categories of thought into the pristine purity of faith.[12]

This is a loaded and stilted assault that warrants a response.[13] That is forthcoming, but for now it needs to be noted that I am a biblical fideist and the reason I believe in God's existence, the truthfulness of the Bible and the gospel of Jesus Christ is because of "the evidence." If there were no logical, reasonable, objective, verifiable evidence for Christianity, then I would reject it. One of the main problems here is that Sproul *et al* define "faith" and "evidence" differently than I do. And there is also a difference between the two parties as to what evidence is required in order to believe. Traditional apologists say the needed evidence to believe comes from natural theology; biblical apologetics says the prerequisite evidence for salvation is defined and determined by special revelation.

In addition to the smears of Sproul *et al*, negative caricatures of fideism abound. Feinberg says fideists "claim that God's existence and the truth of Christianity are matters that are justified by faith alone" apart from reason—fideists oppose the "rational."[14] Craig claims fideists believe in "Christianity because it is absurd."[15] Geisler says fideists believe "truth in religion, then, rest[s] solely on faith and not on a reasoning process,"[16] that "truth is subjectivity" and "objectively Christianity has absolutely no existence."[17] Another pop apologetics book piles on, "fideism says that you should come to faith by believing in God apart from reason and evidence. Faith in God cannot be rooted in rational argument because faith is a matter of the heart, not the head."[18] Many traditional apologists used Van Til as the whipping boy as an example of an irrational fideist to illustrate their derogatory version of fideism.[19] Bahnsen gives a helpful summary of other typical strained, disparaging and derogatory definitions:

> One dictionary describes it as "a pejorative term for subjectivist theories which are based upon religious experience and which undervalue reason in theology." Others are just as clear: fideism holds that "religious truths are inaccessible to human reason," thus amounting to a "reduction of religion to an irrational faith." Fideism is the "view which assumes knowledge originates in a fundamental act of faith, independent of rational presuppositions." According to this view, "Christian assertions are matters of blind belief and cannot be known or demonstrated to be true." Fideism, we are told, is "based upon a leap of faith and a negation of rational constructions." The fideist's faith is "exclusively determined by the emotions."[20]

Too bad critics of fideism cannot agree on a definition. Earlier it was shown that Sproul said fideism was strictly "an act of the will (a choice)," but above, one authoritative anti-fideist says fideism is strictly "determined by the emotions." Well, which one is it? The will, or the emotions?

Healthy Fideism

Now it is time to look at the alternative definition of fideism, for not everyone in philosophy, theology and apologetics defines fideism from a strictly negative or pejorative point of view. Fideism can be positive too; after all fideism derives from the Latin word for "faith" and the last time I checked, faith was a positively valued and esteemed virtue (1 Cor 13:13; 2 Cor 5:7)! Technically, fideism comes from the Latin, *fīdō*, "I trust." *Fidēs* is the nominative singular meaning, "faith, belief, trust, reliance, confidence." So etymologically, fideism is strictly a positive term that simply means "faith." And all words only have meaning as they are defined in a context. Depending on the context fideism can be understood to be negative or positive—just like a flurry of biblical terms. The word "angel" can be either positive or negative. An angel of God is good; an angel of Satan is bad.

Note some examples of scholars who understand this important distinction when fairly and objectively trying to define fideism:

> Fideism is the view that the religious commitment is based primarily upon the intuitive apprehension of God by faith (Lat.: *fides*, trust), rather than rational arguments (moderate fideism) or contrary to rational arguments (extreme fideism). Paul appears to be advocating the latter in 1 Corinthians 1:20-21...the evangelical Christian faith does seem to be an example of a moderate fideism.[21]

Zemek writes, "For the biblical fideist, faith is *above* reason. In contrast, for the rationalist, faith is *according to* reason, and for the existential 'fideist,' faith is *contrary to* reason."[22] A standard dictionary of the Bible says the following:

> FIDEISM. The doctrine that humanity is saved by faith alone. This is God's freely willed gift through the atonement of Jesus Christ.
>
> The doctrine took concrete form in the writings of Augustine, who insisted that the knowledge of God came only through the response of faith...It was not anti-

intellectual, but it gave faith precedence over reason. Luther raised the doctrine as a rallying cry of the Reformation....

Others have disagreed, stating that the intellect is God-given and can be used to understand God. In reverse order, knowing about God could lead to faith in God. Fideism then becomes a disparaging word signifying viewpoints of those who are unwilling or unable to use reason for faith.[23]

One dictionary gives an objective summary, noting the positive and the negative nuances:

The view that faith takes precedence over reason. The word is often used as a term of abuse to designate a view considered by a critic to be a form of irrationalism. Tertullian and Søren Kierkegaard are often cited as fideists.[24]

And finally, Elwell's classic dictionary gives a sober perspective on the whole issue:

A theological term coined at the turn of the century by Protestant modernists in Paris (Menegoz, Sabatier) to describe their own thought, but since used pejoratively to attack various strands of Christian "irrationalism." Fideists, following Kant (who argued that reason cannot prove religious truth), are said to base their understanding of the Christian faith upon religious experience alone, understanding reason to be incapable of establishing either faith's certitude or credibility. Among others, Luther, Kierkegaard, Van Til, Schleiermacher, and Barth have been accused of fideism. The term, however, is used too imprecisely to be of much value. Certainly none of these theologians would deny the use of reason altogether.[25]

A Case for Biblical Fideism

So, am I a fideist? Yes...and no—depending upon how one defines the term. I am not a Kantian/Kierkegaardian/Barthian/existential/mystical/subjective-only brand of fideist. I am a fideist who believes, along with Augustine, Luther and Calvin...and the Apostle Paul, that faith is a supernatural gift from God and a by-product of special revelation. Sinners are saved by grace through faith (Eph 2:8). Jesus said, "Your faith has saved you" (Luke 7:50). I will not disparage the virtue of *sola fide* like the traditional apologists do: I believe in order to understand. Human logic apart from special revelation cannot produce saving faith. Human reason apart from divine revelation cannot produce saving faith. Natural theology cannot produce saving faith. Natural revelation apart from special revelation cannot produce saving faith. Intuition apart from Scripture cannot produce saving faith. Experience apart from the gospel cannot produce faith. Emotion apart from objective heavenly truth cannot produce faith.

When I say, "I believe in order to understand," it means (1) that the ability to believe and (2) the process of believing both require the involvement of the intellect. Believing, or "to have faith," cannot be extricated from thinking. Romans 10 says "faith comes from hearing." "Hearing" in this context means taking in information, thinking about the objective truth that was "heard" as it was given ("preached") in propositional statements and then coming to a conclusion using the mind, the will, the heart and all that the Bible describes as the "inner man." To compartmentalize the inner man into separate categories, pitting man's will against his mind, intellect, emotions and soul, is unbiblical and a Greek pagan understanding and interpretation of anthropology. Unfortunately many traditional apologists fall into such a trap and false notion.[26]

Elusive "Evidence"

It should be noted that traditional apologists who deplore fideism state in their definitions that fideists have no need for "evidence" or that fideists even disdain evidence. For a biblical fideist, that simply is not true. I believe in Christianity because of the evidence. I reject all forms of false religion and aberrant ideologies because of the evidence. My faith is justified by objective reality and immutable ontological truth—which amounts to indisputable, rock-solid evidence. I believe that the evidence for Christianity demands a verdict! One dictionary well notes the following:

> No Christian apologist can function without the use of evidence. Not all have agreed, however, on what types of evidence are valid for Christians to use. Some would be prepared to use any type of evidence to bolster their

318

argument: with the scientist they would use scientific evidence; with the philosopher, philosophical; with the New Age person, the sense of the spiritual—seeking by all possible means to convince some. Others, emphasizing that it is the work of the Holy Spirit to do the convincing, would limit themselves to evidence that is more clearly his specific work; the witness and trustworthiness of the Scriptures, the evidence of the presence of God in Christian individuals, and the personal experience of the Spirit's work.[27]

But what is the "evidence"? Here is another area where traditional apologetics differs from biblical apologetics. Most apologetics books talk about "evidence"—few define what they mean by "evidence." For example, in the popular *Five Views on Apologetics* Craig mentions "evidences" several times but never clearly defines what he means by the term. He refers to "evidences for the...Gospels,"[28] "Christian evidences,"[29] "reason in the form of rational arguments and evidence,"[30] "natural theology and Christian evidences,"[31] "arguments and evidence,"[32] "rational argument and evidence,"[33] "arguments for the existence of God and evidence for the credibility of the Gospels."[34] Through deduction and trying to connect the dots, the reader is left trying to interpret what Craig means by "arguments" and "evidence." Apparently for him, "arguments" refers to natural theology and human reason apart from Scripture in general[35] and the theistic proofs in particular, especially the *kalam* cosmological argument.[36] By "evidences" he is referring to using human reason in an inductive way,[37] wielding the Laws of Logic, especially "the inference to the best explanation"[38] to establish the historicity of the New Testament, particularly the resurrection account.[39]

Further, "evidences" can refer to any non-scriptural testimony, be it a person or an event, which favors the credibility of the Bible's authenticity. With this line of reasoning, Craig concludes that the resurrection of Jesus is "plausible" because "the majority of New Testament critics today" recognize his three main lines of argument.[40] In other words, we can say Jesus probably rose from the dead because the majority of modern New Testament critics allow us to do so. Craig makes it clear that a Christian cannot tell an unbeliever that the resurrection of Jesus is true simply "because the Bible says so." To Craig, that is "irrational."

It is apparent that most traditional apologists understand the meaning of "arguments" and "evidences" in the same manner as Craig.[41] Although "evidences" frequently refers specifically to the argument for Scripture's reliability based on historical evidences, miracles and prophecy,[42] evidentialist Gary Habermas, uses "evidences" to establish the New Testament's credibility. For him the evidence we should believe amounts to what liberal scholars believe, or what they allow to be true, or what they don't deny. Sound confusing? That's because it is. To simplify, Habermas says we should believe in the resurrection of Jesus and His deity, not because "the Bible says so," but rather because select quasi-liberal New Testament scholars say it's OK to do so—guys like Oscar Cullman, I. H. Marshall, Royce Gruenler, Raymond Brown, Rudolph Bultmann, Wolfhart Pannenberg, and William Strawson, as well as Tacitus, Josephus, Lucian and Phlegon.[43]

Bickel and Jantz are a rare exception as they actually give a definition for "evidence" in their pop apologetics survey:

> *Evidence.* This is the data presented to prove the facts (especially in a court case). In a broader sense, evidence is anything that tends to prove or disprove something. From a positive perspective, evidence gives us grounds for belief. From a negative perspective, evidence gives us grounds to no longer believe something previously thought to be true.[44]

The evidence they go on to give includes the typical machinations of the traditional apologists like the theistic arguments for God's existence, natural theology, arguments from intelligent design, miracles and prophecy, historical evidences, scientific theories, including some of their personal heterodoxical musings, like saying hell is not a place of torture, not a place like a dungeon or a place of fire and "not a lake of fire"[45]—even though the Bible says hell is a "lake of fire" (Rev 20:14).

So traditional apologists say the validity of Christianity is based on evidence. As a matter of fact, the entire discipline of Christian apologetics hinges on "evidence": "apologetics is the process of providing reasonable explanations—or evidence—for the truth claims of the Christian faith."[46] They submit that the legitimate evidence includes natural theology, the theistic arguments for God's existence, the Laws of Logic, scientific theories, history, archaeo-logical discoveries, theories from neo-orthodox theologians and human reason apart from divine revelation—just about anything except Scripture! They do say one can use Scripture—but first you have to "prove" Scripture before you can use Scripture.

The Biblical Evidence

Biblical apologetics also says the truthfulness of Christianity is based on evidence, but from the polar opposite perspective. Biblical apologetics teaches that Christianity is to be embraced because of the evidence of special revelation, not apart from it. As a biblical fideist I believe in Christianity based on at least seven lines of evidence, all affirmed and defined by special revelation, and they include the following:

(1) I believe in God's existence because of the evidence of internal general revelation.

(2) I believe in God's existence because of the evidence of external general revelation.

(3) I believe Christianity is true because of the evidence of the personal ministry of the Holy Spirit.

(4) I believe Christianity is true because of the evidence that Jesus saved me and changed my life and produces good works through me.

(5) I believe Christianity is true because of the evidence that Jesus rose from the dead.

(6) I believe Christianity is true because of the evidence of and from Scripture.

(7) I believe Christianity is true because of supernatural faith.

There are actually many more reasons I could give as evidence of why I believe, but I'll keep it to these seven. I have chosen these seven because the Bible explicitly says these seven reasons are called "evidence." Traditional apologists will reject my seven lines of evidence because they will say that I cannot believe in Christianity "because the Bible says so." But I say just the opposite—the only reason I believe in the deity of Jesus, His death, resurrection and ascension is because the Bible says so. The only reason I believe in heaven, an eternal conscious hell, that God is triune, the reality of election, an indwelling Holy Spirit, Christ's second coming, creation in seven real days, Satan, good and evil angels, the inerrancy of Scripture and the efficacy of prayer is because the Bible says so. I will briefly examine all seven lines of evidence in light of the questions, "Why should anyone believe in Christianity? What evidence is there?"

The Evidence of Internal General Revelation

(1) First, every person should believe in Christianity because he has the evidence of internal general revelation. We saw this in detail in chapter four when discussing natural revelation. In Romans Paul stated that every person has the evidence of God's existence "within them" and as a result has the innate imprint of God's existence embossed on his or her soul in the form of a conscience and the moral law in the heart. This is inescapable internal "evidence" of God's existence for every person. Romans 1:18-21 reads as follows:

> [18]For the wrath of God is revealed from heaven against all ungodliness and unrighteousness of men who suppress the truth in unrighteousness, [19]because that which is known about God is evident within them; for God made it evident to them. [20]For since the creation of the world His invisible attributes, His eternal power and divine nature, have been clearly seen, being understood through what has been made, so that they are without excuse. [21]For even though they knew God, they did not honor Him as God or give thanks; but they became futile in their speculations, and their foolish heart was darkened.

This passage reeks of evidence given to the unbeliever by God— evidence God gave them from two fronts: from the beginning of time at creation to all people, and to each individual from the time they were born. This passage clearly says God has revealed Himself inside every person—"God made it evident to them"—that is "evidence"! The evidence is in their conscience since all people have been made in God's image (Rom 2:15; Gen 1:26). Every unbeliever is without excuse. No one can claim ignorance and say, "I don't believe in God because there is no evidence to prove He exists." When they say that, they are lying. They have the truth, or "evidence," but through sin and rebellion, this passage says they have "suppressed" the truth they know intuitively.

Here is a helpful exercise. Think of any unbeliever you know, from the world-class God-hating atheist Richard Dawkins, to your next door neighbor, the nice and friendly agnostic who loans you sugar any time you ask, to the isolated pygmy in Africa, and put their name in the context of Romans 1:18-21. Here's what it looks like with Richard Dawkins:

> [18]For the wrath of God is revealed from heaven against all ungodliness and unrighteousness of Richard Dawkins, who suppresses the truth in unrighteousness, [19]because that which is known about God is evident within him; for God made it evident to Richard. [20]For since the creation of the world His invisible attributes, His eternal power and divine nature, have been clearly seen by all people like Richard, being understood through what has been made, so that Richard the self-proclaimed atheist is without excuse. [21]For even though he knew God, Dawkins did not honor Him as God, or give thanks; but Richard became futile in his speculations, and his foolish heart was darkened.

This was Paul's intent when he wrote this passage. Romans 1:18-21 is a biography of every unbeliever—whether religious, atheist or agnostic. They have enough evidence to know God exists, but in their willful sin they push away the evidence. Regarding this innate witness of evidence given to all people by God, Paul says unbelievers "show the work of the Law written in their hearts, their conscience bearing witness and their thoughts alternately accusing or else defending them" (Rom 2:15).

The Evidence of External General Revelation

(2) Second, all people are expected to believe in the true God because of the evidence of external general revelation. In Romans 1:18-21 Paul says unbelievers know God exists because God has made it plain to them through external creation—His attributes are "clearly seen" by them. The evidence is perspicuous. They just deny it

because they love their sin. "They are without excuse." Paul told the pagan unbelievers the same thing in Acts 14 when he said that God "did not leave Himself without witness (or "evidence," tangible, objective and empirical at that), in that He did good and gave you rains from heaven and fruitful seasons, satisfying your hearts with food and gladness" (Acts 14:17).

We saw earlier in chapter four that Psalm nineteen teaches the same truth. God has given universal, inescapable, tangible, objective witness of His existence through His creation that is intuitively apprehended by all people, including unbelievers. Believers give God glory in light of this truth; unbelievers either suppress this truth in denial because of sin and satanic blindness, or they misinterpret it and practice some form of idolatry or false religion. Psalm 19:1 says, "The heavens are telling of the glory of God; and their expanse is declaring the work of His hands." That is rock-solid, tangible, empirical evidence! Such evidence demands a verdict.

The Evidence of the Holy Spirit's Ministry

(3) The third reason people should believe in the Bible is because of the evidence of the Holy Spirit's personal ministry. Jesus said that the Holy Spirit is working on the heart, mind, soul, will and conscience of every unbeliever, continually, convicting them of their sin and wooing them to Christ, calling them to repent. That is what John 16:8-11 means:

> [8]And He, when He comes, will convict the world concerning sin and righteousness and judgment; [9]concerning sin, because they do not believe in Me; [10]and concerning righteousness, because I go to the Father...[11]and concerning judgment, because the ruler of this world has been judged.

Right now the Holy Spirit of God is convicting the heart of Richard Dawkins and every other unbeliever about the truth of God, the certainty of death and eternal judgment. This is an ongoing reality. And the Spirit works in conjunction with biblical truth and the gospel shared by believers, to cut even deeper into the heart of an unbeliever regarding their obligation to forsake their sin and turn to Christ.

Just because the unbeliever is oblivious to this ongoing reality does not mean it is not happening. Just because they deny the evidence, or misinterpret the evidence, does not mean it is not real evidence. True evidence is dismissed, misinterpreted or ignored all the time. Like the "evidence" of the dirty ice cream dish in our living room that is occasionally interpreted in different ways by various "witnesses." My wife will say, "My husband is probably the guilty party," whereas when I see the same "evidence" I will interpret it by saying, "That was probably one of the kids...or the dog."

The Evidence of Changed Lives and Doing Good Works

(4) Fourth, unbelievers should believe in Christianity because of the evidence of Jesus saving people and radically changing their lives and enabling them to do good works. That's what Jesus said. Jesus taught that there were apologetical implications attached to the way believers live in the world. He said, "You are the light of the world...Let your light shine before men in such a way that they may see your good works, and glorify your Father who is in heaven" (Matt 5:14, 16). When God miraculously turns a sinner into a saint, stuff changes ...and people notice. Paul said the same thing: "Therefore if anyone is in Christ, he is a new creature; the old things passed away; behold, new things have come" (2 Cor 5:17). Living with godly words, attitudes, and actions will get you noticed in this dark, fallen, hopeless sinful world.[47] As a believer you will be incarnate "evidence" for Christ. Jesus also said, "By this all men will know that you are My disciples, if you have love for one another" (John 13:35). When believers love one another in word and deed, that love becomes evidence for the truthfulness of Christ to unbelievers who are watching.

I remember when I was a freshman in college I got saved early in the school year. It was a radical transformation. A month or so after I got saved I was walking down the hall of the third floor of my dorm on the way to brush my teeth when Kevin stopped me in my tracks. Kevin and I used to occasionally cut it up together, ditch class and chapel together, share crude and sarcastic humor together. We were both lost. But this night Kevin said to me, "Hey Cliff. I've been meaning to ask you lately...you are really different. You've changed. What happened to you?" In less than ten minutes I shared with Kevin that I had become a Christian. I committed my life to Jesus and that I asked Him to forgive me of my sins and that I had been running from Him for about two years, and that Kevin could become a Christian too. He did not say much that night. Three months later Kevin got saved!

God used my transformed life as evidence for lost Kevin. I was a living testimony of the truthfulness of Christ's gospel. That is not to say that I am the gospel, because I'm not. I am bad news, not good news. The only good news is Jesus and what He did. And what He does is save people and change people. And those changes can be seen and observed objectively. I was a living epistle for Jesus, as Paul says is true of all Christians: "You are our letter, written in our hearts, known and read by all men; being manifested that you are a letter of Christ, cared for by us, written not with ink but with the Spirit of the living God, not on tablets of stone but on tablets of human hearts" (2 Cor 3:2-3). Kevin noticed the change in my life—it was undeniable. But Kevin did not get saved by just watching my life. He could "read" me as a living epistle, but he could not "interpret" me without the illumination of special revelation I gave him in the form of the gospel and the concomitant work of the Holy Spirit working on his heart. No one gets saved by just watching someone's life. Paul said they will not get saved without a preacher (Rom 10:13-17).

Along these lines, more evidence for the truth of Christianity is in the *good works* produced by these radically changed lives. Ephesians says that God saves people so that they will do good works on behalf of Christ (2:10). The Bible calls these good works spiritual fruit, or "the fruit of the Spirit"—supernatural manifestations generated by the indwelling Holy Spirit that flow from those who are born-again (Gal 5:22-23). Only true believers have this capacity. Unbelievers cannot produce these heavenly-quality good works (Matt 7:15-18). Unbelievers can do relative good works on a natural level due to common grace but they cannot produce supernaturally endowed good works like believers can. Jesus declared that the good works of believers are tangible evidence for unbelievers who are looking on. Heavenly-generated good works in the life of a Christian are apologetical in nature, used by God to put Himself on unmistakable display before those in the world. Good works in the life of a Christian are evidence.

A corollary truth to redeemed individuals being evidence on behalf of Christ is the reality that corporately the Church exists as evidence to the unbelieving world as well. Jesus promised to build His Church, the redeemed people of God (Matt 16:18). And He said

326

the Church would continue through history in perpetuity, as an unbroken testimony on His behalf. And that is exactly what has happened. For two thousand years, Christ's Church has always been in existence as His witness to the world. Paul said, "I write so that you will know how one ought to conduct himself in the household of God, which is the church of the living God, the pillar and support of the truth" (1 Tim 3:15).

A comment needs to be made here about "pre-evangelism." Earlier we debunked the typical definition of the need for pre-evangelism advanced by traditional apologists. They say pre-evangelism is "required" to help prepare unbelievers for the gospel because they believe you can't just spring the gospel on unbelievers cold-turkey. They opine that Christians need to grease the slide first with pre-evangelistic natural theology and the theistic proofs before preaching the gospel. We have to "warm up" the unbeliever's heart in order to make biblical truth "acceptable" or "palatable." Although I rejected their fabricated notion of pre-evangelism, I do believe there is a biblical pre-evangelism of sorts—a preparatory or propaedeutic work of God on the hearts of unbelievers to prepare them for the gospel.

That preparatory work amounts to the first four lines of evidence I just delineated—that is the true "biblical pre-evangelism" that God uses on unredeemed people: (1) general revelation of Himself that is innate in the form of the conscience and the heart; (2) general revelation in external creation that universally cries out relentlessly to unbelievers, declaring the glory of God; (3) the ongoing personal, convicting ministry of the Holy Spirit, who is constantly weighing down on unbelievers in their sin (John 1:9; 3:36; 16:8-11) while at the same time wooing them to Christ; (4) and the display of countless redeemed lives of people God has saved shining as lights of righteousness, truth and morality in a dark world. These four coalesce when the gospel goes out, and God sovereignly uses them to help illuminate the sinner's understanding, enabling him to believe and repent by God's grace (Matt 13:23; 2 Tim 3:15).

The Evidence of Jesus' Resurrection

(5) Fifth, unbelievers should believe in Christianity because of the evidence that Jesus has risen from the dead. That's what Peter and Paul said. When Peter preached to the unbelieving "men of Israel" (2:22) in Acts he did not present to them natural theology or

"Christian evidences." He preached the gospel and he declared truth straight from Scripture (2:25-28). Before he started preaching, the men did not believe. After he was done preaching, they were "pierced to the heart" (2:37) and ready to believe. They became convinced of the truth because of the "evidence." What was Peter's evidence? The gospel, the truth of Scripture, and specifically the truth of Christ's resurrection, was the coercive evidence that brought them to the point of conviction and belief. When the gospel of Christ is preached, supernaturally it is its own apologetic.

Traditional apologists will cry, "Foul!" saying that these Jews Peter preached to already had an allegiance to the Old Testament and were eyewitnesses to Jesus' ministry and miracles—so they are not the same as Greek pagans. Enter Paul in Acts seventeen preaching to Greek pagans who never witnessed Christ's ministry or miracles personally. Paul presented to them biblical truth—special revelation —culminating in the truth of Jesus' resurrection, calling them to repent and believe. Paul told the Greeks that Christ's resurrection from the dead proved that He should be believed.

Christ's resurrection was the "evidence," even though these men never saw Christ risen from the dead—nor had they seen Paul do any kind of miracle up to this point. By sheer proclamation of the gospel, God's Spirit enabled some of these Greek pagans to get saved right there on the spot. That is how powerful the gospel is (Rom 1:16)! We can proclaim it anywhere cold-turkey, and invisible miracles follow (Heb 4:12; Isa 55:8-11). So for Paul, Christ's resurrection was sufficient evidence for pagans to believe. Paul told them the following:

> Therefore having overlooked the times of ignorance, God is now declaring to men that all people everywhere should repent, because He has fixed a day in which He will judge the world in righteousness through a Man whom He has appointed, **having furnished proof to all men** by raising Him from the dead (Acts 17:30-31).

Notice the phrase in bold type. Jesus' resurrection is considered by God sufficient "proof" or "evidence" for "all men" to believe in Christianity. In response to Paul's preaching Christ's gospel, the text says, "some men joined him and believed" (17:34).

328

The Evidence of Scripture

(6) Sixth, unbelievers should believe Christianity because of the evidence of Scripture as found in the Bible. The Bible is autopistic, or self-authenticating. That was the point of chapter five. God's Word is the ultimate authority on truth for it is God's thoughts written down. When Scripture speaks, God speaks. What Scripture says, God says. There is no higher authority. This reality drives traditional apologists batty. But Van Til and Bahnsen were right—we must view Scripture as the pre-supposed, self-authenticating Word of God.

Paul said Scripture was breathed out by God Himself and has inherent efficacy to change human hearts (2 Tim 3:16-17). Hebrews says the Word of God is living and active, penetrating the human heart when it is spoken, read or taught (4:12). The Psalmist said that Scripture has the ability to restore or save the human soul and impart spiritual enlightenment (19:7-8). Isaiah said God's Word is living, always working and will never return void (55:10-11). Paul said when the gospel of Scripture is preached, power from heaven is unleashed onto the human heart (Rom 1:16).

When wielded in defensive apologetics or in evangelism, Scripture has inherent life, authority and power to accomplish miraculous ends—be it conviction, defense, exposure or salvation. Scripture is its own apologetic and needs to be used accordingly.

The critics, unbelievers and believing traditional apologists, will blow the whistle loud at the notion of saying Scripture is evidence for the truth of Christianity. Why do they balk? Because they will cry foul, alleging, "You can't use the Bible to prove the Bible! That is circular reasoning! That violates the Laws of Logic! Aristotle would never allow it!" But their accusation is actually fallacious—legally and logically. When Jesus quotes the Old Testament as a legal witness to validate His teaching (which became the New Testament; see John 5:39) He was in effect arguing from the Bible (the OT) to validate the Bible (the NT).

Again, in Matthew 19:5 Jesus quotes Genesis 2 to validate His own teaching in Matthew 19:6. Jesus is not using circular reasoning because Moses wrote Genesis in 1400 BC, long before Jesus was born. Genesis is a different book than Matthew—written by different authors at different times in a different location. The Bible is not technically one book—it's 66 books by over forty different authors written over the course of 1,500 years. To quote from the book of

Isaiah written in 700 BC as a legal witness to validate the truthfulness of the events that are mentioned in the Gospel of Matthew that was written in AD 50 by a different author is not arguing in a circle. They are two different books. One independent book can be an acceptable witness of another totally different book. No circular reasoning here.

The Evidence of Faith

(7) Seventh, another line of evidence for the truth of Christianity is "faith." Yes, that is right... faith. That seems odd and too subjective to many. But Hebrews 11:1 is clear: *"Now faith is...the evidence."* Faith is the evidence! Faith is the evidence of *"things not seen,"* or the evidence of invisible spiritual realities we cannot see but certainly transpired in the past (like creation), occur now (like the reality of hell and angels) or will indeed be true in the future (like the Millennium and the Second Coming). For example, Jesus will return a second time to the earth. It's a fact. The evidence for the sure reality of Jesus' future return is the faith to believe that reality that results from hearing about that truth as it is taught in the Bible. Supernatural faith is a by-product of hearing the objective content of Scripture, which is then quickened by the Holy Spirit in the inner man. Supernatural "faith" is a verb (*pisteuo*) and a noun (*pistis*) in Scripture depending upon the context.

When we hear God's Word, He enables us to believe (verb/ action) which then results in more faith (noun) (cf. Rom 10:17). The resultant faith spawned from the heavenly transaction is the evidence. Hebrews 11:1 is talking about faith as a noun—that which God imparts as a result of believing His Word. This verse is talking about a specific and unique kind of faith; a quality of faith; a faith unknown and inaccessible to the world—faith that is a supernatural gift from God given to those who respond in belief when they hear God's divine revelation. And it is a faith that enables a greater increase in having more divine faith. This kind of faith issues only from exposure to the content of Scripture, the Word of God or divine revelation (Rom 10:17). It is alien to the natural world. It is beyond human intuition, experience, knowledge, or discovery. Nevertheless, this other-worldly faith is real evidence for "those who have eyes to see and ears to hear." Anyone who rejects God's Word in unbelief will not be given this kind of supernatural faith and therefore will not experience the evidential impact of this divine exchange by which God has determined to operate. That's why the same chapter of

Hebrews says that without faith it is impossible to please God (11:6). There is a prerequisite disposition to be a partaker of this kind of evidence. And just because this kind of evidence is an *a posteriori* enterprise and has a subjective, experiential element, does not mean that it is not real evidence.

If I am standing in cold water, I experience the truth that the water is cold. I can tell my friend who is not in the cold water that the water is cold and he can choose to believe or not to believe; but until he enters the water, then and only then does he experience the evidence of the truth that the water is cold. So yes, there are objective and subjective lines for the truth of the Bible and Christianity. This kind of faith is not evidence to the scoffer, but is indeed real evidence and assurance for the one who takes God at His Word.

Evidence and Presuppositions
A Tale of a Whale

I remember when I was in seminary my Hebrew class was studying Jonah. One day my Hebrew prof read a modern-day story about a man who supposedly got swallowed by a whale and was spit out a day later, and lived to tell about it. A large majority of the class thought the story was very cool and "proved" that the book of Jonah was true after all. The Hebrew teacher took a different position—he said that the Jonah story in the Bible was still true even if the modern day story was fabricated, and further he said if the modern day story was true, it did not prove or validate anything at all about the Jonah story. My classmates were shocked by the teacher's comments...the class got derailed and a thirty minute debate ensued. Personally I was just watching, quite confused, not knowing which side to take.

Initially, I thought it was cool that someone could live after being swallowed by a whale...and that such an incident was "evidence" for the Bible's historicity and truthfulness. Twenty-plus years later, I have landed in a different position: I now agree with what my Hebrew teacher was saying. I believe the Jonah story because that is what the Bible says happened (cf. Matt 12:38-41). Modern day "evidence" does not "prove" that the Bible is true. The Jonah story is true even if there is no modern day evidence that humans can live for days inside a whale. The Jonah story was a supernatural miracle performed by God the Creator—it was not a naturalistic event. God performed other miracles in the Jonah story—He appointed a storm (1:4), a plant (4:6) and a worm (4:7), all to do His bidding.

Now We Can Finally Believe...?

J. P. Moreland is an example of a well-known traditional apologist arguing for believing the Bible based on modern-day evidence. He argues that because of current secular scientific consensus on the expansion of the universe, Christians can now, for the first time, reasonably believe that the universe had a beginning (notice, he does not say it is now reasonable to believe that the universe was created by God). He said,

> Now we know beyond reasonable doubt that the universe of space-time and matter had a beginning. It is now no longer reasonable to believe that the universe has always been here. That is now an irrational belief. Instead, we now know beyond reasonable doubt that the physical cosmos, of matter, and of space and of time, came into existence some time ago. At this point, it doesn't matter how long that was—some estimates are 15 to 20 billion years—that is not relevant to my concerns. What is relevant is that it is now beyond reasonable doubt that the universe came into existence a finite period of time ago.[48]

Notice how many times Moreland says "now." This means that according to him, prior to 2002 it was rational to believe that the earth was infinite and had no beginning, or it was rational to reject the clear teaching of Genesis 1:1. But "now," based on current scientific theory that says the earth is expanding, and therefore must have a beginning, Christians have a rational justification for the first time to be pretty sure, or fairly certain, that the universe has not always existed. So apparently, when I was in seminary back in 1989 and believed indubitably that Genesis 1:1 was a "fact" and that God created the world, I was not fully justified in believing so because the current theory of the expanding universe had not been fully developed yet.

A Whale of a Tale

I grew up Catholic for eighteen years—twelve years of Catholic school, baptized, confirmed, altar boy—the whole package. I remember when the Shroud of Turin became a hot topic in 1978 because of new, scientific studies conducted on the full-length burial cloth. The Shroud dates back to at least 1390. The nuns that were my teachers at the time, as well as our local parish, told us it was Jesus' burial cloth. We believed it.

We were told that the Shroud now "proved conclusively" that the Bible can be trusted and finally, 1,900 years later, it was "scientifically proven" that Jesus really did die and rise again as the Bible said. We were told that we could believe in the Bible because of the supposed historical evidence. But what about all those people who believed that Jesus died, was buried and rose again before 1978? Did they believe in vain? And what if the Shroud turns out to be a phony, or real but just not Jesus' burial cloth? Can we still trust the Bible? This gets to the core issue: what should the evidence be that serves as the foundation of our faith? What evidence is required to produce true faith and salvation?

Jesus said that the saving evidence is special revelation and the truth of the gospel. Seeking "evidence" or "signs" for Jesus' truthfulness apart from His special revelation is condemned by Scripture, and condemned by Jesus Himself. He told the Pharisees who were looking for further "evidence," asking Him to "prove" Himself, "An evil and adulterous generation craves for a sign" (Matt 12:39). His point was that some people won't believe even if they have all the "evidence" possible, including miracles, because they are puffed up with pride, steeped in sin and cannot see the truth because of satanic blindness. He made the same point in Luke when He said, "If they do not listen to Moses and the Prophets, they will not be persuaded even if someone rises from the dead" (16:31).

Unlike many traditional apologists who say that what unbelievers simply need is more evidence, or evidence outside of the Bible, and then they will believe, Jesus said that was not true. What they need is not more Christian evidences, but a merciful and gracious Savior Who can save them from their own debilitating sin and the death grip of Satan based on the supernatural saving power that issues from the gospel as found in Scripture as it is preached, taught and wielded by the Holy Spirit who works on the hearts of people.

The Bottom Line

The discussion on evidences exposes the inescapable reality that we need to always get back to ultimate presuppositions. What is the ultimate basis by which any person bases reality? What is a person's ultimate standard of authority? Is it God's Word or human reason? Is Scripture probably true because we can "prove" it to be so? Or is

Scripture provable because it is true? Two different questions—two different presuppositions—two different approaches to apologetics. Consider more examples of the clash between the presuppositions of Traditional Apologetics (TA) versus Biblical Apologetics (BA):

> TA = the Bible is God's Word because it can be proven by evidences;
> vs.
> BA = there are evidences because the Bible is God's Word.
>
> ----------------
>
> TA = the Bible is God's Word because it is logical;
> vs.
> BA = the Bible is logical because it is God's Word.
>
> ----------------
>
> TA = the Bible is God's Word because of the impossibility to the contrary;
> vs.
> BA = all contrarian views are impossible because the Bible is God's Word.
>
> ----------------
>
> TA = the cosmological argument makes sense, therefore God probably exists;
> vs.
> BA = God absolutely exists, therefore the cosmological argument makes sense.
>
> ----------------
>
> TA = there is universal morality, therefore God exists;
> vs.
> BA = the God of the Bible certainly exists, therefore there is universal morality.

Evidences: Justifying or Edifying?

In light of the previous discussion some might conclude that evidences have no place in biblical apologetics. But that is not the case.

Countless archaeological discoveries have been made over the centuries that are consistent with what the Bible teaches. The theistic arguments make sense, are reasonable and complement what the Bible says about God the Creator. It is apparent that there is indeed an Intelligent Designer. But these do not prove that God exists. But rather, God exists and these are all tangible manifestations of that great reality. God is not true because man can prove it. God remains true whether man can prove it or not.

So what of these evidences? How should we view them and use them? Christians should see true evidences as edifying to their personal faith, not as justifying an unbeliever's faith. True evidences are illustrations of Scripture's truth, not the basis of Scripture's truth.[49] Good science does not validate Christianity; good science complements Christianity.[50] The Laws of Logic flow from God's existence; they don't establish His existence. True archaeological findings bolster my faith; they don't create my faith. True Christian evidences are edifying, not justifying.

Summary

Traditional apologetics and biblical apologetics differ over the meaning and the use of "evidences." Traditional apologists often accuse non-traditionalists of being irrational "fideists." Fideists are said to be those who believe in Christianity without the need for any evidence. But fideism can mean different things based on how it is defined. Fideism comes from the Latin word for "faith." Biblical apologetics gives priority to faith that results from the hearing of the gospel and God's truth revealed in special revelation. But that faith, or the ability to believe, is based on real evidence and is processed through reasoning capacities. There is a legitimate biblical fideism— and it is based on real evidence and objective realities.

Traditional apologetics says "evidence" for true religion is composed of natural theology, human reason, secular history, science, and archaeology among other things apart from Scripture. Biblical apologetics says efficacious evidences are delineated and defined in Scripture, not apart from Scripture. At least seven lines of biblical evidence were given that testify to the truthfulness of Christianity: (1) internal general revelation; (2) external general revelation; (3) the convicting work of the Holy Spirit; (4) redeemed, changed lives that produce good works; (5) Jesus' resurrection; (6) the Christian Scriptures; and (7) supernatural faith that results from exposure to special revelation. God uses the first four realities as a legitimate form of "pre-evangelism" to convict sinners.

One's definition and use of evidences is determined by ultimate presuppositions. Every person has an allegiance to an ultimate source of authority in determining what is true—for biblical apologetics that ultimate source of authority is God Himself and the revelation of His Word. For traditionalists, that ultimate authority is autonomous human reason. Non-Scriptural evidences do not prove that the Bible is true. The Bible is true and as a result there are manifestations of that truth in the form of evidences. Non-Scriptural evidences, that are evidences indeed, are primarily for the believer's edification and practical use in negatively[51] combating erroneous worldviews.

Notes

1. R. C. Sproul, John Gerstner and Arthur Lindsley, *Classical Apologetics: A Rational Defense of the Christian Faith and a Critique of Presuppositional Apologetics*, (Grand Rapids, MI: Zondervan Publishing House, 1984), 25.

2. Ibid., 27.

3. Ibid., 28. It's ironic, and inexplicable, that Sproul categorically rejects "*fide*ism" yet clings to the phrase, "*Sola fide!*" as his life's mantra—the two are inextricably related. *Fideism* comes from *fide*...a huge dilemma for Sproul. One of his best-known books is called, *Faith Alone*, i.e. *Sola Fide*. In the modern vernacular it sounds like, "Fideism alone."

4. Ibid.

5. Ibid., 28-29.

6. Ibid., 29.

7. Ibid.

8. Ibid., 30.

9. Ibid., 31.

10. Ibid., 32.

11. Ibid., 33.

12. Ibid., 34.

13. For an excellent review of Sproul, Gerstner and Lindsley's work see Review Article: *Classical Apologetics: A Rational Defense*, by George J. Zemek, Jr. in *Grace Theological Journal* 7.1 (1986) 111-123; Zemek summarizes, "They certainly cannot be charged with ambivalence, but they frequently may be perceived by the reader as being arrogantly dogmatic...From this inflexible perspective they often criticize such apologetical 'compromisers' as Geisler, Montgomery, Pinnock, and others."

14. Paul Feinberg, *Five Views On Apologetics*, ed. Steven B. Cowan, (Grand Rapids: Zondervan, 2000), 150.

15. William Lane Craig, *Five Views*, 27.

16. Norman Geisler, *Christian Apologetics* (Grand Rapids, MI: Baker Book House, 1976), 47. Geisler rejects fideism as a systematic approach to apologetics, but he does at least recognize some of its legitimate contributions.

17. Ibid., 51.

18. Bruce Bickel and Stan Jantz, *Evidence for Faith 101: Understanding Apologetics in Plain Language* (Eugene, Oregon: Harvest House Publishers, 2008), 32.

19. Greg Bahnsen, *Van Til's Apologetic: Readings & Analysis* (Phillipsburg, NJ: P & R Publishing, 1998), 72-78.

20. Ibid., 73. Bahnsen understood that words have more than one meaning from context to context; this is true of fideism. Fideism is not always bad,

and it does not always mean the same thing. Sadly some self-professed presuppositionalists don't understand this basic truth about words. Words have many meanings; that's why some words listed in a dictionary have ten or more definitions. Presuppositionalist William Edgar has a deficient and myopic view on this matter with respect to fideism; his definition of it is frozen and strained: he alleges that fideism, "is blind authority"..."a leap of faith which denies reason"; see William Edgar, "Why I am a Presuppositionalist" (Westminster Theological Seminary, <www.watch? v=SrlDJGUsLha>.

21. J. W. Ward, *New Dictionary of Christian Apologetics,* eds. W. C. Campbell-Jack and Gavin McGrath (Downers Grove, IL: InterVarsity Press, 2006), 265, 267. Cf. James E. Taylor, *Introducing Apologetics: Cultivating Christian Commitment,* and his use of "responsible fideism," (Grand Rapids, MI: Baker Academic, 2006), 12.

22. George J. Zemek, Jr. "Christian Apologetical Methodology," unpublished syllabus (Sun Valley, CA: The Master's Seminary, 1992), 32.

23. Iris V. Cully, *The Dictionary of Bible and Religion,* ed. William H. Gentz, (Nashville, Tennessee: Abingdon Press, 1986), 360.

24. C. Stephen Evans, *Pocket Dictionary of Apologetics and Philosophy of Religion,* (Downers Grove, IL: InterVarsity Press, 2002), 45. In another place Evans is not as fair or objective in defining fideism, when he fallaciously alleges that "the fideist cannot...even attempt to engage in rational dialogue with those who disagree." And then he goes on to liken Christian fideists to "orthodox Marxists"! This is a blatant example of guilt by association, straw-man argumentation, and caricaturization run amok. C. Stephen Evans and R. Zachary Manis, *Philosophy of Religion* (Downers Grove, IL: InterVarsity Press, 2009), 24-25.

25. R. K. Johnston, 415, *Evangelical Dictionary of Theology,* ed. Walter A. Elwell, (Grand Rapids, MI: Baker Book House, 1987), 415.

26. Zemek well notes Sproul, Gerstner and Lindsley's greatest irreparable crack—or chasm—in their apologetical foundation is their compromised anthropology: "This assumption is that there is a dichotomy between 'mind' and 'heart' (cf. pp. ix, 21, 219, 243, 297, etc.). However, if one conducts a careful investigation of *lev* (Hebrew)/*kardia* (Greek) (i.e., the seat of *both* rational *and* volitional functions) in anthropologically and hamartiologically significant contexts, the endeavor yields more than sufficient evidence to render their above assumption a biblically false dichotomy. Not so incidentally, it is in this area of theological exegesis that presuppositionalism displays its *preeminent* attribute: 'Thus, for the presuppositionalist, theology and apologetics are inseparable. A sound theology is essential for a sound apologetic' (p. 187)"; Zemek, "Review

Article: *Classical Apologetics*, 112. Zemek goes on to show how the alleged heart/mind dichotomy was popularized by Edwards, 122.

27. P. Hicks, *New Dictionary of Christian Apologetics*, 247.
28. Craig, *Five Views*, 26.
29. Ibid., 27.
30. Ibid., 28.
31. Ibid.
32. Ibid., 30, 36, 37, 44.
33. Ibid., 33, 39.
34. Ibid., 38.
35. Ibid., 36-37; 40-41.
36. Ibid., 48.
37. Ibid., 51.
38. Ibid., 52.
39. Ibid., 51-52.
40. Ibid., 52.
41. Cf. Bernard Ramm, *Protestant Christian Evidences* (Chicago: Moody Press, 1953); Gary Habermas, "Evidential Apologetics" *Five Views*, 92 ff.; Josh McDowell, *The New Evidence that Demands a Verdict* (Nashville, Tennessee: Nelson Publishers, 1999).
42. James Strong, *Cyclopedia of Biblical, Theological, and Ecclesiastical Literature*, eds. John McClintock and James Strong, (Grand Rapids, MI: Baker Book House, 1981), III:375.
43. Gary Habermas, *Five Views*, 92-107.
44. Bickel and Jantz, *Evidence for Faith*, 44.
45. Ibid., 235-36.
46. Ibid., 16.
47. Stott notes the reality that Christians are first-hand witnesses of knowing Christ the Savior; that cannot be downplayed or ignored just because the skeptics discount it. "The biblical idea of Christian witness presupposes a firsthand, living experience of the salvation of Jesus Christ. The apostles saw and heard the historical Jesus objectively. But the words of the risen Jesus to St. Paul already suggest the propriety of extending the notion of witness to a subjective and mystical experience of Christ, for He said to Paul: 'I have appeared to you for this purpose, to appoint you to serve and bear witness to the things in which you have seen me and to those in which I will appear to you' (Acts 26:16). There is no reason to suppose that these future experiences of Christ were objective appearances such as he says the Damascus Road revelation was. Rather were they inward and spiritual, and to these too he must bear witness. So must we. In our preaching, we do not just expound words which have been committed to

our stewardship. Nor do we only proclaim as heralds a mighty deed of redemption which has been done. But, in addition, we expound these words and proclaim this deed as witnesses, as those who have come to a vital experience of this Word and Deed of God. We have heard His still, small voice through His Word. We have seen His redeeming Deed as having been done for us, and we have entered by faith into the immeasurable benefits of it. Our task is not to lecture about Jesus with philosophical detachment. We have become personally involved in Him. His revelation and redemption have changed our lives. Our eyes have been opened to see Him, and our ears unstopped to hear Him, as our Saviour and our Lord. We *are* witnesses; so we must *bear* witness"; John Stott, *The Preacher's Portrait* (Grand Rapids: Eerdmans, 1961), 73-74.

48. *Reasons to Believe*, <www.reasons.org>, "The Age of the Earth," 1; Feb 2, 2002.

49. Understood from this perspective—having the right presuppositions in order—then the believer can make great use of a tool like *The New Evidence that Demands a Verdict* by Josh McDowell. His years of excellent research should be used to edify believers and arm them with ammo to put in their arsenal to help destroy false worldviews; legitimate evidences can be used as a wrecking-ball in casting down all ideologies that oppose Christ. McDowell's evidences should not be used with the notion that they will create faith in the unbeliever, make the gospel more palatable, make the Bible more acceptable or "prove" that the Bible is true. With unbelievers these kinds of "evidences" are to be used defensively, not offensively. The gospel of Jesus Christ and His Word is the only offensive apologetic we have or need. Traditional "evidences" are edifying for the believer but not efficacious for the unbeliever. In this light, another helpful book is *When Skeptics Ask: A Handbook On Christian Evidences* by Geisler and Brooks.

50. Some great resources that show how the Bible does not contradict science but rather complements and even defines what true science is include the following: John C. Whitcomb and Henry M. Morris, *The Genesis Flood: The Biblical Record and Its Scientific Implications* (Phillipsburg, NJ: P & R, 1960); Henry Morris, *Scientific Creationism* (Green Forest, AR: Master Books, 1985); Terry Mortenson and Thane H. Ury, *Coming to Grips with Genesis: Biblical Authority and the Age of the Bible* (Green Forest, AR: Master Books, 2009). In addition, there are countless books on biblical archaeology that are excellent and edify the believer while at the same time confound the skeptics who argue that the Bible is myth and not based on true history. Some recent ones by James Hoffmeier are helpful, *The Archaeology of the Bible, Ancient Israel In Sinai: The Evidence for the Authenticity of the Wilderness*

Tradition, and *Israel In Egypt: The Evidence for the Authenticity of the Exodus Tradition*.

51. By "negatively" I mean "defensively." There are many ways to describe the two-fold nature of biblical apologetics that I describe as "advancing" and "defending" the faith. Other synonymous couplets have been used: positive/negative; offensive/defensive; creative/destructive; protective/edifying; undeniability/unaffirmability; the transcendental argument/impossibility of the contrary. House and Holden write, "Within the apologetic task of defending the faith there emerge at least two distinct aspects. The destructive aspect seeks to 'dismantle' or explain away arguments against Christianity (2 Corinthians 10:3-5; Titus 1:9-11). The creative aspect offers evidence and proofs to support arguments for the truthfulness of the Christian faith (Acts 1:3; Luke 24:39; Romans 1:19-20)"; H. Wayne House and Joesph M. Holden, *Charts of Apologetics and Christian Evidences* (Grand Rapids, MI: Zondervan, 2006), chart 1. In chapter five of the present volume I refer to "destructive" apologetics as a "wrecking ball." I have argued that only special, biblical revelation can be used positively (or efficaciously toward salvation) in apologetics, whereas human arguments and evidences (apart from Scripture) can be used to edify the believer and also negatively for the purpose of destroying false notions propagated by anti-theists and anti-Christians.

10

Evil? No Problem for God

Christianity's Greatest Challenge?

Few believers alive today have fielded more questions from skeptics of Christianity than the popular evangelist and apologist, Ravi Zacharias. For more than three decades he has taught and preached all over the world and is in constant demand as a speaker at prominent universities like Oxford, Princeton, Harvard and countless others. He enjoys interacting with heady, aggressive unbelieving and skeptical collegiates. They ask challenging questions about the validity of theism and Christianity in particular. Ravi attests that the number one issue that the skeptics bring up wherever he goes, hands down, is the classic dilemma—the problem of evil.

No discussion on apologetics is complete without addressing the problem of evil. Opponents have long held that the problem of evil is the most impregnable charge confronting Christianity. It is the critic's ultimate trump card against the Bible's credibility...so we are told. Popular atheist, and best-selling author, Victor J. Stenger says, "The problem of evil remains the most powerful argument against God."[1] Many evangelical philosophers and theologians have embraced the skeptic's notion. E. J. Carnell, theologian and former president of Fuller Seminary, believed the problem of evil was "the most stimulating challenge to the logic of the Christian faith."[2] John Frame, theologian and professor at Reformed Theological Seminary, asserts the problem of evil is "the most serious and cogent objection that unbelievers have brought against Christian theism."[3] William Lane Craig, a notable Christian apologist, agrees: "Undoubtedly the greatest intellectual obstacle to belief in God—for both the Christian and the non-Christian—is the so-called problem of evil."[4] Kelly James Clark goes even further by alleging, "The problem of evil is the most formidable and apparently intractable obstacle to belief in God, and it is easy to see why. It is difficult to imagine that God could exist given the various kinds and amounts of evils that exist in the world today...there still seems to be too much evil for God to exist."[5]

Several Christian philosophers undermine the sufficiency of Scripture on this issue by asserting that "the Bible...does not explicitly reveal why God allows [evil]."[6] Bickel and Jantz allege Christians "don't have some kind of special insight into the mind of God and know what His purpose is."[7] That blatantly contradicts the Bible which says, "we have the mind of Christ" (1 Cor 2:16). In other words, Christians do in fact have special insight into the mind of God in Scripture—Scripture amounts to God's thoughts incarnated permanently in writing for us to read and know.

The highly influential and popular theologian, N. T Wright, similarly says the Bible does not give full answers to questions such as: What is evil? Why is there evil? Why is evil allowed to continue? And when will evil end? He goes on to say, "The Bible simply doesn't appear to want to say what God can say about evil."[8] Sproul is equally disappointing when he alleges that, "we cannot explain the existence of evil."[9] Craig says, "We are just so ignorant of God's designs. We are simply not in a position to know why God permits various evils to occur," and again, "we don't know why God permits evil."[10] Evans and Manis are just as doubtful as they concede, "When all is said and done, it is difficult for the theist to be confident that she truly understands why God allows all the evil we find in the world."[11]

In contrast to such ill informed scholarly pessimism, this chapter will show that the Bible says otherwise: evil is not a problem for God. God tells us very clearly in the Bible where evil came from, why it is here, why He allows it, and how He is going to banish it in the future. He has everything under control. "Our God is in the heavens; He does whatever He pleases" (Ps 115:3). God is in control of all things, including evil, and He even has a plan for evil: "The LORD has made everything for its own purpose, even the wicked for the day of evil" (Prov 16:4). Scripture specifically, thoroughly and satisfactorily addresses the supposed problem of evil and, as a result, it is not the unassailable juggernaut against the faith that so many have been led to believe. Jay Adams was correct when he said,

The Christian is not left speechless; God *has* revealed Himself concerning this matter. And, He has done so unequivocally, satisfyingly. The problem is not stated properly. It should be put this way: when God has given an unmistakably clear and sufficient reply to such questions, why do theologians persist in saying that He has not? Why do they go through the foot shuffling routine only to hem and haw about a fact that is plain as the way of salvation itself? The answer, I am afraid, is that they are so heavily loaded with humanism that they are either blinded to the truth, or, understanding it, refuse to teach it out of fear of what others may say.[12]

The Problem Stated

The problem of evil has been articulated in many ways for thousands of years, from the days of the ancient Greek deist Epicurus (341-270 BC), to the Enlightenment era, by the eighteenth-century Scottish skeptic David Hume, to today, from the likes of the crude atheist-comedian Bill Maher. The problem of evil simply asks, "If God is absolutely good, then why is there evil?" It has been expressed axiomatically as follows:

(1) If God is all-powerful, then He would prevent evil.
(2) If God is all-good, then He would desire to prevent evil.
(3) But there is evil.
(4) Therefore, there is no all-powerful, all-good God.

Said another way, if God really exists, wills only good and is powerful enough to get everything He wills, then evil would not exist. But evil does exist; therefore, God is either impotent, not good or does not exist at all. So goes the skeptic's most potent syllogism.

Proposed Solutions

Virtually every belief system has tangoed with the problem of evil. Five classic approaches prevail as options for wrestling with this longstanding philosophical canard. First, there is *atheism* which says evil is real but God is not. Second, there is *pantheism* which says God is real but not all-good. Third, there is *naturalism* in its various forms which says God is not all-powerful. This is the view of process theology, Open Theism, liberation theology and its ilk. This was the view of the highly popular book by Harold Kushner, *When Bad Things Happen to Good People*. The liberal Jewish rabbi concluded: "There are some things God does not control...can you learn to love and forgive Him despite His limitations?"[13] Fourth, there is *idealism* that says evil is not real, but God is. This includes religious systems like Hinduism, Buddhism, Christian Science and various New Age beliefs. Fifth and finally is *theism*, or Christianity in particular, that affirms that God is all-powerful and all-good while evil exists. All three realities are true and are not mutually exclusive or contradictory to each other. Option five is the only viable option as will be shown from the Bible.

There is Evil

Christians are realists about the problem of evil. The world is rife with pain, evil and suffering. And it is manifest in many horrific ways. Man's self-inflicted inhumanity towards each other abounds. Senseless random acts of violence are reported daily in the news. Hatred, prejudice, rape, murder, theft, child abuse and countless other acts of violence are universal, transcending cultural boundaries. Diseases, cancer and bodily deformities are commonplace, many of which defy explanation or justification, like babies born with chronic birth defects, being deaf, blind or having defective limbs or inadequate life-sustaining organs. Natural disasters—earthquakes, tsunamis, tornadoes, floods, fires, famine and the like—plague the world, claiming the lives of countless millions. How do Christians account for all this misery? How can the Bible explain this horror? Why does God sit back and let all this happen?

The first observation to note is that skeptics usually raise the issue of the "problem of evil" as though it's an issue that Christians have never thought of before. Supposedly for us theists, the problem of pain and suffering is an afterthought...or we've actually never considered the issue at all. The anti-theist says, "A hah! Gotcha on that one." Contrary to their ignorance, the Bible is actually a book about pain and suffering—that is actually one of Scripture's major themes. God and the Bible are experts on pain, suffering and evil. Evil is described in all sixty-six books of the Bible. Examples of it abound from Genesis to Revelation. The Bible details the following real-life horrific historical events: the first murder in human history (Gen 4:8); Lamech the first serial killer (Gen 4:23); a universal flood that killed all living beings on earth save eight people (Gen 7:23); war (Gen 14:2); theft (Gen 14:11); kidnapping (Gen 14:12); gang rape

(Gen 19); prostitution (Gen 38); famine (Gen 41:54); slavery (Exod 1:11); infanticide (Exod 1:16); homicidal bodily dismemberment (Judges 19); a crippled child (2 Sam 4:4); forty-two children mauled by two vicious bears (2 Kgs 2:24); a sudden tornado that killed an entire family (Job 1:19); a baby born blind (John 9:1); a stillborn child (Ps 58:8); a mother dying while giving birth (Gen 35:19); sword, famine, pestilence and wild beasts that kill one fourth of the earth's population (Rev 6:8); countless earthquakes and more. The Bible is no stranger to evil, pain and suffering. Actually, the Bible is the authority on the matter.

Shaky Ground

Antagonists to Christianity say that the religion of the Bible and the reality of the problem of evil cannot co-exist, for they are mutually exclusive. But the problem of evil as typically stated is technically not a logical contradiction or in conflict with the Christian worldview. Saying so doesn't make it so. This is true for two reasons. First of all, for something to be a logical contradiction, it must be internally inconsistent, not simply be in conflict with another view. In this case, the atheist says that the Christian view of God is in conflict with the atheist's view of evil. That is not a contradiction. One view may simply be wrong. Christianity and the Bible allow for evil and a good and omnipotent God to co-exist. Therefore there is no internal inconsistency.

Second, the atheist's traditional anti-theistic assertion is actually based on other implied, unspoken assumptions or presuppositions that are left out of the syllogism. As a result, on the surface the argument seems to be impervious to attack, and hence the smoke-screen of the argument continues to daze, choke and even intimidate Christians. But the skeptic's presupposed, unstated auxiliary assumptions need to be exposed. These assumptions include the following:

(1) The atheist's definition of "evil" is the correct one and must be accepted.
(2) The atheist's definition of "good" is the correct one and must be accepted.
(3) The atheist's definition of "God" is the correct one and must be accepted.
(4) Evil has always existed.
(5) God cannot use evil for good purposes.

(6) Evil will always exist.

(7) The only attributes of God that are relevant are His goodness and power.

We will see from Scripture that these unstated assumptions that serve as the latent foundation and scaffolding for the historic problem of evil are fallacious, and as a result the argument collapses upon closer scrutiny. The skeptic's argument is based on a plurality of implied erroneous definitions (1-3) and wrong views of origins (premise 4), destiny (premise 6), and theology (premises 5 and 7). In other words, the atheist has an errant view of reality.

Who's Framing the Debate?

My daughter was on the debate team. I was her coach. One key to winning debates is to try to get your opponent to accept your premise. If you can frame the discussion, establish the rules and the definitions, and get your enemy to accept all the terms—you'll win. That is what atheists and skeptics have successfully been able to do for centuries with the problem of evil—they typically get Christians to accept their premise, buy into all their definitions and lull them into limiting the argument to the parameters of their tri-fold, concocted syllogism. And in the end, in many cases, Christians think there is no answer to the age-old problem of evil.

Instead, Christians need to reject the atheist's trap. How can believers allow atheists to define "evil" and "good"? Atheists have no ultimate standard by which to define these terms. Worse still, how can atheists tell us what God is like? They define God by saying He is limited to two (or sometimes three)[14] attributes: goodness (or love) and omnipotence (or power). That is not an accurate view of God, but a truncated, unbiblical, warped and blasphemous view of God. God is more than just goodness and omnipotence.

Here is the atheist's equation of what constitutes God:

$$GOD = \heartsuit + \text{💪}$$

But God is much more than this myopic depiction. So from the beginning we need to expose the hidden presuppositions and assumptions of the atheist, critique his false definitions of "evil," "good," and "God," and counter his trite syllogism with the full arsenal of the composite truth on the matter as revealed so richly in Scripture.

Defining Evil

We begin by defining "evil." To call something evil is to make a moral judgment. To make a moral judgment, one must have a moral standard. To enforce your moral standard on someone else, the standard must be universal. The atheist rejects a universally binding standard of morality. The atheist lives in an amoral world—there is no such thing as evil. Therefore, the atheist's "problem of evil" syllogism makes no sense, for he cannot make judgments about what is "good" or "evil."

Accommodating the Skeptic

When engaged in such controversial and sensitive matters, clear definitions need to be established as a basis of fruitful dialogue between clashing viewpoints. Most books I have read by Christian philosophers trying to tackle the problem of evil fail to carefully define just what evil is from a biblical point of view. Many just concede with the atheist, acknowledging, "Yes, evil is real and it is bad," and leave evil undefined. A good example is Greg Bahnsen, the late presuppositionalist, who, in his chapter on the problem of evil, never defines what evil is; rather he just acknowledges that it exists.[15]

Defining Evil Without the Bible

Other traditional apologists, in an attempt to create neutral ground with the atheist or unbeliever, typically try to define evil apart from religion or God. Geisler defines evil with the medieval concept of Aquinas and other Catholic theologians by saying it is "a lack or privation of what ought to be present and is not."[16] Groothuis says, "Evil is 'privation' of the good."[17] Powell says, "evil is where good should be but is not."[18] In the same vein, N. T. Wright says evil is a "moral black hole."[19] Craig and Moreland equate evil with "pain and suffering...in the world."[20] Kreeft says, "Evil is not a thing. Things are not evil in themselves...Evil is...not an entity...[evil is]... disordered love, disordered will."[21] Evans says evil is "pain and suffering of any kind."[22] Some confound the matter by never defining evil at all, but rather speak presumptuously about it relative to the problem of evil.[23]

All these definitions are woefully deficient. The greatest deficiency is that they are all missing God and the Bible in the equation—as a result, ironically, their definitions are therefore "a"-theistic in a technical sense. Kreeft says "things are not evil" and evil "is not an entity."[24] Really? What about all those Bible verses where God and Jesus call all kinds of people evil? "Assuredly, the evil man will not go unpunished" (Prov 11:21). Men are evil—they are things and entities. Jesus said, "the evil man out of the evil treasure brings forth what is evil" (Luke 6:45). Christian apologist, Dean Hardy, defines evil as "simply something missing that the thing is expected to have."[25] This is even more obtuse. Based on this vacuous definition he is able to assert that inanimate things can be evil. He avers, "A chair that is missing a leg is evil. A car without an engine is evil."[26] Then in an inexplicable, bizarre twist of logic he goes on to say, "you cannot have a fully evil entity. Even Satan is not completely evil! He does have a few good qualities."[27] Satan—the destroyer, deceiver and accuser of the brethren; the father of lies and the destroyer of souls; the primary occupant of the place of eternal damnation called eternal hell—is not totally evil and has good qualities? Do not be deceived: Jesus categorically pronounced the utterly intrinsic, and repugnant nature of Satan by saying the devil "was a murderer from the beginning…there is no truth in him" (John 8:44). The devil is incorrigible and eternally condemned.

Another basic point needs to be made about evil and God. The Bible in a sense is a book about evil. Evil is mentioned in every book of the Bible, from Genesis to Revelation. God is well aware of the reality of evil and has a plan for it. Evil is illustrated, defined, highlighted, condemned, and counteracted time after time. The Bible goes into graphic detail, delineating the worst kinds of evils imaginable, from murder, to rape, to slavery, to genocide, to every kind of natural disaster. An entire, long book was written about the problem of evil and suffering—Job. The whole theme of the Bible is "Evil, and How God Intends to Eradicate it in His Perfect Time." It is not like the atheist has caught the Christian—or God—off guard by raising the topic of evil as though it is some afterthought to biblical religion.

God Defines Evil in Scripture
To satisfactorily address this issue, a clear biblical definition of evil needs to be delineated. God defines what evil is. Evil is what God says is evil (2 Chron 21:6). Evil is anything contrary to God's nature,

will or Word (Ps 119:9-11). Sin is the greatest evil. Scripture says, "He is pure...sin is lawlessness" (1 John 3:3-4). The only way we can know what is evil today is by understanding what Scripture defines as evil. Without Scripture, trying to define evil becomes a futile exercise in relative ethics. Apart from Scripture we could not know whether anything was evil. For example, secular humanists would say, "Yes we can. Killing, war, floods and earthquakes are all evil." The Bible says that is not true. Not all killing is evil. God killed the whole world save eight people with a worldwide flood (Gen 7:23). God sent ten plagues against the wicked Egyptians, including the plague of death, where God Himself went out at midnight and killed the firstborn in all the homes of the Egyptians (Ps 105:36). Scripture says the proper response to God for doing this is one of celebration, not repulsion: "Sing to Him, sing praises to Him; speak of all His wonders. Glory in His holy name" (Ps 105:2-3). Jesus will kill His enemies when He returns at His second coming (Rev 19:15-21)—that is not evil; that is good, righteous and deserved. Not all war is evil. The Bible says, "There is...a time for war" (Eccl 3:1, 8). At the end of the age Jesus will make war with His enemies (Rev 20:7-10; Ps 2); believers will celebrate and rejoice in God's victory over His enemies. Not all earthquakes are evil: God killed Korah and all his relatives in an earthquake in Numbers 16:31-34.

We cannot resort to sheer human reason, conscience, natural law, the laws of logic, or common sense to define evil or define good. And we especially can't allow unbelievers to define evil for us as they dictate the conversation. Using only human reason, would we tell Abraham to kill his son as a sacrifice (Gen 22), or tell Moses to execute a man for gathering sticks on a Sabbath (Num 15), or command Israelites to slaughter thousands of innocent animals and spread and sprinkle their blood all over (Lev 16)? Or, what about the ultimate example of pain and suffering...hell? Hell is a real place of physical, conscious suffering, torment, and isolation, worse than anything ever experienced in the present life (Luke 16:19-31). Yet the Bible says hell is deserved for those who go there (Rev 20:11-15). Hell was created by God (Matt 25:41) and is ruled by God (Matt 10:28). Many people will go there (Matt 7:13) along with the devil and his angels. Jesus talked about the awfulness and the reality of hell. He called it a place of judgment—a "fiery hell" (Matt 5:22), "weeping and gnashing of teeth" (Matt 25:30). Hell will last forever (Matt

25:46). And somehow God will be glorified by hell's existence (Rev 14:9-11), "because His judgments are true and righteous" (Rev 19:2). God's definition of what is good and bad often differs from man's perspective. Jesus warns that having a man-centered perspective, rather than a God-centered one, is satanic (Matt 16:23).

Relative Evil

Left to human reason apart from Scripture, humanity is awash in relative ethics on any given issue. Consider the institution of marriage and intimacy for example. The Qur'an allows a man to marry up to four women[28] and condones beating them[29] if deemed necessary. This is considered to be "good" by traditional Muslims. Hindus say abstaining from intimacy with your wife is best, and Catholic priests say not getting married is the highest virtue. Mormons say they'll be married for eternity in heaven, and today's America says gay is OK. In contrast, God's Word says it is not good for man to be alone (Gen 2:18) and marriage is God-ordained, monogamous, permanent, intimate, heterosexual (Gen 2:22-24) and an earthly picture of Christ's eternal relationship to His precious Bride, the Church (Eph 5:22-32). Defining morality and ethics apart from God's thoughts in Scripture is hazardous and misleading. Using relative human standards, Hindus say the pig is an ancestor, the vegetarian says pork is evil, the orthodox Jew says pigs are unclean, but Jesus, in Scripture (Acts 10:13), told Peter, "Medium rare, and pass the barbeque sauce!" How liberating Scripture is.

Categories of "Evil"

When addressing the problem of evil, Scripture needs to drive the conversation and the definitions, starting with what is truly evil and what is the source of evil. According to the Bible, what humans typically call evil comes from five sources:

(1) the very nature of man;
(2) sinful activities of humans;
(3) natural disasters;
(4) satanic and demonic activity;
(5) the decrees and activities of God.

We need to be careful here because many of the events that the world may define as evil may actually result from points (3) and (5) which are not always actually evil. God used earthquakes in the Old Testament (Num 16:31-35) and He will use them at the end of the age to accomplish His perfect will (Rev 16:17-19). As has been shown, God issues decrees of war, capital punishment and the like, which are righteous acts of justice, and are not evil.

The only legitimate way to address the question of "God and evil" is from a biblical perspective. But historically the topic is typically confronted on strictly philosophical grounds—this is true even among Christians as well as secularists. Gordon Clark, for example, addressed this dilemma in his classic book on apologetics, *Religion, Reason, and Revelation* from a Reformed and Calvinistic perspective. Yet, in his nearly fifty-page dissertation, Bible verses are elusory as he tackles the subject from a primarily philosophical and historical vantage point instead of an expositional and exegetical one.[30] The same is true for Craig[31] and Evans.[32] But it is the Bible, not man, that must define evil if we are going to truly address this issue.

Letting the Bible Define God

After defining evil from a biblical point of view, we now must define "God" from a biblical point of view. Letting atheists like Stenger define God for us with the formula "God = love + power" is fallacious. When confronting the problem of evil, traditional apologists typically go with the paired down definition of God in trying to defend Christianity. They usually say that the greatest good is to love God.

What God Wants

But there are other requirements equally important to God. He also wants us to fear Him (Eccl 12:13) and worship Him (Luke 4:8), in addition to loving Him. And those actions are distinct, although they can envelope each other. We should love our fellow man, as we are commanded (Mark 12:31), but we are not to fear man (Prov 29:25), nor are we to worship man (Exod 20:4-5). But we are to fear and worship God. According to the Bible the greatest good is to know God and give Him glory, technically speaking. Jesus said, "This is eternal life, that they may know You, the only true God, and Jesus Christ whom you have sent" (John 17:3). Conversely, the people that Jesus will condemn at the end of the age by casting them into hell are those whom He did not know: "And then I will declare to them, 'I never knew you; *Depart from Me, you who practice lawlessness*'" (Matt

7:23). So the greatest good is to know God.

When God created humanity His ultimate goal was to create people with the greatest capacity to know Him, which entails revealing the fullness of His character so that humans can know Him in the most personal, intimate and comprehensive way (1 Cor 13:12). This means God's intention is for us to know Him for who He truly is, in His fullness, in light of all of His attributes (Eph 1:17-18), and in response, to worship and glorify Him. And His attributes are manifold. He wants us to know Him fully so we can worship Him accurately. Jesus said the Father is seeking true worshippers, who will worship "in...truth" (John 4:24). Knowing God means knowing Him truthfully, for who He truly is, which includes knowing Him in light of all of His virtues.

God has More than Two Attributes

Many people say they worship a God of love, but reject the idea of a God who is jealous and full of wrath. When addressing the problem of evil, traditional apologists are virtually silent about God's wrath being relevant. As a matter of fact, they usually apologize for God's wrath.

But the Bible is clear—God's wrath is fundamental to His nature and all He does and allows needs to be seen through the prism of His retributive acts of holiness, in addition to all of His attributes. In Nahum God says, "A jealous and avenging God is the LORD; the LORD is avenging and wrathful; the LORD takes vengeance on His adversaries, and He reserves wrath for His enemies" (1:2). In Deuteronomy God gives His own biography, saying, "See now that I, even I, am He, and there is no god beside Me; I kill and I make alive; I wound and I heal...I will take vengeance on My adversaries and will repay those who hate Me" (32:39, 41; ESV).

We must love and worship God for who He is, and He is a God of wrath just as much as He is a God of love and omnipotence. This is why the traditional syllogism for the problem of evil is flawed—it's a red herring of the first order. It defines God as being only good and all-knowing. That is a deficient, unbiblical view of God.

Remember the atheist's anemic equation for God:

$$\text{GOD} = \heartsuit + 💪$$

Contrast that with the real biblical equation for who God is: God is personal (Exod 3:14), good (Ps 136:1), love (1 John 4:8), gracious (Neh 9:17), merciful (Ps 145:8), forgiving (Num 14:18), compassionate (Deut 4:31), a spirit (John 4:24), infinite (1 Kgs 8:27), immutable (James 1:17), immanent (Acts 17:27), transcendent (1 Tim 6:16), omnipotent (Gen 35:11), omniscient (Ps 139:1-6), omnipresent (Ps 139:7-12), independent (Ps 115:3), self-sufficient (Acts 17:25), triune (2 Cor 13:14), one (Deut 6:4), holy (Isa 6:3), righteous (Deut 32:4), jealous (Nah 1:2), wrathful (Nah 1:6), eternal (Isa 9:6) and sovereign (Isa 46:10; Rom 8:28). To know God is to know God experientially in light of all these characteristics that are intrinsic to His nature.

God Uses Evil

This brings us to the problem of evil. How could we ever know God as a forgiving, gracious, merciful saving God if we have never experienced His forgiveness through salvation? How could we have ever experienced His salvation without ever sinning? The angels are creatures of God who have volition, the ability to choose, but they have never experientially come to know God's mercy and grace through salvation. They don't know God in the same capacity that forgiven humans know God. We know Him in a fuller sense. That's why Scripture says angels look from on high, scratching their heads, or wings, trying to figure out this salvation and forgiveness thing, because they have never experienced it (1 Pet 1:12).

So why did God create a world with the potential for sin and evil? He did so to fully reveal His character and so that we could come to know Him experientially as a loving, powerful, merciful and holy God. This is exactly what God tells us in Romans 9. "What if God, although willing to demonstrate His wrath and to make His power known, endured with much patience vessels of wrath prepared for destruction?" (9:22).

God created a world with the potential for sin and evil to "demonstrate His wrath." He desired to put His holy wrath on display. Wrath is one of God's basic attributes. It flows from His holiness. He is perfect and sinless and cannot tolerate evil and must punish it (Ezek 18:4; Hab 1:13). The outworking of His holiness against sin is His wrath. Without the existence of sin and evil we would never come to know God as a holy God of wrath. Similarly, God desired "to make His power known." He wanted to put His power on display before His creatures. What power? His power to punish and overcome evil. That's why He created people and angels who have the capacity to choose evil. The existence of evil beings like Pharaoh (Rom 9:17) and Satan (Matt 25:41) allows God to demonstrate His power of justice as He overcomes them and ultimately punishes them with death and eternal hell (Ps 105:26-45; Rev 14:9-11; 20:13-15). Hence the inspired proverb: "The LORD has made everything for its own purpose, even the wicked for the day of evil" (Prov 16:4).

Those are attributes of God's justice. He also created a world with the potential for sin and evil to display His attributes of grace: "And He did so to make known the riches of His glory upon vessels of mercy, which He prepared beforehand for glory" (Rom 9:23). God's "glory" is mentioned twice in this verse. God's glory refers to the full manifestation of all His combined attributes (Rev 21:23). The positive, gracious attribute highlighted here is God's "mercy." God allowed a world of sin and evil so that He could rescue helpless sinners and thus prove Himself to be a merciful, saving God. Mercy refers to the act when God withholds punishment against those who deserve it. Every person who sins deserves death and hell (Rom 3:23). Because God is gracious and loving, He has chosen to be merciful to undeserving sinners by saving them from His holy wrath and punishment in hell. If humans were created without the potential of sin, they would never experience God in His fullness as a forgiving, merciful, gracious, saving God. They would not know God in His fullness. In other words, God uses evil; and He uses it for His glory and our good. Calvin said it this way:

> In short, since our mind cannot lay hold of life through the mercy of God with sufficient eagerness, or receive it with becoming gratitude, unless previously impressed with fear of the divine anger, and dismayed at the thought of eternal death, we are so instructed by divine truth, as to perceive that without Christ God is in a manner hostile to us, and has His arm raised for our destruction. Thus taught, we look to Christ alone for divine favor and paternal love.[33]

Jesus addressed this issue as well. There was a very sinful woman who came to believe in Christ and showed her adoration by washing His feet with her tears and her hair and kissing His feet. Yet Simon, a self-righteous Pharisee, despised the woman's unrestrained and unsophisticated expression of love. Simon thought it was embarrassing. Jesus rebuked Simon telling Him that the woman had a greater capacity for loving and worshipping Christ in light of all the sin she once had that was now forgiven. Unlike Simon, the woman now had a greater sensitivity to the heinousness of her sin and as a result she experienced a deeper sense of Christ's love, mercy and grace. Jesus concluded: "For this reason I say to you, her sins, which are many, have been forgiven, for she loved much; but he who is forgiven little, loves little" (Luke 7:47). Why did God create a world with the potential for sin and evil? So He could reveal His true character through all of His attributes including His holiness, power and mercy. None of those attributes could be known experientially by humans without having been saved and forgiven of sin by God. This reality allows us to know God for who He is and as a result allows us to love and worship Him to the greatest degree. And all this is for His glory alone (Eph 1:14) and because of His good pleasure (Col 1:19).

The Traditional Response
The Inadequacy of Human Wisdom
Traditional apologetics has put much ink to paper grappling with the problem of evil. There seems to be a consensus that a cumulative case of compelling reasons has been proposed to serve as an adequate rebuttal to the problem. Some helpful suggestions have been made, but too often anemic solutions are offered in lieu of the most persuasive ones. This results from Christian apologists who try to address the issue using human wisdom instead of God's wisdom. Christian apologist Winfried Corduan is a typical example. In his apologetics book, *Reasonable Faith*, he spends twenty-three pages grappling with the problem of evil but never uses the Bible to diagnose or offer solutions to the supposed dilemma.[34] He relies strictly on raw, human wisdom. Similarly, William Lane Craig devotes an entire chapter in his book, *Hard Questions*, to solving the problem of evil using only human wisdom and no Bible. Amazingly, he concludes the chapter by confidently alleging that logic and philosophy have finally dispelled the challenge posed by the problem of evil: "I'm extremely pleased to report to you that after centuries of discussion, contemporary philosophy has come to recognize...that the logical problem of evil has been solved."[35] Wow, case closed! I don't think so. Carl Henry diagnosed this oft-repeated problem by

Christian philosophers and theologians accurately: "Not even theistic arguments can fully vindicate God's righteousness in the face of human evil if they appeal simply to empirical considerations or to philosophical reasoning devoid of revelational illumination."[36]

The Free Will Theory

The most common argument given by Christians in response to the problem of evil is philosophical and anthropocentric, or man-centered. It is the argument based on the preservation of the free will of man. It posits that the greatest good in the universe is the infinite God. And the greatest experience we can have as finite beings is to have a loving relationship with God. For that reason, God offers all people His love; it is God's love that defines humanity and makes people complete.

Conversely, the greatest evil imaginable for humans is being separated from God's love. However, before we can enter into a real loving relationship with God, we must first be truly free to either choose or reject His love, for true love is always persuasive and never coercive. Therefore, the paramount virtue of any loving relationship is freedom—the ability to choose. In light of this logic, Geisler concludes, "In order for God to make a universe where the greatest good (a loving relationship with Him) was feasible, He would also have to create free creatures who would be capable of choosing or rejecting the greatest good."[37] The idea is that God could not have created a world where people could freely choose to love Him without also having the free choice to reject His love, which is the greatest evil. If God created people with the ability to only choose His love and with no ability to choose evil then they would not be humans—they would be robots or animals. As a result, Geisler *et al*, reason, "There is no way to create a world where people are free to love God in order to experience the greatest good but are not free to reject God's love—the greatest evil."[38] This is also one of C. S. Lewis' main arguments against the problem of evil—the preservation of human freedom: "The happiness which God designs for His creatures is the happiness of being freely, voluntarily united to Him and to each other."[39] Lewis goes on to say that God even took a "risk" to create a free people who might choose to do evil and reject His love. Charles Colson uses this line of reasoning, concluding that, "Free will is the basis of our human dignity."[40] But that simply is not true. The basis of human dignity is the image of God (Gen 9:6; James 3:9).

A chorus of other Christian theologians sing a similar refrain on the matter. Powell chimes in, saying, "for God to destroy evil would ultimately be evil itself since it would take away the greatest good— the ability to love God."[41] Similarly, John Feinberg conjectures that if God eliminated the possibility of evil then humans would be deprived of morality and volition and "He would have to contradict His intentions to create man and the world as He has."[42] Hardy argues God allowed evil because if He didn't, then God would have had to "create a deterministic world where agents would not have true free choice and God would make the choices for them."[43] Kreeft and Tacelli say God created humans with the ability to choose evil, otherwise "that would have been a world without humans, a world without hate but also without love. Love too proceeds only from free will."[44] They go on: God "could not have created a world in which there is genuine human freedom and yet no possibility of sin, for our freedom includes the possibility of sin within its own meaning." Bickel and Jantz echo the same mantra: "what is the highest good for all free beings? It's love (Matt 22:36-40), which is impossible without freedom."[45] Plantinga makes a similar contention.[46] Craig also sings the classic Arminian refrain here: "If God grants people genuine freedom to choose as they like, then it is impossible for Him to determine what their choices will be."[47]

The Bible on Free Will

Ironically, what is purported to be the strongest argument to counter the problem of evil actually creates many more problems in the process. The priority of preserving free will may pacify those with Arminian proclivities, but scripturally this view falls short. First of all, the free will view says that God could not have created a world without evil because that eliminates human volition. I have some follow-up questions for that view: (1) Do saints in heaven have volition or the ability to make real choices? (2) Can saints in heaven sin? Scripture is clear—people in heaven have free will and make real choices (Rev 21:24-27). And the Bible also makes it clear that saints in heaven will never choose to sin (1 John 3:2; Rev 19:7-8). The absence of evil does not automatically negate true humanity or volition. So the above assertions by these theologians and philosophers stand on a faulty premise. Contrary to what they say, it is possible for there to be a world where true humans (possessing genuine volition) exist with the ability to make free choices while at the same time it will be impossible for them to choose evil. That world is called heaven. And Scripture says that God is even going to create a new earth in the future where that reality will be the rule for free, loving humans:

> Then I saw a new heaven and a new earth; for the first heaven and the first earth passed away, and there is no longer any sea. And I saw the holy city, new Jerusalem, coming down out of heaven from God, made ready as a bride adorned for her husband...And He will wipe away every tear from their eyes; and there will no longer be any death; there will no longer be any mourning, or crying, or pain; the first things have passed away (Rev 21:1-2, 4).

Another question the free will advocates must answer is as follows: If people can live in heaven with a real free will and yet never choose to sin, then why didn't God create people in a heavenly glorified state in the first place? If Adam is in heaven now, has a will, and never chooses to sin, then why did God allow him to go through the phase of temptation, sin, suffering and death the first time around on earth? Why not just create him from the get-go in a perfected heavenly state? The answer is because when God created Adam and Eve the first time in Genesis 1 and 2, that was not God's ideal. This is what free will apologists posit—the world God created in Genesis 1 and 2 is the best possible world God could create. Such a view is short-sighted. Adam and Eve were created sinless, but not perfect in the ultimate sense. God's creation in the beginning was "good" (Gen 1:10) and even "very good" (1:31), but not yet in the ideal glorified state God ultimately intends.

Adam and Eve were created without sin, but they were created with vulnerabilities. Frame is incorrect when he says, "Adam was not created morally immature."[48] Although originally sinless, Adam and Eve were still vulnerable to temptation, sin, compromise and death (Gen 3). They were not yet "perfected" in the eschatological sense (Rom 8:23; Rev 20:5-6). Some theologians mistakenly assert that God's ideal for humanity is Genesis 1 and 2. Van Til gave that impression when he said Christ came, "to restore what man...was in paradise."[49] But that is erroneous. God's ideal for humanity is not

Genesis 1 and 2, but rather Revelation 21 and 22. Some would have us believe that God intends to bring us back to the original garden. But God's ideal for humanity is not to become pre-Fall humanity all over again, but rather to become resurrection humanity. Jesus declared, "The sons of this age marry and are given in marriage, but those who are considered worthy to attain to that age and the resurrection from the dead, neither marry nor are given in marriage; for they cannot even die anymore, because they are like angels, and are sons of God, being sons of the resurrection" (Luke 20:34-36).

Paul discusses this reality as well in 1 Corinthians 15. Paul says Adam's original physical body was "natural," "weak," and not God's ultimate ideal. Rather, the resurrection body after the likeness of the glorified Christ is God's ideal:

> All flesh is not the same...There are also heavenly bodies and earthly bodies...So also is the resurrection of the dead. It is sown a perishable *body*, it is raised an imperishable *body*; it is sown in dishonor, it is raised in glory; it is sown in weakness, it is raised in power; it is sown a natural body, it is raised a spiritual body. If there is a natural body, there is also a spiritual *body* (15:39-44).

God's ultimate goal for believers is to bring them to full glory (Rom 8:30). That glory is replicated after the model of Jesus' glorious, physical resurrection body (Phil 3:20-21). Jesus achieved His glorious resurrection status through the path of suffering, pain, evil, sorrow and death (Matt 16:21; Phil 2:5-11). And it is God's eternal, divine, wonderful plan of the ages to bring humanity to ultimate, Christ-like glory through the refining fire of the toils of suffering (Heb 2:9-10). So why did God and why does God continue to allow evil and suffering in the world? One reason is that God has chosen to use it, according to His incomparable wisdom, to accomplish His perfect plan for humanity—perfected resurrection glory.

Another defect in the free will view has to do with defining freedom. To say that humans have free will is a misnomer. At best humans have "freedom on a leash." To say that the essence of humanity is absolute freedom or that God prizes man's volition over all else is overstating the case. Geisler's axiom does not stand biblical scrutiny that says, "to stop evil, God must stop free will, and to stop free will is to stop the greatest good—which is the greatest evil."[50]

Man's freedom is limited and even thwarted in many ways. Our freedom is inhibited and limited by Satan. God allowed Satan to torture Job and his family against Job's free will: "the LORD said to Satan, 'Behold, all that he has is in your power'" (Job 1:12). Our freedom is further limited by our finitude, by our contingency as dependent beings, by the fallen world we live in and by indwelling sin. Sinners aren't free—we are slaves of sin. Jesus declared, "Truly, truly, I say to you, every one who commits sin is the slave of sin" (John 8:34). Even as a Christian Apostle, Paul lamented the reality of indwelling sin that hampered his ability to make his desired free choices: "the good that I want, I do not do; but I practice the very evil that I do not want" (Rom 7:19). So much for free will.

A final contention against the free will view is that it is hedonistic and anthropocentric instead of theocentric and doxological. The overriding emphasis in this view is all on man—man's choices, man's happiness, man's consequences, man's relational capacities. Biblically speaking, the emphasis needs to be on God—His purposes, His goal, His will, His glory.

One of the clearest examples of the problem of evil illustrated in the Bible is in John 9. As Jesus was ministering in Jerusalem He came across a man born blind (9:1). A baby born blind is the quintessential poster-child for the atheist's problem of evil scenario. Babies are helpless, innocent, harmless, fragile—why would a good God allow a baby to be born into the world blind?

This is a real dilemma and even Jesus' disciples struggled with this painful reality. They actually had a proposed solution which they offered to Jesus in the form of a question. They asked Jesus, "Rabbi, who sinned, this man or his parents, that he would be born blind?" (9:2). They basically had an illegitimate and myopic man-made religious solution to the problem of evil. They in effect were saying, "This man was born blind as a baby because he had bad karma or his parents had bad karma—he deserved to be born blind." The disciples' diagnosis was grossly off base. They no doubt inherited that view from their religious teachers, the Pharisees, who later on in the chapter say the same thing, in effect, directly to the man born blind: "You were born entirely in sins" (9:34).

Jesus corrects the disciples' pragmatic, shortsighted, man-centered view of the problem of evil. In response, Jesus proclaimed one of the most profound utterances ever declared by saying, "*It was* neither *that* this man sinned, nor his parents; but *it was* so that the works of God might be displayed in him" (John 9:3). What was "the work of God" to be displayed? It was when Jesus, the God-Man, immediately after His comment, healed the man born blind by restoring his sight (9:6-7)—a miracle unprecedented up until that moment (9:32). Jesus said that God allowed this man to be born blind for the sole purpose that God's healing power would be put on display. In this case, God allowed evil, not to preserve man's free will, but to glorify Himself. That is theocentric. That is doxological. That is the highest virtue. That is what Jesus clearly taught.

Contrary to popular Christian apologist Doug Powell, who says, "the Bible...does not explicitly reveal why God allows evil,"[51] Jesus clearly explained here why God allowed this evil. So one key answer to the question, "Why does a good, all powerful God allow evil?" is, "So that He can display His power over evil and as a result reveal His matchless glory." Here's where Van Til was refreshingly right on, going against the seven-hundred-year-old anthropocentric stronghold of traditional apologetics. He wrote: "[I]t was God's will that sin should come into the world. He wished to enhance his glory by means of its punishment and removal."[52]

The Reality and the Severity of the Fall

The answer to the questions, "Why do people die? Why are their natural disasters? Why is there disease? Why is their pain and suffering?" is actually a simple one. The reason for all of these realities is that God cursed the earth at the time Adam and Eve sinned. All evil, pain, suffering, sorrow and tragedy are by-products of sin. This historical event is documented clearly in Genesis 3 and expounded upon throughout the rest of the Bible. This explanation is in stark contrast to the one given by traditional apologists like Dean Hardy who believes that "evil sometimes is merely an accidental by-product of good, and not necessarily a choice...humans can make free good choices that result in evil."[53] To Hardy, there is no direct correlation between evil and the Fall.

In the beginning God created the world out of nothing in six days (Gen 1). The original creation was "very good" and without sin; all on earth was harmonious. Adam and Eve disobeyed and incurred the promised consequence of sin (Gen 2:17), namely death (Rom 6:23). A holy God must punish sin, and He did. Traditional apologists don't like talking about the wrath of God in this context. Nevertheless, it's at the heart of the issue. In His anger, God punished all of creation with a curse (Gen 3:14-19; 5:29; 8:21). God cursed the constitution of man, human relationships, nature, and the angelic world. Since the Fall of Adam and Eve, God promised life would be characterized by "enmity" (3:15), "pain" (3:16), "toil" (3:17), hardship (3:18), and death (3:19).

God explains the effects and cause of the curse in the New Testament. Paul tells us the "sufferings of this present time" are a result of the curse, for "the creation was subjected to futility, not of its own will, but because of Him who subjected it" (Rom 8:18, 20). Why is there pain and suffering in the world? Because God cursed the creation. Why did He do this? As a punishment for sin. How long will the earth be cursed? Temporarily, for God cursed the earth "in hope, that the creation itself also will be set free from its slavery to corruption into the freedom of the glory of the children of God" (8:20-21). God has a perfect plan; He's the Author of history (Isa 46:9-10); He works all things together for good and in accord with His divine will (Rom 8:28). The curse will be terminated in the future, at the end of the age, because of the saving work of Jesus Christ, who is Savior of the world. Christ's redeeming work on the cross had more than personal soteriological implications; it also had cosmic implications. Jesus created this universe (Col 1:16) and He will also redeem this universe. At the end of the age, God declares, "there will no longer be any curse" (Rev 22:3).

The Fall was a Historical Event

One key reason traditional apologists struggle so much with the classic dilemma of the problem of evil is because so many of them deny the historicity and reality of Genesis 1-3, in whole or in part. This is where Cornelius Van Til was unique and at his best in establishing a solid foundation for apologetic methodology. He warned evangelicals that if you compromise with the beginning (Gen 1-3) then you concede the rest: "I have frequently argued...that the historicity of Christianity cannot be maintained unless the historicity of the Old Testament and in particular the historicity of the Genesis account be also maintained."[54] Where did evil come from? Genesis is clear. Van Til goes on: "I hold sin to be that which the Confession and catechisms say it is. This involves the historicity of the Genesis account."[55] He concludes, "I believe in the infallibility of the Bible.

How could I believe in that unless I believed the historicity of the Genesis story."[56]

Compromise Run Amuck

A literal view of Genesis 1-3 should be a basic litmus test for vetting Christian apologists' views, theology and methodology. If scholars, theologians, philosophers or apologists botch the first chapters of Genesis and deny, marginalize or dismiss its literal historicity then that is a telltale sign that they are operating with a mangled hermeneutic. The preponderance of Christian apologists who have compromised in this area is startling. For example, Geisler says, "Most scientific evidence sets the age of the world at billions of years."[57] Similarly, J. P. Moreland speculates, "if science seems to point to a universe of several billions of years, it seems allowable to read Genesis in this light."[58] That's preposterous! No one can come to that conclusion reading Genesis at face value. These two Christian philosophers are basically saying, "Most secular, atheistic, humanistic, anti-biblical, Darwinian proponents tell us all their so-called invalidated hypotheses of origins suggest the world is billions of years old, and we believe the meaning of Scripture can be stretched to align with them."

Everywhere he speaks, William Lane Craig rejects the biblical perspective of a young earth, calling it naïve and not plausible, while wholeheartedly embracing the secular humanist's notion that the universe is 13-plus billion years old. Kelly James Clark unabashedly embraces Darwinian theory with respect to the origin of the universe and humanity, and therefore outright rejects the literal history of Genesis 1-3. In his discussion on the problem of evil, Clark claims Christians need to explain the way God acts "naturalistically," using "the truth of evolutionary theory."[59] This comes from a professing Christian apologist who claims he follows in the footsteps of Calvin![60] Tremper Longman, one of the most influential evangelical theologians today, goes so far as to say that Adam was not even a real person but a concept.[61] Space does not allow a detailed exposé of all the other well-known evangelicals who have compromised in this area over the years, including Bible scholars such as B. B. Warfield, Gleason Archer, James Montgomery Boice, Meredith Kline, Douglas Groothuis, Walt Kaiser and R. C. Sproul, to name a few.[62]

By contrast, God (Gen 2:16), Eve, Adam's wife, Cain, Abel and Seth, Moses (Gen 5:5), Job (Job 31:33), the prophet Hosea (Hos 6:7),

Paul's companion Luke (Luke 3:38), the Apostle Paul (Rom 5:14), Jude, the half brother of Jesus (Jude 1, 14), Jesus (Matt 19), the Jews of Jesus' day, and the Church for 1,800 years, all believed Adam was a real man and that Genesis 1-3 was all history. Even Adam believed he was a real man (Gen 2:23). When one takes the same view as God, Jesus and the saints of the ages on Genesis, then the problem of evil has a rational historical context and a future with perfect resolution.

Hebrew scholar, Bill Barrick, sets the record straight on the importance of maintaining biblical fidelity in the area of origins with this powerful admonition:

> ...in spite of the revelatory nature of the biblical record, many evangelical scholars continue to give up valuable ground to secular scientists and liberal biblical critics. Evangelicals too often attempt to baptize secular and humanistic theories in evangelical waters without realizing that those theories and their methodologies have never been converted. While there are valuable kernels of truth buried within contemporary critical and so-called "scientific" studies, evangelicals must take great care to irradiate the material with the Word of God so as not to unknowingly and unintentionally introduce secularized thinking into the Church.[63]

God, Mystery and Evil

A basic common denominator between Arminian theologians and Christian philosophers is that they don't like mystery, and as a result tend to downplay mystery. They want to diffuse all apparent tension, paradoxes and antinomies from religion. This is especially true when they confront the problem of evil. To eradicate any tension or mystery when it comes to the problem of evil or the conflict between God's sovereignty and human responsibility they concoct man-made doctrines like "middle knowledge" (Craig), Open theism (Pinnock), Arminianism (Geisler), pre-evangelism (Schaeffer) and natural theology (Sproul). Erickson gives an impeccable diagnosis on the matter:

> ...natural theologians tend to be Arminian...Natural theologians assiduously avoid paradoxes and logical contradictions, considering them something to be removed by a more complete logical scrutiny of the issues under con-

sideration. A paradox is a sign of intellectual indigestion; had it been more completely chewed, it would have disappeared.[64]

They seem to be bothered by the fact that God knows more than they do. If a Christian makes any reference to "mystery," then that Christian is quickly labeled a "fideist," a "mystic" or an "anti-intellectual." This is a dangerous mistake. God is infinite; we are finite. God is perfect; we are fallen. God is omniscient, we are ignorant and see through a glass dimly (1 Cor 13:12).

In this life we can only "know in part" and what we can know about ultimate realities are only the things that God has revealed (Matt 16:17). God has not revealed everything to us: "The secret things belong to the LORD our God, but the things revealed belong to us and to our sons forever" (Deut 29:29). All the major Christian doctrines have elements of "apparent" irresolvable mystery. This attests to God's infinity and our humanity. "It is the glory of God to conceal a matter" (Prov 25:2). That's mystery. This is good, not bad. God is smarter than me...I like that.

Too often philosophers are like five-year-old children, asking endless questions, and worse, demanding answers for every one of them. This is human pride. Not every question is a legitimate question, especially when it comes to the deep things of God and His unrevealed mysteries. That's why in Romans 9, when an antagonist keeps questioning why God does what He does with respect to human free will versus His sovereign choices, God the Creator stops the inquisitor in his tracks with this resounding divine rebuke:

On the contrary, who are you, O man, who answers back to God? The thing molded will not say to the molder, "Why did you make me like this," will it? Or does not the potter have a right over the clay, to make from the same lump one vessel for honorable use, and another for common use? What if God, although willing to demonstrate His wrath and to make His power known, endured with much patience vessels of wrath prepared for destruction? (Rom 9:20-22).

It is blasphemous to question God about His behavior. He's the one who has the right to ask the questions. Remember the book of Job,

God's divine answer to the problem of evil. The lesson at the end of the book is that God is the Almighty sovereign One: "Then the LORD said to Job, 'Will the faultfinder contend with the Almighty? Let him who reproves God answer it'" (Job 40:1-2). Job got the message. In the end he acknowledged his pathetic limitations in light of God's infinite splendor: "Then Job answered the LORD, and said, 'I know that You can do all things, and that no purpose of Yours can be thwarted. Who is this that hides counsel without knowledge?' Therefore I have declared that which I did not understand, things too wonderful for me, which I did not know" (42:1-3). In his wisdom Job conceded that there was mystery that defied human comprehension.

Jesus also illustrates that not every query is legitimate. Some questions are veiled, insincere attacks on God Himself. The Christ-hating Pharisees routinely asked Jesus questions in public for the sole purpose of making Him look foolish. They were "testing Him" (Matt 19:3; cf. John 8:5-6). Their ongoing strategy was to ask Him trick questions so "they might trap Him in what He said" (Matt 22:15).

Not every religious question is a legitimate question. "Jesus perceived their malice, and said, 'Why are you testing Me, you hypocrites?'" (22:18). Like Jesus, Paul was aware of illegitimate questions and gave Timothy this warning: "But refuse foolish and ignorant speculations, knowing that they produce quarrels" (2 Tim 2:23).

Romans 9-11 is the New Testament answer to the problem of evil and God concludes the discussion by saying: "For God has shut up all in disobedience so that He may show mercy to all. Oh, the depth of the riches both of the wisdom and knowledge of God! How unsearchable are His judgments and unfathomable His ways! For *who has known the mind of the LORD, or who became His counselor?*" (11:32-34).

God chose to create a world that allowed for sin, evil and suffering. He did so based on His "wisdom." This passage says His wisdom is "unsearchable" and "unfathomable." Ultimately, all the intricacies and questions about the problem of evil are incomprehensible to the finite, fallen, ignorant human mind. That's why the Christian is called to "walk by faith, not by sight" (2 Cor 5:7). God Himself has decreed that, "without faith it is impossible to please Him, for he who comes to God must believe that He is, and that He is a rewarder of those who seek Him" (Heb 11:6).

me free from the body of this death?" (Rom 7:19, 21, 24). And future tribulation saints who will get beheaded for believing in Jesus cry out, "O Sovereign Lord, holy and true, how long before you will judge and avenge our blood on those who dwell on the earth" (Rev 6:10; ESV).

The faith of believers needs to be protected, bolstered and encouraged. Protecting the sheep is the primary job of the pastor and the Church (Acts 20:28-31; 1 Tim 3:15). And God has given us His sufficient Word, the Scriptures, to fulfill that task (2 Tim 3:16-17). That is what I do as a pastor. I am fully committed to apologetics— yet not primarily as a means of convincing atheists to believe in God, but for proclaiming the gospel and encouraging the faith of Christians, protecting them from the constant barrage of heresy, worldly ideologies, demonic doctrines, secular scientific theories and philosophical dilemmas that threaten to weaken and undermine their faith.

You Ain't Seen Nothing Yet!

One supposed insurmountable stumbling block presented by the problem of evil dilemma is the amount of evil present in the world. Traditional apologists routinely give credence to this allegation. Regarding pain and suffering, Geisler asks, "Why does God allow *so much* of it to exist in the world?"[68] Christian philosopher, Kelly Clark, sympathizes with the atheist here when he says, "It is difficult to imagine that God could exist given the various kinds and amounts of evils that exist in the world today."[69] But the Bible clearly teaches why there is so much evil in the world and even says that evil will grow exponentially worse as history moves forward. If people are having a hard time reconciling God's existence in light of the current evil in the world, then this will only be exacerbated in light of God's diagnosis of the future. Evil is going to go from bad to worse.

Jesus predicted that at the end of the age, as world history winds up, "there will be a great tribulation, such as has not occurred since the beginning of the world until now, nor ever will" (Matt 24:21). This will be a time of unprecedented, universal, worldwide evil, death, destruction, natural disasters and tragedy like the world has never seen. Jesus said, "nation will rise against nation, and kingdom against kingdom, and in various places there will be famines and earthquakes" (24:7). Hatred, murder and brutality will abound at an epic level (24:9-12). Paul echoes Jesus' sobering diagnosis of the future when he says, "But realize this, that in the last days difficult times will come. For men will be lovers of self, lovers of money, boastful, arrogant, revilers, disobedient to parents...without self-control, brutal, haters of good, treacherous, reckless, conceited" (2 Tim 3:1-4).

This is what the whole book of Revelation is about. It's a prophecy delineating the details of the devastating Great Tribulation (7:14) that God will inflict on the whole world. John describes it as "the hour of trial, that hour which is about to come upon the whole world, to test earth-dwellers" (Rev 3:10; author's translation). At the beginning of the Tribulation one fourth of the people on earth will be killed—by today's number that is almost two billion people (6:8). There will be cataclysmic natural disasters like never before (6:12). A third of the earth will be burned up, a third of the seas will be turned to blood and a third of all rivers will be poisoned from meteors smashing to earth (8:7-11).

An evil dictator will rise to power, ruling the whole world with a ruthless iron fist (Rev 13). He will consolidate and wield political and military power like none before him. His influence will be universal and his evil tyranny will make Hitler and Stalin look like pesky gnats. He will kill, maim and behead all who resist his will. The Old Testament says he will be, "dreadful and terrifying and extremely strong," devouring, trampling and crushing all in his path (Dan 7:7). The New Testament calls him "the man of lawlessness" and "the son of destruction" (2 Thess 2:3). He will exercise the supernatural power of Satan, performing miracles and false wonders, effectively leading the whole world astray into unmitigated and unparalleled wickedness (2:9-12). There will be no peace on earth (Rev 6:4). Out of shear fear, countless people will pursue suicide as a means of escape (Rev 6:16). If you think evil abounds in the world now, then you ain't seen nothing yet.

How can we explain this coming worldwide, universal, cosmic reign of terror? The Bible says God is the one who will bring all this evil to the world. God inflicts wrath (Rom 3:5). Revelation says it's the expression of "the wrath of the Lamb" (Rev 6:16). Paul says that God will enact the horrors of the Great Tribulation "in order that they all may be judged who did not believe the truth, but took pleasure in wickedness" (2 Thess 2:12). Revelation says it is a time of God's righteous wrath purposing to "destroy those who destroy the earth" (Rev 11:18). God will use evil, moral and natural, to display

His righteous, holy character to the entire creation.

The proper response of Christians in the face of skeptics who drum up the problem of evil to deflect accountability of the truth needs to be straightforward. Believers can't water down the reality of evil, but rather need to accentuate it in stark detail as the Bible does, using it to persuade unbelievers to flee from the wrath to come.

This is the urgency with which John the Baptist confronted unbelievers when he warned, "His winnowing fork is in His hand, and He will thoroughly clear His threshing floor; and He will gather His wheat into the barn, but He will burn up the chaff with unquenchable fire" (Matt 3:12). Jesus used the problem of evil as a means of calling sinners to repentance: "Or do you suppose that those eighteen on whom the tower in Siloam fell and killed them were worse culprits than all the men who live in Jerusalem? I tell you, no, but unless you repent, you will all likewise perish" (Luke 13:4-5). Paul was motivated by the problem of evil to evangelize the lost: "knowing the fear of the Lord, we persuade men" (2 Cor 5:11). God Himself is not willing for any to perish but desires all to come to repentance (2 Pet 3:9).

Man's Greatest Evil, God's Greatest Good

The greatest act of evil in the history of the world was used by God to accomplish the greatest good ever achieved. In fact, God was overseeing the most egregious act of injustice known to man. God planned it in eternity past, He predicted it in the Old Testament, He orchestrated all the events leading up to it in the New Testament, and He carried out its execution to the bitter end.

Mel Gibson's 2004 film, *The Passion of the Christ*, became a public scandal. Although it brought in over $600,000,000 worldwide, it was boycotted by standard American distribution companies, Hollywood elites, and even by a few countries like Saudi Arabia, Kuwait and Bahrain. The controversy was over the question: "Who was responsible for Jesus' death?" In Gibson's film it was the Jewish leadership that spearheaded Christ's death. As a result, Gibson was branded an anti-Semite. All the pundits chimed in with their opinions. Most suggested it was either the Romans, or Pilate, or Judas or the Sanhedrin who killed Jesus. Few, if any, in the public arena were consulting the Bible for the answer. But the Bible is clear on who was responsible for killing Jesus. Those responsible include the following: (1) the Jewish Sanhedrin (John 11:47-53), (2) Judas (John 18:1-3), (3) Herod (Acts 4:27), (4) Pilate (John 19:16), (5) the Roman soldiers (John

19:17-18, 23) and all sinners, including you and me (Isa 53:5). Christ's execution was a corporate act.

Amidst the furious debate at the time of Gibson's movie, one candidate was entirely left out of the discussion regarding whom had Christ executed—and that was God the Father. God was never associated with the betrayal, arrest, torture and death of Christ, the greatest act of evil humanity has ever known. Yet Scripture teaches that God the Father was in charge every step of the way. God planned Jesus' death in eternity past: "blood, as of a lamb unblemished and spotless, the blood of Christ. For He was foreknown before the foundation of the world" (1 Pet 1:19-20; cf. Rev 13:8). God announced 4,000 years before His death that Jesus would suffer a fatal "bruise" (Gen 3:15). One thousand years before the crucifixion, God said Jesus would be pierced in the hands and the feet (Ps 22:16). God predicted 700 years before Christ that Jesus would be murdered by evil men even though He, Himself, would be absolutely innocent (Isa 53:9).

Not only did the Father plan Jesus' death in eternity past and predict it in the Old Testament, the Father was active in the death of Christ and even punished Jesus, His own Son, while Christ hung on the cross for nearly six hours. Isaiah clearly says that God the Father was the One who punished Jesus on the cross: "Smitten of God, and afflicted...the LORD was pleased to crush Him, putting Him to grief" (53:4, 10). Smitten, afflicted, crushed...by God the Father Himself! Some evangelicals blatantly deny this key truth about the atonement. Many others misplace the emphasis of Christ's sufferings either by overemphasizing the physical pain He endured or by saying He was passively abandoned by the Father. Tim Keller says at the cross Jesus experienced "cosmic rejection and pain," but never explicitly says it was the Father who punished Jesus.[70] Christian philosopher, Douglas Groothuis, says Jesus did not even really know why He was dying on the cross at the time of the crucifixion![71] What made Christ's death on the cross so horrendous was not just the physical pain as much as the invisible transaction that took place as the Father poured out His full fury of wrath and hatred toward sin on Christ as He hung on the cross.

This is also the clear teaching of the New Testament: "O Lord...For truly in this city there were gathered together against Your holy servant Jesus, whom You anointed, both Herod and

Pontius Pilate, along with the Gentiles and the peoples of Israel, to do whatever Your hand and Your purpose predestined to occur" (Acts 4:24, 27-28). God predestined, or planned in eternity past, the death of Christ by means of evil wicked sinners to accomplish His perfect plan of salvation for the world. At the cross, God poured out His full fury of holy torment toward sin on Jesus. It was the cup of the Father's wrath that Jesus would absorb (Mark 14:36). Jesus was punished by the Father as the perfect substitute for sinners and thus conquered Satan, subdued death, overcame the world and appeased God's holy hatred of sin. The most heinous evil human act in history—the death of Christ—achieved the greatest good ever known—salvation for sinners.

Neither raw human logic, nor esoteric philosophy can answer the dilemma of the problem of evil. Only God can. And He has chosen to reveal what we need to know about it in the Bible. There is much about it that God has chosen not to reveal, and that is to His glory. In the end, with humility and faith, we must submit our hearts to God and solicit the prayer of Abraham who said to God: "Shall not the Judge of all the earth deal justly?" (Gen 18:25).

Summary

The problem of evil is considered by many the strongest argument against the truth of Christianity and the Bible. Simply stated, the problem of evil asks, "If God is good and all powerful, then why is there evil and suffering in the world?" Historically, many Christians have attempted to answer this question from a philosophical and theoretical point of view instead of a biblical and theological one. As a result, typical answers offered are man-centered, Arminian, insufficient and even at times unbiblical. The doctrine of the sufficiency of Scripture, or *sola Scriptura*, needs to be invoked on this matter.

Biblical truth needs to define and drive this discussion. The believer cannot allow the critics to frame the debate by granting them their sterile definition of evil and their myopic definition of who God is. Evil is what God says it is as revealed in Scripture—not what some atheist or evolutionist says it is, for they have no binding universal standard by which to define anything. God needs to define His nature—not the atheist. The atheists blasphemously define God with only two attributes—love (goodness) and power. They conveniently deny God His essential nature of holiness as revealed in His justice, wrath, jealousy, righteousness, glory and sovereignty.[72]

The doctrine of God's sovereignty is typically neglected in discussions on the problem of evil. The Bible clearly reveals that God is absolutely sovereign, in control of all things including evil, pain and suffering, and has a plan for it all in His perfect timing for His glory. In addition, the reality of the Fall of man and God's resultant devastating curse on the earth and the human race is usually downplayed or ignored altogether in discussions of the problem of evil. Why is there pain and suffering and evil in the world? Because Adam and Eve disobeyed God and willfully sinned as rebels and God punished them with the curse as a result. Ever since then, all creation has been groaning in turmoil awaiting the redemption yet to come. This world is currently fallen and under God's judgment.

Jesus the Savior is the answer to the problem of evil. He came to seek and to save that which was lost. He was all good and omnipotent, yet was subject to pain, suffering and the evil of others. He subjected Himself willingly to the most heinous evil act in the history of the universe—crucifixion—to accomplish the greatest good ever—salvation. All who believe in Him as Savior and Lord will have eternal life, eventually in heaven where all pain, suffering and evil will be banished forever. Those who reject Christ will live in the worst place of suffering, pain, and evil ever known—eternal hell, a real place which will exist for all eternity. And both heaven and hell will simultaneously reveal for all creation, for all time, the full, true, glorious nature of the one Almighty God of the universe. To Him alone be all the glory, forever and ever.

Notes

1. Victor J. Stenger, *God, the Failed Hypothesis: How Science Shows that God Does Not Exist* (Amherst, New York: Prometheus Books, 2007), 216. "German playwright Georg Büchner (1813-37) called the problem of evil 'the rock of atheism.' Atheists point to the problem of evil as proof that the God of the Bible doesn't exist. Every day the ancient argument gets raised in college philosophy classes, coffee shops, dinner discussions, e-mail exchanges, blogs, talk shows and best-selling books"; Randy Alcorn, *If God Is Good: Faith in the Midst of Suffering and Evil* (Colorado Springs, CO: Multnomah Books, 2009), 11.

2. E. J. Carnell, *An Introduction to Christian Apologetics* (Grand Rapids, MI: Eerdmans, 1956), 305.

3. John Frame, *Apologetics to the Glory of God* (Phillipsburg, NJ: P & R, 1994), 149.

4. William Lane Craig, *Hard Questions, Real Answers* (Wheaton, IL: Crossway, 2003), 75.

5. Kelly James Clark, *Five Views On Apologetics*, ed. Steven B. Cowen (Grand Rapids, MI: Zondervan, 2000), 251. Alcorn gives other examples of Christian writers who agree: Richard Swinburne says the problem of evil is "the most powerful objection to traditional atheism"; Ronald Nash says, "the most serious challenge to theism was, is, and will continue to be the problem of evil"; John Stott wrote, "The fact of suffering undoubtedly constitutes the single greatest challenge to the Christian faith"; Alcorn, *If God is Good*, 11.

6. Doug Powell, *Holman Quick Source Guide to Christian Apologetics*, (Nashville, TN: Holman Reference, 2006), 336.

7. Bruce Bickel and Stan Jantz, *Evidence for Faith: Understanding Apologetics in Plain Language* (Eugene, OR: Harvest House Publishers, 2008), 101.

8. N. T. Wright, *Evil and the Justice of God* (Downers Grove, IL: InterVarsity Press, 2006), 44-45. For a thorough exposé of Wright's heterodox views in this book see the book review by Cliff McManis in *The Master's Seminary Journal*, Fall, 2010, 270-272.

9. R. C. Sproul, *Objections Answered* (Glendale, CA: Regal Books, G/L Publications, 1978), 129.

10. Craig, *Hard Questions*, 91, 109.

11. C. Stephen Evans and R. Zachary Manis, *Philosophy of Religion: Thinking about Faith* (Downers Grove, IL: IVP Academic, 2009), 167.

12. Jay Adams, *The Grand Demonstration: A Biblical Study of the So-Called Problem of Evil* (Santa Barbara, CA: EastGate Publishers, 1991), 15.

13. Harold Kushner, *When Bad Things Happen to Good People* (New York: Avon, 1981), 84.

14. Stenger says three = omnibenevolence, omnipotence and omniscience, *God*, 216.

15. Greg L. Bahnsen, *Always Ready: Directions for Defending the Faith*, ed. Robert R. Booth (Texarkana, TX: Covenant Media Foundation, 1996), 163-75.

16. Norman Geisler and Peter Bocchino, *Unshakable Foundations: Contemporary Answers to Crucial Questions about the Christian Faith* (Minneapolis, MN: Bethany House, 2001), 233.

17. Douglas Groothuis, *Christian Apologetics: A Comprehensive Case for Biblical Faith* (Downers Grove, IL: IVP Academic, 2011), 618.

18. Powell, *Holman Quick Source*, 334.

19. Wright, *Evil and the Justice of God*, 113.

20. J. P. Moreland and William Lane Craig, *Philosophical Foundations for a Christian Worldview* (Downers Grove, IL: InterVarsity, 2003), 536.

21. Peter Kreeft and Ronald Tacelli, *Pocket Handbook of Christian Apologetics* (Downers Grove, IL: InterVarsity Press, 2003), 46-47.

22. Evans and Manis, *Philosophy of Religion*, 158.

23. Bickel and Jantz, *Evidence for Faith*, 177-95.

24. Kreeft, *Pocket Handbook*, 46-47.

25. Dean Hardy, *Stand Your Ground: An Introductory Text for Apologetics Students* (Eugene, OR: Wipf & Stock, 2007), 106.

26. Ibid.

27. Ibid.

28. Qur'an 4:3.

29. Qur'an 4:34.

30. Gordon Clark, *Religion, Reason, and Revelation*, (Hobbs, New Mexico: The Trinity Foundation, 1995), 194-242.

31. Craig, *Hard Questions*, 75-88.

32. Evans and Manis, *Philosophy*, 156-82.

33. Calvin, *Institutes*, 326.

34. Winfried Corduan, *Reasonable Faith* (Nashville, TN: Broadman and Holman Publishers, 1993).

35. Craig, *Hard Questions*, 86-87.

36. Carl F. Henry, *God, Revelation and Authority* (Wheaton, IL: Crossway Books, 1999), VI:282. Randy Alcorn is a welcomed exception in tackling the problem of evil. He says up front in his book, "We need our worldview realigned by God's inspired Word: 'All Scripture is God-breathed and is useful for teaching, rebuking, correcting and training in righteousness' (2 Timothy 3:16)...I quote Scripture frequently in this book because God promises that his Word 'will not return to me empty, but will accomplish what I desire and achieve the purpose for which I sent it' (Isaiah 55:11). God never makes such a promise about my words or your words. I want

this book to accomplish God's purpose—and that will happen only if it remains faithful to his words"; *If God Is God: Faith In the Midst of Suffering and Evil* (Colorado Springs, CO: Multnomah Books, 2009), 5.

37. Geisler and Bocchino, *Unshakable Foundations*, 235.

38. Ibid., 235.

39. C. S. Lewis, *Mere Christianity* (San Francisco: Harper, 2002), 52-53.

40. Charles Colson, *Answers to Your Kid's Questions* (Wheaton, IL: Tyndale House Publishers, 2000), 22.

41. Powell, *Holman Quick Source*, 348.

42. John Feinberg, *Theologies and Evil* (Washington, DC: University Press of America, 1979), 125.

43. Hardy, *Stand Your Ground*, 107.

44. Kreeft and Tacelli, *Pocket Handbook*, 51.

45. Bickel and Janz, *Evidence for Faith*, 183.

46. Alvin Plantinga, *God, Freedom, and Evil* (Grand Rapids, MI: Eerdmans, 1977).

47. Craig, *Hard Questions*, 83.

48. John Frame, *Apologetics to the Glory of God: An Introduction* (Phillipsburg, NJ: P & R Publishing), 164.

49. Cornelius Van Til, *Christian Apologetics* (Phillipsburg, NJ: P & R Publishing, 2003), 40.

50. Geisler and Bocchino, *Unshakable Foundations*, 241.

51. Doug Powell, *Holman Quick Source Guide to Christian Apologetics* (Nashville, TN: Holman Reference, 2006), 336.

52. Cornelius Van Til, *The Defense of the Faith*, (Phillipsburg, NJ: P & R Publishing, 1967), 160.

53. Hardy, Stand, 108.

54. Van Til, *Defense of the Faith*, 192.

55. Ibid., 190.

56. Ibid., 191.

57. Norman Geisler, *Baker Encyclopedia of Christian Apologetics* (Grand Rapids, MI: Baker Books, 1999), 272.

58. J. P. Moreland, *Scaling the Secular City* (Grand Rapids, MI: Baker Book House, 1987), 220.

59. Clark, *Five Views*, 281.

60. Unlike Clark, who supposedly presents the "Reformed" epistemology view of apologetics, Calvin, one of the original Reformers, believed in a literal Genesis, a real Adam and Eve and taught that Genesis 1-11 was true, reliable history. He came to that conclusion based on thorough exegesis of the Hebrew text and also taking God's Word at face value. He called those who believed in an old earth "mad" and he labeled as

"miscreants" those who questioned whether Moses wrote Genesis or questioned whether Moses even existed; *Institutes*, 40, 91.

61. Tremper Longman, <www.youtube.com/watch?v=I8Pk1vXL1WE>. Recently, a pack of evangelical scholars has "come out," categorically denying the historicity of Adam. Fortunately, true biblical apologists are being raised up to expose such calumnious teaching. Some good resources defending the historicity of Adam and Genesis include *Coming to Grips with Genesis*, Terry Mortenson and Thane H. Ury, eds; *What Happened In the Garden*, ed. Abner Chou; *The Battle for the Beginning* by John MacArthur; *Grappling with the Chronology of the Genesis Flood*, ed. Steven W. Boyd and *Searching for Adam: Genesis and the Truth about Origins*, ed. Terry Mortenson.

62. See *Coming to Grips with Genesis*, Terry Mortenson and Thane H. Ury, eds. (Green Forest, AR: Master Books, 2009) where the whole Evangelical compromise is thoroughly catalogued.

63. Ibid., 252.

64. Millard Erickson, *Christian Theology* (Grand Rapids, MI: Baker Book House, 1985), 156. The Church has had no greater intellect and scholar than John Calvin, yet in humility he welcomed mystery and irresolvable tensions in Scripture and life because (1) he knew he was a pathetic, fallen, finite sinner, and (2) that Moses declared that "the secret things belong to the LORD" (Deut 29:29). He exposed arrogant philosophers, theologians and Christian thinkers in his day and in Church history who trespassed into God's inscrutable mysteries, being driven by pride and intellectual autonomy: "many display monstrous infatuation, presuming to subject the works of God to their calculation, and discuss His secret counsels, as well as to pass a precipitate judgment on things unknown, and that with greater license than on the doings of mortal men. What can be more preposterous than to show modesty toward our equals, and choose rather to suspend our judgment than incur the blame of rashness, while we petulantly insult the hidden judgments of God, judgments which it becomes us to look up and revere...Hence it is, that in the present day so many dogs tear this doctrine with envenomed teeth, or, at least, assail it with their bark, refusing to give more license to God than their own reason dictates to themselves...For it is not right that man should with impunity pry into things which the Lord has been pleased to conceal within Himself, and scan that sublime eternal wisdom which it is His pleasure that we should not apprehend but adore, that therein also His perfections may appear. Those secrets of His will, which He has seen it meet to manifest, are revealed in His Word—revealed insofar as He knew to be conducive to our interest and welfare"; *Institutes*, 124, 608.

65. Richard Dawkins, *The God Delusion* (New York: Houghton Mifflin, 2006), 36.

66. Christopher Hitchens, *God is Not Great: How Religion Poisons Everything* (New York: Hachette, 2007).

67. Clark, *Five Views*, 273.

68. Geisler and Bocchino, *Unshakable Foundations*, 241.

69. Clark, *Five Views*, 281.

70. Tim Keller, *The Reason for God* (New York, NY: Dutton, 2008), 30.

71. He writes, "Nor did Jesus himself fully understand his own redemptive sufferings while he agonized on the cross. Otherwise he would not have cried out in dereliction, 'My God, my God, why have you forsaken me?' (Matthew 27:46)"; Groothuis, *Christian Apologetics*, 643. This is a ghastly interpretation from an evangelical on the true meaning of Jesus' words here. Jesus knew full well why He was dying. He said, "My God, my God," because He knew He was fulfilling every detailed prophecy about the crucifixion of the Messiah as stated in Psalm 22 that was written 1,000 years before Jesus' death. Jesus was purposely quoting Psalm 22:1, thus declaring to everyone at the foot of the cross, and to the world, that He was indeed the promised Messiah and Suffering Servant, who was absorbing the Father's wrath for the sins of the world by virtue of His death.

72. Morely rightly observes that, "love is not the only form of goodness. Justice is also goodness"; Brian Morley, *God in the Shadows: Evil in God's World* (Ross-Shire, Scotland: Christian Focus, 2006), 241.

his mentor, anything can become the Word of God if what is said is true and efficacious on a subjective level. For Craig the gospel is "whatever truth works."

The Gospel According to Pinnock

For decades Clark Pinnock has been a recognized seminary professor, evangelical philosopher, theologian and traditional apologist.[7] As a traditional apologist he was the quintessential example of all that is wrong with the historic and popular approach to defending the faith. The area where he became most compromised was in respect to the gospel.

Like other traditionalists, the gospel played no part in Pinnock's apologetics proper. He also eschewed the notion that Scripture is self-authenticating and the starting point for defending the faith. As a matter of fact, Pinnock held the most deficient and questionable view of Scripture of all the so-called popular contemporary Christian apologists. His view of Scripture's sufficiency, inerrancy and authority was more than suspect. As such, his view of the gospel was equally suspect.

With respect to the salvation of sinners, Pinnock called himself an "inclusivist."[8] Simply stated, Pinnock believed people all over the world are being saved apart from the special revelation of Scripture or the gospel message. He said God is imparting salvific grace and faith apart from the Church or the gospel. Pinnock purported that the only thing necessary to bring salvation to a sinner is the ubiquitous work of the Holy Spirit. Like Craig, Pinnock bifurcated the Spirit's utilization of the gospel message to save people. He said the Spirit can save people without the specific content of the gospel message about Jesus' death, burial and resurrection.

The Christian seminary professor and apologist alleged that people get saved simply by having a generic faith in God. He wrote: "The Bible does not teach that one must confess the name of Jesus to be saved."[9] Yet the Bible says just the opposite: "Believe in the Lord Jesus, and you will be saved" (Acts 16:31). And the Gospel of John declares categorically that "He who believes in the Son has eternal life" and those who do not believe in Jesus "will not see life, but the wrath of God abides on him" (John 3:36; cf. Acts 4:12 and 1 John 4:15).

Pinnock went so far as to say that people are being saved all over the world in different religions other than Christianity.[10] Pinnock

387

praised Hinduism "which celebrates a God of love";[11] he endorsed Buddhism, claiming the Buddha was a "righteous" man,[12] and he fawned over Muhammad, claiming he was a true prophet of the Old Testament order.[13]

He rejected the biblical view of eternal hell in favor of conditional immortality and annihilationism.[14] He also believed that people will get another chance to get saved after they die. He wrote, "Scripture does not require us to hold that the window of opportunity is slammed shut at death."[15] Pinnock claimed he got these inclusivist views of salvation, which are tantamount to a quasi-universalism, from C. S. Lewis.[16]

Pinnock's distortion of God's grace and love was unparalleled in the evangelical community and continues to be dangerous and damning. Jesus said salvation was "exclusive," only through Christ and the truth of the gospel: "I am the way, and the truth, and the life; no one comes to the Father but through Me" (John 14:6). But for the traditional apologist, Pinnock, the good news was that people don't need the gospel to be saved.

The Gospel According to Sproul

On the Reformed side of apologetics, there is R. C. Sproul and his unique handling of the gospel in the vortex of apologetics. Unlike most apologists, Sproul has written, preached and taught much about the gospel over the years. To some he is one of the staunchest defenders of the true saving gospel. Oddly, the gospel has never been part of his apologetics philosophy. He is one of the many who creates a firewall between apologetics and gospel proclamation. When it comes to apologetics proper he is actually staunchly philosophical. His books on apologetics are for the most part void of the gospel.

In a chapter entitled, "Apologetics and Saving Faith," Sproul argues that Christians cannot just proclaim the gospel to unbelievers.[17] Believers must first lay the groundwork through "pre-evangelism." He writes, "Though apologetics may not be evangelism, it is a vital part of pre-evangelism."[18] He is wrong on two counts here: (1) apologetics does in fact entail evangelism; and (2) there is no such thing as pre-evangelism. Such a notion is not in the Bible.

He goes on to say pre-evangelism entails creating pre-faith faith through the philosophical enterprising of reason and logic. This comes from mastering three Latin concepts, all supposedly related to the word "faith." He says we need to understand the multi-faceted character of faith that includes three separate components: *notitia*, *assensus*, and *fiducia*. The first two terms are supposedly related to the work of apologetics and they lead up to the third term, *fiducia*. This third term is allegedly saving faith, whereas the other two by themselves are not. This can all sound very impressive, scholarly and important—especially if you don't know Latin. Unfortunately many evangelicals have unwittingly bought into Sproul's oft-repeated, artificially fabricated trichotomy of faith.

A biblical understanding of faith does not come from etymological studies of obscure Latin words, but rather from the languages of the Bible, which include Hebrew and Greek. All the nuances of saving faith are bound up in just one word in the Greek New Testament—*pistis* and its verb form, *pisteuo*. This word and its cognates are used several hundred times in the New Testament. Its multi-faceted nuances and implications don't come from isolated word studies about its root meaning, but rather from its usage in each passage with the meaning being determined by the context in light of syntactical relationships with other words and phrases.

When it comes to the gospel and apologetics, Sproul fails to shoot straight on two counts. First of all, he over isolates the issue of faith, injects the word with unbiblical nuances and fails to make reference to other concomitant components of the gospel like "repentance" and belief in the resurrection.[19] Second, Sproul illegitimately banishes evangelism from the work of apologetics proper. For Sproul, the gospel is a Latin version of *"sola fide"*—but we will see that the biblical gospel is much more than that.

The Gospel According to Van Til

Presuppositionalist, Cornelius Van Til, made many helpful, unique contributions to the debate on Christian apologetics. But like his predecessors and his traditionalist contemporaries he never made a comprehensive delineation of the gospel a part of his system of apologetics. He majored in the realm of theological prolegomena and sophisticated philosophical ratiocinations rather than in biblical exegesis and theology.

In his classic work on apologetics, *The Defense of the Faith*, out of 300 pages he dedicated only two pages to gospel matters under the title of, "The Doctrine of Salvation."[20] Amazingly in this short section he never explains the gospel. He never refers to any Bible

verses either and he fails to mention expected fundamental soteriological terms of the gospel including "justify," "righteous," "law,"
"punish," "propitiation," "forgiveness," "eternal life," "heaven,"
"cross," "believe," "faith," "grace," "love," "hell," and "repent." He
mentions the word "gospel" but never mentions Christ's death,
resurrection, burial or ascension. Without these terms there can be no
theology of salvation or soteriology—no true gospel. His point of
emphasis in the discussion is that we need to reject Arminianism.[21]
But that is not the gospel message.

The Gospel According to Bahnsen

Presuppositionalist, Greg Bahnsen, enhanced the life's work of Van
Til and improved it by popularizing it into accessible concepts and
vocabulary, systematizing it into a synthetic and consistent corpus
and by providing many of the biblical and theological underpinnings
that were often lacking in Van Til's writings. Bahnsen's classic work
on apologetics, *Always Ready*, was published posthumously.[22] It is a
breath of fresh air in many respects. Scriptural passages are sprinkled
throughout every page. His presentation of biblical epistemology is
unparalleled. His refutation of the myth of neutrality is incontestable.
His bibliology is rock solid. Nevertheless, Bahnsen, like the rest, does
not incorporate an explication of the gospel into his apologetics
scheme. The actual content of the gospel is almost non-existent in his
290 pages.

This makes sense in view of Bahnsen's strange theonomic perspective regarding the Old Testament Law and the gospel. As a
Reconstructionist, Bahnsen melded too much continuity between the
Law and the gospel, infusing too much grace into the Law and
undermining the simplicity and purity of the gospel by weighing it
down with legal encumbrances. Here's an example of his fundamental confusion as he conflates Law and gospel: "we are compelled
to conclude that the old covenant—indeed, the Mosaic law—was a
covenant of *grace* that offered salvation on the basis of grace through
faith".[23] Contrary to Bahnsen, the Mosaic Law was not a covenant of
grace (although it is not absent of God's grace toward sinners). And
it did not have the power to impart salvation. The Bible clearly
teaches that, "a man is not justified by the works of the Law" (Gal
2:16). For Bahnsen, the gospel was "the whole Bible." Such a view
overgeneralizes and actually smothers the distinctive features of the
true, saving gospel.

The Gospel According to Wright

Few have made a bigger splash in the evangelical scholarly community in the past generation than the always Right Reverend Dr. Nicholas Thomas Wright Lord Bishop of Durham, more popularly known as N. T. Wright. He has now retired from his influential position as Research Professor of New Testament at St. Mary's College, St. Andrews in Scotland. He has authored more books than many folks will read in a lifetime. He is known in apologetics circles for books he's authored defending the resurrection, as well as taking a shot at explaining, and even redefining, the age old conundrum of "the problem of evil." At the same time he has specialized in the topic of "justification," which historically would be inseparable from the gospel. Yet Wright made his mark as an evangelical by redefining the meaning of justification and popularizing it on a grand scale.

Wright is a slippery writer and hard to pin down at times about what he actually means, but some things have become clear over the past decades as to where he stands with respect to gospel truths ...and they are alarming. Here are just a few: (1) he says we need to read the Gospels in a new way, in a political way; (2) he says the doctrine of justification has nothing to do with soteriology but rather ecclesiology; (3) he says Christ's death was not a penal substitution but rather a confrontation with political and cosmic forces; (4) he says Jesus did not die for the sins of individuals but rather "Jesus died in a representative capacity for evil"[24]; (5) he says that Jesus' death did not secure a once-for-all spiritual salvation for the sinner, but rather Christ's death merely "began the process of redemption" which humans are to complete by "implementing the achievement of the cross"[25] through social justice and gook works; (6) and he rejects a literal, physical, eternal hell as taught in Scripture. In the end Wright's good news, or gospel, is that Jesus' death was primarily an ideal human example for Christians to follow as they seek to mete out social justice in the world. Here, sadly, Wright is wrong.

Back to the Gospel

Peter was clear. Apologetics is about giving answers for the hope that is in you. The believer's "hope" is in Christ, and Christ Himself is our hope—our only hope. Apologetics is about giving answers regarding the gospel—the good news about Jesus Christ. In studies on apologetics it is customary for theologians and philosophers to unwittingly ignore, marginalize or shortchange the gospel—some even confuse or misrepresent it altogether. That needs to change. In the work of apologetics, the gospel needs to be front and center. With the apostle Paul we need to declare with boldness, "For I am not ashamed of the gospel, for it is the power of God for salvation to everyone who believes" (Rom 1:16). To that glorious end we now look to Scripture's explanation of the gospel of Jesus Christ.

The Gospel According to Timmy

Years ago, I had a discussion with an older Christian who was a seasoned Bible teacher. The topic of conversation was "the gospel," about which there was disparity between the two of us. After some interactive interchange I finally posed the direct question to him and asked, "What is the gospel? If you had the opportunity to share the gospel with an inquiring unbeliever, in a nutshell, what would you tell him?"

His first response was, "Well...(pause)...I don't know what I would tell him."

I was amazed. I pressed the issue further. "Come on. You have a willing candidate who wants to know how to get to heaven—what do you tell him?"

This time he said, "Well, I'd tell him that God is a holy God and totally sovereign and that He cannot tolerate any evil and that He must punish sin. And that all of our human works, no matter how good we think they are, are actually nothing but filthy rags!"

I asked, "Is that it?"

He said, "Yep."

I proceeded to point out to him that the word "gospel" means "good news" and that his response entailed no good news whatsoever. I reminded him also that he failed to mention Jesus' name, Jesus' crucifixion, Jesus' resurrection; and that he did not tell the unbeliever how one might appropriate the good news and actually receive eternal life.

Shortly after that conversation, around 2003, on a casual family drive, my five-year old son, Timothy, noticed a building outside the window as we drove by. The building was emblazoned with a huge moniker that the novice reader actually recognized. Timmy blurted out with enthusiasm: "Mommy—that building has the letters G-O-S-P-E-L on it."

My wife affirmed, "That's right Timmy. And what does that spell?"

Savior was predicted in the Old Testament (Isa 52:7; Gal 3:6-9), announced at the advent of Christ (Matt 3:1-3; Mark 1:14-15) and fulfilled after His resurrection and ascension (Acts 2:14-41). It is all one message,[31] albeit, it progressed quantitatively throughout redemptive history, but not qualitatively. There has always been only one saving message for sinful humanity (Rom 1:1-4; Eph 4:5-6).

The fact that there is only one gospel is important, because there are those who erroneously suppose that there is more than one gospel. Some eccentric dispensationalists assert that there was "the gospel of Jesus" and then there was "the gospel of Paul." Or there was "the gospel of Peter" which was different than Paul's gospel. Over the years, on several occasions I have had visitors at my church confront me right after the sermon telling me I am confused about the gospel. They purport that Jesus preached the "gospel of the kingdom" and Paul preached the "gospel of grace." They say the two were different gospels, with different requirements on the part of the recipients.

Jesus and Peter preached an Old Testament "gospel of works" to the Jews while Jesus was alive, and after Acts chapter 2 Paul preached a new gospel, a gospel of grace apart from works, which was different from Jesus' gospel. This crazy view is surprisingly widespread in popular American evangelical Christianity. For decades, a major proponent of this false distinction regarding gospels has been Charles Ryrie. He has written much positing that when Jesus preached the gospel, it was only for the Jews, was only in reference to the earthly Millennial Kingdom, is not being preached during the Church age, will only be preached again during the future seven year Great Tribulation, and is to be distinguished from Paul's gospel that we read about in his epistles.[32]

This is an astonishing assertion in light of the warning of Galatians 1:6-9:

> [6] I am amazed that you are so quickly deserting Him who called you by the grace of Christ, for a different gospel;[7] which is *really* not another; only there are some who are disturbing you and want to distort the gospel of Christ. [8] But even if we, or an angel from heaven, should preach to you a gospel contrary to what we have preached to you, he is to be accursed! [9] As we have said before, so I say again now, if any man is preaching to you a gospel

contrary to what you received, he is to be accursed!

Ryrie did not invent the theory of two gospels. He got it from his predecessor, Lewis Sperry Chafer, co-founder of Dallas Seminary. Chafer said, "the 'gospel of the kingdom,'...should in no wise be confused with the Gospel of saving grace."[33] Chafer was known for making such antithetical and dichotomizing statements in the area of soteriology; not only did he propose more than one gospel—at one time he proposed there were *two* New Covenants! He said, "To suppose that these two covenants—one for Israel and one for the Church—are the same is to assume that there is a latitude of common interest between God's purpose for Israel and His purpose for the Church. Israel's covenant, however, is new only because it replaces the Mosaic, but the Church's covenant is new because it introduces that which is God's mysterious and unrelated purpose." [34]

Despite what Chafer wrote, there is no exegetical support for the idea of "two New Covenants"—there is only one! Chafer went even further than Ryrie, for he posited three distinct eras, with *three* distinct messages/proclamations/gospels. They included the following: (1) the time of pure law under Moses; (2) the kingdom portions of the Gospels; (3) and the Church age. The message differs with each respective era: (1) the key words for the Mosaic period are "law" and "obedience"; (2) the key words for the period Christ was teaching are "righteousness" and "peace"; and (3) the key words during the Church age are "believe" and "grace." Chafer definitely paved the way for Ryrie's eventual gospel bifurcation of the one true gospel of biblical history by constructing false distinctions during the respective historical eras. So in effect, Chafer postulates three distinct gospels![35] This explains Chafer's apparent paradoxical and antithetical style of writing, especially in the area of soteriology. In his systematic theology, Chafer wrote the following about being "justified" or being saved under the Mosaic Law versus being saved or "justified" during the Church age, the "age of grace":

> A distinction must be observed here between just men of the Old Testament and those justified according to the New Testament. According to the Old Testament men were just ['*saved*'] because they were true and faithful in keeping the Mosaic Law....Men were therefore just ['*saved*'] because of their own works for God, whereas New

lated, minimalist, ineffectual reductionist gospel. Like the guy on the side of the road holding the card-board sign trying to communicate his need with the fewest words possible, so the Church is more and more holding out a pared down, indiscernibly meager message with the least common denominators of truth to be believed. One author puts it this way:

> In the twentieth century the church has tried to see how little it could say and still get converts. The assumption has been that a minimal message will conserve our forces, spread the Gospel farther, and of course, preserve a unity among evangelicals. It has succeeded in spreading the truth so thinly that the world cannot see it. Four facts droned over and over have bored sinners around us and weakened the church as well....Now is the hour to recover the full, rich Gospel of Christ....Needed most of all, then, is the demolition of the dreadful trend that sees the Gospel as simply a few facts. True evangelism preaches the whole counsel of God with explanation and application to sinners.[39]

Jesus Preached the Complete Gospel

Jesus was the Master and Model of preaching the gospel, the full gospel, "according to the Scriptures." A classic example is in Luke 24 when Jesus meets two disciples on the road to Emmaus on Resurrection Sunday. They spoke with the resurrected Lord, not knowing it was Jesus, and were downcast about Jesus' death. Jesus rebuked them for their lack of faith and said,

> "O foolish men and slow of heart to believe in all that the prophets have spoken! Was it not necessary for the Christ to suffer these things and to enter into His glory?" Then beginning with Moses and with all the prophets, He explained to them the things concerning Himself in all the Scriptures (Luke 24:25-27).

A few comments are in order. First of all what Jesus explained to them at length was the gospel—i.e., Jesus' death and resurrection—the very same content Paul summarizes in 1 Corinthians 15. Second, Jesus explained the gospel "according to the Scriptures" by referring to "all the Scriptures" (v. 27). He explained the significance and need of His death and resurrection in light of "all the Scriptures." He began with Genesis, and preached the gospel, went through the whole Torah, then explained the gospel as revealed in "all the Prophets" (v. 27). This was no fly-by-night, hurried minimalist presentation of the gospel. To go through the key truths in all the Scriptures takes a long time. This may have been a personal Bible study that lasted for hours. Third, in giving the gospel, Jesus did not simply spit out a canned spiel of gospel facts in less than sixty seconds. He opened up "the Scriptures," (v. 32) "explaining" all the pertinent information relative to the gospel. We need to do likewise. We need to thoroughly preach, teach, explain, highlight, accentuate, illustrate, and explicate the gospel using the totality of Scripture.[40]

Paul Preached the Complete Gospel

This is what Paul did. When he preached the gospel to unbelievers he was thorough, comprehensive and he labored long hours, days and even weeks in his presentation. For Paul, the gospel was not a pithy one-line mantra like, "Turn or Burn!" or "Believe in Jesus" as some today would have us believe. These statements are trite, inadequate and ineffectual truncations of gospel truth. They are not "the gospel." They are not attended by "all the Scriptures." In contrast, look at a typical gospel-preaching scenario of Paul's ministry:

> Now when they had traveled through Amphipolis and Apollonia, they came to Thessalonica, where there was a synagogue of the Jews. And according to Paul's custom, he went to them, and for three Sabbaths reasoned with them from the Scriptures, explaining and giving evidence that the Christ had to suffer and rise again from the dead (Acts 17:1-3).

This passage shows how Paul labored for three consecutive Sabbath days with the same group of people, fully explaining the gospel to them. It was hard work. Contrast Paul and Jesus' methodology of exhaustively teaching a complete gospel, "according to [all] the Scriptures," with some popular versions today. For example, Zane Hodges has written a trilogy on what he purports to be the true gospel. Note some of his conclusions:

To be saved, all the unsaved person needs to do is to believe on the Lord Jesus Christ (Acts 16:31)![41]

And when a man or woman is ready to hear the message of grace—no matter how God has worked to prepare them for that—then there is no need to speak to him or her at that point about repentance. Instead one may simply say, 'Believe on the Lord Jesus Christ, and you will be saved' (Acts 16:31, NKJV)![42]

Thank God there is only one answer to the question, 'What must I do to be saved?' That of course, is the answer not only of Paul and all the apostles, but of Jesus Himself. The answer is: 'Believe!'[43]

In his books on the gospel, Hodges never says that we are supposed to preach about the resurrection to unbelievers, or about who Jesus is, or about sin, or about the character of God who is holy. He says the gospel we present to unbelievers is simply, "Believe in Jesus. That's all." But that is inadequate. Mormons and Jehovah's Witnesses believe that statement.

When Paul defined the gospel in 1 Corinthians 15 he mentioned who Jesus is, what Jesus did, why Jesus did what He did, the reality of sin, the need for Christ's death, the reality of Christ's resurrection. We need to thoroughly explain what it means to believe in Jesus. Hodges comes up with his reductionist gospel by isolating Acts 16:31 and showcasing it as an absolute and comprehensive statement by Paul. But it is not. It is an umbrella summary statement. It gives the essence of how to be saved, but it does not reveal the prerequisites of the gospel contents. Paul said a lot more to that Philippian jailer about the gospel that night. 16:32 clearly shows that Paul and Silas "spoke the word of the Lord to him and to all who were in his house."

A cohort of Hodges presents a similarly minimalist gospel when he writes the following:

Tell unbelievers that if they simply believe in Christ they will at that moment have eternal life. That is justification by faith alone....If an unbeliever asks if he must give up his sinful ways to have eternal salvation, tell him no. The only condition is faith in Christ....Paul's answer to the question, 'What must I do to be saved?' was, 'Believe on the Lord Jesus Christ, and you will be saved' (Acts 16:30-31, NKJV). If repentance is the condition, then Paul got it wrong! That is, of course, absurd. The only condition is to believe in Christ. Believe. Not repent. Not believe plus repent. Just believe. It's that simple.[44]

To expose the folly of the above minimalist statements, consider two statements from Christ Himself that debunk such a trivialized and simplistic notion of how to get saved. First, according to Jesus there were other conditions to be saved in addition to the one given above. In John 5:24 Jesus said, "Most assuredly, I say to you, he who hears My word and believes in Him who sent Me has everlasting life." So Jesus adds two more stipulations: to be saved one must hear Jesus' word and one must believe in God the Father. Nowhere will you read those prerequisites in "the gospel according to Hodges."

Second, someone did in fact ask Jesus the question, "What must I do to be saved?" It was the rich young ruler (Matt 19:16-26; Mark 10:17-27; Luke 18:18-27). When he asked Jesus that question, Jesus did not say, "Believe on the Lord Jesus Christ and you shall be saved," as Hodges and Wilkin insist we must always respond. Rather Jesus told him to keep the commandments, to be perfect, to sell all his possessions and give to the poor and to follow Christ. Quite a scandalous response![45] What Hodges and company propose as *the gospel* is found wanting—they give part of the truth, but not the whole truth.

The Gospel is about Knowing the Identity of Jesus

The gospel as stated in 1 Corinthian 15 is Christo-centric. Paul showcases "Christ" as the subject of the gospel (v. 3). After all, in Paul's inspired definition of the gospel, "Christ" is the first word. The good news is all about who Jesus is and what He did. As little Timmy proclaimed, the gospel is "Jesus!" Paul said, "we preach Christ" (1 Cor 1:23). Before Philip baptized the Ethiopian eunuch on the desert road, "he preached Jesus to him" (Acts 8:35). When we preach the good news, we are first and foremost telling people about a Person; we are introducing them to the God and Savior of the world. We must clearly explain to people who Jesus is. We are not in the business of simply spewing out a little data and a few facts. We are charged with the mandate to reveal the nature of an infinite God. That can't be done with a one-sentence mantra, "Believe in Jesus." Bumper-sticker Christianity is ineffectual. Becoming a Christian or getting saved is about having "eternal life." What is the essence of eternal life? Jesus told us clearly in John 17:3: "This is eternal life, that they may know You, the only true God, and Jesus Christ whom You have sent."

To gain eternal life one must first come to know who God the Father and Jesus Christ really are. That takes some time, a prerequisite amount of information and some thorough explaining. John the apostle understood this. His Gospel was written for an explicitly evangelistic purpose—to introduce people to Jesus Christ, for he stated, "but these [*miracles of Jesus*] have been written so that you may believe that Jesus is the Christ, the Son of God; and that believing you may have life in His name" (John 20:31).

John went to great lengths in his Gospel to thoroughly explain who Jesus was and what Jesus did—twenty-one chapters' worth, one of the longest books in the New Testament. He was not a shallow, superficial evangelist with a handful of spiritual laws. Also notice in John's purpose statement of 20:31 that he does not say that he wrote so people would "believe in Jesus," but rather that they would believe "that Jesus is the Christ, the Son of God." There's a big difference. He was compelled to explain fully who Jesus was. People can't "just believe in Jesus" if they don't know who He is.

In his Gospel, John explained thoroughly who Jesus was: he says that Jesus was uncreated (1:1a), co-equal with the Father (1:1b; 10:30), God (1:1c), the Creator (1:3, 10), the Author of salvation (1:12), all-glorious Incarnate Deity (1:14; 17:5), the Unique Son of God (1:18, 34), the Savior from sin (1:29), the Eternal One (1:30; 8:58), the Teacher (1:38), the Messiah of the Old Testament (1:45), omniscient (1:48-50; 2:24; 4:18; 21:17), supernatural (2:1-11), a holy God of wrath (2:12-17), sovereign over death (2:19; 11:43-44), from Heaven (3:13), the Son of Man (3:14), the Savior of the World (3:17; 4:42), the Judge of all souls (3:18; 5:22), the Light of the world (3:19), hated by men (1:11; 3:19-20; 5:18; 15:18), the Bridegroom (3:29), Sovereign over all (3:31), a Jew (4:9), greater than Jacob (4:12), the Messiah (4:25), a Prophet (4:44), omnipotent (4:50; 19:11), the theme of the Scriptures (5:39), the Bread of Life (6:35), sinless (8:46; 18:38) greater than Abraham (8:56), worthy of worship (12:1-7; 20:28), the only way to Heaven (10:1-10; 14:6), the Good Shepherd (10:11), the Resurrection and the Life (11:25), the fulfillment of prophecy (12:37-41), the Coming One (14:3), the Truth (14:6), the only way to the Father (14:6), the True Vine (15:1), the King of Heaven (18:36-37), the Suffering Servant (19:1-17), the crucified Savior (19:18-42), and the Risen Lord (20-21)! That is who Jesus is. And to believe in that Jesus is to have eternal life.

To say that the gospel is simply, "Believe in Jesus" without explanation or qualification is not the gospel. Mormons "believe in Jesus," but they believe Jesus is a created being, that He was the spirit-brother of Lucifer, who worked His way to godhood, that He was not born of a virgin, is not co-equal with the Father, had multiple wives on earth and is now a polygamist in heaven, and is not to be worshipped. They believe in a false Jesus. Mormons adhere to a pseudo-gospel.

Jehovah's Witnesses "believe in Jesus," but they believe Jesus is a created being (not eternal or co-equal with the Father), that He is Michael the Archangel reincarnated (not Almighty God), that He did not die on the cross and that He is not to be worshipped. They believe in a false Jesus and a false gospel.

Muslims "believe in Jesus" but they believe that He is a created being and not eternal, that He was not a Jew, that He is not God nor is He to be worshipped, that He was not virgin born, that He is inferior to Muhammad and Allah, and that His death on the cross does not provide forgiveness of sin. Islam believes in a counterfeit Jesus and a false gospel.

Many Protestants today who claim to "believe in Jesus" don't believe Jesus was born of a virgin, was sinless, was uncreated, is eternal, is a holy God of wrath or the only and exclusive way to the Father in heaven. Such people believe in a false Jesus—they don't know the true gospel. Every false religion and cult on planet earth "believes in Jesus" in some manner or another. But they don't believe the correct things about who He is and what He did. This should not be surprising for Jesus warned us this would happen: "Jesus answered: 'Watch out that no one deceives you. For many will come in my name, claiming, 'I am the Christ,' and will deceive many....For false Christs and false prophets will appear...See, I have told you ahead of time" (Matt 24:4-5, 24-25). The true gospel is about proclaiming fully who Jesus is.

The Gospel is about Knowing What Jesus Did

The Meaning of Christ's Death

Preaching the gospel means telling people what Jesus did and why He did it. Paul wrote, "For I delivered to you as of first importance what I also received, that Christ died for our sins" (1 Cor 15:3). The death of Christ is of "first importance." Jesus' crucifixion is the cornerstone of the good news and gives significance to every other truth about Him. That's why Paul made statements like, "For I determined to know nothing among you except Jesus Christ, and Him crucified" (1 Cor 2:2) and "But may it never be that I would boast, except in the cross of our Lord Jesus Christ, through which the world has been crucified to me, and I to the world" (Gal 6:14). That's why John spent half of his entire Gospel (chapters 12-21) on the last week of Christ's ministry, culminating with His death.

Christ's death is the central feature of Christianity.[46] It is the central feature because it is Christ's death on the cross as a sacrifice that provides forgiveness of sins. Christ's death absorbed God's wrath[47] against sin (Rom 3:25). God the Father punished Jesus at the cross. In Isaiah's words, God the Father "crushed," "scourged," and "chastened" the Messiah (53:5). In addition, Christ's death redeemed[48] sinners by fulfilling the penal requirements of God's holy law and satisfied His justice (Gal 4:5). It was through Christ's death that God purchased[49] sinners (Rev 5:9). Christ's death was the ransom[50] that liberated us from the slavery of sin (Titus 2:14). Christ's death reconciled[51] us to God (Rom 5:10). Christ died as the substitute[52] for sinners (2 Cor 5:15). Christ's death became the grounds for our justification[53] before God the Judge (Rom 5:18). Without death, or the shedding of blood, there is no forgiveness of sin (Heb 9:22). That is what God requires. When we preach the gospel, we preach the meaning of Christ's death.

Jesus Died for Sins

But why did Christ have to die? Paul says because of "sins" (1 Cor 15:3). We must talk about sin when we preach the gospel with unbelievers. This is not a popular notion. People get mad when you tell them they are sinners. But in order for people to be receptive to the "good news" they must first know the bad news. We must tell people where sin came from (Rom 5:17) and that we are all sinful (Rom 3:23). We must tell people what sin is. Sin is a personal offense against God. We must tell people sin has separated us from God.

They need to understand their desperate need for the forgiveness of sin and salvation. They need to be told that God is holy and cannot tolerate sin and that He must punish sin (Ezek 18:4). People need to know they can't save themselves from their sin (Rom 3:19-20). They must be told that the wages of sin is death and that without the total forgiveness of sin, no one can please God, know God or enter into heaven (John 8:24; Rom 6:23). Clearly diagnosing humanity's spiritual terminal illness of sin on a personal level with people will help them understand their need for a Savior. When we preach the gospel, we must preach about sin! Jesus did:

> I go away, and you will seek Me, and will die in your sin...Truly, truly, I say to you, everyone who commits sin is the slave of sin (John 8:21, 34).

> If your right eye makes you stumble, tear it out and throw it from you; for it is better for you to lose one of the parts of your body, than for your whole body to be thrown into hell. If your right hand makes you stumble, cut it off and throw it from you; for it is better for you to lose one of the parts of your body, than for your whole body to go into hell (Matt 5:29-30).

The Gospel is a Call to Repentance[54]

Not only must we preach about sin and its deleterious effects, but we must also call unbelievers to repent of their sins. Preaching repentance is part of the gospel. This is a basic biblical truth. Again Jesus is the Master and Model for us: "Now after John had been taken into custody, Jesus came into Galilee, preaching the gospel of God, and saying, 'The time is fulfilled, and the kingdom of God is at hand; repent and believe in the gospel'" (Mark 1:14-15).

The first word Jesus proclaimed as He preached the "good news" or "the gospel" was "repent"! The call to repentance was the heart of Jesus' saving message. He summarized His whole purpose for coming as the Savior in this way: "And Jesus answered and said to them, 'It is not those who are well who need a physician, but those who are sick. I have not come to call the righteous but sinners to repentance'" (Luke 5:31-32).

And Jesus commissioned the Church to do the same—to preach the gospel of repentance. In Luke 24 Jesus gave the contents of the gospel thusly: "He said to them, 'Thus it is written, that the Christ would suffer and rise again from the dead the third day, and that repentance for forgiveness of sins would be proclaimed in His name to all the nations, beginning from Jerusalem'" (Luke 24:46-47). If we were to ask the familiar question today, "What Would Jesus Do? (WWJD)" relative to evangelizing the lost, the clear answer from Scripture tells us, "He would preach repentance!"

The apostles also preached repentance in their gospel presentations. The apostles and the early church were to continue what "Jesus began to do and teach" (Acts 1:1). And relative to the gospel they did just that. On the Day of Pentecost, Peter preached an evangelistic message, the gospel of Christ, and the listeners responded positively by asking, "Brethren, what shall we do?" (Acts 2:37). Peter responded by saying, "*Repent* and be baptized, every one of you, in the name of Jesus Christ for the forgiveness of your sins. And you will receive the gift of the Holy Spirit. The promise is for you and your children and for all who are far off—for all whom the Lord our God will call" (2:38-39). This verse makes it clear that "forgiveness" is contingent upon repentance. Peter said, "Repent!" And this call for repentance is a timeless message, still applicable today, for Peter said it was "for all" whom the Lord will call.

Similarly, in Acts 3, when Peter was preaching the gospel in the temple courts, Peter proclaimed, "Repent, then, and turn to God, so that your sins may be wiped out" (v. 19, NIV; cf. Acts 8:22). Again, "forgiveness" results from repentance. Peter even equates getting saved with "coming to repentance" in 2 Peter 3:9 when he says that the Lord is "not wishing for any to perish but for all to come to repentance."

Paul also clearly taught and modeled that repentance was part of the gospel. Paul summed up his evangelistic ministry with the following statements: "Therefore having overlooked the times of ignorance, God is now declaring to men that all *people* everywhere should repent" (Acts 17:30). God commands "all people" "everywhere" to repent. It is a universal demand—no one is excluded:

> I did not shrink from declaring...solemnly testifying to both Jews and Greeks of repentance toward God and faith in our Lord Jesus Christ (Acts 20:20-21).

So, King Agrippa, I did not prove disobedient to the heavenly vision, but *kept* declaring both to those of Damascus first, and *also* at Jerusalem and *then* throughout all the region of Judea, and *even* to the Gentiles, that they should repent and turn to God, performing deeds appropriate to repentance (Acts 26:19-20).

So clearly repentance is a basic component of the gospel of Jesus. But unfortunately there is a growing trend in evangelicalism that flat-out denies this truth. And it is gaining popularity. Note a recent example from one Bible teacher:

Tell unbelievers that if they simply believe in Christ they will at that moment have eternal life....If an unbeliever asks if he must give up his sinful ways to have eternal salvation, tell him no. The only condition is faith in Christ. Tell him, however, that sin never pays, for the believer or the unbeliever, and that he should turn from his sinful ways whether or not he is convinced that Jesus gives eternal life to all who merely believe in him for it...Paul's answer to the question, "What must I do to be saved?" was, "Believe on the Lord Jesus Christ, and you will be saved" (Acts 16:30-31, NKJV). If repentance is the condition, then Paul got it wrong! That is, of course, absurd. The only condition is to believe in Christ. Believe. Not repent. Not believe plus repent. Just believe. It's that simple.[55]

That statement is unbelievable in light of biblical truth. Jesus emphatically said, "repent and believe" (Mark 1:15) and yet this author says, "Not believe plus repent." Peter said, "Repent!" (Acts 2:38), but this author says, "Not repent." Paul said, "Repent" (Acts 17:30), but this author says, "Not repent." Who will you believe?

Wilkin also says that if an unbeliever asks if they must give up their sinful ways to have eternal life, he says to tell them, "No"! On the other hand, Jesus said, "If your right eye causes you to sin, then gouge it out and throw it away...if your right hand causes you to sin, cut if off and throw it away." Further, Jesus said, "If anyone would come after Me [*anyone who wants eternal life*], he must deny himself [*give up your sins and self desires*], and take up his cross [*be willing to die*], and follow Me [*obey Jesus, commit to Him, do what He says, go where He goes*].

For whoever wants to save his life [*inherit eternal life and forgiveness*] will lose it [*turn from sin and self*], but whoever loses his life for Me will save it [*if an unbeliever asks if he must give up his sinful ways to have eternal salvation, tell him Jesus said, 'Yes—absolutely!'*]." (Luke 9:23-24). Jesus also said, "If anyone comes to Me, and does not hate his own father and mother and wife and children and brothers and sisters, yes, and even his own life, he cannot be My disciple" (Luke 14:26).

So, the gospel of Jesus is clearly a call to repentance. Nevertheless, there are those who insist otherwise. Zane Hodges for example, makes the following assertions despite the clear testimony of Scripture:

> ...repentance is *not* a condition for eternal life.[56]

> ...the view that 'repentance is necessary for eternal life'... cannot be demonstrated from Scripture.[57]

> No text in the New Testament...makes *any direct connection* between repentance and eternal life. No text does that. Not so much as one![58]

But Jesus said "Repent and believe," (Mark 1:15) plain and simple.

> Those who teach that repentance is necessary for eternal salvation can have no true assurance of their eternal destiny. And if they claim to have this, they are either fooling themselves or us or both![59]

But Jesus repeatedly said otherwise—salvation is directly related and contingent upon repentance. That is why the popular *Evangelical Celebration* of the Gospel of Jesus (which is signed by more than 125 distinguished representative evangelicals), says, "We affirm that saving faith includes...acknowledgement of our own sin and need."[60] That is a good definition of repentance—"acknowledgement of our own sin." That just goes to show that Hodges' view is theologically spurious, outside the mainstream of evangelical Christianity and even historically unprecedented in the Christian Church.

Why does Hodges hold this skewed view on repentance? Several reasons. First of all he argues that the Gospel of John never mentions the word "repentance" and it is the Gospel about evangelism and salvation; therefore "repentance" has nothing to do with evangelism and salvation. He avers,

> ...repentance...is totally absent from John's gospel. There is not even so much as one reference to it in John's twenty-one chapters!....The fourth evangelist explicitly claims to be doing evangelism (John 20:30-31).... Only a resolute blindness can resist the obvious conclusion: John did not regard repentance as a condition for eternal life. If he had, he would have said so. After all, that's what his book is all about: obtaining eternal life (Jn 20:30-31).[61]

This is a classic illegitimate "argument from silence." John's Gospel also failed to employ the words "gospel," "redemption," "propitiation," "justification," "reconciliation," "atonement," or the noun "faith." So are we to assume that none of these truths are related to Christ's saving message because they are absent in John? Absurd! Jesus never mentions the word "grace" in the Gospels. Do we conclude grace is not a part of Jesus' saving gospel? The Bible never uses the word "Trinity" but that doctrine is what distinguishes true biblical Christianity from other religions. We don't argue from silence to prove a point—that is dangerous and misleading. Hodges' argument also assumes that the Synoptics were not written for the purpose of evangelizing the lost, which is another absurdity (cf. Matt 26:13; 28:19-20; Mark 13:10; 16:15; Luke 24:45-48).

The second reason Hodges holds the non-repentance view of the gospel is because of his hermeneutic.[62] Because of his hyper-dispensationalism, he is prone to making numerous false distinctions in the Bible, often pitting complementary doctrines against one another, which results in false dichotomies, exaggerated discontinuities, contrived theological distinctions and a botched hermeneutic. He pits "the Kingdom" vs. "the Church age," "the Kingdom of God" vs. "the Kingdom of Heaven," inheriting the kingdom of God vs. inheriting salvation, overcomers vs. normal Christians, law vs. grace, temporal salvation vs. eternal salvation, the gift of eternal life vs. the gift of the Holy Spirit, false teachers vs. unbelievers, justification vs. sanctification, Christians vs. disciples, faith vs. repentance, perseverance vs. assurance, apostasy vs. unbelief, "the gospel of Jesus" vs. "the gospel of Paul," "the gospel of Israel" vs. "the gospel to the Gentiles", etc. He even pits "forgiveness" against "eternal life" when he says this amazing statement:

...eternal life and forgiveness of sins are *not the same thing!*[63]

And this one:

"forgiveness...is personal and not judicial."[64]

And another:

"Paul...received eternal salvation (1 Jn 5:1). But *not* forgiveness of sins."[65]

The third reason Hodges holds the non-repentance view is because he inherited it. He did not invent all this zany thinking by himself. He got it from Chafer.[66] Again, contrast that view with Jesus Himself who came preaching, saying, "repent and believe in the gospel" (Mark 1:15)! Chafer taught at times that there was more than one gospel—one for the Jews and one for the Church. Repentance was the gospel for Israel, but repentance was not the gospel for the Church:

> It is an error to require repentance as a preliminary act preceding and separate from believing. Such insistence is too often based on Scripture which is addressed to the covenant people, Israel....The preaching of John the Baptist, of Jesus and the early message of the disciples was "repent for the kingdom of heaven is at hand"; but it was addressed only to Israel (Matthew 10:5-6).[67]

The fourth reason Hodges holds the non-repentance view is because he has a wrong definition of repentance. He maintains that repentance is a human work and therefore violates the doctrine of *sola fide*. He confuses biblical repentance with medieval-Catholic "penance," which in fact is a humanly-contrived, meritorious view of earning forgiveness. Biblical repentance is the human response in faith, and attitude change, toward one's sin which results from the inner working of the Holy Spirit, Who convicts the human heart (John 16:8-11; Acts 16:14). Repentance is not a work of man, but a work wrought by God manifest by man. Repentance is a gift from God— just as faith, grace, forgiveness, and every good thing regarding salvation is a gift from God (Eph 2:8-9).[68] So Hodges confounds the whole issue.

A definitive example from the teachings of Jesus illustrating that "repentance" is at the heart of the saving gospel is in Luke 18. The self-righteous Pharisee prayed to and praised himself. At a distance from him was the outcast tax collector who prayed a prayer of repentance in faith that saved him:

> But the tax collector, standing some distance away, was even unwilling to lift up his eyes to heaven, but was beating his breast, saying, 'God, be merciful to me, the sinner!' I tell you, this man went to his house justified rather than the other; for everyone who exalts himself will be humbled, but he who humbles himself will be exalted (vv. 13-14).

Jesus clearly says that the penitent sinner went home "justified."[69] So when we preach the gospel of Jesus, we must preach about the nature of sin and call sinners to repentance.

The Gospel is about the Resurrection

The truth of Jesus' resurrection from the dead is at the heart of the gospel of Jesus. That is what Paul says in 1 Corinthians 15:4—Jesus "was raised on the third day according to the Scriptures." That is Paul's whole argument in chapter fifteen for fifty-eight verses. If Jesus did not rise from the dead, then there is no Christianity, no salvation, no forgiveness of sins—our faith would be futile (15:14). But by rising from the dead, Jesus secured victory over sin, death, hell, the devil and the world and assumed the preeminence in all things (Phil 2:9-11; Rev 1:5, 17-18). Christ's resurrection validates all of God's promises and secures our eternal salvation. This is good news. Jesus is alive! This is the saving gospel. Because He lives, we also will live! (John 14:19).

Jesus commanded the Church to preach the gospel of the resurrection. Jesus set the example in Luke 24 when He said, "Thus it is written, that the Christ shall suffer and rise again from the dead the third day, and that repentance for forgiveness of sins shall be proclaimed in His name to all nations, beginning from Jerusalem" (vv. 46-47). Notice the parallels of Christ's message here with what Paul says in 1 Corinthians 15 about the gospel—they are identical. Jesus' gospel includes "good news" (forgiveness) and "one gospel" (all the nations). His message is Christo-centric. And He mentions "sin," "repentance," and the reality of His death and the glory of His resurrection.

The early church preached the resurrection as an essential component of the gospel.[70] The first sermon Peter ever preached after Christ's ascension was a gospel presentation, the cornerstone of which is the reality of Christ's resurrection, which he mentions more than four times (Acts 2:22-36). Paul also preached the gospel of the resurrection. Acts 17:18 declares that Paul was accustomed to "preaching Jesus and the resurrection." Similarly, in Philippians, Paul says the essence of being a Christian is "that I may know Him and the power of His resurrection" (3:10). There is no gospel without the truth of the resurrection. There is no salvation if one neglects this truth. Paul said unequivocally, "if you confess with your mouth Jesus as Lord, and believe in your heart that God raised Him from the dead, you will be saved" (Rom 10:9). Being saved is contingent upon believing in the *risen* Christ.[71]

Despite the blatant truth that Jesus' resurrection is at the very heart of the full gospel message, unfortunately this truth is grossly neglected in the evangelical Church today. Just a cursory overview of many gospel tracts will reveal the reality of the ongoing dissemination of an emasculated gospel, as many omit the resurrection (or some other essential element of the gospel) in their presentation of the good news.

Trite gospel tracts are not the only culprits here. Pastors and theologians who should know better have done the same. For example, in a special issue of *Christianity Today*,[72] nine evangelical "experts" were asked to give a written summary of the essential gospel in 300 words. Two of the nine did not even mention the resurrection! (Only one of the nine referred to 1 Corinthians 15 in reference to the gospel. Four of the nine gave no Bible verses whatsoever. Only three of the nine refer to "repentance." Two experts failed to mention "sin." Only one refers to Jesus as God. And one expert apparently had a modalistic view of God! So much for the "experts"). These nine gospel experts perfectly illustrate the crisis in the Evangelical Church today regarding the confusion about what constitutes the gospel. These nine may have neglected key elements of the gospel by default. But there are others who are deliberate in their gospel truncation. For example, Robert Wilkin has gone on record to say the following: "it is possible to believe savingly in Christ without understanding the reality of His resurrection."[73] To the contrary, the Bible is clear—one must understand the reality of the resurrection to be saved. No resurrection, no salvation. The *Evangelical Celebration* got it right, for it declares the resurrection to be indispensable to the gospel:

> This Gospel further proclaims the bodily resurrection, ascension, and enthronement of Jesus as evidence of the efficacy of his once-for-all sacrifice for us, of the reality of his present personal ministry to us, and of the certainty of his future return to glorify us (1 Cor. 15; Heb. 1:1-4, 2:1-18, 4:14-16, 7:1-10:25)....10. We affirm that the bodily resurrection of Christ from the dead is essential to the biblical Gospel (1 Cor. 15:14).[74]

The Gospel is Appropriated by Faith

Paul says in 1 Corinthians 15:2 that the Corinthian Christians were "saved" because they "believed" in the gospel. "Believed" is from *pisteuō* and means "to believe, also to be persuaded of, and hence, to place confidence in, to trust, signifies in this sense of the word, reliance upon, not mere credence."[75] Paul said, "For I am not ashamed of the gospel, for it is the power of God for salvation to everyone who *believes*" (Rom 1:16). So salvation is received or appropriated by believing or by exercising faith in the gospel.[76]

To believe in the gospel means to believe in all the elements of the gospel. To become a Christian people must believe in who Jesus is—that He is God incarnate, the Lord (Acts 16:31; 18:8; Rom 10:9), the Savior (Luke 2:11), and the only way to the Father (John 14:6). They must believe in God the Father (John 5:24). They must believe that they are sinners in need of forgiveness. They must believe that Jesus died for their sins. They must believe that Jesus rose from the dead and is the living Lord (Matt 22:32). One must act on his faith and ask God to forgive him of his sins (Rom 10:13)—i.e. one must repent.[77] That's what it means to believe in the gospel. There are no human works here in this scenario. People bring nothing to the equation of salvation except their sin and the prayer of faith and repentance. Salvation is totally of God—a free gift from Him (Ps 80:3; Jonah 2:9). But one must believe in the whole package, not just the wrapping.

Summary

First Peter 3:15 exhorts Christians to defend "the hope" that is in them when unbelievers inquire about that hope. Scripture says the hope we defend is the hope we have in the gospel—"the hope of the gospel that you have heard" (Col 1:23). And it is the hope we have in Christ Himself, for "Christ Jesus is our hope" (1 Tim 1:1). According to the Bible, apologetics is the act of advancing and defending our hope in Christ and the gospel. But traditional apologists typically avoid the gospel altogether in their apologetic endeavors. Christian apologetics urgently needs a drastic reformation, and needs to begin by making the advancement and defense of the gospel the preeminent priority.

Not only is a recalibration of a foundational starting point necessary for apologetics, there also needs to be a fresh biblical examination of what the gospel message actually entails. There is confusion in the evangelical Church today about what constitutes the "gospel of Jesus Christ." Although the true gospel is simple, many versions of it are anemic, insufficient, and convoluted. Such versions of the gospel are ineffectual. Such versions result by straying from the compass of Scripture. It has been proposed that 1 Corinthians 15:1-4 should be paradigmatic for Christians when it comes to understanding, articulating, and proclaiming the gospel.

In 1 Corinthians 15, Paul explicitly says "this is the gospel." We should take note of what follows as he delineates the flashpoints of gospel truth—the indispensable priorities and essentials of the saving message of Jesus. First, the gospel is "good news." It is a specific message, with specific content, about hope. The good news is that God has provided a way for hell-bound sinners[78] to be totally forgiven, accepted, reconciled and adopted into the family of God, and they can enjoy eternal life with Him, beginning now and extending into eternity.

Second, Paul says the gospel is about "Christ." Our gospel message orbits around the Person of Christ—all that He is and all that He did. He is the eternal God who took on human flesh; He is the only way to have forgiveness, the only way to know God, the only way to get to heaven. In simplest terms, the gospel is "Jesus"!

Third, the gospel entails preaching about "sin." That's what Paul said in 1 Corinthians 15:3. Sin entered the world through Adam. Sin separates us from God. Every person is a sinner from birth. Sin deserves to be punished. We cannot save ourselves from sin. Death and hell are the wages of sin.

Fourth, the gospel entails preaching about the meaning and significance of Christ's death. Sin has been conquered by Christ's atoning death. He "died for sins." Jesus willingly got punished for the sins of the world. Jesus' death was the only acceptable sacrifice that could appease God's holy wrath and justice because Jesus was God (so He provided an infinite sacrifice) and Jesus was sinless (He provided a perfect sacrifice). Jesus' death is the only thing that can forgive sin and reconcile a sinner to God. Jesus' death provides eternal life, forgiveness, redemption, reconciliation, acquittal and adoption.

Fifth, the gospel entails preaching about Jesus' resurrection from the dead. Jesus' resurrection fulfilled prophecy, validated all the promises of God, conquered sin, death, the devil, hell and the world, and vindicated Jesus Christ as the rightful King over all the universe. Jesus' resurrection guarantees that He will likewise redeem our lowly bodies after the pattern of His glorious body. To be saved, a sinner must believe that Jesus rose from the dead.

Sixth, the gospel is appropriated and made efficacious by "faith" —by believing in the truths of the good news listed above. Believing also includes "repenting" whereby one agrees with God's verdict that we are all undeserving sinners. Repenting entails asking God to forgive one's sins in Christ. Confessing sins is a prayer of faith (Luke 18:13). Repentance is not a human work, for salvation is a gift from God. Repentance is the result of the Holy Spirit's convicting work on the human heart that manifests itself in a heart and attitude change, enabling one to believe in the gospel (John 16:8-11; Acts 16:14). So repentance, along with the whole work of salvation, is a gift (Jonah 2:9) from God.

Finally, the gospel is "according to the Scriptures" (1 Cor 15:3-4). The gospel is a specific, yet comprehensive message, sufficiently explained in God's written Word, the Bible. The gospel is therefore from God—supernatural revelation. Being "according to the Scriptures," the gospel is one consistent message, for all people, for all time. And because it is "according to the Scriptures" it entails more than any one isolated Bible verse or truth, that might be set forth in contradistinction from the rest of written revelation—which results in an insufficient, misrepresentative, truncated gospel. In other words, the gospel of Jesus needs to be taught, preached, understood and appropriated in light of the "whole purpose of God" (Acts 20:27).

Do you want to do the work of an apologist? Then begin and end with the life-changing power of the gospel of Jesus Christ. It is the most potent weapon against unbelief that God has entrusted to the Church. One of the most influential pastors of all time knew this to be true. We do well to heed his inimitable exhortation:

> Brethren, if you want to answer infidelity, preach the gospel; tell the people that Jesus Christ is able to save sinners. Lift high the blood-stained cross, proclaim liberty to the captives, and the opening of the prisons to them that are bound. This will make a stir, this will agitate the masses. There is nothing like it. Christ's gospel is like the fire flung amongst the standing corn, it makes a wondrous conflagration. Preach Jesus Christ and him crucified, the people must come to hear it, they are not masters of themselves, they cannot stay away; and as they hear it, and as they feed upon it, and joy comes unto them, and peace, and new life, facts will answer theories, salvation will be the test reply to the witticisms and the sophistries of unbelief. Do not enter into arguments, but test the gospel practically. Somebody says that yonder lifeboat is not of the right colour. I see a number of men in the rigging of yonder sinking vessel: they cannot hold on much longer. Here, good fellows, do not stand debating about the boat, jump into it, pull out to the vessel, get the men on board, and bring them to shore. Hurrah! Here they are! If they tell us that the gospel which we preach is not true, we point to many here present whose stories of reclamation from vice and deliverance from despair and uplifting into light and life and holiness are proofs that the gospel is divine. There they are! Facts, facts, facts, these are God's replies.[79]

Notes

1. Steven B. Cowan, ed., *Five Views On Apologetics* (Grand Rapids: Zondervan, 2000).

2. Ibid., 229.

3. Ibid., 314.

4. Ibid., 28, 29, 37, 38, 43, 53-55, 134.

5. Ibid., 53.

6. Ibid., 315. See Pannenberg's lengthy, convoluted treatise on his elusive definition of the "Word of God" in his systematic theology (pp. 230-257). In it he makes the absurd assertion that, "the Word of God never has in the Bible the direct sense of the self-disclosure or self-revelation of God"; Wolfhart Pannenberg, *Systematic Theology, vol. 1*, translated by Geoffrey W. Bromiley (Grand Rapids, MI: Eerdmans Publishing Company, 1991), 240. For a reliable expose of Barthian, neo-orthodox and related proposed, subjective dichotomies made between the Bible and God's revelation, see Cornelius Van Til, *Christianity and Barthianism* (Philadelphia, PA: 1962), 117-145.

7. Some of Pinnock's more pertinent writings include the following: *A Defense of Biblical Infallibility* (Philadelphia: P & R, 1967); *Set Forth Your Case: An Examination of Christianity's Credentials* (Nutley, NJ: Craig Press 1968); Pinnock wrote an essay in the *Festschrift* dedicated to Cornelius Van Til in *Jerusalem and Athens: Critical Discussions on the Philosophy and Theology of Cornelius Van Til* (Philadelphia: P & R, 1971); *Biblical Revelation: The Foundation of Christian Theology* (Chicago: Moody, 1971); *Reason Enough: A Case for the Christian Faith* (Downers Grove, Ill.: InterVarsity, 1980); *A Wideness in God's Mercy* (Grand Rapids: Zondervan, 1992); *The Grace of God and the Will of Man*, ed. (Minneapolis: Bethany House, 1995); *Most Moved Mover: A Theology of God's Openness* (Grand Rapids: Baker, 2001).

8. Dennis L. Okholm, ed. *Four Views on Salvation in a Pluralistic World* (Grand Rapids: Zondervan, 1996), 100.

9. *A Wideness in God's Mercy*, 158.

10. *Four Views on Salvation*, 107.

11. Ibid., 110.

12. Ibid., 110.

13. Ibid., 110.

14. *A Wideness in God's Mercy*, 157.

15. Ibid., 171.

16. *Four Views on Salvation*, 107.

17. R. C. Sproul, *Defending Your Faith: An Introduction to Apologetics* (Wheaton: Crossway, 2003), 23.

18. R. C. Sproul, John Gerstner and Arthur Lindsley *Classical Apologetics: A Rational Defense of the Christian Faith and a Critique of Presuppositional Apologetics* (Grand Rapids: Zondervan, 1984), 21.

19. For example, in R. C. Sproul's helpful treatise on biblical justification, any discussion of 1 Corinthians 15 and the topic of the resurrection is conspicuously neglected; see, *Faith Alone: The Evangelical Doctrine of Justification* (Grand Rapids: Baker Books, 1995).

20. Cornelius Van Til, *The Defense of the Faith* (Phillipsburg, NJ: P & R, 1967).

21. Ibid., 18-19.

22. Greg Bahnsen, *Always Ready: Directions for Defending the Faith*, edited by Robert R. Booth (Texarkana, AR: Covenant Media Foundation, 1996).

23. Greg Bahnsen, *Five Views on Law and Gospel*, edited by Stanley Gundry (Grand Rapids MI: Zondervan, 1996), 97.

24. N. T. Wright, *Evil and the Justice of God* (Downers Grove, IL: InterVarsity, 2006), 90.

25. Ibid., 102-104, 107; see also the many good works exposing Wright's skewed, subtle and highly misleading soteriology: *The Master's Seminary Journal*, 16/2, Fall, 2005; John Piper, *The Future of Justification: A Response to N. T. Wright* (Wheaton, IL: Crossway Books, 2007); Phil Johnson, "What's Wrong with Wright?" in *The Grace Life Pulpit*, *www.thegracelife pulpit.com/Articles.aspx?code=PJ-A15.*

26. Calvin, *Institutes*, 269, 275. Calvin summarizes the comprehensive meaning of a Christ-centered gospel like no other in this paragraph from 500 years ago: "If we seek salvation, we are taught by the very name of Jesus that He possesses it; if we seek any other gifts of the Spirit, we shall find them in His unction; strength in His government; purity in His conception; indulgence in His nativity, in which He was made like us in all respects, in order that He might learn to sympathize with us: if we seek redemption, we shall find it in His passion; acquittal in His condemnation; remission of the curse in His cross; satisfaction in His sacrifice; purification in His blood; reconciliation in His descent to hell; mortification of the flesh in His sepulcher; newness of life in His resurrection; immortality also in His resurrection; the inheritance of a celestial kingdom in His entrance into heaven; protection, security, and the abundant supply of all blessings, in His kingdom; secure anticipation of judgment in the power of judging committed to Him. In fine, since in Him all kinds of blessings are treasured up, let us draw full supply from Him, and none from any other quarter"; *Institutes*, 338.

27. John MacArthur, *Hard to Believe* (Nashville: Thomas Nelson, 2003), 187.

28. See Walter Chantry's classic, *Today's Gospel: Authentic or Synthetic?* (Carlisle, Pennsylvania: The Banner of Truth Trust, 1970). In what is an otherwise

helpful little book on the gospel, Chantry never mentions the resurrection as an essential element of the saving gospel, nor does he make mention of 1 Corinthians 15 at all. Ironically, Chantry concludes his book with the stern words, "True evangelism preaches the whole counsel of God with explanation and application to sinners" (91), but he never mentions the resurrection! Similarly, in another polemic against easy-believism, James Boice made some helpful soteriological observations, but regrettably neglects the priority of the resurrection as a priority of the gospel message; see *Whatever Happened to the Gospel of Grace?: Rediscovering the Doctrines that Shook the World* (Wheaton, IL: Crossway Books, 2001). Also, the ECT accord, *Evangelicals and Catholics Together: The Christian Mission in the Third Millennium* (1994); [Printed in First Things, no. 43 (May 1994):15-22] and ECT II, also known as *The Gift of Salvation*, it is the follow-up document to ECT signed by fifteen Roman Catholics and eighteen Evangelicals (including Bill Bright, Charles Colson, Max Lucado, and J. I. Packer, among others), the purpose of which is to elucidate their common understanding in salvation and the truth of the gospel. In their nineteen assertions they never mention or quote the gospel as delineated in 1 Corinthians 15. The document has been printed in *Christianity Today*, 8 December 1997, 35-36, 38. Further, John Piper exhorts fellow preachers to make a priority of preaching the true gospel, but when he delineates what the message is, it entails no resurrection truth!; see, *Brothers, We Are Not Professionals:* "Brothers, Live and Preach Justification by Faith" (Nashville: Holman Publishers, 2002), 17-32. This is apparently an all too common occurrence of a default on an all too important and essential element of the gospel.

29. Hodges was a New Testament professor for almost thirty years at Dallas Seminary. His prominent works on salvation include *The Gospel Under Siege* (Dallas: Redencion Viva, 1981); *Absolutely Free* (Dallas: Redencion, 1989) and *Harmony With God* (Dallas: Redencion Viva, 2001). In these works he never refers to the resurrection of Christ as an essential component of the gospel. Although he championed himself as a guardian of the purity of the one true gospel, he gave nary a word on 1 Corinthians 15 in all his discussions on what he said constituted the true gospel. Yet plainly, Paul makes it clear in 1 Corinthians 15 that the resurrection of Christ is at the very core of the gospel.

30. Trent C. Butler, ed. *Holman Bible Dictionary* (Nashville: Holman Bible Publishers, 1991), 569.

31. The "gospel of Christ" (1 Cor 9:12) is described in many ways in the NT, illustrating its multi-faceted beauty and complexity like a fine diamond, i.e.: "the gospel of God" (Mark 1:14); "the gospel of His Son" (Rom 1:9);

"the gospel of the kingdom" (Matt 4:23); "the gospel" (11:5); "the gospel of the grace of God" (Acts 20:24); "the gospel of the glory of Christ" (2 Cor 4:4); "the gospel of ...salvation" (Eph 1:13) "the gospel of peace" (6:15); the "eternal gospel" (Rev 14:6).

32. Charles C. Ryrie, *So Great Salvation* (Wheaton, IL: Victor Books, 1989) 38-39.

33. Lewis Sperry Chafer, *Grace: The Glorious Theme* (Grand Rapids: Dunham Publishers, 1922), 132.

34. Chafer, *Systematic Theology*, (Dallas: Dallas Seminary Press, 1948), VII: 98-99.

35. Chafer, *Grace*, 122-135; John D. Hannah, long-time professor of Historical Theology at Dallas Seminary, posits that Chafer "seemed to denigrate the revelation of God in the Old Testament" which "created in his mind...a discontinuity between the two testaments that became a defining characteristic in his understanding of the Bible," <'Chafer, Lewis Sperry' dirnOnline: Lewis Sperry Chafer, 5>.

36. Chafer, *Systematic Theology*, VII:219.

37. John MacArthur, *Faith Works: The Gospel According to the Apostles* (Dallas: Word Publishing, 1993), 279; for details, see *The Scofield Reference Bible* (New York: Oxford, 1917), 1115.

38. Robert L. Thomas, *Evangelical Hermeneutics: The New Versus the Old* (Grand Rapids: Kregel, 2002), 64-65.

39. Walter Chantry, *Today's Gospel: Authentic or Synthetic* (Carlisle, Pennsylvania: The Banner of Truth Trust, reprint, 2001) 45, 91-92. MacArthur's words are profound on this matter of preaching the whole gospel in all its requisite components: "the gospel is not a message that can be capsulated, abridged, and shrink-wrapped, then offered as a generic remedy for every kind of sinner. Ignorant sinners need to be instructed about who God is and why He has the right to demand their obedience. Self-righteous sinners need to have their sin exposed by the demands of God's law. Careless sinners need to be confronted with the reality of God's impending judgment. Fearful sinners need to hear that God in His mercy has provided a way of deliverance. All sinners must understand how utterly holy God is. They must comprehend the basic truths of Christ's sacrificial death and the triumph of His resurrection. They need to be confronted with God's demand that they turn from their sin to embrace Christ as Lord and Savior"; John MacArthur, *Evangelism: How to Share the Gospel Faithfully* (Nashville, TN: Thomas Nelson, 2011), 152.

40. An excellent example of how to do this is given by J. I. Packer in *Evangelism and the Sovereignty of God* (Downers Grove, IL: InterVarsity, 1961) 37-73; also, see other help Will Metzger, *Tell the Truth* (Downers

Grove, IL: InterVarsity, 1996); Mark Dever, *The Gospel and Personal Evangelism* (Wheaton: Crossway Books, 2007); Greg Gilbert, *What is the Gospel?* (Wheaton: Crossway Books, 2010); Ray Comfort, *The Way of the Master* (Alachua, FL: Bridge-Logos, 2006).

41. Hodges, *Harmony with God*, 29.

42. Ibid., 55.

43. Ibid., 123; see also Zane Hodges, *Absolutely Free*, 144, 154, 202-203.

44. Robert N. Wilkin, *Confident In Christ: Living by Faith Really Works* (Irving, Texas: Grace Evangelical Society, 1999), 210.

45. See, Walter Chantry, *Today's Gospel*, for a thorough exegesis of this passage and why Jesus gave such a response.

46. Bruce Demarest says, "Christ's death on the cross…is the central, indeed crucial doctrine of the faith….The importance of the cross is reflected in part by the attention Scripture gives to the death of Jesus Christ….there are 175 direct references to his death in the NT"; *The Cross and Salvation* (Wheaton, IL: Crossway Books, 1997) 166-67.

47. Christ's death was a "propitiation" (*hilasterion*) that satisfied God's wrath because of His hatred of sin as a holy God; see, George J. Zemek, *A Biblical Theology of the Doctrines of Sovereign Grace: Exegetical Considerations of Key Anthropological, Hamartiological and Soteriological Terms and Motifs* (Little Rock, AR: B.T.D.S.G., 2002) 129-131.

48. *exagorazo*, "buy back."

49. *agorazo*, "paid for and taken home."

50. *lutrosetai*, "purchased from the slave market."

51. *katellasso*, our relationship "changed" with God—we are now at peace.

52. *huper*, "instead of " or "in behalf of."

53. *dikaiosis*, a forensic term meaning "acquit," "declare righteous" the opposite of "condemn"; soteriologically, "justification" for the believer is legal, personal, immediate, complete, final and irrevocable; see, Leon Morris, *The Apostolic Preaching of the Cross* (Grand Rapids: Eerdmans, 2001), 251-298; James R. White, *The God Who Justifies* (Minneapolis: Bethany House, 2001), 64-92; Henry W. Holloman, *Kregel Dictionary of the Bible and Theology* (Grand Rapids: Kregel, 2005), 266-68. The reader needs to be aware and leery of the recent distortion of the biblical teaching on "justification" as seen in *The New Perspective* movement. An example is N. T. Wright's explanation of "justification" in *New Dictionary of Theology*, edited by Sinclair Ferguson, David Wright, and J. I. Packer (Downers Grove: InterVarsity, 1988), 359-361.

54. Since the 1970's, prominent anti-Lordship salvationists have tried to redefine the historic definition of "repentance" as taught in the Bible by over-emphasizing the etymological root of *metanoia*, which means "to

change the mind." They allege "repentance" simply entails one changing one's mind about who Jesus is and they say it has no relation to one's view of personal sin whatsoever. They also purport that repentance has nothing to do with changing one's behavior. But such a notion is fallacious. "*Metanoia* can be said to denote that inward change of mind, affections, convictions, and commitment, rooted in the fear of God and sorrow for offenses committed against Him, which, when accompanied by faith in Jesus Christ, results in an outward turning from sin to God and His service in all of life," Charles F. Pfeiffer, Howrd F. Vos, John Rea, editors, *Wycliffe Bible Dictionary* (Peabody: Hendrickson, 1999), 1453; cf. Holloman, *Kregel Dictionary*, 453-455. Repentance is a call to turn from sin. Ray Comfort sets the record straight by reminding Christians of the priority of calling the sinner to repentance in the work of evangelism with unbelievers: "Jesus used the Moral Law to reveal the man's hidden sin—his love of money above all else. Why did Jesus use the Ten Commandments? His method seems a bit archaic compared to the quick and easy modern methods of making instant converts. Dr. Martyn Lloyd-Jones gives us the answer: 'A gospel which merely says "Come to Jesus," and offers Him as a Friend, and offers a marvelous new life, without convincing of sin, is not New Testament evangelism. (The essence of evangelism is to start by preaching the Law; and it is because the Law has not been preached that we have had so much superficial evangelism.) True evangelism...must always start by preaching the Law....'" When you use the Law to show lost sinners their true state, be prepared for them to thank you. For the first time in their lives, they will see the Christian message as expressing love and concern for their eternal welfare rather than merely proselytizing for a better lifestyle while on this earth. They will begin to understand why they should be concerned about their eternal salvation. The Law shows them that they are condemned by God. It even makes them a little fearful—and 'the fear of the Lord is the beginning of wisdom' (Ps 111:10; Prov 9:10)"; *The Way of the Master* (Alachua, FL: Bridge-Logos, 2006), 48-49.

55. Wilkin, *Confident in Christ*, 210; Wilkin has also gone on record to say, "I do not believe that one *must* recognize that he is a sinner to be saved"; 'Letters to the Editor', *The Grace Evangelical Society News* (August, 1990), 3.

56. Hodges, *Harmony With God*, 3.

57. Ibid., 9, 49, 57, 62, 93, 109.

58. Ibid., 10. Earl Radmacher, former President of Western Seminary, has also embraced the "non-repentance" view; he says, "Repentance is not necessary...for entering into an eternal saving relationship with Jesus"; *Salvation* (Nashville: Thomas Nelson, 2000), 135. Unfortunately, Chuck

Swindoll also adopted Wilkin's "non-repentance" view; see, *Understanding Christian Theology* (Nashville: Thomas Nelson, 2003), 938-944. Similarly, John Walvoord, another Dallas Seminary guy, says, "The divine message is not...'believe and repent,'" *Major Bible Themes* (Grand Rapids: Academic, 1974), 187.

59. Hodges, *Harmony*, 123.

60. "The Gospel of Jesus Christ: An Evangelical Celebration," Affirmations and Denials, #16.

61. Zane Hodges, *Absolutely Free!* (Grand Rapids: Zondervan, 1989), 147-148.

62. D. A. Carson has done an excellent job of exposing Hodges' hermeneutical foibles in his helpful little book, *Exegetical Fallacies* (Grand Rapids: Baker, 1984).

63. Hodges, *Harmony*, 99.

64. Ibid., 97.

65. Ibid., 100.

66. Chafer's theology influenced countless professors and students who followed at Dallas Seminary over the years. For example, J. Dwight Pentecost, long-time Professor of Biblical Exposition at Dallas, perpetuated Chafer's unbiblical "non-repentance" view in his teachings and writings. While Pentecost has contributed much helpful material in areas like eschatology and theology in general, unfortunately he did not escape the Chafer curse on simple soteriology. In, *Things Which Become Sound Doctrine*, Pentecost goes so far as to say it is "Satanic" to require the unbeliever to repent in order to be saved: "Satan's method of deceiving men has been to add to the simplicity of the gospel. That is why some will teach that salvation is by...faith plus repentance" (Grand Rapids: Zondervan, 1965, 1969, 1976), 61.

67. Chafer, *Salvation* (Grand Rapids: Dunham, 1917), 48. Strangely, five years later Chafer said the following: "*Repentance*, which means 'a change of mind,' is never *excluded* from the terms of salvation; it is *included* as an essential part of believing....It is impossible for a person to believe who does not repent," *Grace*, 18.

68. Even on this point Hodges goes astray from historical orthodoxy and exegetical consistency when he alleges that "faith" is not a gift from God!; see, *Absolutely Free!*, 259. Here Hodges is even in direct conflict with his predecessor, Chafer who affirmed that, "Even the faith by which [salvation] is received is itself a *gift* from God"; *The Ephesian Letter* (Findly, Ohio: Dunham, 1935), 79.

69. Literally, "the sinner," [Gk. *toi hamartoloi*] the presence of the article before the noun is emphatic. Also of note, this is one of the only two times the word "justified" is used in the Gospels, and in this context it is used soter-

iologocially. The Greek is *dedikaiomenos*, from *dikaioō*, perfect passive participle, "to justify, to declare righteous. Perf. looks at the completed state; i.e., the state of having been declared to be in the right....Theol. pass. indicating that God is the One justifying"; Cleon L. Rogers, Jr. *The New Linguistic and Exegetical Key to the Greek New Testament* (Grand Rapids: Zondervan, 1998), 155.

70. 26 of the 27 New Testament books refer explicitly to the reality and importance of Christ's resurrection by either declaration or by reference to "Jesus" as the living Savior and Lord; Third John is the one exception, although it does make reference to "the Name" (v. 7).

71. Refer to the several examples already delineated in the beginning of this chapter.

72. *Christianity Today*, (vol 44. num. 2, Feb. 7, 2000); 46-51; the "gospel experts" include Myron Augsburger, Darrell Bock, David Dockery, Ajith Fernando, Cheryl Johns, Roberta Hestenes, Dennis Kinlaw, Robert Smith Jr. and Steven Voth.

73. Robert Wilkin, "Tough Questions About Saving Faith", *The Grace Evangelical Society News* (June 1990), 1.

74. *Christianity Today*, "The Gospel of Jesus Christ: An Evangelical Celebration," (vol. 43, num. 7; June 14, 1999), 52, 55.

75. Zemek, *Sovereign Grace*, 177. Few have written more definitively, clearly and biblically on the nature of true, "saving faith" than John Calvin. For a masterful and unparalleled tutorial on "faith" the reader is referred to three chapters in his *Institutes*: "Of Faith: The Definition of It," "Regeneration by Faith," and "Of Justification by Faith." A few jewels to consider: "Faith itself is produced only by the Spirit"; "Faith has respect to God only"; "Faith has all its stability in Christ"; "Faith consists not in ignorance, but in knowledge—knowledge not of God merely, but of the divine will"; "Take away the Word and no faith will remain"; "Faith...is the instrument of receiving justification"; "the power of justifying is ascribed to faith"; "To have faith is not to fluctuate, to vary, to be carried up and down, to hesitate, remain in suspense, vacillate, in fine, to despair; it is to possess sure certainty and complete security of mind, to have whereon to rest and fix your foot"; "For, in regard to justification, faith is merely passive, bringing nothing of our own to procure the favor of God, but receiving from Christ everything that we want."

76. And faith comes only from hearing the Word of Christ, or from Scripture, Romans 10:17.

77. At times "repent" is used synonymously for "believe" and vice versa; cf. Matthew 3:2 with Acts 19:4 as an example where "repent" means "to believe"; for a thorough study on this issue, see James E. Rosscup, "The

Relation of Repentance to Salvation and the Christian Life," unpublished paper delivered at ETS (Arrowhead Springs, CA, 1988). Another thorough and excellent study on this truth is Richard Owen Roberts, *Repentance: The First Word of the Gospel* (Wheaton: Crossway Books, 2002); cf. Acts 11:21; 19:18.

78. The fact that Jesus saves some from going to hell implies that others are going there—that is what the Bible teaches (Matt 7:13-14; 2 Thess 1:7-9; Rev 14:9-11; 19:20; 20:14-15). Contrast this with the very popular universalist, Brennan Manning, who talks about gospel truth, but affirms that everyone is going to heaven because God's love is "unconditional." He says, "the Father of Jesus loves all, no matter what they do...Have you learned to think of the Father as the judge...? If you think that way, you are wrong," *The Ragamuffin Gospel* (Sisters, Oregon: Multnomah, 2000), 22, 75. Manning is not alone in his rejection of the biblical teaching on an eternal, conscious, physical, deserved hell of torment, some others include E. G. Selwyn, John Stott, Michael Green, Philip Hughes, John Wenham, Stephan Travis, N.T. Wright, Brian McLaren, to name a few.

79. C. H. Spurgeon, "Beware of Unbelief," a sermon delivered at the *Metropolitan Tabernacle*, Newington, London, England, June 6, 1875.

Appendix 1

Presuppositions of Biblical Apologetics
vs.
Traditional Apologetics

Biblical	Traditional
1. assumes God exists; no need to prove His existence	1. tries to prove God probably exists
2. uses the Bible as the ultimate authority for truth	2. human reason & laws of logic are ultimate authority for truth
3. human reason is subject to biblical scrutiny	3. Bible is subject to scrutiny of human reason & laws of logic
4. apologetics is an action; it's what we do	4. apologetics is a noun, i.e., either a person (apologist) or field of study
5. *apologia* is broad, informal and in reference to the gospel	5. *apologia* is formal, forensic, secular and isolated from the gospel
6. apologetics is a mandate for every Christian	6. is primarily reserved for philosophers & scholars
7. apologetics is in the domain of biblical theology	7. apologetics is in the domain of philosophy & metaphysics
8. apologetics begins with religionists inside the Church	8. apologetics is primarily for skeptics outside the Church
9. apologetics is directed toward all unbelievers	9. apologetics is primarily geared toward atheists & agnostics
10. pastors are called to be specialized in apologetics	10. pastors should leave apologetics to the professional philosophers

Biblical	Traditional
11. apologetics is holistic/a lifestyle	11. primarily an intellectual exercise
12. 1 Peter 3:15 needs to be understood in the biblical context	12. does not exegete 1 Peter 3:15 in a biblcal context
13. Acts 20 is a major apologetics passage	13. ignores Acts 20 as a paradigm for apologetics
14. assumes Christianity is certain/true and other religions are false/evil	14. Christianity is merely the most plausible of all the competing worldviews
15. defends the whole Christian faith and the gospel	15. defends theism & the possibility of miracles
16. faith results only from hearing God's Word in Scripture/divine revelation	16. saving faith can result from natural theology and general revelation
17. Scripture is autopistic/self-validating	17. Scripture has to be proven to be true & is not self-validating
18. today, only Scripture is the Word of God	18. the Word of God includes more than the Bible
19. the greatest impediment to belief is personal sin and satanic blindness	19. the greatest impediment to belief is ignorance and intellectual speculations
20. the *sensus divinitatis* is intuitive	20. the *sensus divinitatis* is learned/discovered
21. natural revelation is only sufficient to condemn	21. natural revelation produces faith & is the basis of natural theology
22. natural revelation is always rejected by unbelievers	22. natural revelation is welcomed by unbelievers
23. special revelation is essential for true faith	23. special revelation is not the only source for saving faith

Biblical	Traditional
24. there is no natural theology	24. natural theology is foundational
25. there is metaphysical common ground	25. common ground is more than metaphysical
26. no epistemological common ground	26. epistemological common ground
27. no neutrality with the unbeliever	27. there is neutral ground with the unbeliever
28. all people are innately religious	28. some people are not religious
29. total depravity has skewed the mind	29. the fallen mind is neutral
30. there is common ground in the *imago Dei*, conscience & *sensus divinitatis*	30. no *sensus divinitatis* (for some); *imago Dei* not the basis for common ground
31. apologetics, preaching, evangelism & theology are all organically interrelated	31. apologetics is typically separated from theology, preaching and evangelism
32. Plato & Aristotle were lost pagans	32. Plato & Aristotle are models for Christians to follow
33. Augustinian and Calvinistic in soteriology and anthropology	33. Arminian/Thomistic/Romanist in soteriology and anthropology
34. champions total sufficiency, inspiration and perspicuity of Scripture	34. undermines bibliology, sufficiency and perspicuity
35. consistent use of grammatical-historical hermeneutics	35. allegorical hermeneutics and the analogy of Scripture
36. priority given to Hebrew/Greek	36. priority given to Latin
37. the *Testimonium* includes the Holy Spirit working with Scripture	37. Misinterprets the Reformers' view of the *Testimonium*

Biblical	Traditional
38. hamartiology determinative	38. hamartiology not developed
39. efficacious evidences derive from special revelation	39. efficacious evidences derive from natural theology
40. theistic arguments are edifying for the believer; help establish unaffirmability with unbelievers	40. theistic arguments are positively helpful, establishing undeniability with unbelievers, creating faith
41. no prerequisites for evangelism	41. prerequisites for evangelism
42. pre-evangelism includes general revelation & the work of the Spirit	42. pre-evangelism includes natural theology; no special revelation
43. truth is certain	43. truth is probable
44. the 'hope' we defend is the gospel	44. the 'hope' we defend is theism
45. internal apologetics is paramount	45. ignores internal apologetics
46. Satan is a real person and blinds unbelievers	46. Satan is not a factor in apologetics
47. the starting point of apologetics is the knowledge of God	47. the starting point of apologetics is the knowledge of man
48. "faith" is *amen* and *pistis*	48. "faith" is *noticia, assentia* and *fiducia*
49. a literal and historical Genesis 1-3 is presupposed and determinative	49. a literal Genesis 1-3 is not required; Adam's fall and God's curse not determinative
50. welcomes biblical mysteries and antinomies where Scripture is silent	50. eschews biblical mysteries; seeks answers through philosophical conjecture
51. the Bible has inherent authority	51. the Bible's authority is derivitive

Appendix 2

Apologia and *Apologeomai* in the New Testament

Acts 22:1-3

[1]"'Brethren and fathers, hear my **defense** (*apologias*) which I now offer to you'. [2]And when they heard that he was addressing them in the Hebrew dialect, they became even more quiet; and he said, [3]'I am a Jew, born in Tarsus of Cilicia, but brought up in this city, educated under Gamaliel, strictly according to the law of our fathers, being zealous for God just as you all are today'."

Acts 25:16-19

[16]"I answered them that it is not the custom of the Romans to hand over any man before the accused meets his accusers face to face and has an opportunity to make his **defense** (*apologias*) against the charges. [17]So after they had assembled here, I did not delay, but on the next day took my seat on the tribunal and ordered the man to be brought before me. [18]When the accusers stood up, they *began* bringing charges against him not of such crimes as I was expecting, [19]but they *simply* had some points of disagreement with him about their own religion and about a dead man, Jesus, whom Paul asserted to be alive."

1 Corinthians 9:1-4

"Am I not free? Am I not an apostle? Have I not seen Jesus our Lord? Are you not my work in the Lord? [2]If to others I am not an apostle, at least I am to you; for you are the seal of my apostleship in the Lord. [3]My **defense** (*apologia*) to those who examine me is this: [4]Do we not have a right to eat and drink? [5]Do we not have a right to take along a believing wife, even as the rest of the apostles and the brothers of the Lord and Cephas?"

2 Corinthians 7:10-11

[10]"For the sorrow that is according to *the will of* God produces a repentance without regret, *leading* to salvation, but the sorrow of the world produces death. [11]For behold what earnestness this very thing, this godly sorrow, has produced in you: what **vindication** (*apologian*)

436

of yourselves, what indignation, what fear, what longing, what zeal, what avenging of wrong! In everything you demonstrated yourselves to be innocent in the matter."

Philippians 1:6-7, 15-16

"⁶*For I am* confident of this very thing, that He who began a good work in you will perfect it until the day of Christ Jesus. ⁷For it is only right for me to feel this way about you all, because I have you in my heart, since both in my imprisonment and in the **defense** (*apologia*) and confirmation of the gospel, you all are partakers of grace with me... ¹⁵Some, to be sure, are preaching Christ even from envy and strife, but some also from good will; ¹⁶ the latter do it out of love, knowing that I am appointed for the defense (*apologian*) of the gospel."

2 Timothy 4:14-17

¹⁴"Alexander the coppersmith did me much harm; the Lord will repay him according to his deeds. ¹⁵Be on guard against him yourself, for he vigorously opposed our teaching. ¹⁶At my first **defense** (*apologia*) no one supported me, but all deserted me; may it not be counted against them. ¹⁷But the Lord stood with me and strengthened me, so that through me the proclamation might be fully accomplished, and that all the Gentiles might hear; and I was rescued out of the lion's mouth"

1 Peter 3:13-16

¹³"Who is there to harm you if you prove zealous for what is good? ¹⁴But even if you should suffer for the sake of righteousness, you are blessed. AND DO NOT FEAR THEIR INTIMIDATION, AND DO NOT BE TROUBLED, ¹⁵but sanctify Christ as Lord in your hearts, always *being* ready to make a **defense** (*apologian*) to everyone who asks you to give an account for the hope that is in you, yet with gentleness and reverence; ¹⁶and keep a good conscience so that in the thing in which you are slandered, those who revile your good behavior in Christ will be put to shame."

Luke 12:11-12

¹¹When they bring you before the synagogues and the rulers and the authorities, do not worry about how or what you are to speak in **your**

defense (*apologēsēsthe*), or what you are to say; [12] for the Holy Spirit will teach you in that very hour what you ought to say."

Luke 21:12-15

[12] "But before all these things, they will lay their hands on you and will persecute you, delivering you to the synagogues and prisons, bringing you before kings and governors for My name's sake. [13] It will lead to an opportunity for your testimony. [14] So make up your minds not to prepare beforehand to **defend yourselves** (*apologēthēnai*); [15] for I will give you utterance and wisdom which none of your opponents will be able to resist or refute."

Acts 24:10-11

[10] "When the governor had nodded for him to speak, Paul responded: 'Knowing that for many years you have been a judge to this nation, I cheerfully **make my defense** (*apologoumai*), [11] since you can take note of the fact that no more than twelve days ago I went up to Jerusalem to worship'."

Acts 19:32-34

[32] "So then, some were shouting one thing and some another, for the assembly was in confusion and the majority did not know for what reason they had come together. [33] Some of the crowd concluded *it was* Alexander, since the Jews had put him forward; and having motioned with his hand, Alexander was intending to **make a defense** (*apologeisthai*) to the assembly. [34] But when they recognized that he was a Jew, a *single* outcry arose from them all as they shouted for about two hours, 'Great is Artemis of the Ephesians!'"

Acts 25:7-8

[7] "After Paul arrived, the Jews who had come down from Jerusalem stood around him, bringing many and serious charges against him which they could not prove, [8] while Paul said in **his own defense** (*apologoumenou*), 'I have committed no offense either against the Law of the Jews or against the temple or against Caesar'."

Acts 26:1-2, 24

[1] "Agrippa said to Paul, 'You are permitted to speak for yourself.' Then Paul stretched out his hand and proceeded to make his defense

(*apelogeito*): ² 'In regard to all the things of which I am accused by the Jews, I consider myself fortunate, King Agrippa, that I am about to make my defense (*apologeisthaia*) before you today...' ²⁴ While *Paul* was saying this in **his defense** (*apologoumenou*), Festus said in a loud voice, 'Paul, you are out of your mind! *Your* great learning is driving you mad'."

Romans 2:14-15

¹⁴ "For when Gentiles who do not have the Law do instinctively the things of the Law, these, not having the Law, are a law to themselves, ¹⁵ in that they show the work of the Law written in their hearts, their conscience bearing witness and their thoughts alternately accusing or else **defending them** (*apologeomai*)."

2 Corinthians 12:19

¹⁸ "I urged Titus to go, and I sent the brother with him. Titus did not take any advantage of you, did he? Did we not conduct ourselves in the same spirit and walk in the same steps? ¹⁹ All this time you have been thinking that we are **defending ourselves** (*apologoumetha*) to you. Actually, it is in the sight of God that we have been speaking in Christ; and all for your upbuilding, beloved."

Glossary of BIG Words

Ad hominem-a fancy Latin phrase literally meaning "to the man"; an informal fallacy that refers to attacking an opponent's character rather than answering his argument.

Alchemy-a form of chemistry and speculative philosophy practiced in the Middle Ages and the Renaissance and concerned principally with discovering methods for transmuting baser metals into gold and with finding a universal solvent and an elixir of life.

Allegorical-a method of interpreting the Bible in a non-literal, figurative, metaphorical, subjective, spitualized manner, in contrast to the grammatical-historical (literal/face value/normal) approach.

Anachronism-something or someone that is not in its correct historical or chronological time, especially a thing or person that belongs to an earlier time.

Analogical-meaning based on analogy; resemblance in some particulars between things otherwise unlike, e.g., a man's mind is like God's mind; a form of reasoning in which a similarity between two or more things is inferred from a known similarity between them in other respects.

Animus-strong dislike or enmity; hostile attitude; animosity.

Anthropic-of or pertaining to human beings or their span of existence on earth.

Anthropocentric-regarding the human being as the central fact of the universe; assuming human beings to be the final aim and end of the universe; viewing and interpreting everything in terms of human experience and values.

Apologia-the New Testament Greek word for "defense" as used in 1

Peter 3:15 from which we get the term "apologetics;" also used in Luke 12:11; 21:14; Acts 19:33; 22:1; Philippians 1:7; 1:17; 2 Timothy 4:16.

Appeasement-to yield or concede to the belligerent demands of (a nation, group, person, etc.) in a conciliatory effort, sometimes at the expense of justice or other honorable principles.

A posteriori-one of those fancy Medieval Latin phrases that philosophers use; from particular instances to a general principle or law; based upon actual observation or upon experimental data; an *a posteriori* argument that derives the theory from the evidence, in contrast to *a priori*; knowledge gained whose validity depends on experience of things observed through the senses; not existing in the mind prior to or independent of experience; arguments that logically follow from, or are dependent on, sense experience (i.e., the teleological argument).

A priori-the opposite of *a posteriori*; the truth of a statement or proposition is self-evident prior to or independent of experience; arguments that are logically prior to, or independent of, sense perception (i.e., the ontological argument).

Aprioristic-belief in, or reliance upon, *a priori* reasoning, arguments, or principles.

Arminian-from Jacobus Arminius (1560-1609) who taught conditional predestination; the view that says God chose those who would be saved based on God's knowledge ahead of time of how the sinner might choose; the ultimate choice for salvation is in the hands of the fallen, finite sinner; this is in contrast to unconditional election (the view of Augustine, Luther and Calvin), whereby God chooses some to be saved before the foundation of the world based solely on His good pleasure, thus the ultimate choice of salvation is in the hands of a good, perfect, holy sovereign God.

Autonomous-self-governing; independent; subject to its own laws only.

Autopistic-self-authenticating.

Axiology/axiological-the branch of philosophy dealing with values, as those of ethics, aesthetics or religion.

Bibliology-a systematic study of the doctrine of the Bible.

Canard-a false or baseless, usually derogatory story, report, or rumor.

Catechism-instruction by a series of questions and answers, especially a book containing such instruction on the religious doctrine of a Christian Church.

Chimerical-unreal; imaginary; visionary; wildly fanciful; highly unrealistic; illusory.

Circumlocutions-rambling, meandering, verbosity, prolixity; speaking around the topic.

Coherence-a theory of truth stating that the truth of any (true) proposition consists in its coherence with some specified set of propositions; sometimes called the consistency theory and is in contrast to the correspondence theory.

Common ground-a shared starting point between believer and unbeliever as the basis for dialogue about spiritual matters; traditional apologists say the primary area of common ground is in the area of epistemology whereas presuppositionalists say there is no epistemological common ground due to total depravity; but there is ontological common ground between the two parties since both were made in the image of God.

Concomitantly-existing or occurring with something else, often in a lesser way; accompanying; concurrent.

Contextualize/contextualization-a modern approach to hermeneutics adapted from the World Council of Churches from 1972; it incorporates application into the exegesis process and as a result allows for multiple meanings in any given text; this is in contrast to the time-honored approach to hermeneutics called the grammatical-historical method.

Correspondence-the theory of truth that says truth can be defined as those statements, propositions, affirmations, and judgments that correctly correspond to its extra-mental referent in the real world as it exists; truth value is contained in indicative statements about reality regardless of what anyone else thinks or feels about the matter; its traditional com-petitors, coherentist, pragmatist, and verificationist theories of truth, are often associated with idealism, anti-realism, or relativism.

Cosmology-the branch of philosophy dealing with the origin and general structure of the universe, with its parts, elements, and laws, and especially with such of its characteristics as space, time, causality, and freedom.

Derivative-not original; not primary; secondary.

Discursive-proceeding by reasoning or argument rather than in-tuition.

Doxological-God-honoring; praising God by making His glory pre-eminent.

Dualism-a world-view which admits that there are two independent and mutually irreducible ultimate beings, usually one good and one evil; in contrast, monism maintains that there is but one ultimate Being.

Ecclesiastical-of or pertaining to the Church or the clergy; churchly; clerical; not secular.

Efficacious-capable of having the desired result or effect; effective as a means, measure or remedy; in soteriology, that which can effect salvation or regeneration.

Eidetically-of visual, or sometimes auditory, images, exceptionally vivid and allowing detailed recall of something previously perceived; thought to be common in children; relating to or subject to such imagery.

Emerging-a modern version of repackaged theological liberalism based on deconstructionism and postmodern notions.

Empirical-derived from or guided by experience or experiment; evidence must be empirical, or empirically based, that is, dependent on evidence or consequences that are observable by the senses.

Epicurean-view of life based on Epicurus, the Greek philosopher, 341-270 BC; adapted to or fond of luxury or indulgence in sensual pleasures; having luxurious tastes or habits, especially in eating and drinking; hedonistic.

Epistemology-the study of the theory of knowledge; addresses the questions related to the origin, scope and limits of knowledge; religious epistemology grapples with the matters of knowledge and verification of truth claims; one's epistemology usually defines one's approach to apologetics.

Etymological-the study of words; the derivation of a word; a chronological account of the birth and development of a particular word or element of a word, often delineating its spread from one language to another and its evolving changes in form and meaning; the historical development of a word.

Evangelical-broad and inclusivist term referring to non-Catholic Christians, usually of Protestant origin.

Evidences-in apologetics, usually refers to so-called proofs for Christianity from logic, human reasoning, natural theology and science; extra-biblical proofs.

Evidentialist-the "one step" approach to apologetics; tries to demonstrate Christianity is probable or reasonable by use of historical evidences; in contrast to presuppositionalism.

Ex nihilo-another fancy Latin phrase meaning God created everything "out of nothing"; He did not use preexisting material to create the world.

Exegetical/exegesis-applying the rules of biblical interpretation or hermeneutics; interpreting the Bible based on the meaning of the words, grammar, syntax and context in the text of Scripture.

Exemplar-a model or pattern to be copied or imitated; the original or archetype.

Existential-pertaining to what exists, and is thus known by experience rather than reason; empirical as opposed to theoretical.

Fallacy-any of various types of erroneous reasoning that render arguments logically unsound.

Fideism-from the Latin, *fide*, faith; the view that says believing is a priority when it comes to knowing spiritual truth.

Filicidal-killing one's children.

General revelation-the means whereby an attribute of God is made clearly and universally manifest to humanity through conscience and creation; universal revelation; natural revelation.

Genus-a class or group of individuals, or of species of individuals; a kind; sort.

Grammatical-historical-biblical interpretation based on normal interpretation of the text, putting a premium on the meaning of the grammar and context; the process for determining the original meaning of the text is through examination of the grammatical and syntactical aspects, as well as the historical background. The historical-grammatical method distinguishes between the one original meaning of the text and its significance. The significance of the text is essentially the application or contextualization of the principles from text. This approach is in contrast to the historical-critical method, the allegorizing method and contextualization.

Hamartiology-from the Greek word, *hamartia*, an archery or hunting term meaning "fall short"; this is the study of the doctrine of sin.

Hellenized-to make Greek in character; to adopt Greek ideas or customs.

Hermeneutics-the science of literary interpretation; the rules for interpretation.

Heterodoxical-characterized by departure from accepted beliefs or standards; teaching considered to be unorthodox.

Highfalutin-self-important, pompous, arrogant or egotistical; tending to show off or hold oneself in unduly high regard.

Historiography-the study of the discipline and practice of history and the writings of past historians.

Holistic-relating to a study of the whole instead of a separation into parts.

Hortatory-giving exhortation or advice; encouraging; inciting.

Humanism-an ethical system and worldview that centers on humans and their values, needs, interests and abilities; especially used for a secular one which rejects theistic religion and superstition; a man-centered world-view that is hostile to religion in general and Christianity in particular.

Hyper-dispensationalism-taking dispensationalism (changes and distinctions that occur in God's economy in the progress of revelation) to an extreme.

Idealism-an ontological doctrine that holds that reality itself is incorporeal or experiential at its core; the family of views which assert that reality, or reality as we can know it, is fundamentally mental, mentally constructed, or otherwise immaterial, in contrast to physicalist and dualist theories.

Imago Dei-another fancy Latin phrase meaning "the image of God."

Imminent-about to happen, occur or take place very soon; chronologically, the next event to take place; often confused with "eminent" which means prominent or standing out in quality and with "immanence" which is the opposite of transcendence.

Immolation-from Latin, "to sacrifice"; in Roman Catholic dogma, a blood sacrifice, whereby Catholics believe that Christ is actually sacrificed at the Mass during transubstantiation.

Imputation-a theological term related to the atoning work of Christ; from the Latin, *imputare*, literally meaning "to reckon" or "to charge to one's account" and is therefore a rendering of the New Testament Greek word *logizomai*; a forensic or judicial declaration made by God based on the death and resurrection of Christ whereby Christ's righteousness is registered to the spiritual account of the repentant, believing sinner (Gen 15:6; Rom 4:3).

Incorrigible-incapable of being corrected, amended, changed or reformed.

Indubitable-unquestionable; too evident to be doubted.

Ineffable-indescribable; incapable of being expressed in words.

Infallibility-the inability to err; always correct.

Infusion-happening on a continual, slow, incremental (partial) progressive manner; Roman Catholics teach "infused righteousness" whereas the Bible teaches "imputed (instantaneous and complete) righteousness."

Inherent-naturally a part or consequence of something; existing in someone or something as a permanent and inseparable element, quality, or attribute.

Inimitable-that which cannot be duplicated or imitated; unique.

Innate-inborn; native; inherent in the essential character of something.

Inscripturation-when what is communicated in revelation is committed to writing; the process that God orchestrated to put the Bible in writing over the course of history.

Inspiration-from 2 Timothy 3:16 which says Scripture, the very writings, are "God-breathed"; the Scriptures are God's thoughts on paper; what the Bible says, God says.

Integration-mixing Bible truths with man-made philosophy, thoughts or religion, the by-product of which is compromised and lacks fidelity to biblical truth.

Intrinsic-belonging to a thing by its very nature; the essential nature or constitution of something.

Intuitively-immediate apprehension or cognition; knowledge or conviction gained by intuition; the power or faculty of attaining to direct knowledge or cognition without evident rational thought and inference; instant and immediate awareness.

Ipso facto-another cool Latin phrase meaning "by the fact itself"; it means that a certain phenomenon is a direct consequence, a resultant effect, of the action in question, instead of being brought about by a subsequent action such as the verdict of a tribunal.

Irrefragable-beyond refutation; indisputable; clearly right.

Kalam **cosmological argument**-an *a posteriori* argument for God's existence derived from Islamic theologians of the *Kalām* tradition.

Laws of logic-the laws of thought; the three classic laws of thought (noncontradiction, identity, excluded middle) are attributed to Aristotle (384-322 BC) and were foundational in scholastic thought.

Lexical-of or pertaining to the words or vocabulary of a language, especially as distinguished from its grammatical and syntactical aspects; morphemes of a language.

Locus classicus-another cool Latin phrase; an authoritative passage from a standard work that is often quoted as an illustration; a classic case or example.

Malevolent-wishing evil or harm to another or others; showing ill will; ill-disposed; malicious.

Medieval-of the Middle Ages; the Dark Ages; the time period covering AD 476-1453.

Metaphysical/metaphysics-is a branch of philosophy concerned with explaining the fundamental nature of being and the world or the ultimate nature of reality; beyond the physical realm; traditionally, metaphysics attempts to answer two basic questions in the broadest possible terms: "What *is there?*" and "What is it *like?*"; the metaphysician attempts to clarify the fundamental notions by which people understand the world, e.g., existence, objects and their properties, space and time, cause and effect and possibility; a central branch of metaphysics is ontology, the investigation into the basic categories of being and how they relate to each other.

Metonymy-a figure of speech that consists of the use of the name of one object or concept for that of another to which it is related, or of which it is a part, as "right hand" for "power."

Middle knowledge-a form of Molinism, named after 16th Century Jesuit theologian, Luis de Molina; attempts to reconcile the sovereignty of God with human free will; a cross between Calvinism and Arminianism.

Misnomer-a misapplied or inappropriate name or designation; an error in naming a person or thing.

Misogynistic-reflecting or exhibiting hatred, dislike, mistrust, or mistreatment of women.

Modalistic/modalism-a heretical view of the Trinity; says God is one Person not three, who reveals Himself in three different modes—as a Father, then as a Son and then as a Spirit, never at the same time; the three are not distinct persons but the same person changing forms; also called monarchianism, patripassianism and Sabellianism.

Modus operandi-fancy Latin phrase meaning the "mode of operation."

Monotheism-the belief in one God only.

Mumbo jumbo-an English phrase or expression that denotes a confusing or meaningless subject; often used as a sarcastic and humorous expression of criticism; the phrase probably originated from the Mandingo name *Maamajomboo*, a masked dancer that took part in religious ceremonies; Mungo Park's travel journal, *Travels in the Interior of Africa* (1795) describes 'Mumbo Jumbo' as a character, complete with "masquerade habit", that Mandinka males would dress up in order to resolve domestic disputes; in the 18th century mumbo jumbo referred to a West African god.

Natural theology-philosophical theology in contrast to biblical theology; thoughts about God deriving from human thought and speculation as opposed to special revelation; often confused with natural revelation; examples include the theistic arguments.

Natural revelation-general revelation; universal revelation.

Nefarious-extremely wicked or villainous; iniquitous.

Neo-orthodoxy-a post World War I theology of Christianity that taught that the Bible is not the Word of God but it "becomes" the Word of God when it is taught, understood and applied; a subjective approach and application of hermeneutics; the theology of crisis; dialectical theology; Karl Barth was the key originator.

Neoplatonism-the principal form of Greek philosophy from the third to the sixth centuries AD; key proponent was Platonus (AD 205-270); a modification of Platonism; the main pagan antagonist to Christianity in the fourth and fifth centuries.

Noetic-from the Greek, *nous*, which means "mind"; the noetic effects of sin refer to the consequences of the Fall on humanity.

Nominalists/nominalism-the philosophical view that says that neither universals nor essences are real, that is, they have no extramental existence; everything is particular; a universal is a general or class concept that includes all the particulars in it; the class is an abstract concept that exists only in the mind.

Bibliography

Alcorn, Randy. *If God Is God: Faith In the Midst of Suffering and Evil.* Colorado Springs, CO: Multnomah Books, 2009.

Alford, Henry. *Alford's Greek Testament.* 4 vols. London: Gilbert and Rivington Printers, 1861.

Anselm. "Monologion", LXVI, in *Anselm of Canterbury*, ed. and trans. J. Hopkins and H. Richardson. 4 vols. Toronto and New York: Edwin Mellen, 1975-76.

_____. "Proslogion," in *St. Anselm, Proslogium and Monologium,* trans. Sidney Norton Deane. Chicago: Open Court, 1935.

Anthony, Michael J., and Warren S. Benson. *Exploring the History and Philosophy of Christian Education: Principles for the 21st Century.* Grand Rapids, MI: Kregel Academic, 2003.

Arndt, William F., and F. Wilbur Gingrich. *A Greek-English Lexicon of the New Testament.* Chicago and London: The University of Chicago Press, 1979.

Bahnsen, Greg L. *Always Ready: Directions for Defending the Faith,* ed. Robert R. Booth. Texarkana, TX: Covenant Media Foundation, 1996.

_____. *Presuppositional Apologetics: Stated and Defended,* ed. Joel McDurmon. Nacogdoches, TX: Covenant Media Press, 2008.

_____. *Van Til's Apologetic: Readings & Analysis.* Phillipsburg, NJ: P & R, 1998.

_____. *An Answer to Frame's Critique of Van Til: Profound Differences Between the Traditional and Presuppositional Approach.* Glenside, PA: Westminster Seminary Bookstore, n.d.

Baucham, Voddie. *Expository Apologetics: Answering Objections with the Power of the Word.* Wheaton: Crossway, 2015.

Berkouwer, G. C. *Studies in Dogmatics: General Revelation.* Grand Rapids, MI: Eerdmans, 1955.

Bickel, Bruce, and Stan Jantz. *Evidence for Faith 101: Understanding Apologetics in Plain Language.* Eugene, OR: Harvest House Publishers, 2008.

Bigg, Charles. *A Critical and Exegetical Commentary on the Epistle of St. Peter and St. Jude.* Charleston, SC: BilioLife, n.d.

Boa, Kenneth D., and Robert M. Bowman Jr., eds. *Faith Has Its Reasons: An Integrative Approach to Defending Christianity.* Waynesboro, GA: Paternoster, 2006.

Bibliography

Boice, James. *Whatever Happened to the Gospel of Grace?: Rediscovering the Doctrines that Shook the World.* Wheaton, IL: Crossway Books, 2001.

Brand, Chad, Charles Draper, and Archie England, eds. *Holman Illustrated Bible Dictionary.* Nashville, TN: Holman Bible Publishers, 1998.

Brown, Colin Brown. *Miracles and the Critical Mind.* Grand Rapids, MI: Eerdmans, 1984.

Bullinger, E. W. *The Witness of the Stars.* Grand Rapids, MI: Kregel Publications, 1967.

Bush, L. Russ. *Classical Readings in Christian Apologetics—AD 100-1800.* Grand Rapids: Zondervan, 1983.

Calvin, John. *Calvin's Commentaries.* 22 vols. Grand Rapids, MI: Baker Book House, 1999.

_____. *Institutes of the Christian Religion.* Translated by Henry Beveridge. Peabody, MA: Hendrickson Publishers, 2009.

Campbell-Jack, W. C., and Gavin McGrath, eds. *New Dictionary of Christian Apologetics.* Downers Grove, IL: InterVarsity Press, 2006.

Carnell, Edward John. *An Introduction to Christian Apologetics: A Philosophic Defense of the Trinitarian-Theistic Faith.* Grand Rapids, MI: Eerdmans, 1956.

Carson, D. A. *Exegetical Fallacies.* Grand Rapids, MI: Baker Books, 1996.

Carson, Herbert M. *The Epistles of Paul to the Colossians and Philemon: An Introduction and Commentary.* Grand Rapids, MI: Eerdmans, 1960.

Chafer, Lewis Sperry. *The Ephesian Letter.* Findly, OH: Dunham, 1935.

_____. *Grace: The Glorious Theme.* Grand Rapids, MI: Dunham Publishers, 1922.

_____. *Systematic Theology.* 7 vols. Dallas, TX: Dallas Seminary Press, 1948.

Chantry, Walter. *Today's Gospel: Authentic or Synthetic?* Carlisle, PA: The Banner of Truth Trust, 1970.

Charlesworth, M. J. trans. and ed. *St. Anselm's Proslogion.* Notre Dame, IN: University of Notre Dame Press, 2003.

Christianity Today, Vol. 43, num. 7. June 14, 1999.

Clark, Gordon. *Religion, Reason, and Revelation.* Hobbs, NM: The Trinity Foundation, 1995.

Coleman, Robert E. *The Heart of the Gospel: The Theology behind the Master Plan of Evangelism.* Grand Rapids, MI: Baker Books, 2011.

Colson, Charles. *Answers to Your Kid's Questions.* Wheaton, IL: Tyndale House Publishers, 2000.

Comfort, Ray. *The Way of the Master.* Alachua, FL: Bridge-Logos, 2006.

Corduan, Winfried. *Reasonable Faith.* Nashville, TN: Broadman & Holman Publishers, 1993.

Cowan, Steven B., ed. *Five Views On Apologetics.* Counterpoint series. Grand Rapids, MI: Zondervan, 2000.

Craig, William Lane. *Apologetics: An Introduction.* Chicago, IL: Moody Press, 1984.

_____. *Hard Questions, Real Answers.* Wheaton, IL: Crossway, 2003.

Culver, Robert Duncan. *Systematic Theology: Biblical & Historical.* Great Britain: Christian Focus Publications, Ltd., 2005.

Dana, H. E., and Julius R. Mantey. *A Manual Grammar of the Greek New Testament.* New York, NY: Macmillan Company, 1957.

Dakin, Arthur. *Calvinism.* Duckworth, London: Kemp Hall Press, 1941.

Davison, Andrew. *Imaginative Apologetics: Theology, Philosophy and the Catholic Tradition.* Grand Rapids: Baker Academic, 2011.

Dawkins, Richard. *The God Delusion.* New York: Houghton Mifflin, 2006.

Demarest, Bruce. *The Cross and Salvation.* Wheaton, IL: Crossway Books, 1997.

_____. *General Revelation: Historical Views and Contemporary Issues.* Grand Rapids, MI: Zondervan, 1982.

Dever, Mark. *The Gospel and Personal Evangelism.* Wheaton, IL: Crossway Books, 2007.

Douglas, J. D., ed. *The Illustrated Bible Dictionary, Part 1 Aaron-Golan.* Wheaton, IL: Tyndale House Publishers, 1980.

Dowley, Tim., ed. *Introduction to the History of Christianity.* Minneapolis, MN: Fortress Press, 1995.

Duffield, G. E. *John Calvin: A Collection of Distinguished Essays.* Grand Rapids: Eerdmans Publishing Company, 1966.

Dulles, Avery Cardinal. *A History of Apologetics.* San Francisco, CA: Ignatius Press, 2005.

Durant, Will. *Caesar and Christ.* New York: Simon and Schuster, 1944.

Edgar, William, and K. Scott Oliphint, *Christian Apologetics Past and Present: A Primary Source Reader.* Wheaton, IL: Crossway, 2009.

Elwell, Walter, ed. *Evangelical Dictionary of Theology.* Grand Rapids, MI: Baker, 1984.

Erickson, Millard. *Christian Theology.* Grand Rapids, MI: Baker, 1985.

Evans, C. Stephen. *Pocket Dictionary of Apologetics and Philosophy of Religion.* Downers Grove, IL: InterVarsity Press, 2002.

_____, and R. Zachary Manis. *Philosophy of Religion.* Downers Grove, IL: InterVarsity Press, 2009.

Evans, G. R. "Introduction" in *Saint Augustine City of God.* London, England: Penguin Books, 2003.

Feinberg, John S. *Theologies and Evil.* Washington, D.C.: University Press of America, 1979.

Ferguson, Sinclair B., David F. Wright, and J. I. Packer, eds. *New Dictionary of Theology.* Downers Grove, IL: InterVarsity, 1988.

Frame, John M. *Apologetics to the Glory of God: An Introduction.* Phillipsburg, NJ: P & R Publishing, 1994.

_____. *Apologetics: A Justification of Christian Belief.* Phillipsburg, NJ: P & R Publishing, 2015.

Gaebelein, Frank E., ed. *The Expositor's Bible Commentary.* 12 vols. Grand Rapids, MI: Zondervan, 1991.

Geehan, E. R., ed. *Jerusalem and Athens: Critical Discussions on the Philosophy and Apologetics of Cornelius Van Til.* Phillipsburg, NJ: P & R Publishing, 1980.

Geisler, Norman L. *Baker Encyclopedia of Christian Apologetics.* Grand Rapids, MI: Baker Academic, 1999.

_____. *Christian Apologetics.* Grand Rapids, MI: Baker Books, 1976.

_____, ed. *Inerrancy.* Grand Rapids, MI: Zondervan, 1980.

_____. *Systematic Theology.* 4 vols. Minneapolis, MN: Bethany House, 2002.

_____, and Peter Bocchino. *Unshakable Foundations: Contemporary Answers to Crucial Questions about the Christian Faith.* Minneapolis, MN: Bethany House, 2001.

_____, and Ron Brooks. *When Skeptics Ask: A Handbook On Christian Evidences.* Grand Rapids, MI: Baker Books, 1990.

Gentz,William H., ed. *The Dictionary of Bible and Religion.* Nashville, TN: Abingdon Press, 1986.

Gilbert, Greg. *What is the Gospel?* Wheaton, IL: Crossway Books, 2010.

Girdlestone, Robert Baker. *Girdlestone's Synonyms of the Old Testament: Their Bearing on Christian Doctrine.* Edited by Donald R. White. Grand Rapids, MI: Baker Book House, 1991.

Glenn, Paul J. *Apologetics: A Philosophic Defense and Explanation of the Catholic Religion* Rockford, IL: Tan Books, 1980.

Glomsrud, Ryan and Michael Horton. *Justified: Modern Reformation Essays on the Doctrine of Justification.*

Groothuis, Douglas. *Christian Apologetics: A Comprehensive Case for Biblical Apologetics.* Downers Grove, IL: InterVarsity Press, 2011.

Grudem, Wayne. *Systematic Theology: An Introduction to Biblical Doctrine.* Grand Rapids, MI: Zondervan, 1994.

Gundry, Stanley, ed. *Five Views on Law and Gospel.* Counterpoint series. Grand Rapids, MI: Zondervan, 1996.

Habermas, Gary. *The Resurrection of Jesus: An Apologetic.* University Press of America, 1984.

Halsey, Jim S. *For a Time Such as This: An Introduction to the Reformed Apologetic of Cornelius Van Til.* Philadelphia, PA: P & R Publishing, 1976.

Hannah, John. *Our Legacy: The History of Christian Doctrine.* Colorado Springs, CO: Navpress, 2001.

Hardy, Dean. *Stand Your Ground: An Introductory Text for Apologetics Students.* Eugene, OR: Wipf & Stock, 2007.

Harris, Ralph, Stanley Horton, and Gayle Garrity. *The Complete Biblical Library: The New Testament Study Bible*, 10 vols. Springfield, MO: World Library Press, 1989.

Hastings, James, ed. *Hastings Dictionary of the Bible*. New York: Charles Scribner's Sons, 1963.

Headlam, A. C. *Christian Theology*. Oxford: Clarendon, 1934.

Hendriksen, William. *Romans: New Testament Commentary*. Grand Rapids: Baker Book House, 1981.

Henry, Carl. F. *God, Revelation and Authority*.4 vols. Wheaton, IL: Crossway Books, 1999.

Hiebert, D. Edmond. *Second Peter and Jude: An Expositional Commentary*. Greenville, SC: Unusual Publications, 1989.

_____. *1 Peter*. Chicago: The Moody Bible Institute, 1992.

Hillyer, Norman. *1 and 2 Peter, Jude: New International Commentary, vol. 16*. Peabody, Mass: Hendroksin Publishers, 1994.

Hitchens, Christopher. *God is Not Great: How Religion Poisons Everything*. New York: Hachette, 2007.

Hodges, Zane. *Absolutely Free!* Dallas, TX: Redencion Viva, 1989.

_____. *The Gospel Under Siege*. Dallas, TX: Redencion Viva, 1981.

_____. *Harmony With God*. Dallas, TX: Redencion Viva, 2001.

Hoffmeier, James K. The Archaeology of the Bible. Oxford: Lion Hudson, 2008.

_____. Ancient Israel In Sinai: The Evidence for the Authenticity of the Wilderness Tradition. Oxford: Oxford University Press, 2011.

_____. Israel In Egypt: The Evidence for the Authenticity of the Exodus Tradition. Oxford: Oxford University Press, 1999.

Holloman, Henry. *Kregel Dictionary of the Bible and Theology*. Grand Rapids, MI: Kregel, 2005.

Hopkins, Jasper *A Companion to the Study of St. Anselm*. Minneapolis, MN: University of Minnesota Press, 1972.

Horton, Michael. *The Christian Faith: A Systematic Theology for Pilgrims on the Way*. Grand Rapids, MI: Zondervan, 2011.

_____. *For Calvinism*. Grand Rapids: Zondervan, 2011.

House, H. Wayne and Joseph M. Holden. *Charts of Apologetics and Christian Evidences*. Grand Rapids, MI: Zondervan, 2006.

Jackson, Samuel Macauley, and Charles Colebrook Sherman, eds. *The New Schaff-Herzog Encyclopedia of Religious Thought*. 12 vols. New York: Funk & Wagnalls Company, 1908.

Keller, Tim. *The Reason for God*. Dutton New York, NY: Dutton, 2008.

Kelly, J. N. D. *The Epistles of Peter and of Jude*, in *Black's New Testament Commentary*. London: Hendrikson Publishers, 1969.

Keyser, Leander S. *A System of Christian Evidence*. The Lutheran Literary Board, 1953.

Kienel, Paul. *A History of Christian School Education.* Colorado Springs, CO: ACSI, 1998.

Kittel, Gerhard, and Gerhard Friedrich, eds. *Theological Dictionary of the New Testament.* 10 vols. Translated and edited by Geoffrey W. Bromiley. Grand Rapids, MI: Eerdmans Publishing, 1975.

Kreeft, Peter, and Ronald Tacelli. *Pocket Handbook of Christian Apologetics.* Downers Grove, IL: InterVarsity Press, 2003.

Kruger, Michael J. "The Sufficiency of Scripture in Apologetics." *The Master's Seminary Journal* (12/1, Spring 2001): 69-87.

Kushner, Harold. *When Bad Things Happen to Good People.* New York: Avon, 1981.

Lange, John Peter *Commentary on the Holy Scriptures: Critical, Doctrinal and Homiletical.* Vol. 5. Translated by Philip Schaff. Grand Rapids, MI: Zondervan, 1960.

Lawson, Steven J. *The Expository Genius of Calvin.* Lake Mary, FL: Reformation Trust, 2007.

Lenski, R. C. H. *The Interpretation of the New Testament.* 12 vols. Minneapolis, MN: Augsburg Fortress, 2008.

Léon-Dufour, Xavier, ed. *Dictionary of Biblical Theology.* Ijamsville, MD: The Word Among Us Press, 2000.

Lewis, C. S. *The Abolition of Man.* London, 1947.

_____. *Mere Christianity.* San Francisco, CA: Harper, 2002.

Lewis, Gordon R., and Bruce A. Demarest. *Integrative Theology.* Grand Rapids, MI: Zondervan, 1996.

_____. *Testing Christianity's Truth Claims: Approaches to Christian Apologetics.* Chicago, IL: Moody Press, 1976.

Little, Bruce A. and Mark D. Liederbach. *Defending the Faith: Engaging the Culture; Essays Honoring L. Russ Bush.* Nashville: B & H Publishing Group, 2011.

Luther, Martin. *The Bondage of the Will.* Translated by J. I. Packer and O. R. Johnston. USA: Fleming H. Revell Company, 1957.

_____. *Commentary on Romans.* Translated by J. Thedore Mueller. Grand Rapids, MI: Kregel Publications, 1976.

_____. *Luther's Works.* 51 vols. Translated by Timothy F. Lull and William R. Russell. Minneapolis, MN: Fortress Press, 2005.

_____. *Three Treatises.* Translated by Charles M. Jacobs. Philadelphia, PA: Fortress Press, 1970.

MacArthur, John. *Faith Works: The Gospel According to the Apostles.* Dallas, TX: Word Publishing, 1993.

_____. *Evangelism: How to Share the Gospel Faithfully.* Nashville, TN: Thomas Nelson, 2011.

_____. *Hard to Believe.* Nashville, TN: Thomas Nelson, 2003.

_____. *The MacArthur New Testament Commentary.* 29 vols. Chicago, IL: Moody.

_____. *Proclaiming a Cross-Centered Theology*. Edited by Mark Dever, J. Ligon Duncan III., R. Albert Mohler Jr., C. J. Mahaney. Wheaton, IL: Crossway, 2009.

_____. *Slave: The Hidden Truth about Your Identity in Christ*. Nashville, TN: Thomas Nelson, 2010.

_____, and Wayne A. Mack. *Introduction to Biblical Counseling: A Basic Guide to the Principles and Practice of Counseling*. Dallas, TX: Word Publishing, 1994.

MacArthur, John and Richard Mayhue. *Biblical Doctrine: A Systematic Summary of Biblical Truth*. Wheaton: Crossway, 2017.

Manning, Brennan. *The Ragamuffin Gospel*. Sisters, OR: Multnomah, 2000.

Mayers, Ronald B. *Both/And: A Balanced Apologetic*. Chicago, IL: Moody Press, 1984.

McCallum, Dennis. *Christianity, The Faith that Makes Sense: Solid Evidence for Belief in Christ*. Wheaton, IL: Tyndale House Publishers, 1997.

McClintock, John, and James Strong. *Cyclopedia of Biblical, Theological and Ecclesiastical Literature*. 10 vols. Grand Rapids, MI: Baker Book House, 1981.

McDowell, Josh and Thomas Williams. *In Search of Christianity*. Holiday, FL: Green Key, 2003.

_____. *The New Evidence that Demands a Verdict*. Nashville, TN: Nelson Publishers, 1999.

Metzger, Will. *Tell the Truth*. Downers Grove, IL: InterVarsity, 1996.

Moran, Alan. *Climate Change: The Facts*. Woodsville, NH: Stockade Publishing, 2015.

Moreland, J. P., and William Lane Craig. *The Blackwell Companion to Natural Theology*. Malden, MA: Blackwell Publishers, 2009.

_____., and William Lane Craig. *Philosophical Foundations for a Christian Worldview*. Downers Grove, IL: InterVarsity, 2003.

_____. *Scaling the Secular City*. Grand Rapids, MI: Baker Book House, 1987.

Morley, Brian. *God in the Shadows: Evil in God's World*. Ross-Shire, Scotland: Christian Focus, 2006.

Morris, Henry. *Scientific Creationism*. Green Forest, AR: Master Books, 1985.

Morris, Leon. *The Apostolic Preaching of the Cross*. Grand Rapids, MI: Eerdmans Publishing, 2001.

_____. *The Gospel According to Matthew* in *The Pillar New Testament Commentary*. Grand Rapids: Eerdmans Publishing Company, 1992.

Mortenson, Terry, and Thane H. Ury, eds. *Coming to Grips with Genesis: Biblical Authority and the Age of the Earth*. Green Forest, AR: Master Books, 2009.

Mueller, Marc T. "Bibliology: The Doctrine of Authority." Unpublished class syllabus. Sun Valley, CA: The Master's Seminary, 1989.

Muether, John R. *Cornelius Van Til: Reformed Apologist and Churchman*. Phillipsburg, NJ: P & R Publishing, 2008.

Murray, Iain H. *John MacArthur: Servant of the Word and Flock*. Carlisle, PA: The Banner of Truth Trust, 2011.

Newman, A. H. *A Manual of Church History.* 2 vols. Philadelphia, PA: American Baptist Publication Society, 1912.

Nicoll, Robertson, ed. *The Expositor's Greek Testament.* 5 vols. Grand Rapids, MI: Eerdmans, 1990.

Okholm Dennis L., and Timothy R. Phillips, eds. *Four Views on Salvation in a Pluralistic World.* Counterpoint series. Grand Rapids, MI: Zondervan, 1996.

Oliphint, K. Scott. *The Battle Belongs to the Lord: The Power of Scripture for Defending Our Faith.* Phillipsburg, NJ: P & R Publishing, 2003.

_____. *Covenant Apologetics: Principles & Practice in Defense of Our Faith.* Wheaton, Illinois: Crossway, 2013.

Orr, James, ed. *The International Standard Bible Encyclopedia.* 5 Vols. Chicago, IL: The Howard-Severance Company, 1930.

Osborne, Grant R. *Matthew: Exegetical Commentary on the New Testament, vol. 1,* ed. by Clinton E. Arnold. Grand Rapids: Zondervan, 2010.

Packer, J. I. *Concise Theology: A Guide to Historic Christian Belief.* Tyndale House Publishers,1993.

_____. *Evangelism and the Sovereignty of God.* Downers Grove, IL: InterVarsity, 1961.

_____. *'Fundamentalism' and the Word of God.* Grand Rapids, MI: Eerdmans, 1958.

Palmer, Edwin H. *The Five Points of Calvinism.* Grand Rapids, MI: Baker Book House, 1972.

Pannenberg, Wolfhart. *Systematic Theology.* 3 vols. Translated by Geoffrey W. Bromiley. Grand Rapids, MI: Eerdmans Publishing, 1997.

Pazmiño, Robert W. *Foundational Issues in Christian Education: An Introduction in Evangelical Perspective.* Grand Rapids, MI: Baker Academic, 2008.

Pearcey, Nancy. *Total Truth: Liberating Christianity from Its Cultural Captivity.* Wheaton, IL: Crossway Books, 2004

Pentecost, J. Dwight. *Things Which Become Sound Doctrine.* Grand Rapids, MI: Zondervan, 1965.

Pfeiffer, Charles F., Howrd F. Vos, and John Rea, editors. *Wycliffe Bible Dictionary.* Peabody: Hendrickson, 1999.

Pinnock, Clark. *Biblical Revelation: The Foundation of Christian Theology.* Chicago, IL: Moody, 1971.

_____. *A Defense of Biblical Infallibility.* Philadelphia, PA: P & R, 1967.

_____. *The Grace of God and the Will of Man,* ed. Minneapolis, MN: Bethany House, 1995.

_____. *Most Moved Mover: A Theology of God's Openness.* Grand Rapids, IL: Baker, 2001.

_____. *Reason Enough: A Case for the Christian Faith.* Eugene, OR: Wipf and Stock, 1997.

_____. *Set Forth Your Case: An Examination of Christianity's Credentials.* Chicago, IL: Moody Press, 1974.

_____. *A Wideness in God's Mercy: The Finality of Jesus Christ in a World of Religions.* Grand Rapids, MI: Zondervan, 1992.

Piper, John. *Brothers, We Are Not Professionals.* Nashville, TN: Holman Publishers, 2002.

Plantinga, Alvin, and Nicholas Wolterstorff, eds. *Faith and Rationality: Reason and Belief in God.* Notre Dame, IN: University of Notre Dame Press, 1983.

_____. *God, Freedom, and Evil.* Grand Rapids, MI: Eerdmans, 1977.

_____. *Warranted Christian Belief.* New York, NY: Oxford University Press, 2000.

_____. *Knowledge and Christian Belief.* Grand Rapids: Eerdmans Publishing Company, 2015.

Powell, Doug. *Holman Quick Source Guide to Christian Apologetics.*, Nashville, TN: Holman Reference, 2006.

Pratico, Gary D. and Miles V. Van Pelt. *Basics of Biblical Hebrew Grammar.* Grand Rapids, MI: Zondervan, 2007.

Pratt, Richard. *Every Thought Captive.* Phillipsburg, NJ: P & R, 1979.

Radmacher, Earl. *Salvation.* Nashville, TN: Thomas Nelson, 2000.

Ramm, Bernard. *A Christian Appeal to Reason.* Waco, TX: Word, Inc., 1972.

_____. *Protestant Biblical Interpretation.* Grand Rapids, MI: Baker Book House, 1978.

_____. *Protestant Christian Evidences.* Chicago, IL: Moody Press, 1967.

_____. *Varieties of Christian Apologetics.* Grand Rapids, MI: Baker Book House, 1976.

Reid, Daniel G. *The IVP Dictionary of the NT.* Downers Grove, IL: Inter-Varsity Press, 2004.

Reymond, Robert L. *The Justification of Knowledge.* Phillipsburg, NJ: P & R Publishing, 1979.

_____. *A New Systematic Theology of the Christian Faith.* Nashville, TN: Thomas Nelson, 1998.

Richards, Lawrence O. *New International Encyclopedia of Bible Words.* Grand Rapids, MI: 1991.

Roberts, Richard Owen. *Repentance: The First Word of the Gospel.* Wheaton, IL: Crossway Books, 2002.

Robertson, A. T. *A Grammar of Greek New Testament in the Light of Historical Research.* Nashville, TN: Broadman Press, 1934.

_____. *Word Pictures in the New Testament.* 6 vols. Grand Rapids, MI: Baker, 1930.

Rogers, Cleon L., Jr. and Cleon L. Rogers III, *The New Linguistic and Exegetical Key to the Greek New Testament.* Grand Rapids, MI: Zondervan, 1998.

Bibliography

Rosscup, James E. "The Relation of Repentance to Salvation and the Christian Life." Unpublished paper delivered at the Evangelical Theological Society. Aarowhead Springs, CA, 1988.

Ryrie, Charles C. *So Great Salvation.* Wheaton, IL: Victor Books, 1989.

Schlissel, Steven M., ed. *The Standard Bearer: A Festschrift for Greg L. Bahnsen.* Nacogdoches, TX: Covenant Media Foundation, 2002.

Schreiner, Thomas R. *1, 2 Peter, Jude: An Exegetical and Theological Exposition of Holy Scripture* in *The New American Commentary, vol. 37.* Nashville: Broadman and Holman Publishers, 2003.

Scofield, C. I. *The Scofield Reference Bible.* New York: Oxford, 1917.

Selwyn, Edward Gordon. *The First Epistle of St. Peter: The Greek Text with Introduction, Notes and Essays.* London: The Macmillan Press, LTD, 1946, 1971.

Sire, James W. *A Little Primer on Humble Apologetics.* Downers Grove, IL: InterVarsity Press, 2006.

Smith, Jonathan Z. *The Harper Collins Dictionary of Religion.* New York, NY: Harper Collins Publishers, 1995.

Snyder, J. L. *In Pursuit of God: The Life of A. W. Tozer.* Camp Hill, PA: Christian Publications, 1991.

Sproul, R. C., John Gerstner and Arthur Lindsley. *Classical Apologetics: A Rational Defense of the Christian Faith and a Critique of Presuppositional Apologetics.* Grand Rapids, MI: Zondervan, 1984.

Sproul, R. C. *Defending Your Faith: An Introduction to Apologetics.* Wheaton, IL: Crossway Books, 2003.

_____. *Faith Alone: The Evangelical Doctrine of Justification.* Grand Rapids, MI: Baker Books, 1995.

_____. *Objections Answered.* Glendale, CA: Regal Books, G/L Publications, 1978.

_____. *What is Reformed Theology? Understanding the Basics.* Grand Rapids, MI: Baker Books, 1997.

_____. *Willing to Believe: The Controversy over Free Will.* Grand Rapids, MI: Baker Books, 1997.

Spurgeon, Charles H. *Metropolitan Tabernacle Pulpit.* 63 vols. London, England: Banner of Truth.

Stackhouse, John G. Jr. *Humble Apologetics: Defending the Faith Today.* New York, NY: Oxford University Press, 2002.

Steele, David N., Curtis C. Thomas and S. Lance Quinn, *The Five Points of Calvinism: Defined, Defended and Documented.* Phillipsburg, NJ: P & R Publishing, 2004.

Stenger, Victor J. *God, The Failed Hypothesis: How Science Shows That God Does Not Exist.* Amherst, NY: Prometheus Books, 2008.

Steyn, Mark. *A Disgrace to the Profession.* Woodsville, NH: Stockade Publishing, 2015.

Stott, John. *The Preacher's Portrait.* Grand Rapids: Eerdmans, 1961.

Strauch, Alexander. *Biblical Eldership: An Urgent Call to Restore Biblical Church Leadership*. Colorado Springs, CO: Lewis and Roth Publishers, 2005.

Sussman, Brian. *Climategate: A Veteran Meteorologist Exposes the Global Warming Scam*. Washington, D C: WorldNetDaily, 2010.

_____. *Eco-Tyranny: How the Left's Green Agenda Will Dismantle America*. Washington, DC: WND Books, 2012.

Swinburne, Richard. *The Coherence of Theism*. New York: Oxford University Press, 2010.

Swindoll, Charles, ed. *Understanding Christian Theology*. Nashville, TN: Thomas Nelson, 2003.

Taylor, James E. *Introducing Apologetics: Cultivating Christian Commitment*. Grand Rapids, MI: Baker Academic, 2006.

Tenney, Merrill C., ed. *The Zondervan Pictorial Encyclopedia of the Bible*. 5 vols. Grand Rapids, MI: Zondervan.

Thomas, Robert L. *Evangelical Hermeneutics: The New Versus the Old*. Grand Rapids, MI: Kregel, 2002.

Thomas, W. H. Griffith. *How We Got Our Bible*. Dallas, TX: Dallas Seminary Press, 1984. Escondido: Modern Reformation, 2010.

Van Til, Cornelius. *Christian Apologetics*. Phillipsburg, NJ: P & R Publishing, 2003.

_____. *The Defense of the Faith*. Phillipsburg, NJ: P & R Publishing, 1967.

_____. *A Survey of Christian Epistemology: In Defense of Biblical Christianity*. Den Dulk Christian Foundation, 1969.

Walvoord, John. *Major Bible Themes*. Grand Rapids, MI: Academic, 1974.

Warfield, B. B. *The Works of Benjamin B. Warfield: Studies in Theology*, 10 vols. Grand Rapids, MI: Baker Books, 2003.

Whitcomb, John C., and Henry M. Morris. *The Genesis Flood: The Biblical Record and Its Scientific Implications*. Phillipsburg, NJ: P & R Publishing, 1960.

White, James R. *The God Who Justifies*. Minneapolis, MN: Bethany House, 2001.

Wiersbe, Warren W. *The Bible Expository Commentary: An Exposition of the New Testament*. 2 vols. Colorado Springs, CO: Chariot Victor Publications, 1989.

Wilkin, Robert N. *Confident In Christ: Living by Faith Really Works*. Irving, TX: Grace Evangelical Society, 1999.

_____. *The Grace Evangelical Society News*. June, 1990.

Wong, John-Michael. *Opening Up Acts*. Leominster, England: Day One Publications, 2010.

Wright, N. T. *Evil and the Justice of God*. Downers Grove, IL: InterVarsity Press, 2006.

Zacharias, Ravi. *Beyond Opinion: Living the Faith We Defend*. Nashville, TN: Thomas Nelson, 2007.

Zemek, George J. *A Biblical Theology of the Doctrines of Sovereign Grace: Exegetical*

Bibliography

Considerations of Key Anthropological, Hamartiological and Soteriological Terms and Motifs. Little Rock, AR: B.T.D.S.G., 2002.

_____. "Christian Apologetical Methodology." Unpublished class syllabus. Sun Valley, CA: The Master's Seminary, 1992.

_____. *Doing God's Business God's Way: A Biblical Theology of Ministry*. George J. Zemek, 1995.

_____. "Exegetical And Theological Bases For A Consistently Presuppositional Approach to Apologetics." Unpublished Th.D. dissertation. Winona Lake, IN: Grace Theological Seminary, 1982.

_____. "Review Article: Classical Apologetics: A Rational Defense." *Grace Theological Journal* (7.1, 1986):111-123.

_____. "Testimonium Spiritus Sancti." Unpublished class syllabus. Nd.

_____. *The Word of God in the Child of God: Exegetical, Theological, and Homiletical Reflections from the 119th Psalm*. Mango, FL: George J. Zemek, n.d.

Zerwick, Max and Mary Grosvenor. *A Grammatical Analysis of the Greek New Testament*. Rome: Biblical Institute Press, 1981.

Author Index

Author Index

Grosvenor, Mary-261
Grotius, Hugo-19,
Grudem, Wayne-177, 458
Gruenler, Royce-320
Guillet, Jacques-175
Gundry, Stanley-421, 458
Habermas, Gary-7, 10, 25, 27,
  65, 181, 192, 202, 211, 280,
  289, 305, 309, 320, 339, 458
Hall, Basil-263
Halsey, Jim-13, 27, 31, 458
Hanna, Mark-26
Hannah, John-74, 94, 423, 458
Hardy, Dean-12, 16, 27, 29, 32,
  41, 63-65, 159, 162, 173, 176,
  195, 210, 349, 359, 363, 378-
  379, 458
Harris, Ralph-65-66, 95, 458
Hart, J. H. A.-31, 39, 64
Hartshorne, Charles-230
Hastings, James-304, 459
Headlam, A. C.-98, 139, 459
Hegel, Georg-230
Hendriksen, William-304, 459
Henry, Carl-91, 357, 378, 459
Hestenes, Roberta-427
Hicks, P.-339
Hiebert, D. Edmund-65, 94, 459
Hillyer, Norman-66, 459
Hitchens, Christopher-151, 173, 193,
210, 369, 381, 459
Hodge, Charles-227
Hodges, Zane-395, 402-404,
  411-413, 422, 424-426, 459
Hoffmeier, James-341, 459
Holden, Joseph-211, 341
Holloman, Henry-112, 140-141,
  184, 206, 208, 424-425, 459
Hopkins, Jasper-260, 459
Horne, C. M.-141
Horton, Michael-207, 209-210,

217, 219-221, 226-227, 235,
252-253, 255-256, 258-259,
261, 263, 307, 458-459
Horton, Stanley-65, 95
House, H. Wayne-211, 341, 459
Howe, Frederic-12, 30
Hughes, Philip-428
Hume, David-248, 345
Hunsinger, George-307
Irenaeus-19, 32
Jackson, Samuel Macauley-27,
  143, 256, 459
Jantz, Stan-63, 320, 337, 339,
  344, 377-379
Jerome-22, 253-254, 269
Johns, Cheryl-427
Johnson, Phil-421
Johnston, O. R.-134, 145, 262,
  309
Johnston, R. K.-338
Josephus-320
Julian the Apostate-229
Kaiser, Walt-365
Kant-317
Keller, Tim-15, 25, 31, 374, 381,
  459
Kelly, J. N. D.-66, 459
Kenneson, Phillip-174
Keyser, Leander-9, 27, 29, 459
Kienel, Paul-145, 254-255, 259,
  261, 460
Kierkegaard, Søren-298, 305,
  314, 317
Kinlaw, Dennis-427
Kistemaker, Simon-64
Kitttel, Gerhard-66, 460
Kline, Meredith-365
Koukl, Gregory-268, 302
Kreeft, Peter-4, 27, 349, 359,
  378-379, 460
Kroeger, Catherine-222, 255

Scripture Index

2 Thessalonians
1:7-9......................428
2:3-12....................372

1 Timothy
Book........................92
1:1..................84, 417
1:7...........................81
1:1, 18-19..........81, 84
1:9........................182
1:20..................81, 87
3:2...........................83
3:1-7................84, 89
3:8-13...............59, 84
3:15..........84, 327, 371
3:16-17...........83, 115
4:1...........................81
4:2, 13..............83, 192
4:14.......................85
5:17.......................84
6:3, 11-12, 20.....81-82
6:5........................186
6:12-13..................84
6:16.....................355
6:20-21......81, 83, 198

2 Timothy
Book................85, 92
1:15.......................87
2:3.................57, 168
2:17-18..............74, 87
2:23.....................368
3:1-4..............173, 372
3:5...........................18
3:7........................186
3:8........................186
3:13.................88, 192
3:15..............121, 327
3:16-17.....42, 83, 119-
  121, 138, 162, 165-
  166, 246, 329, 371,
  378
4:1-5..................xvi, 83
4:14-17..................87,
  437

Titus
Book........................86
1:5...........................84

Titus
1:9...........................82
1:9-11...................341
1:10-11...................88
1:15.....................186
2:14.....................407
3:2-5.......................61

Hebrews
1:1........................119
1:1-4.....................416
2:9-10...................361
2:1-18...................416
3:13.....................192
4:12....xi, 53, 115, 120,
  166, 296, 328-329
4:14-16.................416
6:13.....................172
7:1-10:15...............416
9:22.....................407
9:24-28..........133, 237
11:1.......274, 282, 299,
  330
11:1-40..................20
11:6........137, 331, 368
11:7.........................19

James
1:5-8................17, 200
1:17.....................355
2:9........................166
2:19........................21
3:9.................103, 359
4:7...........................94
5:16-18.................198

1 Peter
1:1...........................48
1:3, 13......51, 66, 383-
  384
1:12.....................355
1:19-20............66, 374
1:21..............135, 384
1:22-25...................50
1:23.......117, 166, 290,
  386
2:4-25.....................57
3:13-18.....48, 57, 236,
  437

1 Peter
3:15....xi, xiv, 1, 3, 10,
  12, 15, 19-20, 31,
  33, 35-36, 38, 40,
  43, 47, 51-53, 56,
  58-59, 61-64, 72,
  77, 81, 86, 165,
  167, 199, 217, 249-
  250, 285, 383, 417,
  431
3:16.......................47
4:3...........................48
5:1-5.......................89
5:7-8.....................199

2 Peter
Book........................86
1:3.....................3, 245
1:16-18.................126
3:9...............373, 409
3:15-16.................120

1 John
Book................17, 86
1:5-10.....................94
2:21.....................175
2:22-23..........133, 135
3:2........................359
3:3-4..............182, 351
3:8, 10.....60, 133, 183,
  196
3:19.....................175
4:8.................94, 355
4:15.....................387
5:1........................413
5:13.....................166
5:14-15.................199
5:19.....................196

3 John
7..........................427
9-10.......................88

Jude
Book........................92
1..........................366
3-4.....4, 75-77, 81, 86,
  119
12...........................77

ABOUT THE AUTHOR

Clifford B. McManis (MDiv, PhD) is an Elder and the teaching pastor at Grace Bible Fellowship of Silicon Valley in Northern California and serves as Professor of Apologetics and Bible Exposition at The Cornerstone Seminary in Vallejo, CA.

Made in the USA
San Bernardino, CA
24 July 2018